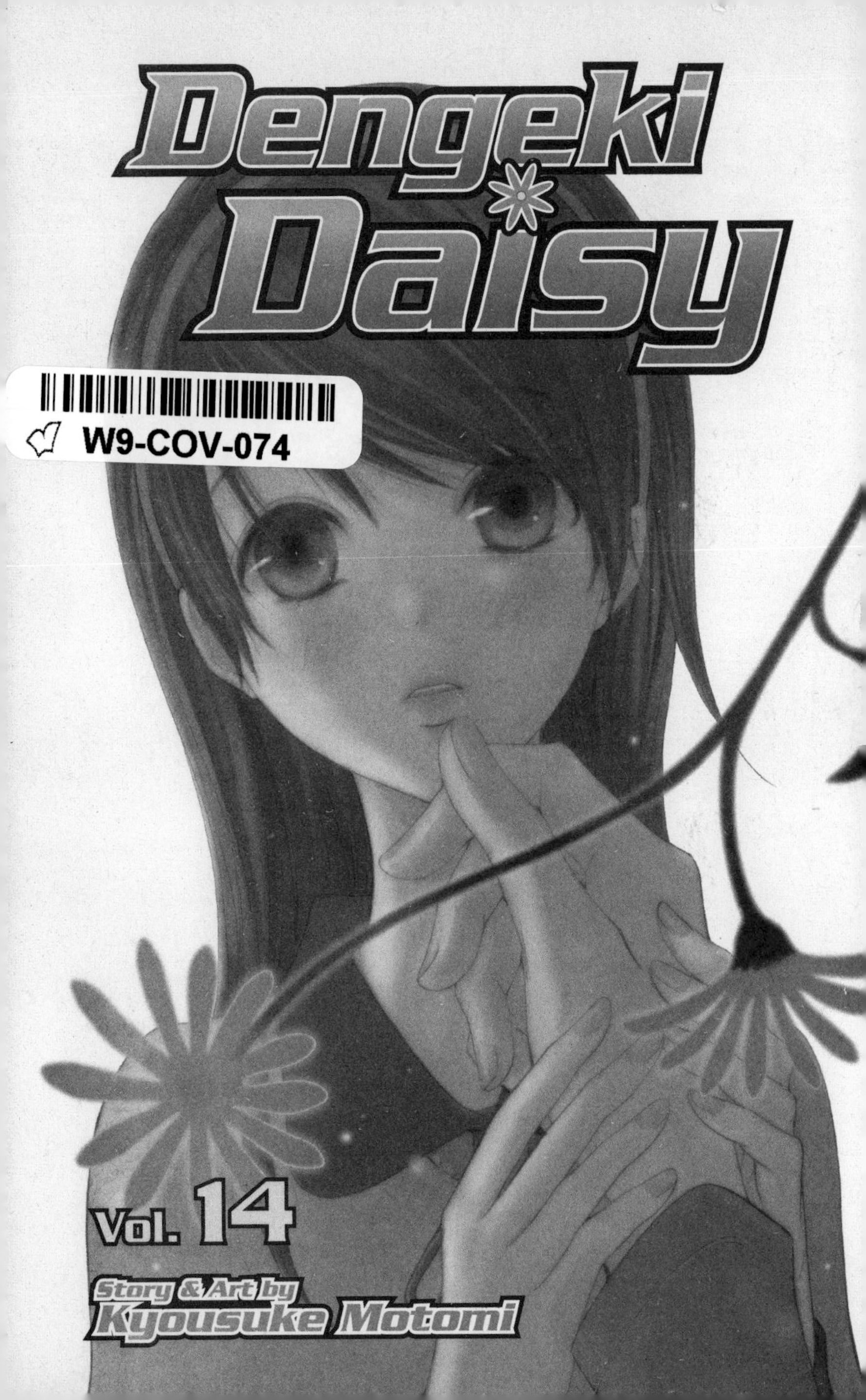
Dengeki Daisy
Vol. 14
Story & Art by
Kyousuke Motomi

Dengeki Daisy Vol. 14

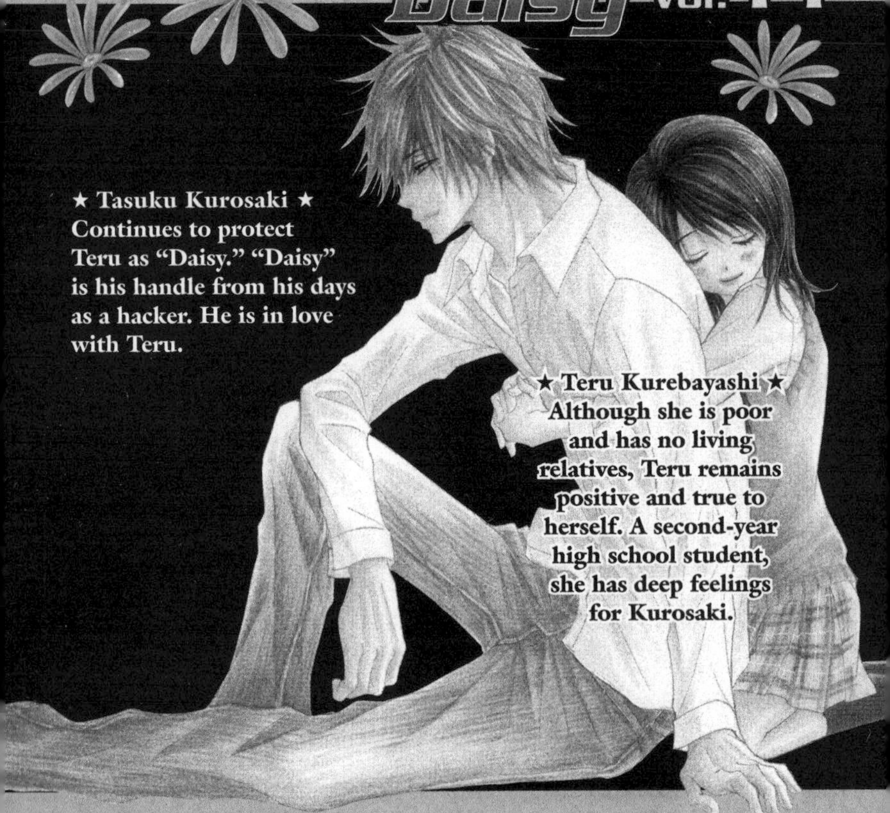

★ Tasuku Kurosaki ★
Continues to protect Teru as "Daisy." "Daisy" is his handle from his days as a hacker. He is in love with Teru.

★ Teru Kurebayashi ★
Although she is poor and has no living relatives, Teru remains positive and true to herself. A second-year high school student, she has deep feelings for Kurosaki.

★ Teru discovers that Kurosaki is Daisy, the mysterious person who supported and encouraged her after her brother Soichiro's death. Thinking that there must be a reason why Kurosaki has chosen to hide his identity, Teru decides to keep this knowledge to herself.

★ During this time, Teru's life is threatened, and strange incidents involving Teru and Kurosaki occur. Kurosaki decides to disclose the truth to Teru, but Akira beats him to it and tells her about Kurosaki's past "sin." Learning what Akira has done, Kurosaki disappears from sight. Seeing Teru so despondent, the Director and Riko tell her about Kurosaki's past.

★ Teru learns that Kurosaki's father was involved with the development of a top-secret government code, and his death was shrouded in mystery. Kurosaki became a hacker to clear his father's

CHARACTERS...

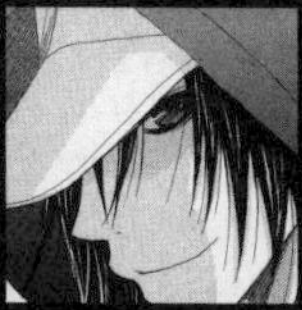

★ Akira ★
Chiharu Mori's partner-in-crime. He continues to stalk Teru and Kurosaki.

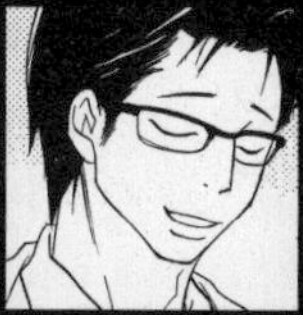

★ Takeda ★
Soichiro's former coworker. He is the owner of Kaoruko, a Shiba dog.

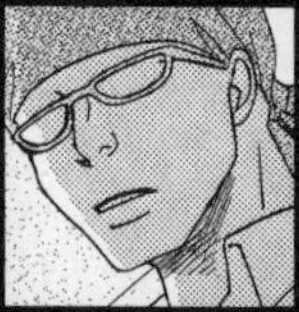

★ Boss (Masuda) ★
Currently runs the snack shop "Flower Garden" but used to work with Soichiro.

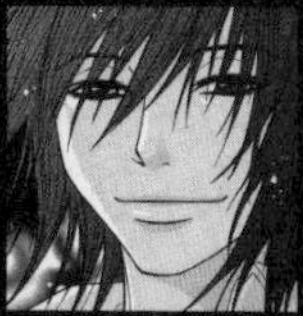

★ Soichiro Kurebayashi ★
Teru's older brother and a genius systems engineer. He died after leaving Teru in Kurosaki's care.

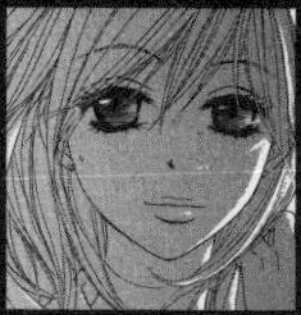

★ Chiharu Mori ★
She used to work at Teru's school. Teaming up with Akira, she continues to target Teru and Kurosaki.

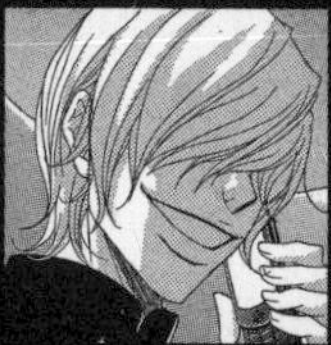

★ Antler ★
He tricked Kurosaki into creating the "Jack Frost" virus.

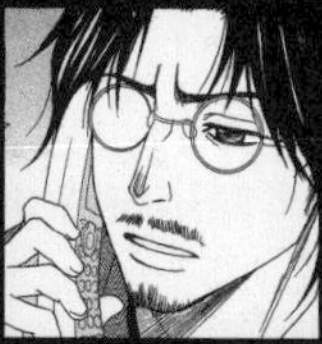

★ Director (Kazumasa Ando) ★
He used to work with Soichiro and is currently the director of Teru's school.

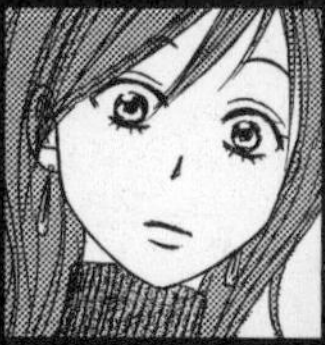

★ Riko Onizuka ★
She was Soichiro's girlfriend and is now a counselor at Teru's school.

STORY...

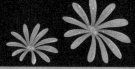

name and created the code virus known as "Jack Frost." In order to save Kurosaki from being charged with a "Jack Frost"-related murder, Soichiro worked nonstop to decipher the code and died in the process. Teru accepts this newfound knowledge about Kurosaki. She thanks him for all that he has done for her and asks him to stay by her side.

★ Kurosaki and company search for M's Last Testament, data that Professor Midorikawa left behind about an incident in the past. Meanwhile, Teru realizes that there is a hidden message from Soichiro on her cell phone. She and her friends follow the message and get their hands on top-secret information regarding M's Last Testament...

Dengeki Daisy

Volume 14 CONTENTS

Chapter 65: Professor Midorikawa's Will

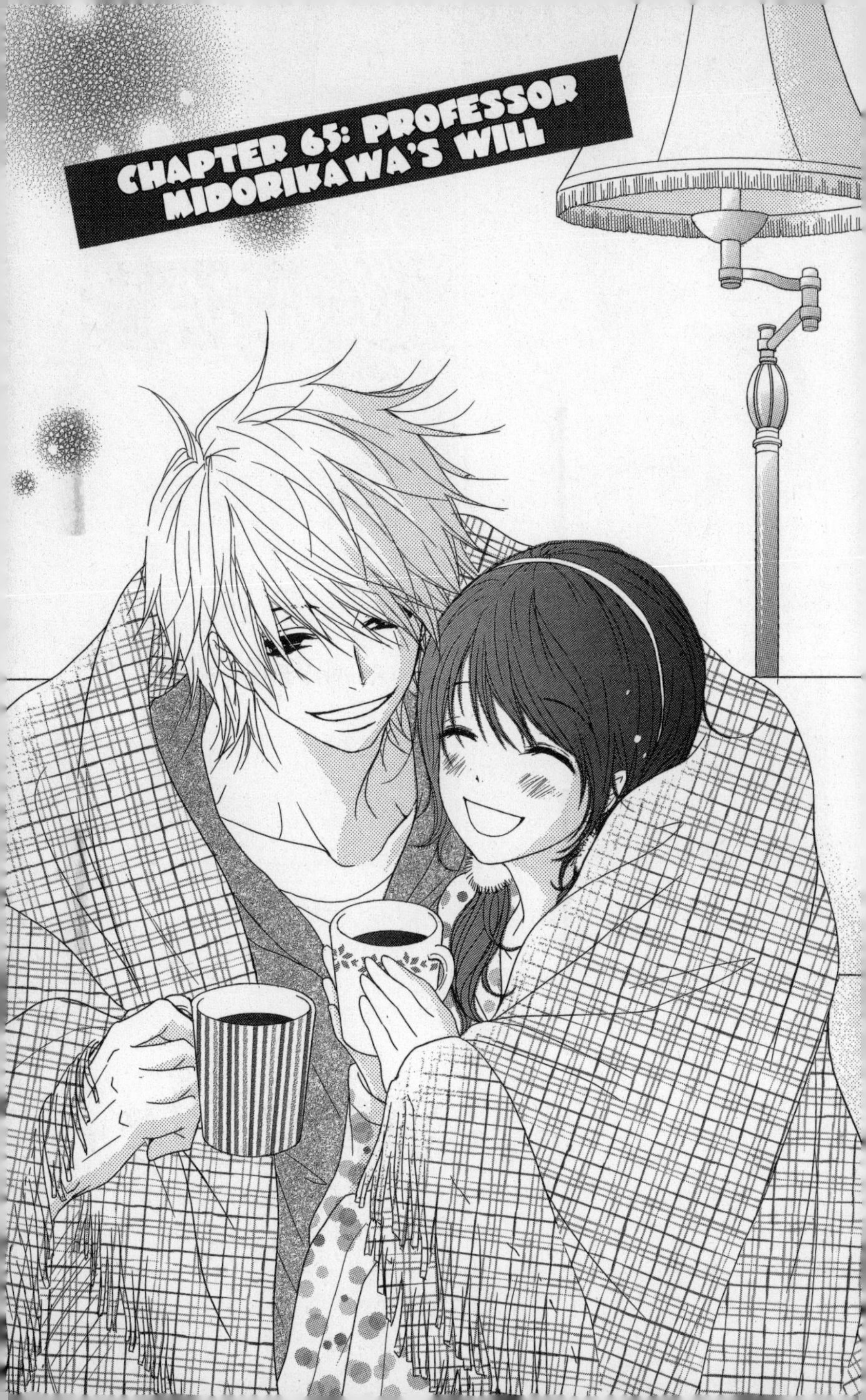

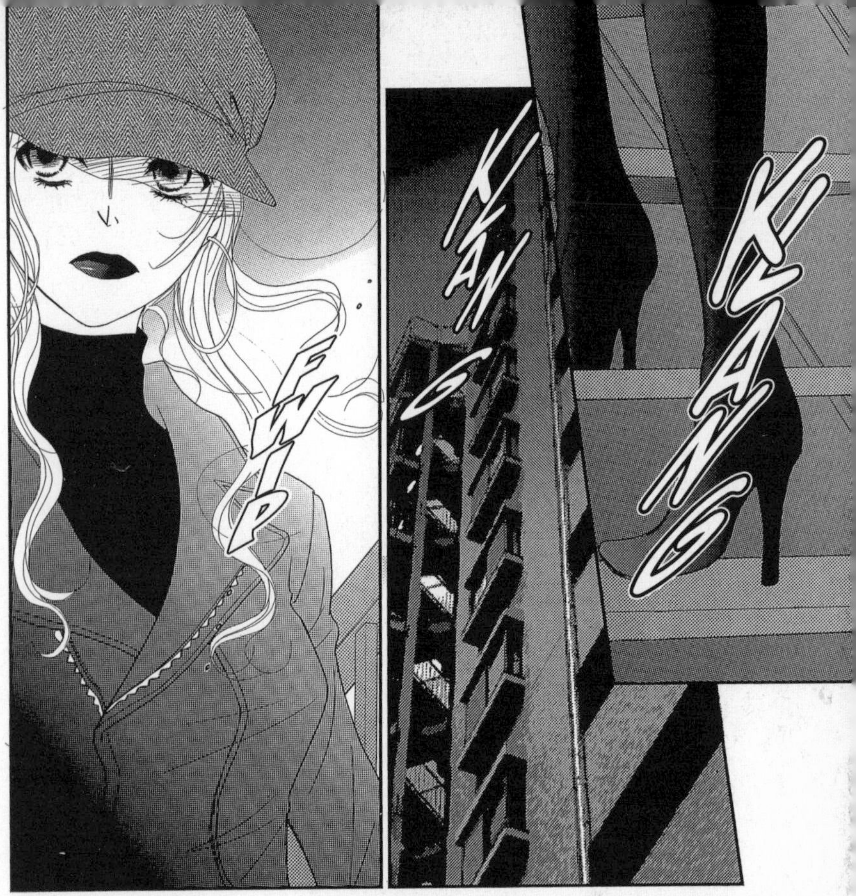
KWANG
KWANG
FWIP

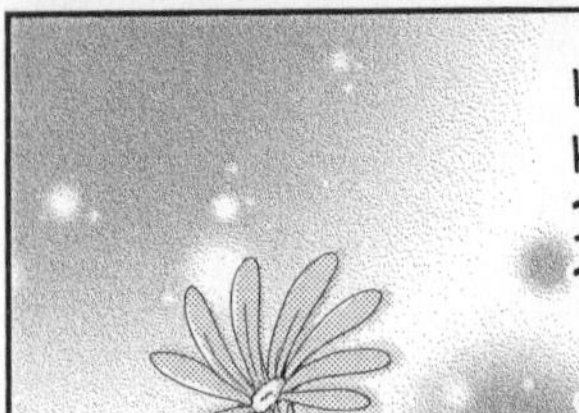

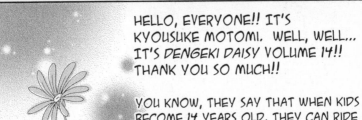

HELLO, EVERYONE!! IT'S KYOUSUKE MOTOMI. WELL, WELL... IT'S *DENGEKI DAISY* VOLUME 14!! THANK YOU SO MUCH!!

YOU KNOW, THEY SAY THAT WHEN KIDS BECOME 14 YEARS OLD, THEY CAN RIDE THE E●A. (UNEXPECTED KNOWLEDGE) SO WITH THAT (?) SAID, I PRESENT TO YOU VOLUME 14. IT'D MAKE ME HAPPY IF YOU ENJOY IT.

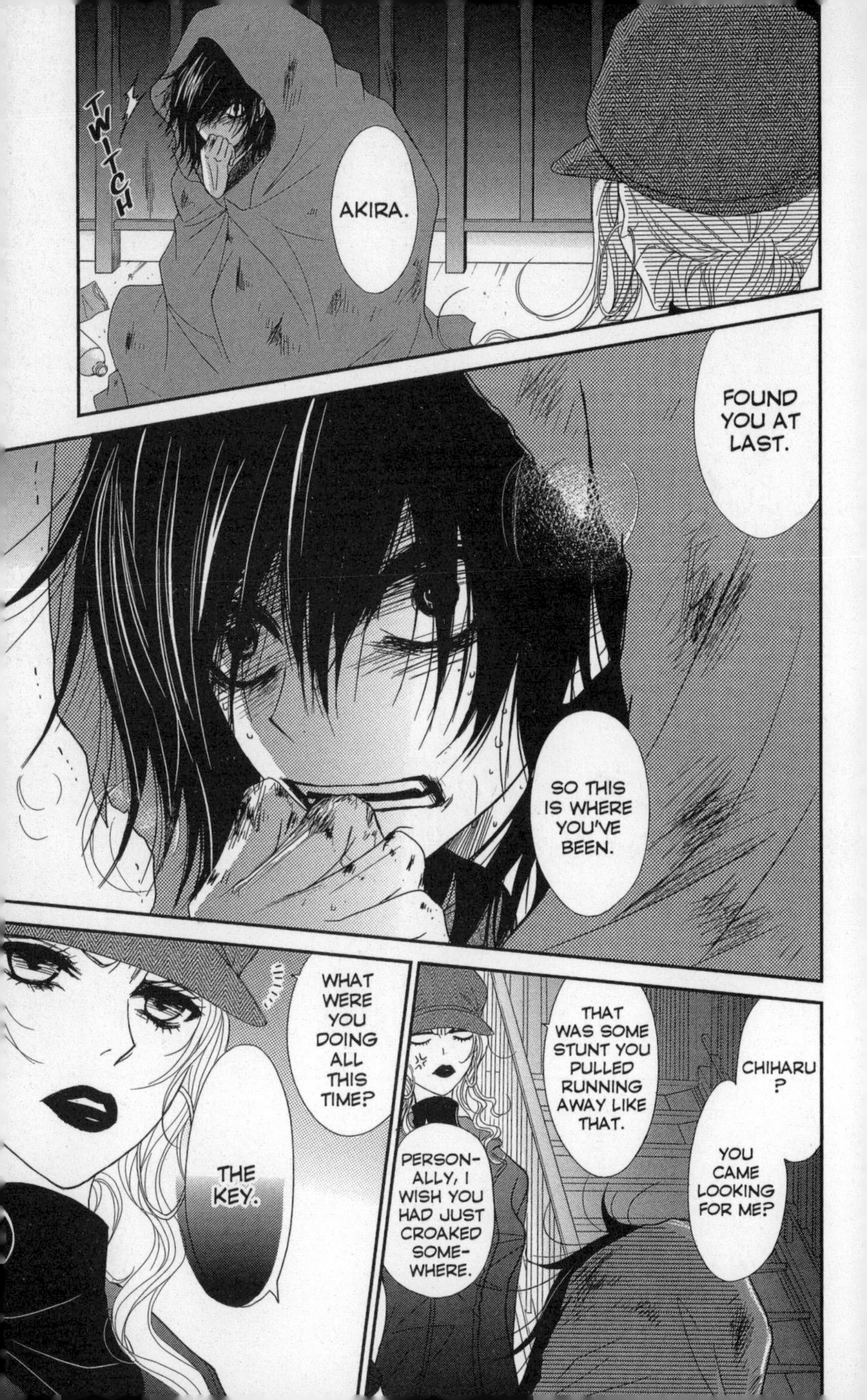
AKIRA.
TWITCH
FOUND YOU AT LAST.
SO THIS IS WHERE YOU'VE BEEN.
CHIHARU?
THAT WAS SOME STUNT YOU PULLED RUNNING AWAY LIKE THAT.
YOU CAME LOOKING FOR ME?
PERSONALLY, I WISH YOU HAD JUST CROAKED SOMEWHERE.
WHAT WERE YOU DOING ALL THIS TIME?
THE KEY.

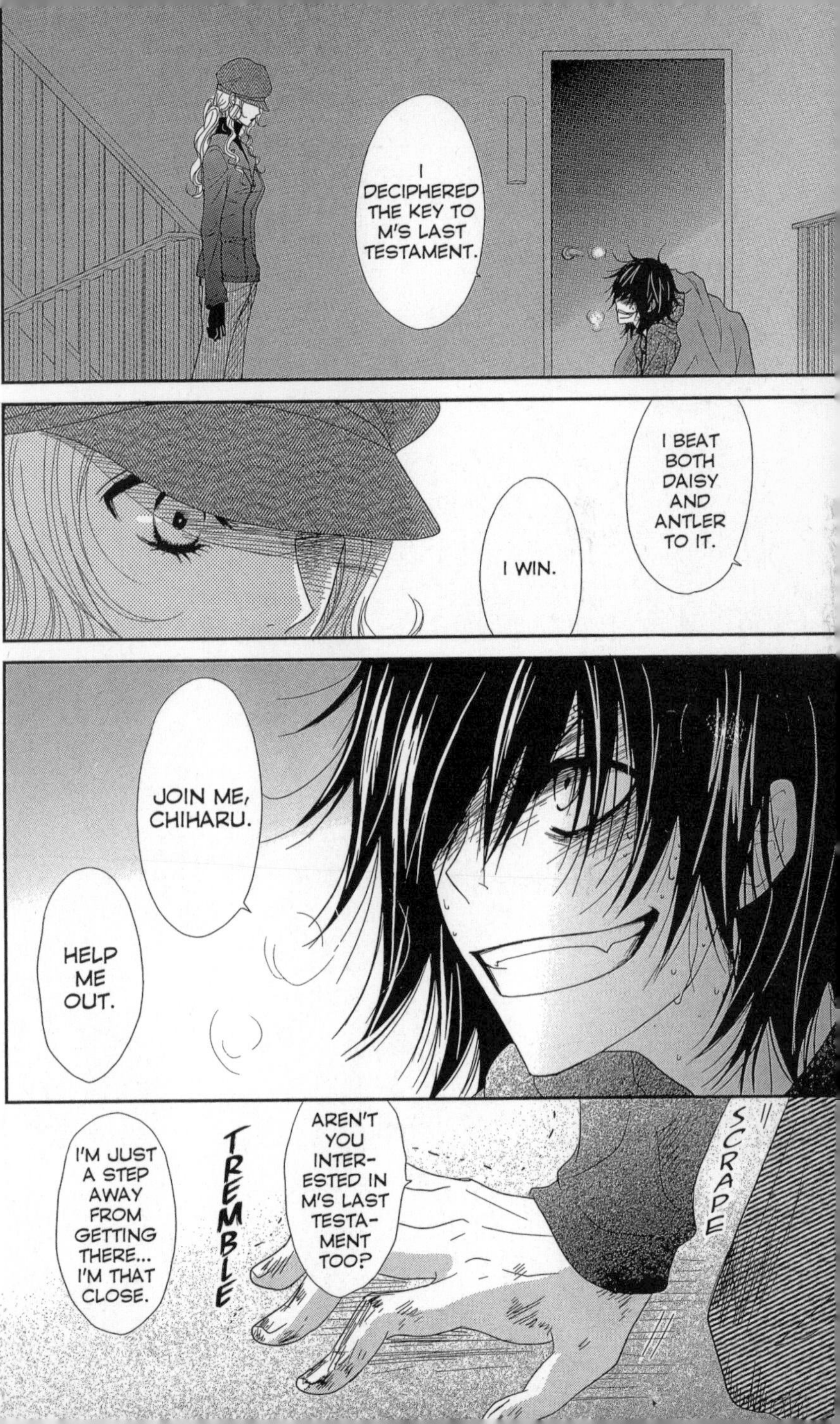
I DECIPHERED THE KEY TO M'S LAST TESTAMENT.
I BEAT BOTH DAISY AND ANTLER TO IT.
I WIN.
JOIN ME, CHIHARU.
HELP ME OUT.
SCRAPE
AREN'T YOU INTER-ESTED IN M'S LAST TESTA-MENT TOO?
TREMBLE
I'M JUST A STEP AWAY FROM GETTING THERE... I'M THAT CLOSE.

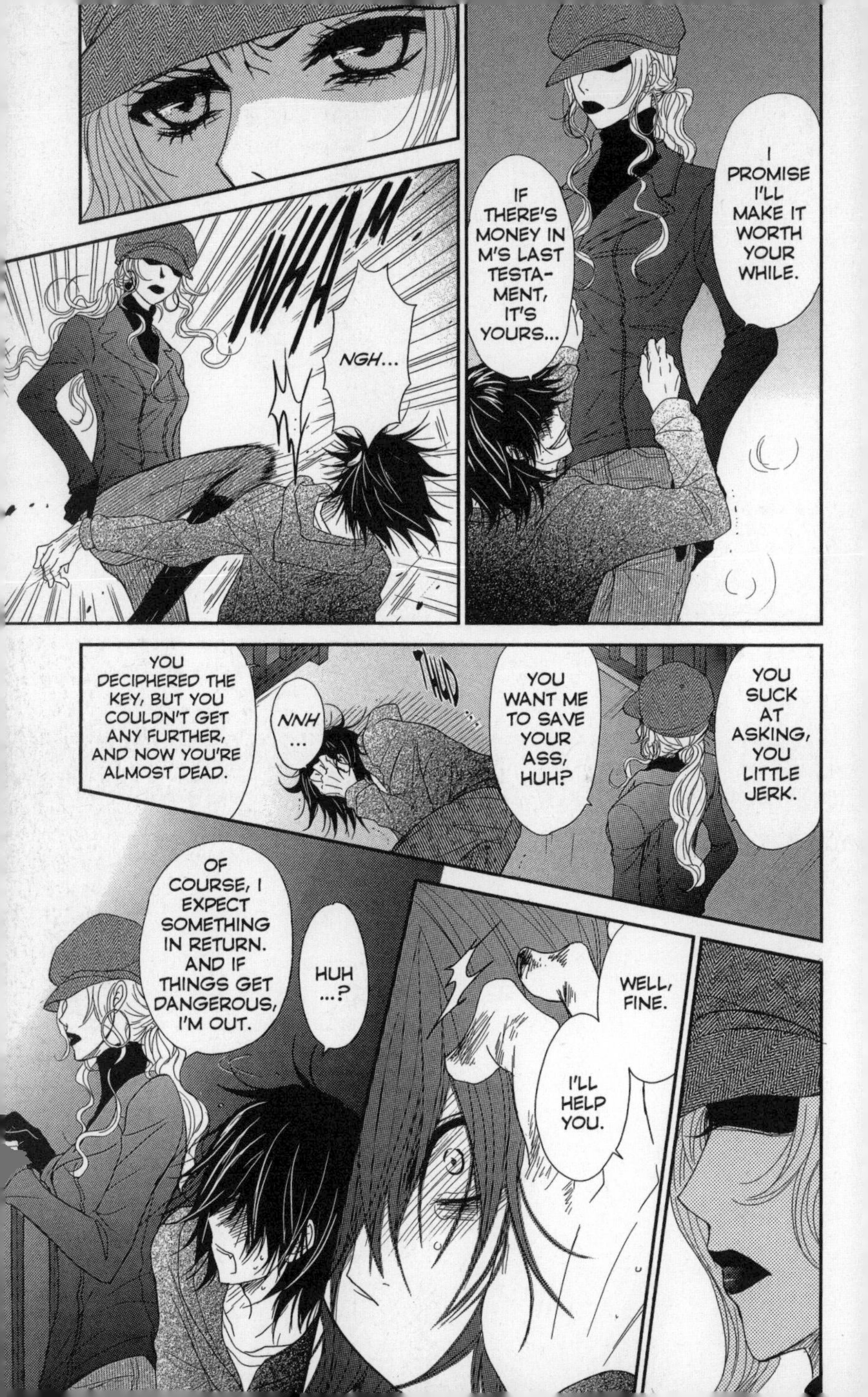
I PROMISE I'LL MAKE IT WORTH YOUR WHILE.
IF THERE'S MONEY IN M'S LAST TESTAMENT, IT'S YOURS...
WHAM
NGH...
YOU SUCK AT ASKING, YOU LITTLE JERK.
YOU WANT ME TO SAVE YOUR ASS, HUH?
THUD
NNH...
YOU DECIPHERED THE KEY, BUT YOU COULDN'T GET ANY FURTHER, AND NOW YOU'RE ALMOST DEAD.
WELL, FINE.
I'LL HELP YOU.
HUH...?
OF COURSE, I EXPECT SOMETHING IN RETURN. AND IF THINGS GET DANGEROUS, I'M OUT.

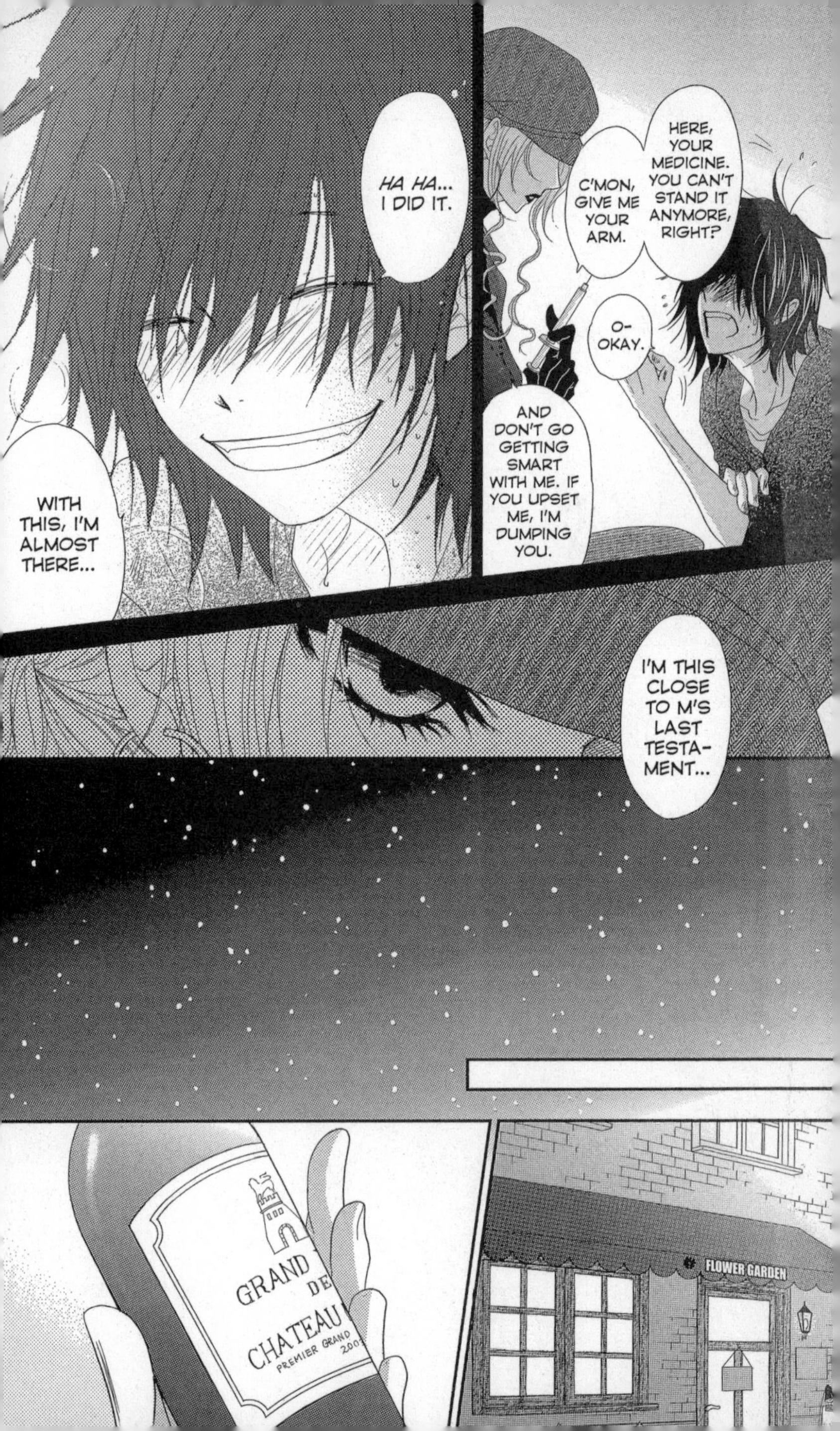
HERE, YOUR MEDICINE. YOU CAN'T STAND IT ANYMORE, RIGHT?
C'MON, GIVE ME YOUR ARM.
O-OKAY.
AND DON'T GO GETTING SMART WITH ME. IF YOU UPSET ME, I'M DUMPING YOU.
HA HA... I DID IT.
WITH THIS, I'M ALMOST THERE...
I'M THIS CLOSE TO M'S LAST TESTAMENT...
FLOWER GARDEN
GRAND
DE
CHATEAU
PREMIER GRAND

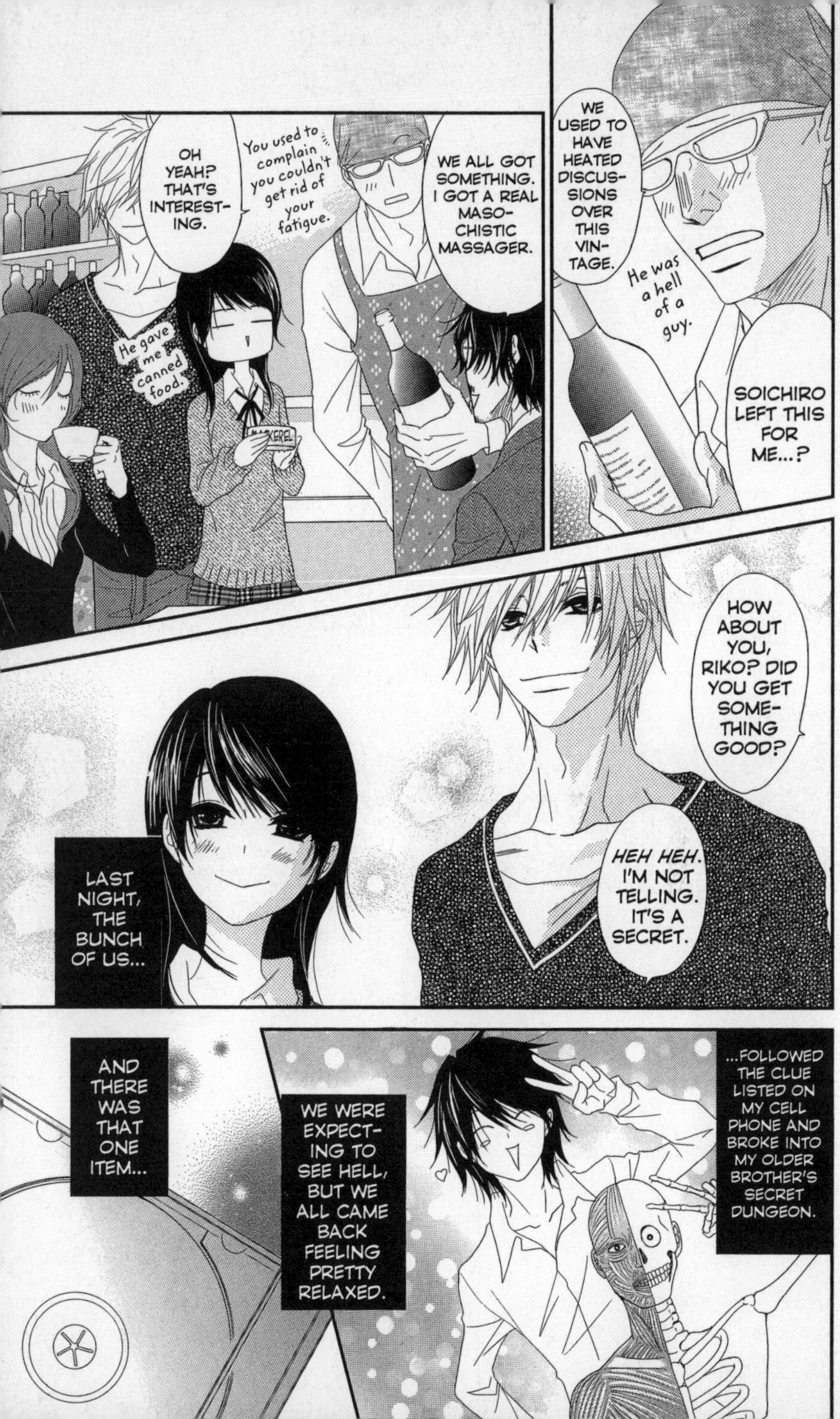
SOICHIRO LEFT THIS FOR ME...?
WE USED TO HAVE HEATED DISCUSSIONS OVER THIS VINTAGE.
He was a hell of a guy.
WE ALL GOT SOMETHING. I GOT A REAL MASOCHISTIC MASSAGER.
You used to complain you couldn't get rid of your fatigue.
OH YEAH? THAT'S INTERESTING.
He gave me canned food.
HOW ABOUT YOU, RIKO? DID YOU GET SOMETHING GOOD?
HEH HEH. I'M NOT TELLING. IT'S A SECRET.
LAST NIGHT, THE BUNCH OF US...
...FOLLOWED THE CLUE LISTED ON MY CELL PHONE AND BROKE INTO MY OLDER BROTHER'S SECRET DUNGEON.
WE WERE EXPECTING TO SEE HELL, BUT WE ALL CAME BACK FEELING PRETTY RELAXED.
AND THERE WAS THAT ONE ITEM...

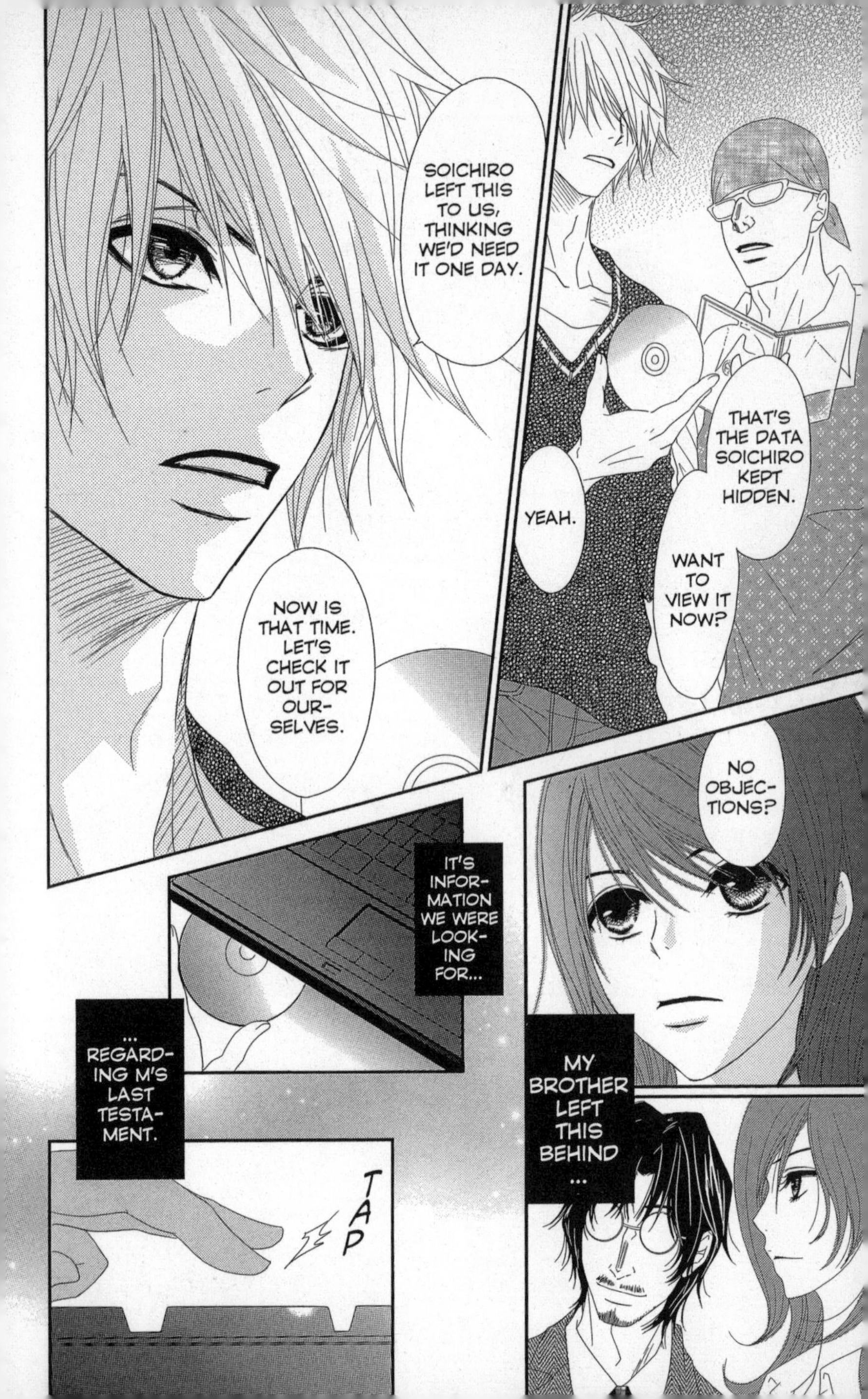
THAT'S THE DATA SOICHIRO KEPT HIDDEN.
YEAH.
WANT TO VIEW IT NOW?
SOICHIRO LEFT THIS TO US, THINKING WE'D NEED IT ONE DAY.
NOW IS THAT TIME. LET'S CHECK IT OUT FOR OURSELVES.
NO OBJECTIONS?
IT'S INFORMATION WE WERE LOOKING FOR...
...REGARDING M'S LAST TESTAMENT.
MY BROTHER LEFT THIS BEHIND...
TAP

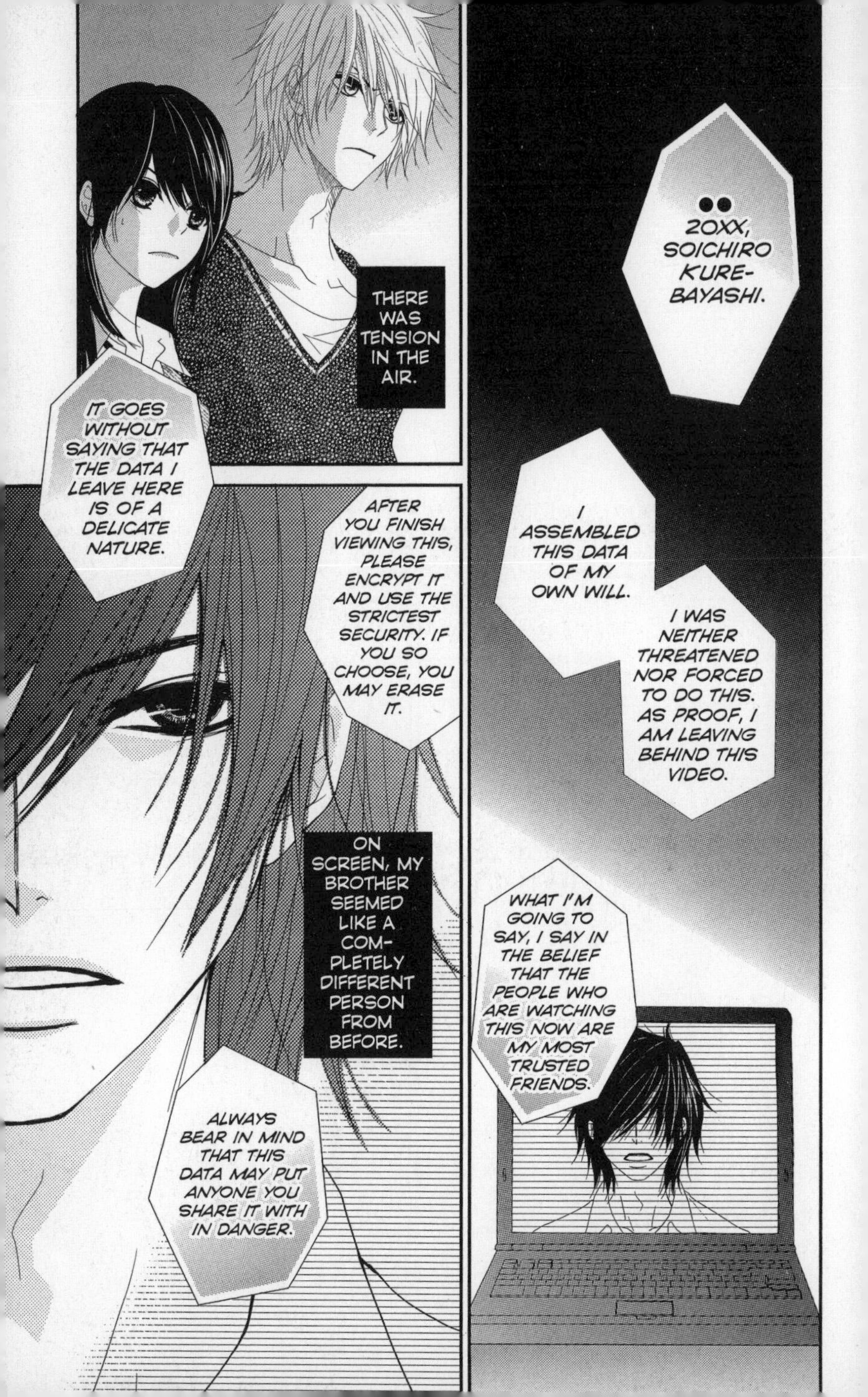
●● 20XX, SOICHIRO KURE-BAYASHI.
I ASSEMBLED THIS DATA OF MY OWN WILL.
I WAS NEITHER THREATENED NOR FORCED TO DO THIS. AS PROOF, I AM LEAVING BEHIND THIS VIDEO.
WHAT I'M GOING TO SAY, I SAY IN THE BELIEF THAT THE PEOPLE WHO ARE WATCHING THIS NOW ARE MY MOST TRUSTED FRIENDS.
THERE WAS TENSION IN THE AIR.
IT GOES WITHOUT SAYING THAT THE DATA I LEAVE HERE IS OF A DELICATE NATURE.
AFTER YOU FINISH VIEWING THIS, PLEASE ENCRYPT IT AND USE THE STRICTEST SECURITY. IF YOU SO CHOOSE, YOU MAY ERASE IT.
ON SCREEN, MY BROTHER SEEMED LIKE A COM-PLETELY DIFFERENT PERSON FROM BEFORE.
ALWAYS BEAR IN MIND THAT THIS DATA MAY PUT ANYONE YOU SHARE IT WITH IN DANGER.

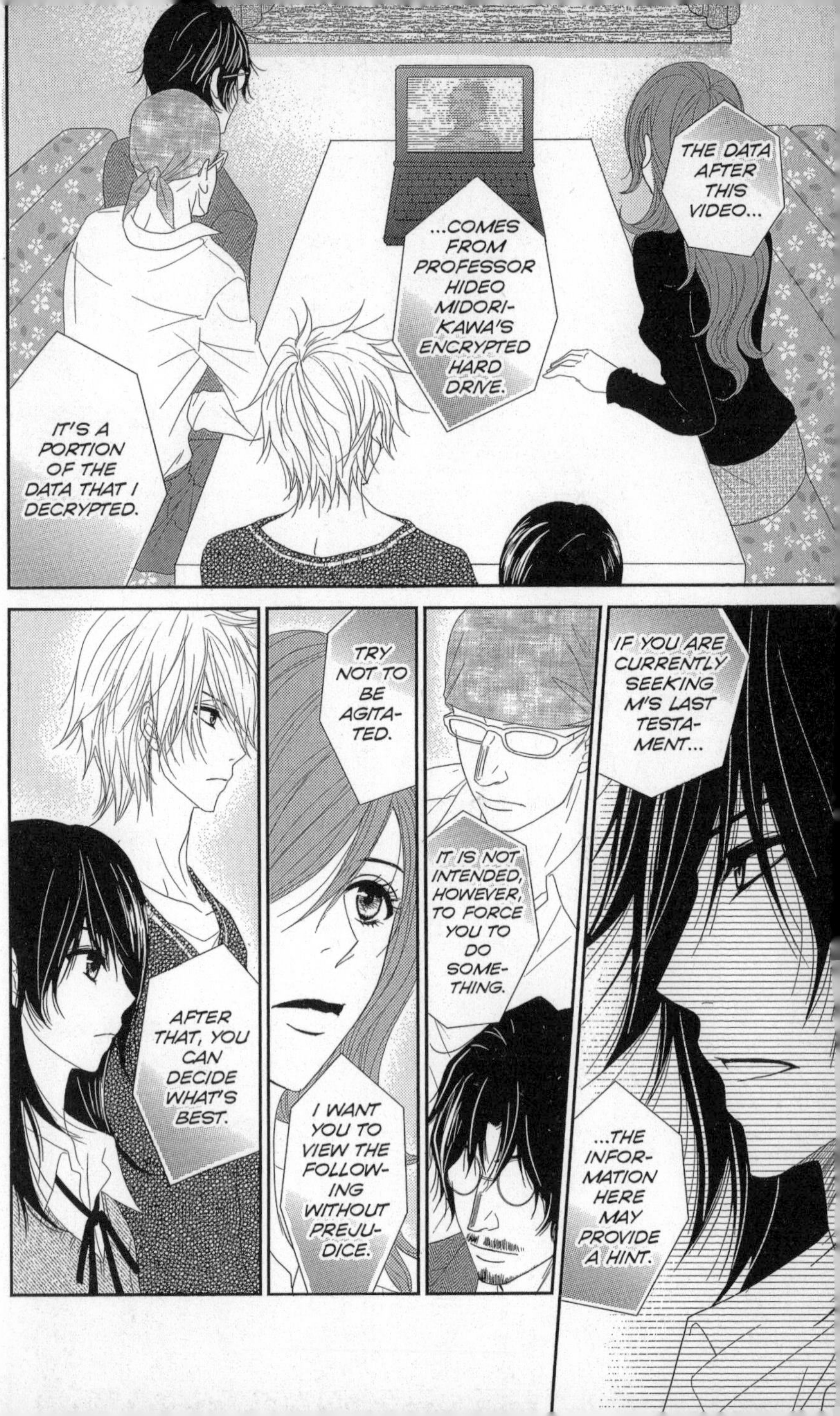
THE DATA AFTER THIS VIDEO...
...COMES FROM PROFESSOR HIDEO MIDORIKAWA'S ENCRYPTED HARD DRIVE.
IT'S A PORTION OF THE DATA THAT I DECRYPTED.
IF YOU ARE CURRENTLY SEEKING M'S LAST TESTAMENT...
...THE INFORMATION HERE MAY PROVIDE A HINT.
IT IS NOT INTENDED, HOWEVER, TO FORCE YOU TO DO SOMETHING.
TRY NOT TO BE AGITATED.
I WANT YOU TO VIEW THE FOLLOWING WITHOUT PREJUDICE.
AFTER THAT, YOU CAN DECIDE WHAT'S BEST.

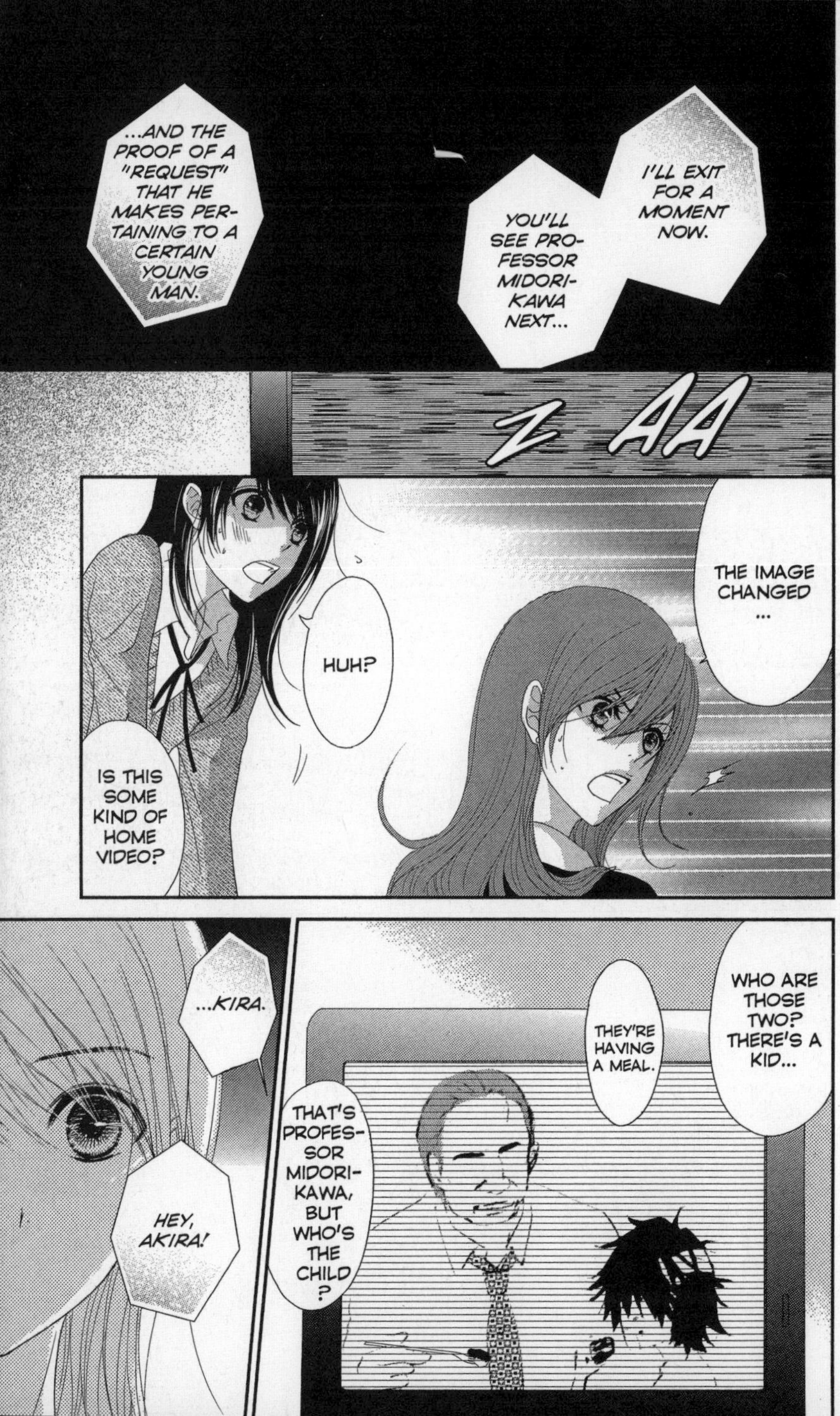
I'LL EXIT FOR A MOMENT NOW.
YOU'LL SEE PRO-FESSOR MIDORI-KAWA NEXT...
...AND THE PROOF OF A "REQUEST" THAT HE MAKES PER-TAINING TO A CERTAIN YOUNG MAN.
ZAA
THE IMAGE CHANGED...
HUH?
IS THIS SOME KIND OF HOME VIDEO?
WHO ARE THOSE TWO? THERE'S A KID...
THEY'RE HAVING A MEAL.
THAT'S PROFES-SOR MIDORI-KAWA, BUT WHO'S THE CHILD?
...KIRA.
HEY, AKIRA!

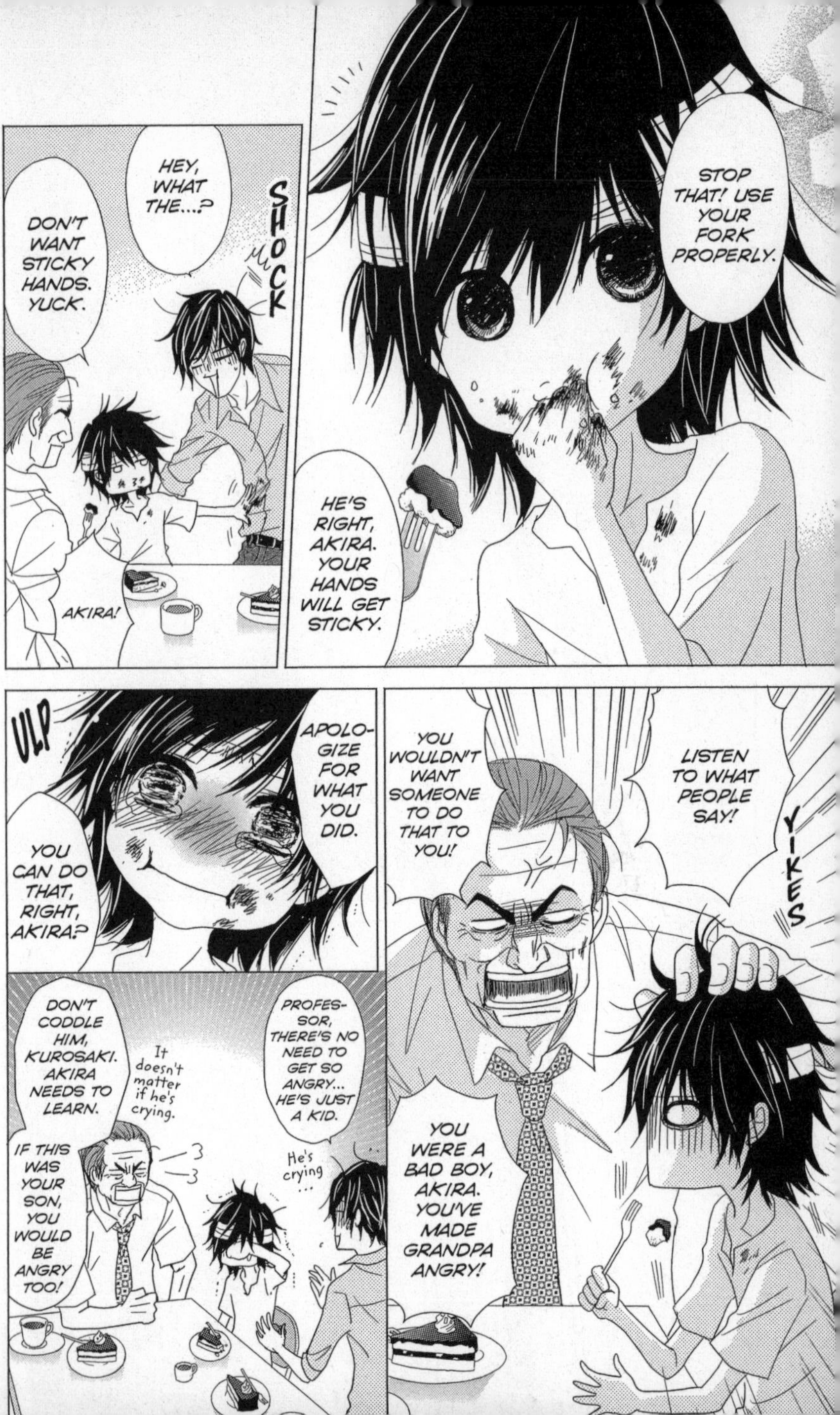
STOP THAT! USE YOUR FORK PROPERLY.
HE'S RIGHT, AKIRA. YOUR HANDS WILL GET STICKY.
SHOCK
HEY, WHAT THE...?
DON'T WANT STICKY HANDS. YUCK.
AKIRA!
LISTEN TO WHAT PEOPLE SAY!
YIKES
YOU WOULDN'T WANT SOMEONE TO DO THAT TO YOU!
YOU WERE A BAD BOY, AKIRA. YOU'VE MADE GRANDPA ANGRY!
APOLOGIZE FOR WHAT YOU DID.
ULP
YOU CAN DO THAT, RIGHT, AKIRA?
PROFESSOR, THERE'S NO NEED TO GET SO ANGRY... HE'S JUST A KID.
He's crying...
DON'T CODDLE HIM, KUROSAKI. AKIRA NEEDS TO LEARN.
It doesn't matter if he's crying.
IF THIS WAS YOUR SON, YOU WOULD BE ANGRY TOO!

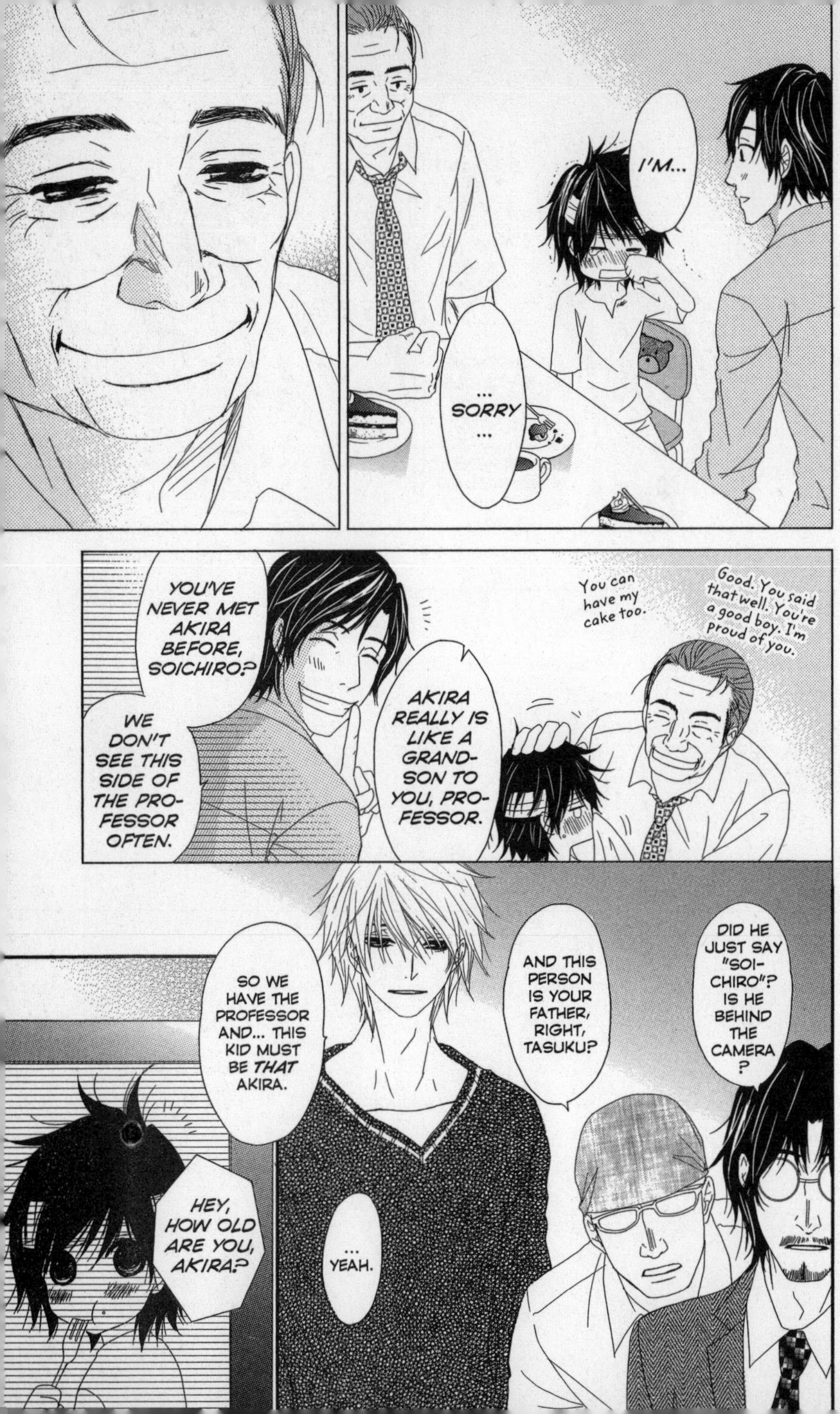
I'M...
...SORRY...
Good. You said that well. You're a good boy. I'm proud of you.
You can have my cake too.
AKIRA REALLY IS LIKE A GRANDSON TO YOU, PROFESSOR.
YOU'VE NEVER MET AKIRA BEFORE, SOICHIRO?
WE DON'T SEE THIS SIDE OF THE PROFESSOR OFTEN.
DID HE JUST SAY "SOICHIRO"? IS HE BEHIND THE CAMERA?
AND THIS PERSON IS YOUR FATHER, RIGHT, TASUKU?
SO WE HAVE THE PROFESSOR AND... THIS KID MUST BE *THAT* AKIRA.
...YEAH.
HEY, HOW OLD ARE YOU, AKIRA?

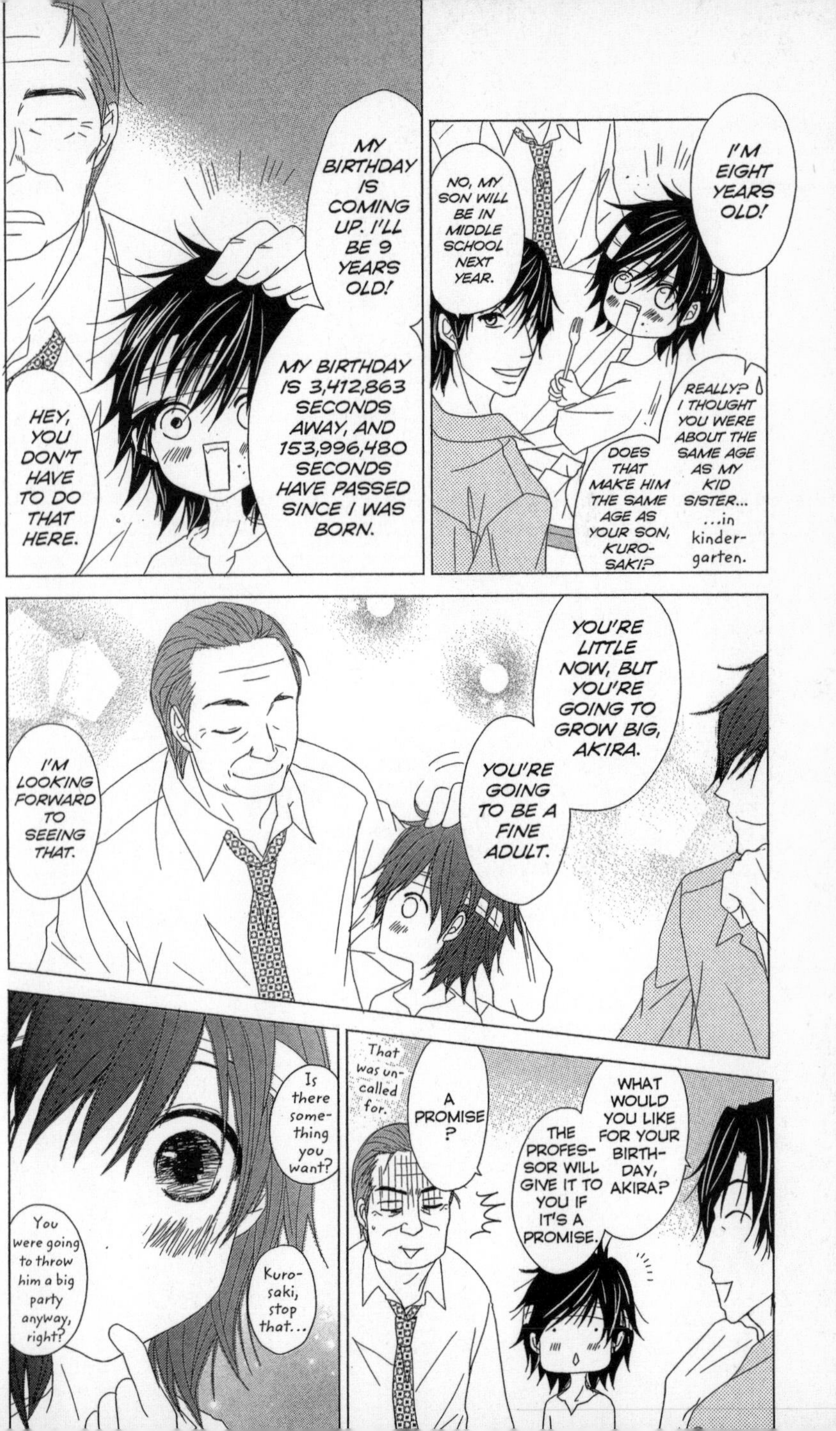
I'M EIGHT YEARS OLD!
NO, MY SON WILL BE IN MIDDLE SCHOOL NEXT YEAR.
REALLY? I THOUGHT YOU WERE ABOUT THE SAME AGE AS MY KID SISTER... ...in kindergarten.
DOES THAT MAKE HIM THE SAME AGE AS YOUR SON, KUROSAKI?
MY BIRTHDAY IS COMING UP. I'LL BE 9 YEARS OLD!
MY BIRTHDAY IS 3,412,863 SECONDS AWAY, AND 153,996,480 SECONDS HAVE PASSED SINCE I WAS BORN.
HEY, YOU DON'T HAVE TO DO THAT HERE.
YOU'RE LITTLE NOW, BUT YOU'RE GOING TO GROW BIG, AKIRA.
YOU'RE GOING TO BE A FINE ADULT.
I'M LOOKING FORWARD TO SEEING THAT.
WHAT WOULD YOU LIKE FOR YOUR BIRTHDAY, AKIRA?
THE PROFESSOR WILL GIVE IT TO YOU IF IT'S A PROMISE.
A PROMISE?
That was uncalled for.
Is there something you want?
Kurosaki, stop that...
You were going to throw him a big party anyway, right?

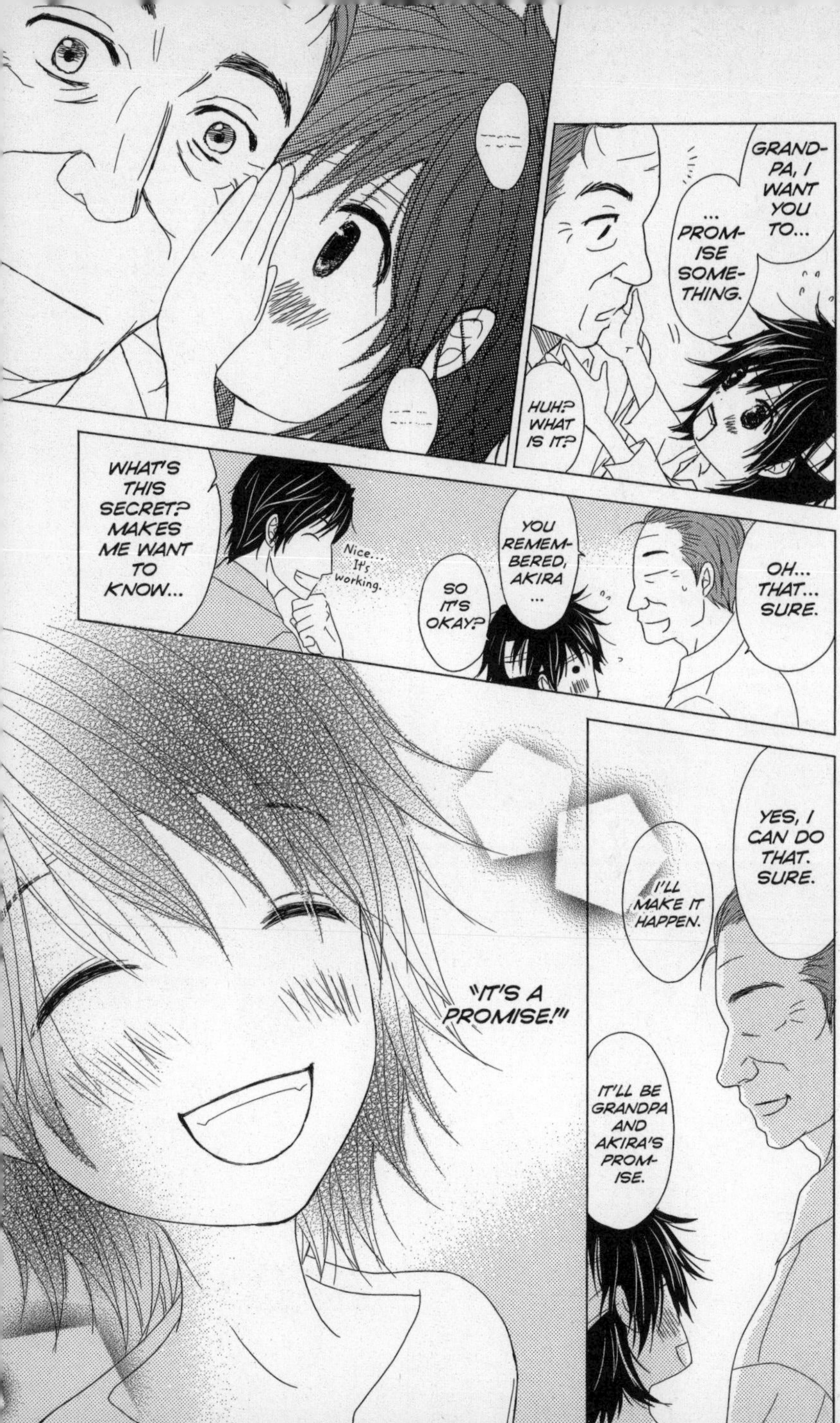
GRAND-PA, I WANT YOU TO...
... PROM-ISE SOME-THING.
HUH? WHAT IS IT?
OH... THAT... SURE.
YOU REMEM-BERED, AKIRA ...
SO IT'S OKAY?
Nice... It's working.
WHAT'S THIS SECRET? MAKES ME WANT TO KNOW...
YES, I CAN DO THAT. SURE.
I'LL MAKE IT HAPPEN.
IT'LL BE GRANDPA AND AKIRA'S PROM-ISE.
"IT'S A PROMISE!"

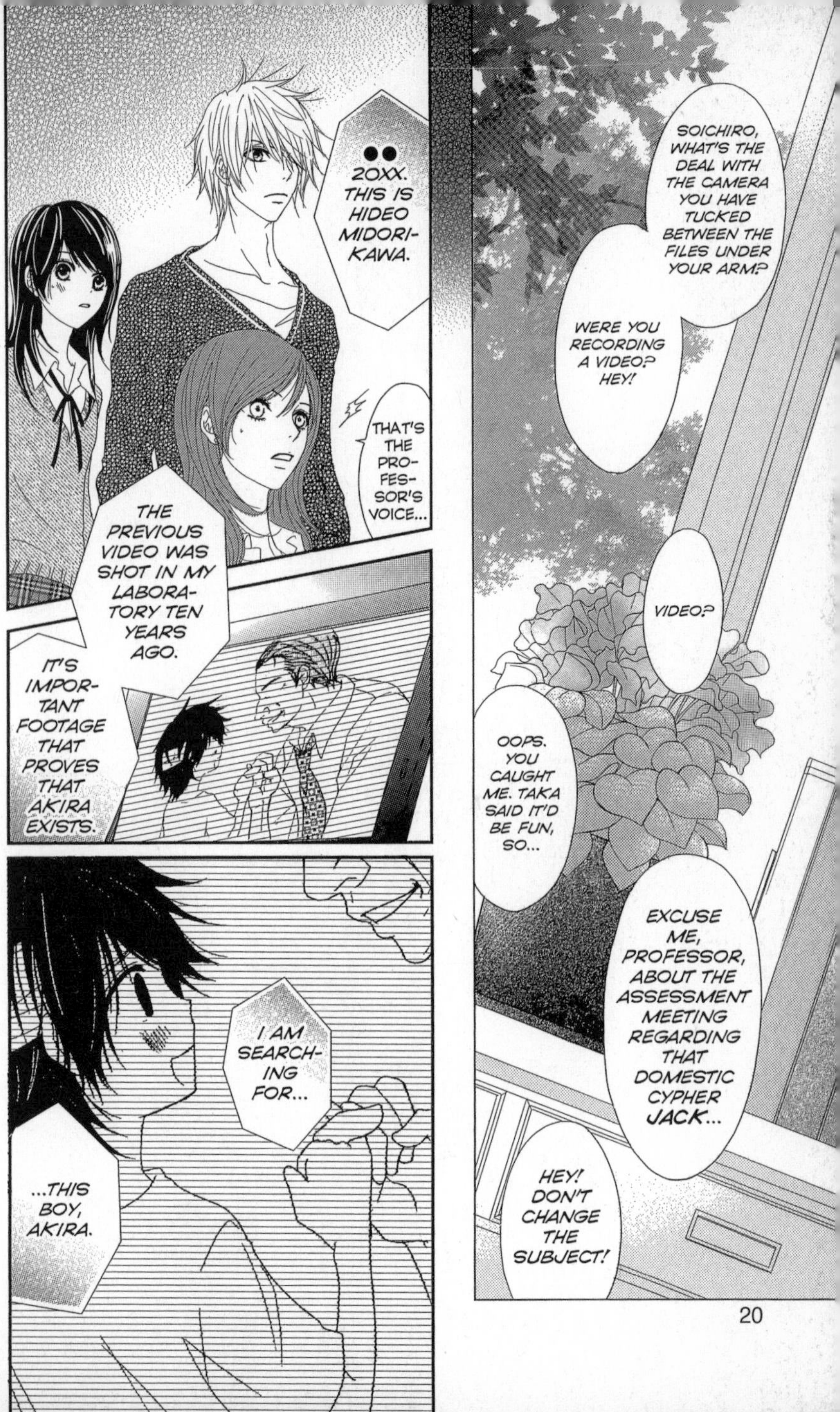
SOICHIRO, WHAT'S THE DEAL WITH THE CAMERA YOU HAVE TUCKED BETWEEN THE FILES UNDER YOUR ARM?
WERE YOU RECORDING A VIDEO? HEY!
VIDEO?
OOPS. YOU CAUGHT ME. TAKA SAID IT'D BE FUN, SO...
EXCUSE ME, PROFESSOR, ABOUT THE ASSESSMENT MEETING REGARDING THAT DOMESTIC CYPHER JACK...
HEY! DON'T CHANGE THE SUBJECT!
●● 20XX. THIS IS HIDEO MIDORIKAWA.
THAT'S THE PROFESSOR'S VOICE...
THE PREVIOUS VIDEO WAS SHOT IN MY LABORATORY TEN YEARS AGO.
IT'S IMPORTANT FOOTAGE THAT PROVES THAT AKIRA EXISTS.
I AM SEARCHING FOR...
...THIS BOY, AKIRA.

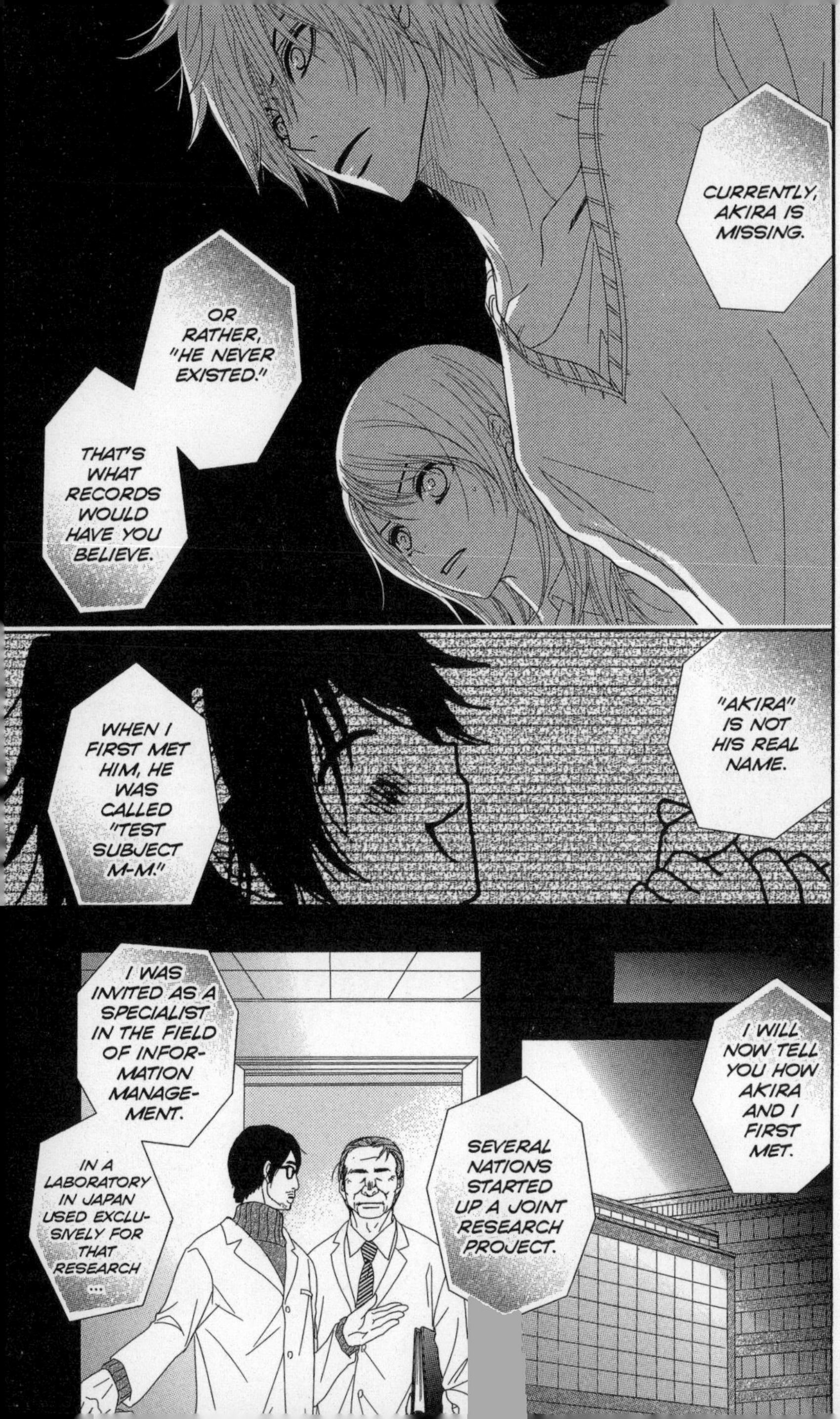
CURRENTLY, AKIRA IS MISSING.
OR RATHER, "HE NEVER EXISTED."
THAT'S WHAT RECORDS WOULD HAVE YOU BELIEVE.
"AKIRA" IS NOT HIS REAL NAME.
WHEN I FIRST MET HIM, HE WAS CALLED "TEST SUBJECT M-M."
I WILL NOW TELL YOU HOW AKIRA AND I FIRST MET.
SEVERAL NATIONS STARTED UP A JOINT RESEARCH PROJECT.
I WAS INVITED AS A SPECIALIST IN THE FIELD OF INFOR-MATION MANAGE-MENT.
IN A LABORATORY IN JAPAN USED EXCLU-SIVELY FOR THAT RESEARCH ...

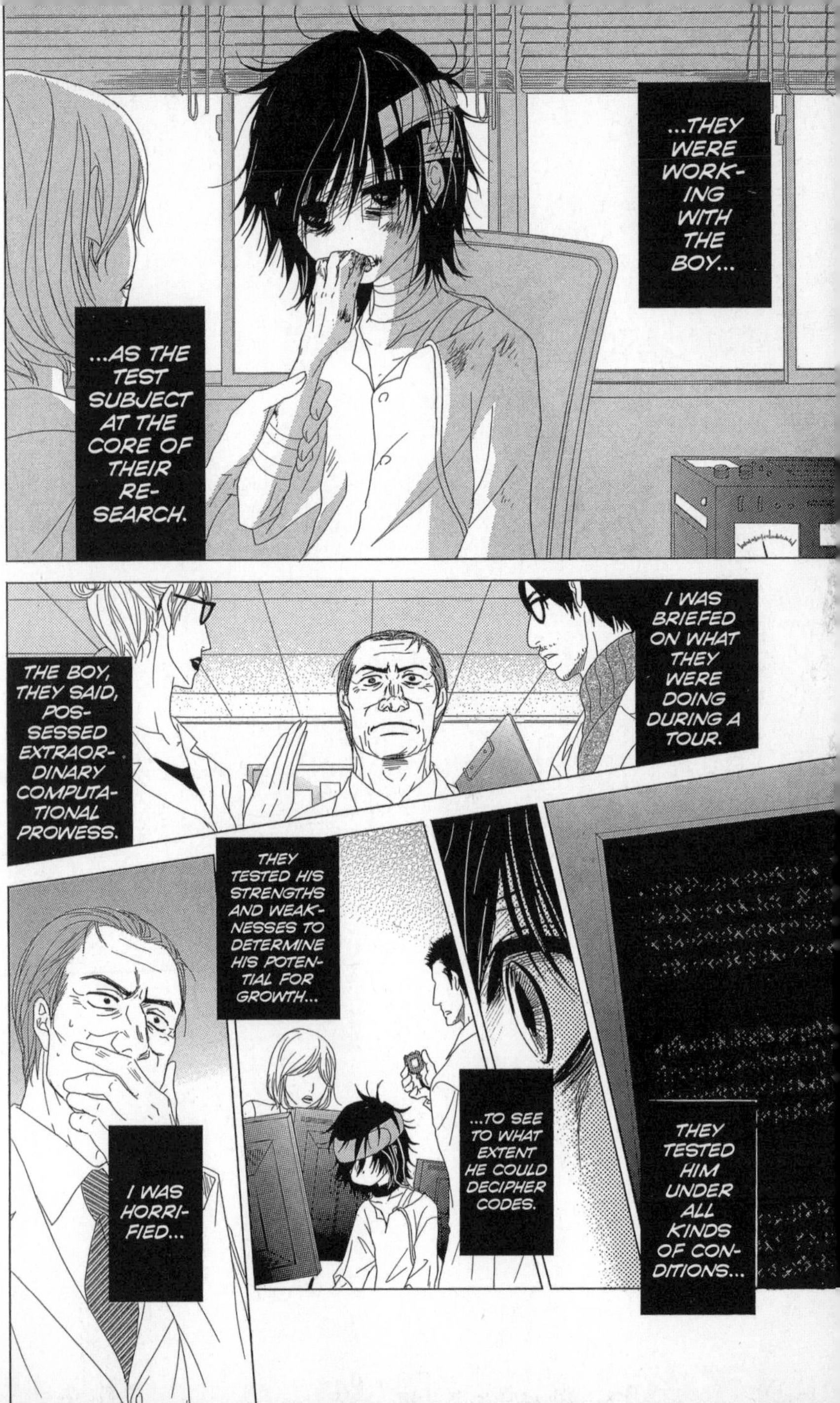
...THEY WERE WORK-ING WITH THE BOY...
...AS THE TEST SUBJECT AT THE CORE OF THEIR RE-SEARCH.
I WAS BRIEFED ON WHAT THEY WERE DOING DURING A TOUR.
THE BOY, THEY SAID, POS-SESSED EXTRAOR-DINARY COMPUTA-TIONAL PROWESS.
THEY TESTED HIM UNDER ALL KINDS OF CON-DITIONS...
THEY TESTED HIS STRENGTHS AND WEAK-NESSES TO DETERMINE HIS POTEN-TIAL FOR GROWTH...
...TO SEE TO WHAT EXTENT HE COULD DECIPHER CODES.
I WAS HORRI-FIED...

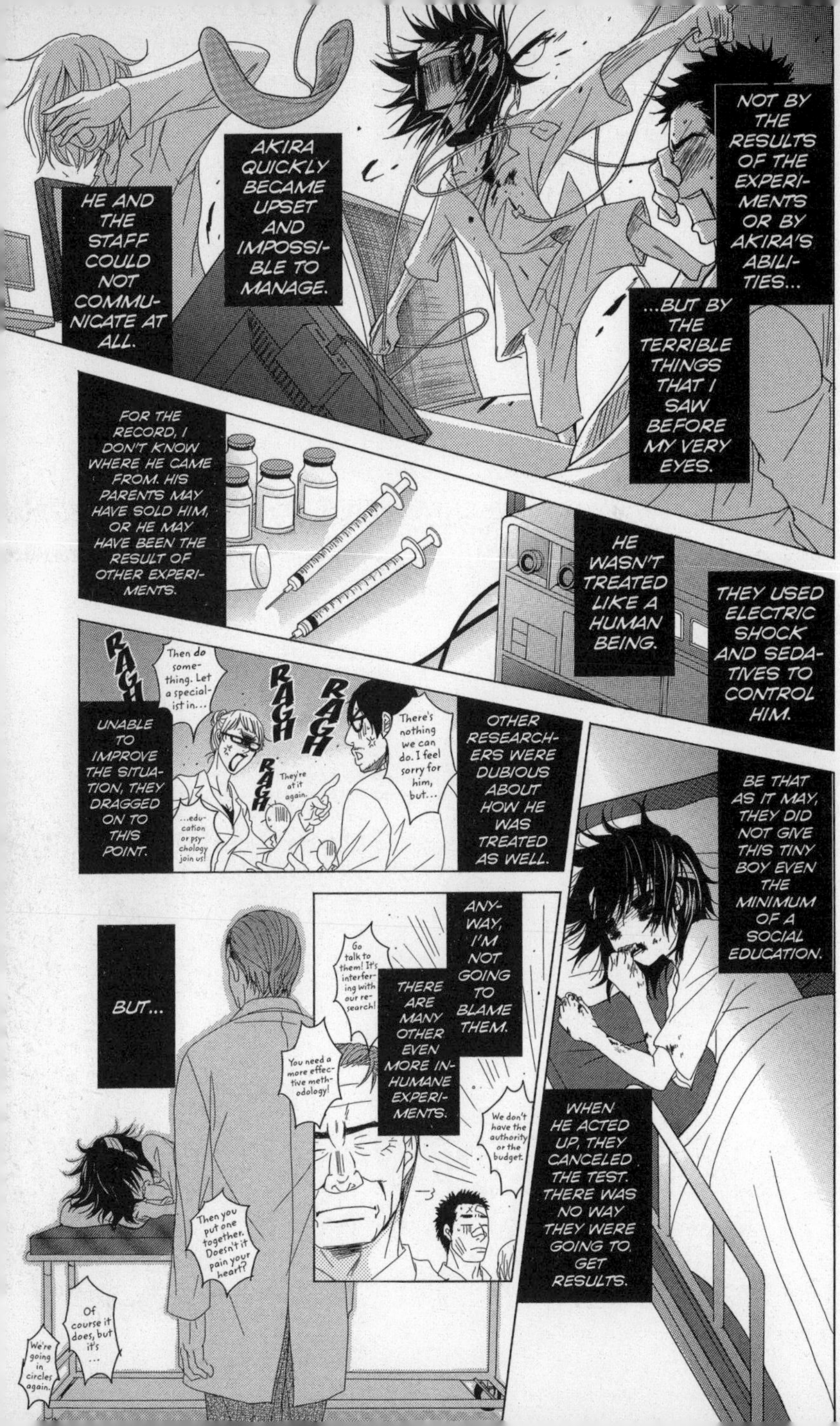
NOT BY THE RESULTS OF THE EXPERIMENTS OR BY AKIRA'S ABILITIES...
...BUT BY THE TERRIBLE THINGS THAT I SAW BEFORE MY VERY EYES.
AKIRA QUICKLY BECAME UPSET AND IMPOSSIBLE TO MANAGE.
HE AND THE STAFF COULD NOT COMMUNICATE AT ALL.
HE WASN'T TREATED LIKE A HUMAN BEING.
THEY USED ELECTRIC SHOCK AND SEDATIVES TO CONTROL HIM.
FOR THE RECORD, I DON'T KNOW WHERE HE CAME FROM. HIS PARENTS MAY HAVE SOLD HIM, OR HE MAY HAVE BEEN THE RESULT OF OTHER EXPERIMENTS.
BE THAT AS IT MAY, THEY DID NOT GIVE THIS TINY BOY EVEN THE MINIMUM OF A SOCIAL EDUCATION.
WHEN HE ACTED UP, THEY CANCELED THE TEST. THERE WAS NO WAY THEY WERE GOING TO GET RESULTS.
OTHER RESEARCHERS WERE DUBIOUS ABOUT HOW HE WAS TREATED AS WELL.
RAGH
RAGH
There's nothing we can do. I feel sorry for him, but...
RAGH
RAGH
They're at it again.
Then do something. Let a specialist in...
...education or psychology join us!
UNABLE TO IMPROVE THE SITUATION, THEY DRAGGED ON TO THIS POINT.
ANYWAY, I'M NOT GOING TO BLAME THEM.
THERE ARE MANY OTHER EVEN MORE INHUMANE EXPERIMENTS.
Go talk to them! It's interfering with our research!
You need a more effective methodology!
We don't have the authority or the budget.
Then you put one together. Doesn't it pain your heart?
Of course it does, but it's...
We're going in circles again.
BUT...

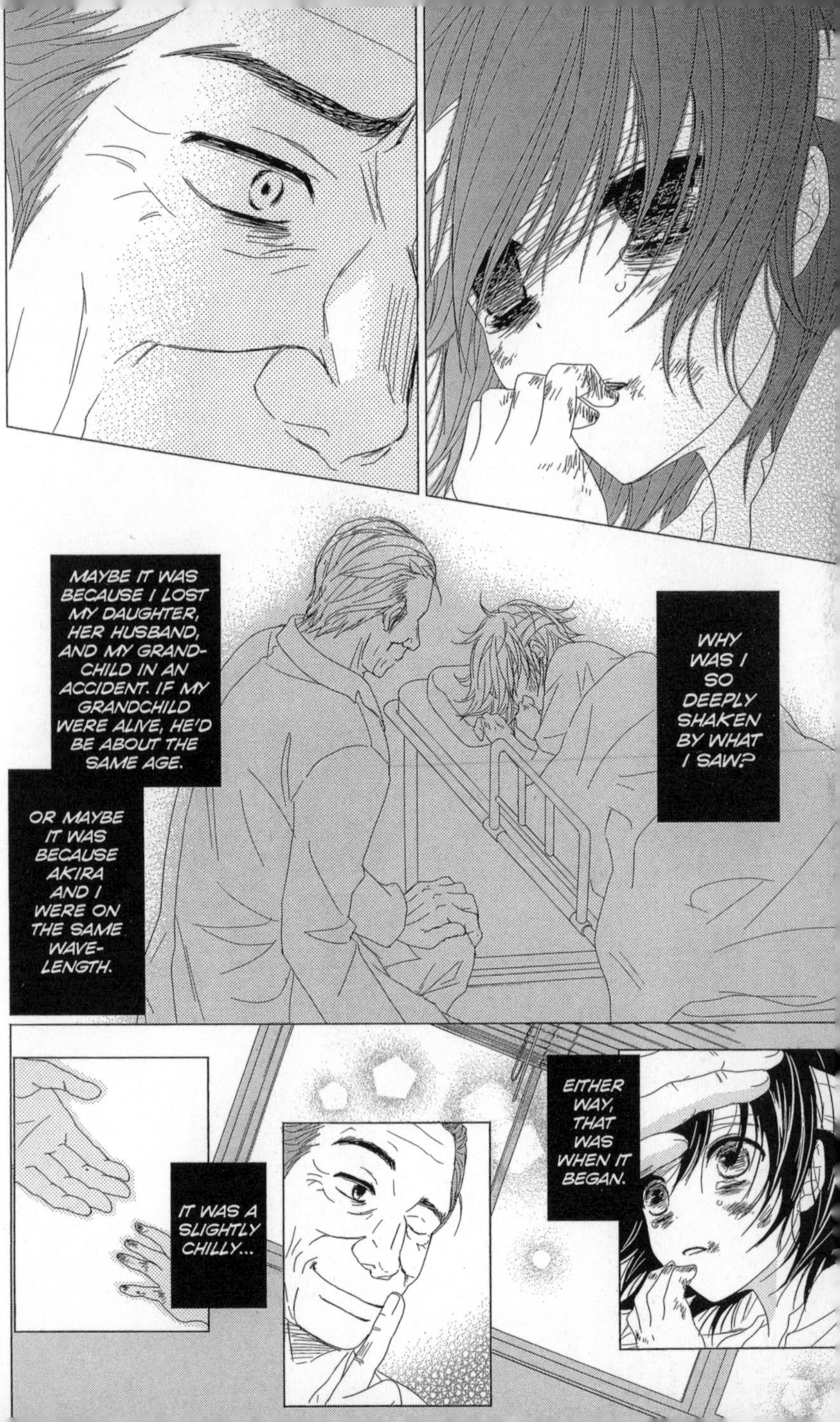
WHY WAS I SO DEEPLY SHAKEN BY WHAT I SAW?
MAYBE IT WAS BECAUSE I LOST MY DAUGHTER, HER HUSBAND, AND MY GRAND-CHILD IN AN ACCIDENT. IF MY GRANDCHILD WERE ALIVE, HE'D BE ABOUT THE SAME AGE.
OR MAYBE IT WAS BECAUSE AKIRA AND I WERE ON THE SAME WAVE-LENGTH.
EITHER WAY, THAT WAS WHEN IT BEGAN.
IT WAS A SLIGHTLY CHILLY...

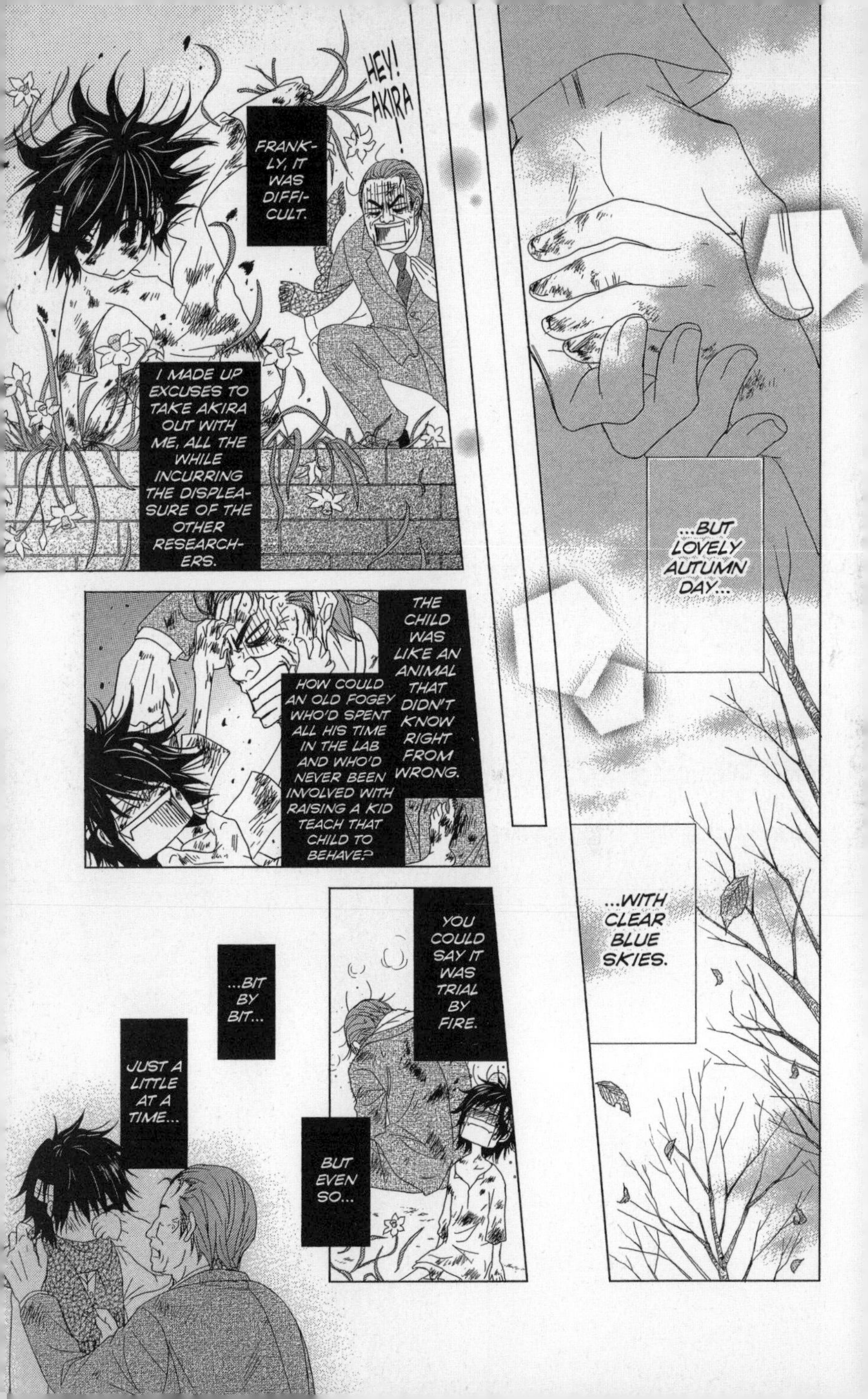
...BUT LOVELY AUTUMN DAY...
...WITH CLEAR BLUE SKIES.
HEY! AKIRA!
FRANKLY, IT WAS DIFFICULT.
I MADE UP EXCUSES TO TAKE AKIRA OUT WITH ME, ALL THE WHILE INCURRING THE DISPLEASURE OF THE OTHER RESEARCHERS.
THE CHILD WAS LIKE AN ANIMAL THAT DIDN'T KNOW RIGHT FROM WRONG.
HOW COULD AN OLD FOGEY WHO'D SPENT ALL HIS TIME IN THE LAB AND WHO'D NEVER BEEN INVOLVED WITH RAISING A KID TEACH THAT CHILD TO BEHAVE?
YOU COULD SAY IT WAS TRIAL BY FIRE.
BUT EVEN SO...
...BIT BY BIT...
JUST A LITTLE AT A TIME...

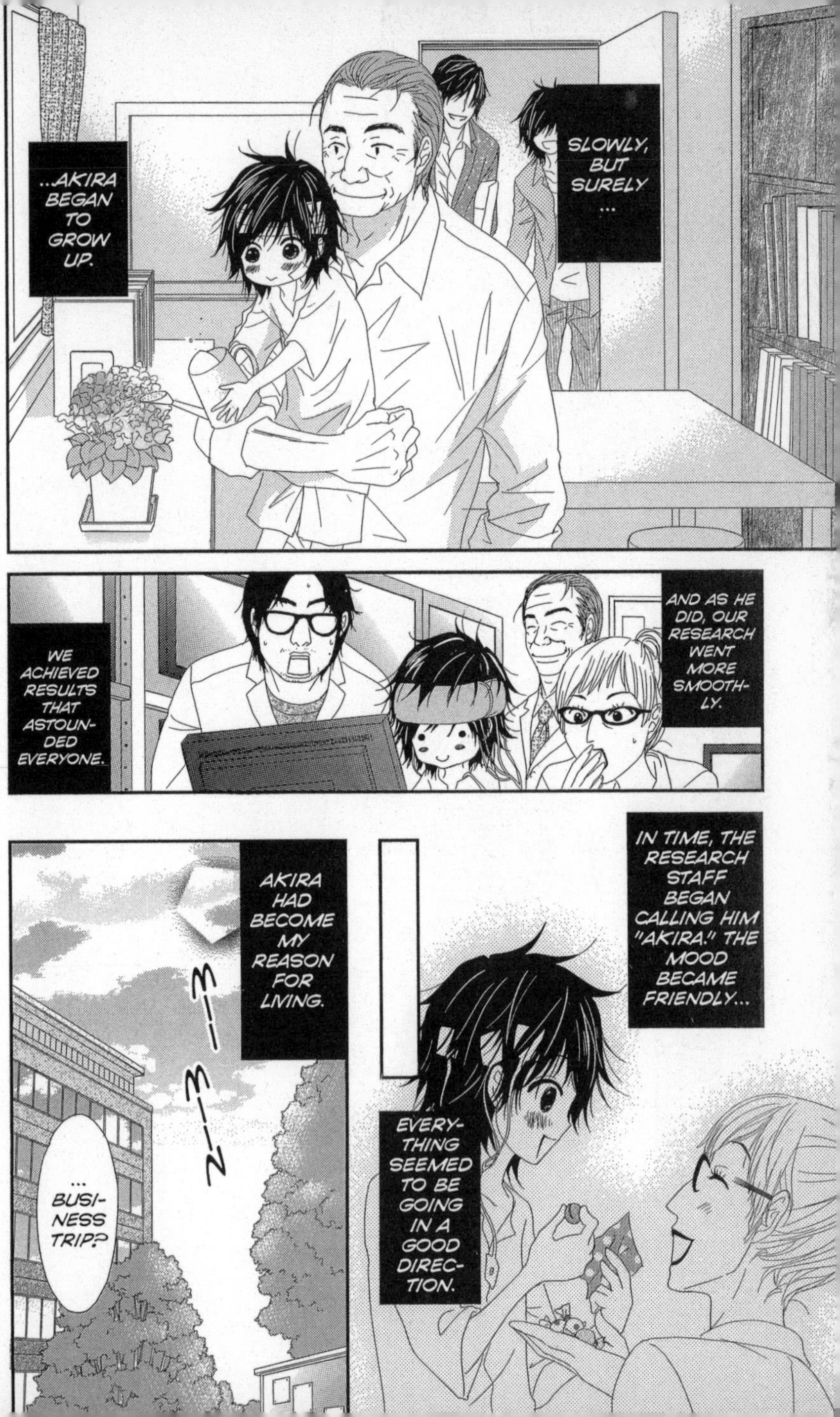
SLOWLY, BUT SURELY ...
...AKIRA BEGAN TO GROW UP.
AND AS HE DID, OUR RESEARCH WENT MORE SMOOTHLY.
WE ACHIEVED RESULTS THAT ASTOUNDED EVERYONE.
IN TIME, THE RESEARCH STAFF BEGAN CALLING HIM "AKIRA." THE MOOD BECAME FRIENDLY...
EVERYTHING SEEMED TO BE GOING IN A GOOD DIRECTION.
AKIRA HAD BECOME MY REASON FOR LIVING.
MI-I MI-I-N
... BUSINESS TRIP?

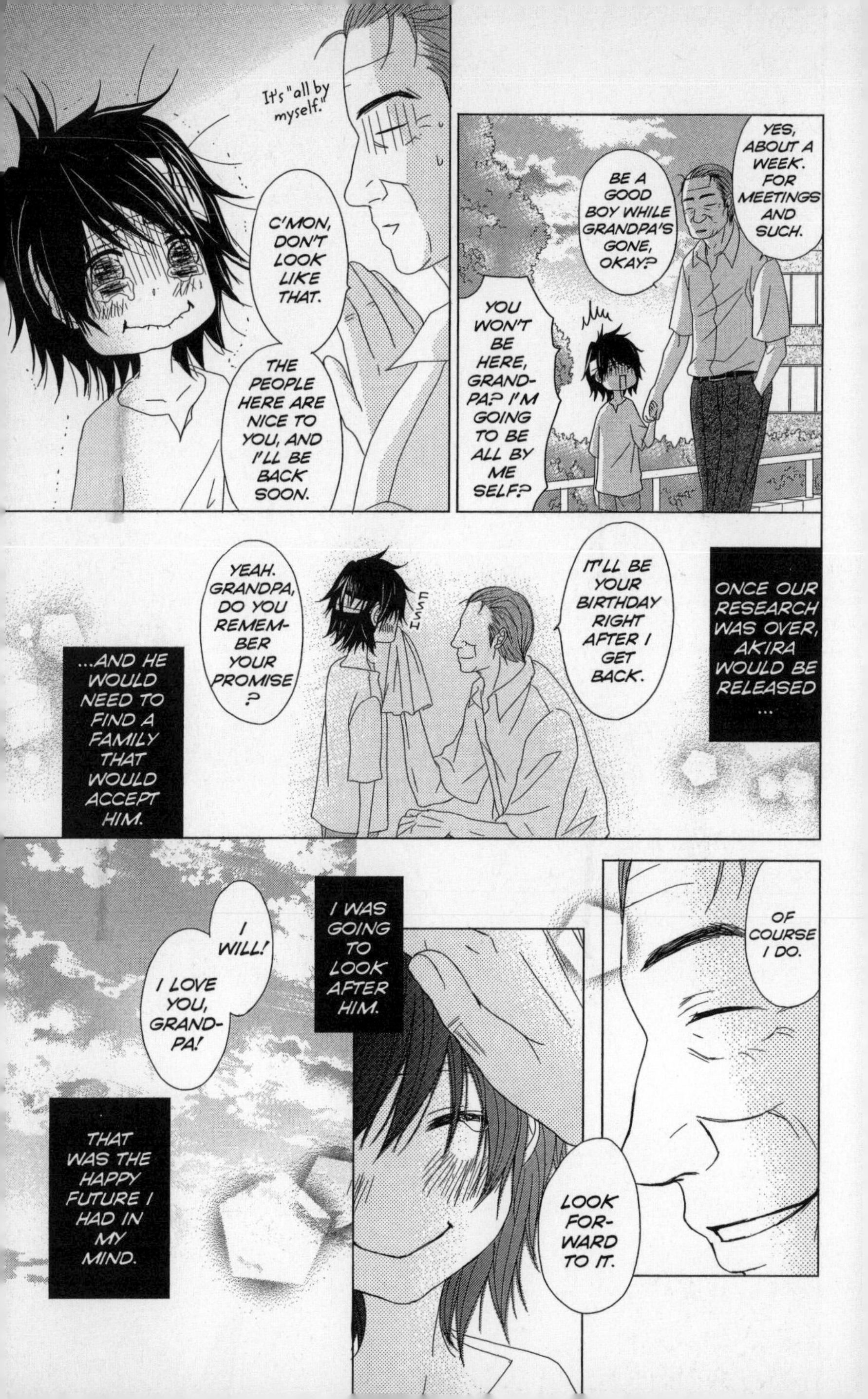
YES, ABOUT A WEEK. FOR MEETINGS AND SUCH.
BE A GOOD BOY WHILE GRANDPA'S GONE, OKAY?
YOU WON'T BE HERE, GRANDPA? I'M GOING TO BE ALL BY ME SELF?
It's "all by myself."
C'MON, DON'T LOOK LIKE THAT.
THE PEOPLE HERE ARE NICE TO YOU, AND I'LL BE BACK SOON.
ONCE OUR RESEARCH WAS OVER, AKIRA WOULD BE RELEASED ...
IT'LL BE YOUR BIRTHDAY RIGHT AFTER I GET BACK.
FSSH
YEAH. GRANDPA, DO YOU REMEMBER YOUR PROMISE?
...AND HE WOULD NEED TO FIND A FAMILY THAT WOULD ACCEPT HIM.
OF COURSE I DO.
LOOK FORWARD TO IT.
I WAS GOING TO LOOK AFTER HIM.
I WILL!
I LOVE YOU, GRANDPA!
THAT WAS THE HAPPY FUTURE I HAD IN MY MIND.

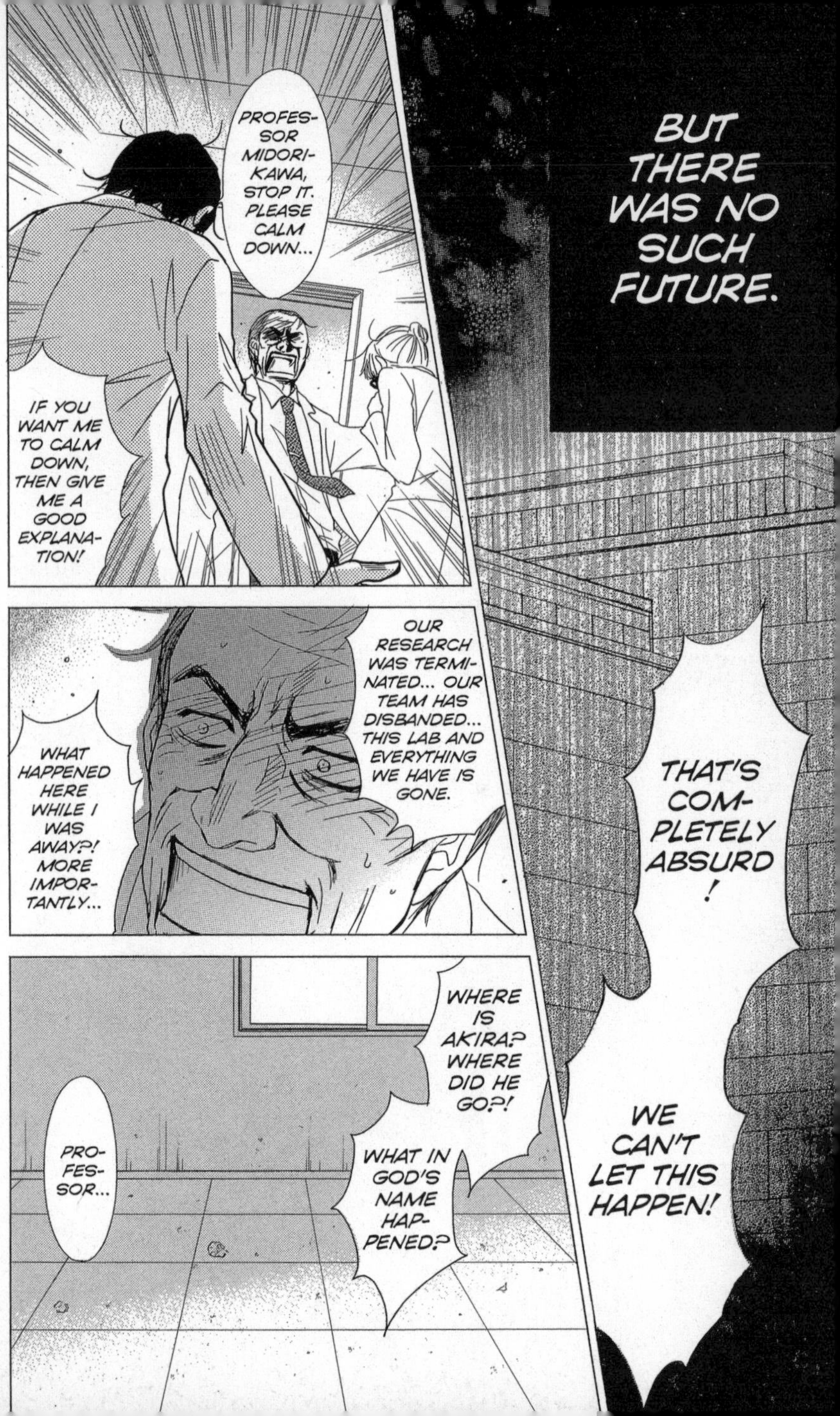
BUT THERE WAS NO SUCH FUTURE.
THAT'S COMPLETELY ABSURD!
WE CAN'T LET THIS HAPPEN!
PROFESSOR MIDORIKAWA, STOP IT. PLEASE CALM DOWN...
IF YOU WANT ME TO CALM DOWN, THEN GIVE ME A GOOD EXPLANATION!
OUR RESEARCH WAS TERMINATED... OUR TEAM HAS DISBANDED... THIS LAB AND EVERYTHING WE HAVE IS GONE.
WHAT HAPPENED HERE WHILE I WAS AWAY?! MORE IMPORTANTLY...
WHERE IS AKIRA? WHERE DID HE GO?!
WHAT IN GOD'S NAME HAPPENED?
PROFESSOR...

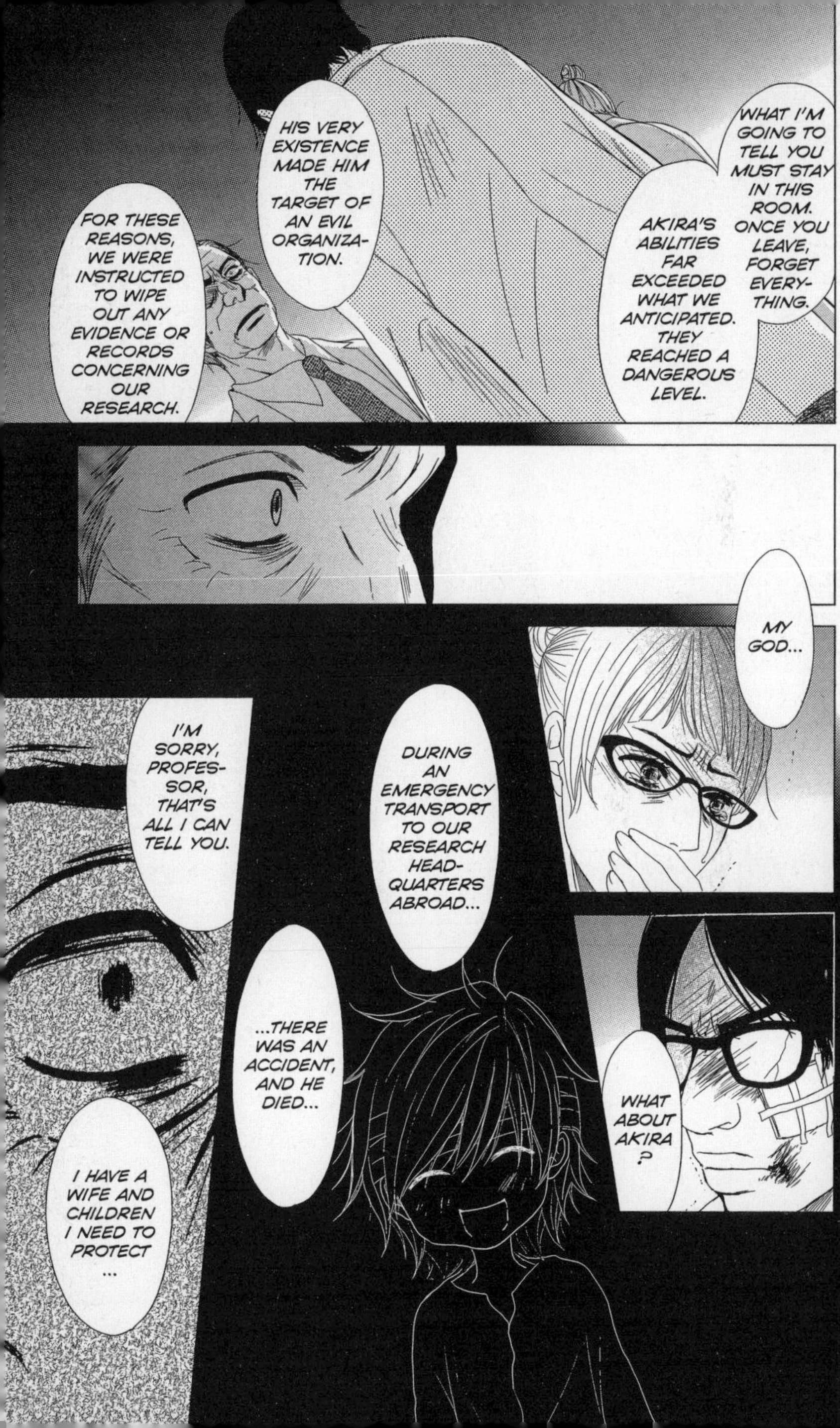
WHAT I'M GOING TO TELL YOU MUST STAY IN THIS ROOM. ONCE YOU LEAVE, FORGET EVERYTHING.
AKIRA'S ABILITIES FAR EXCEEDED WHAT WE ANTICIPATED. THEY REACHED A DANGEROUS LEVEL.
HIS VERY EXISTENCE MADE HIM THE TARGET OF AN EVIL ORGANIZATION.
FOR THESE REASONS, WE WERE INSTRUCTED TO WIPE OUT ANY EVIDENCE OR RECORDS CONCERNING OUR RESEARCH.
MY GOD...
WHAT ABOUT AKIRA?
DURING AN EMERGENCY TRANSPORT TO OUR RESEARCH HEADQUARTERS ABROAD...
...THERE WAS AN ACCIDENT, AND HE DIED...
I'M SORRY, PROFESSOR, THAT'S ALL I CAN TELL YOU.
I HAVE A WIFE AND CHILDREN I NEED TO PROTECT...

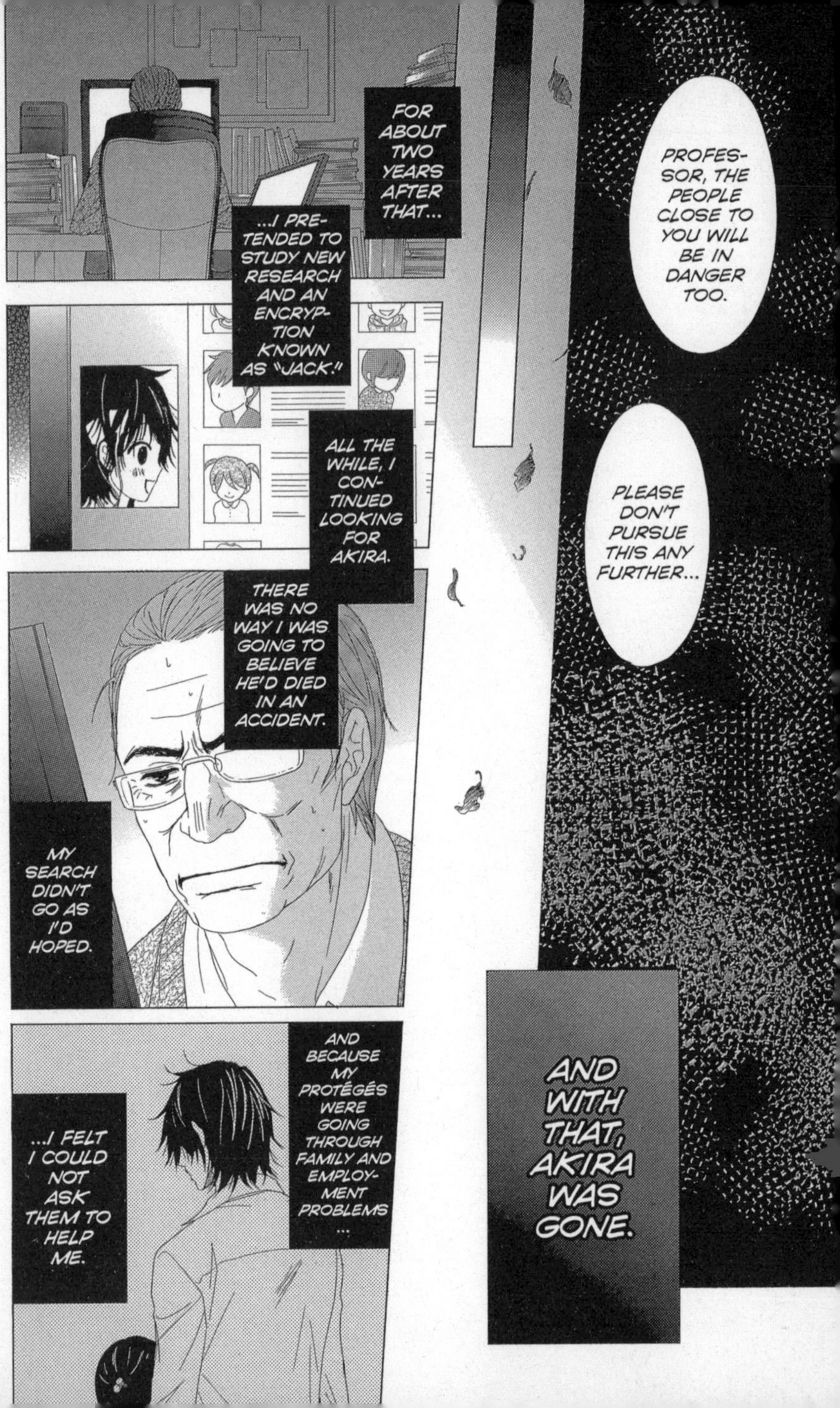
PROFESSOR, THE PEOPLE CLOSE TO YOU WILL BE IN DANGER TOO.
PLEASE DON'T PURSUE THIS ANY FURTHER...
AND WITH THAT, AKIRA WAS GONE.
FOR ABOUT TWO YEARS AFTER THAT...
...I PRETENDED TO STUDY NEW RESEARCH AND AN ENCRYPTION KNOWN AS "JACK."
ALL THE WHILE, I CONTINUED LOOKING FOR AKIRA.
THERE WAS NO WAY I WAS GOING TO BELIEVE HE'D DIED IN AN ACCIDENT.
MY SEARCH DIDN'T GO AS I'D HOPED.
AND BECAUSE MY PROTÉGÉS WERE GOING THROUGH FAMILY AND EMPLOYMENT PROBLEMS...
...I FELT I COULD NOT ASK THEM TO HELP ME.

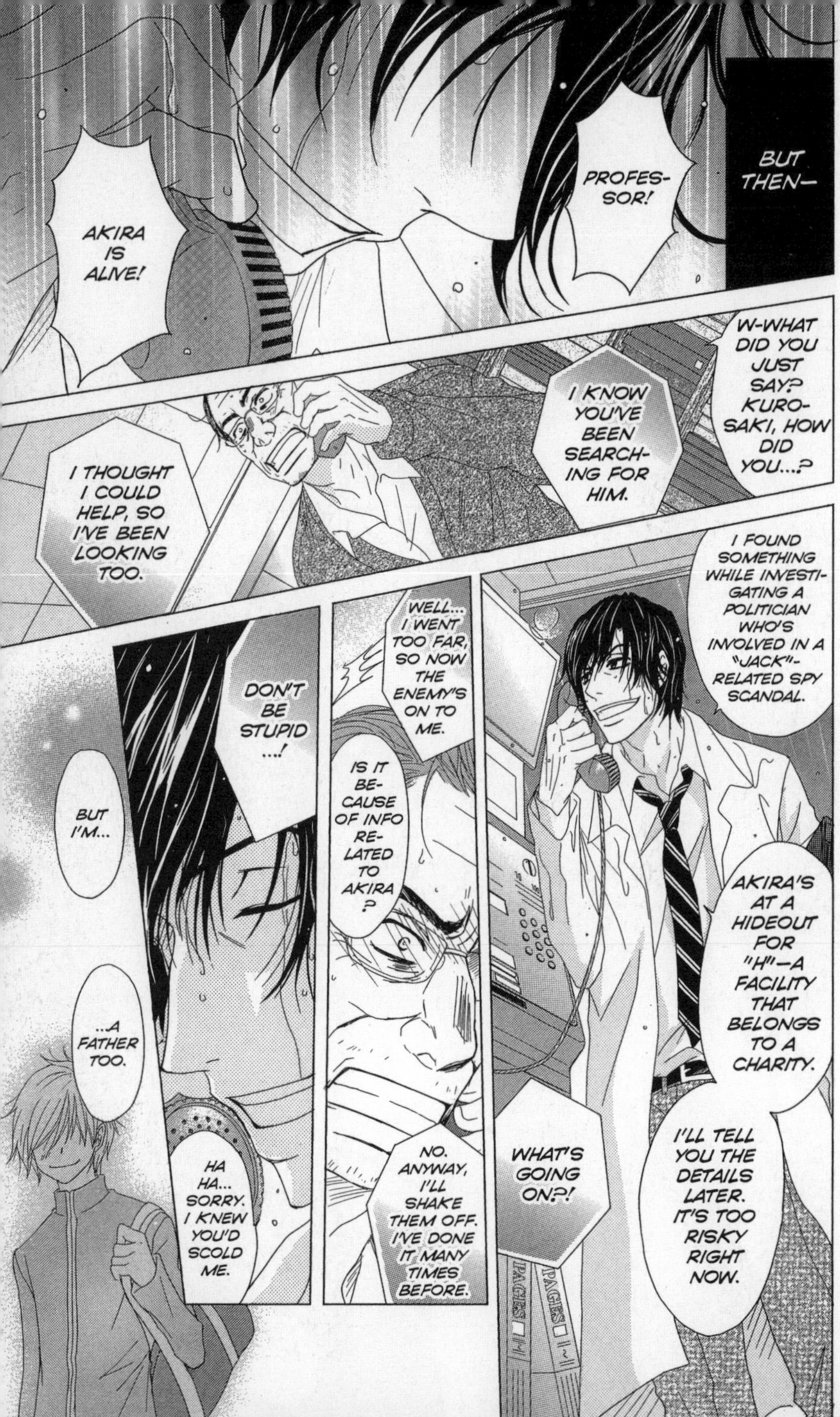
BUT THEN—
PROFESSOR!
AKIRA IS ALIVE!
W-WHAT DID YOU JUST SAY? KUROSAKI, HOW DID YOU...?
I KNOW YOU'VE BEEN SEARCHING FOR HIM.
I THOUGHT I COULD HELP, SO I'VE BEEN LOOKING TOO.
I FOUND SOMETHING WHILE INVESTIGATING A POLITICIAN WHO'S INVOLVED IN A "JACK"-RELATED SPY SCANDAL.
AKIRA'S AT A HIDEOUT FOR "H"—A FACILITY THAT BELONGS TO A CHARITY.
WHAT'S GOING ON?!
I'LL TELL YOU THE DETAILS LATER. IT'S TOO RISKY RIGHT NOW.
WELL... I WENT TOO FAR, SO NOW THE ENEMY'S ON TO ME.
IS IT BECAUSE OF INFO RELATED TO AKIRA?
NO. ANYWAY, I'LL SHAKE THEM OFF. I'VE DONE IT MANY TIMES BEFORE.
DON'T BE STUPID...!
HA HA... SORRY. I KNEW YOU'D SCOLD ME.
BUT I'M...
...A FATHER TOO.

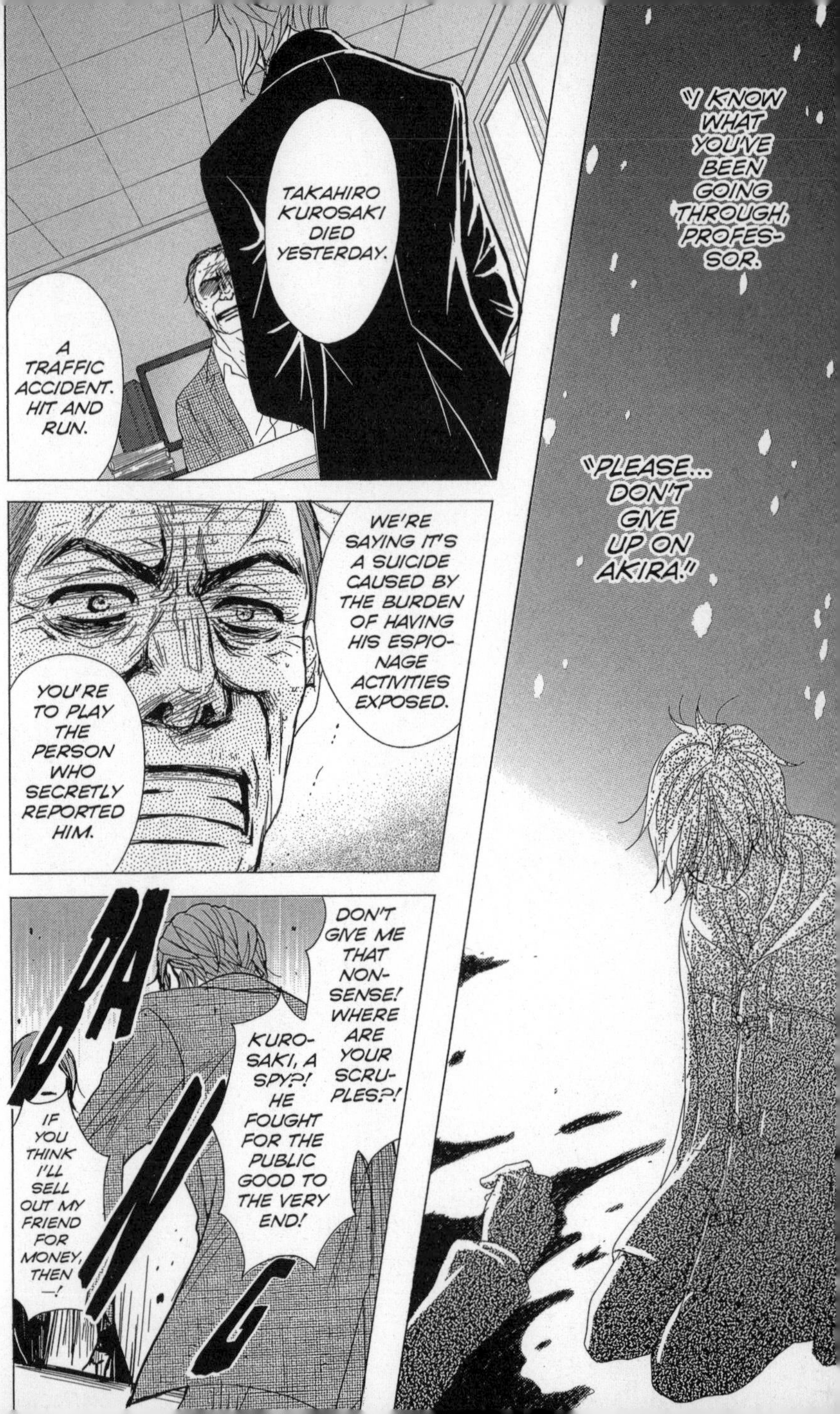
"I KNOW WHAT YOU'VE BEEN GOING THROUGH, PROFES-SOR.
"PLEASE... DON'T GIVE UP ON AKIRA."
TAKAHIRO KUROSAKI DIED YESTERDAY.
A TRAFFIC ACCIDENT. HIT AND RUN.
WE'RE SAYING IT'S A SUICIDE CAUSED BY THE BURDEN OF HAVING HIS ESPIO-NAGE ACTIVITIES EXPOSED.
YOU'RE TO PLAY THE PERSON WHO SECRETLY REPORTED HIM.
DON'T GIVE ME THAT NON-SENSE! WHERE ARE YOUR SCRU-PLES?!
KURO-SAKI, A SPY?! HE FOUGHT FOR THE PUBLIC GOOD TO THE VERY END!
BANG
IF YOU THINK I'LL SELL OUT MY FRIEND FOR MONEY, THEN —!

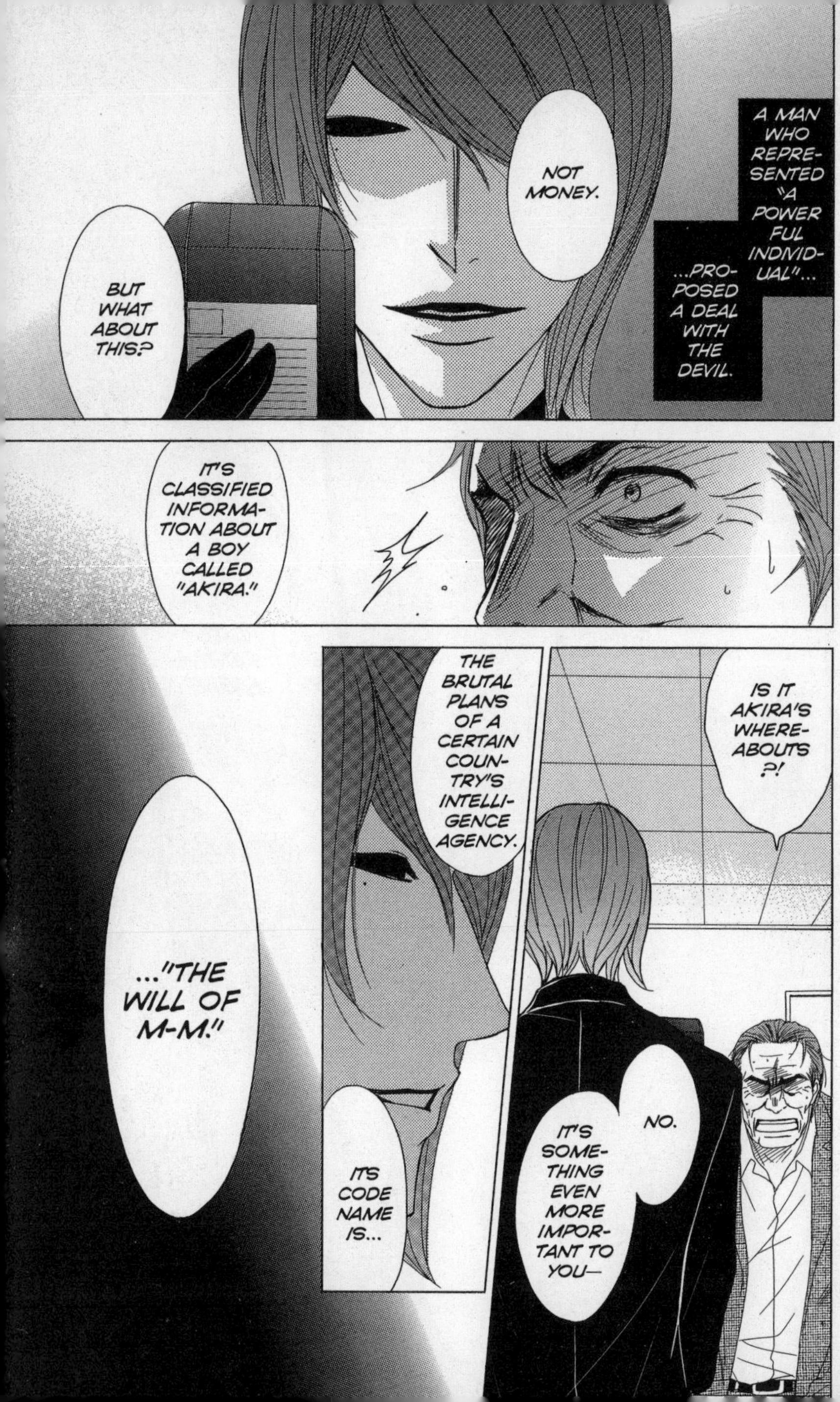
A MAN WHO REPRESENTED "A POWERFUL INDIVIDUAL"...
...PROPOSED A DEAL WITH THE DEVIL.
NOT MONEY.
BUT WHAT ABOUT THIS?
IT'S CLASSIFIED INFORMATION ABOUT A BOY CALLED "AKIRA."
IS IT AKIRA'S WHEREABOUTS?!
NO.
IT'S SOMETHING EVEN MORE IMPORTANT TO YOU—
THE BRUTAL PLANS OF A CERTAIN COUNTRY'S INTELLIGENCE AGENCY.
ITS CODE NAME IS...
..."THE WILL OF M-M."

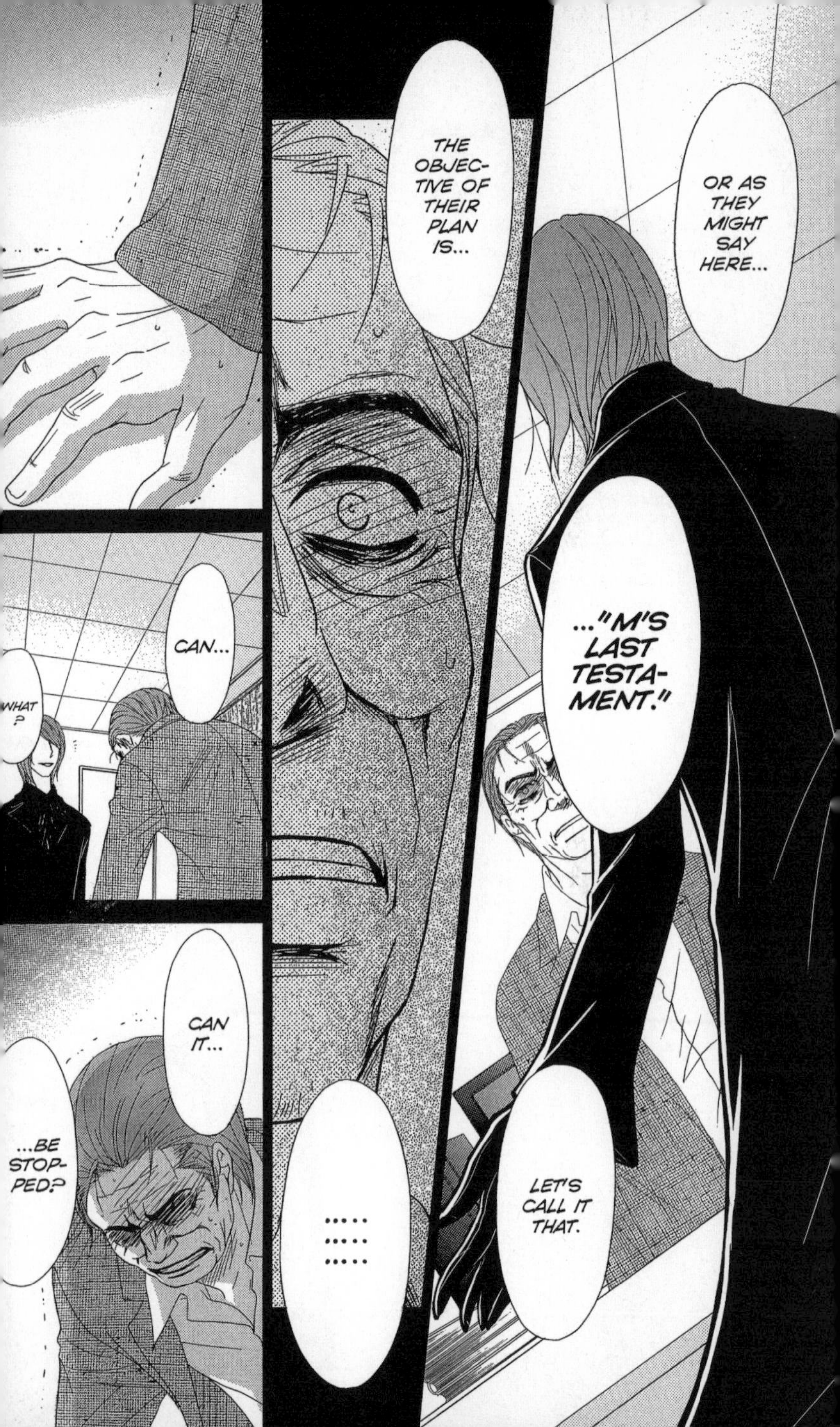
THE OBJECTIVE OF THEIR PLAN IS...
OR AS THEY MIGHT SAY HERE...
..."M'S LAST TESTAMENT."
LET'S CALL IT THAT.
......
CAN...
WHAT?
CAN IT...
...BE STOPPED?

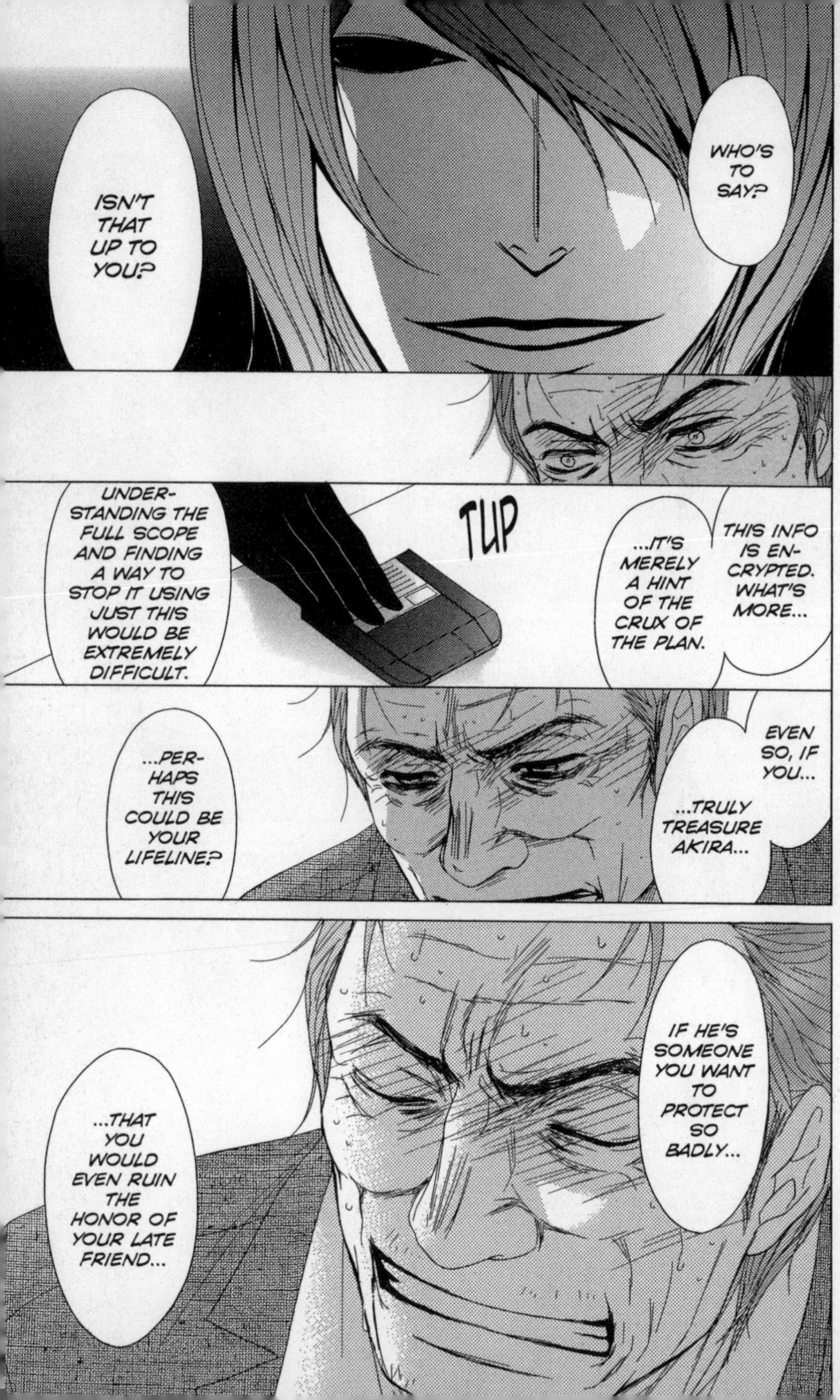
WHO'S TO SAY?
ISN'T THAT UP TO YOU?
THIS INFO IS EN-CRYPTED. WHAT'S MORE...
...IT'S MERELY A HINT OF THE CRUX OF THE PLAN.
TUP
UNDER-STANDING THE FULL SCOPE AND FINDING A WAY TO STOP IT USING JUST THIS WOULD BE EXTREMELY DIFFICULT.
EVEN SO, IF YOU...
...TRULY TREASURE AKIRA...
...PER-HAPS THIS COULD BE YOUR LIFELINE?
IF HE'S SOMEONE YOU WANT TO PROTECT SO BADLY...
...THAT YOU WOULD EVEN RUIN THE HONOR OF YOUR LATE FRIEND...

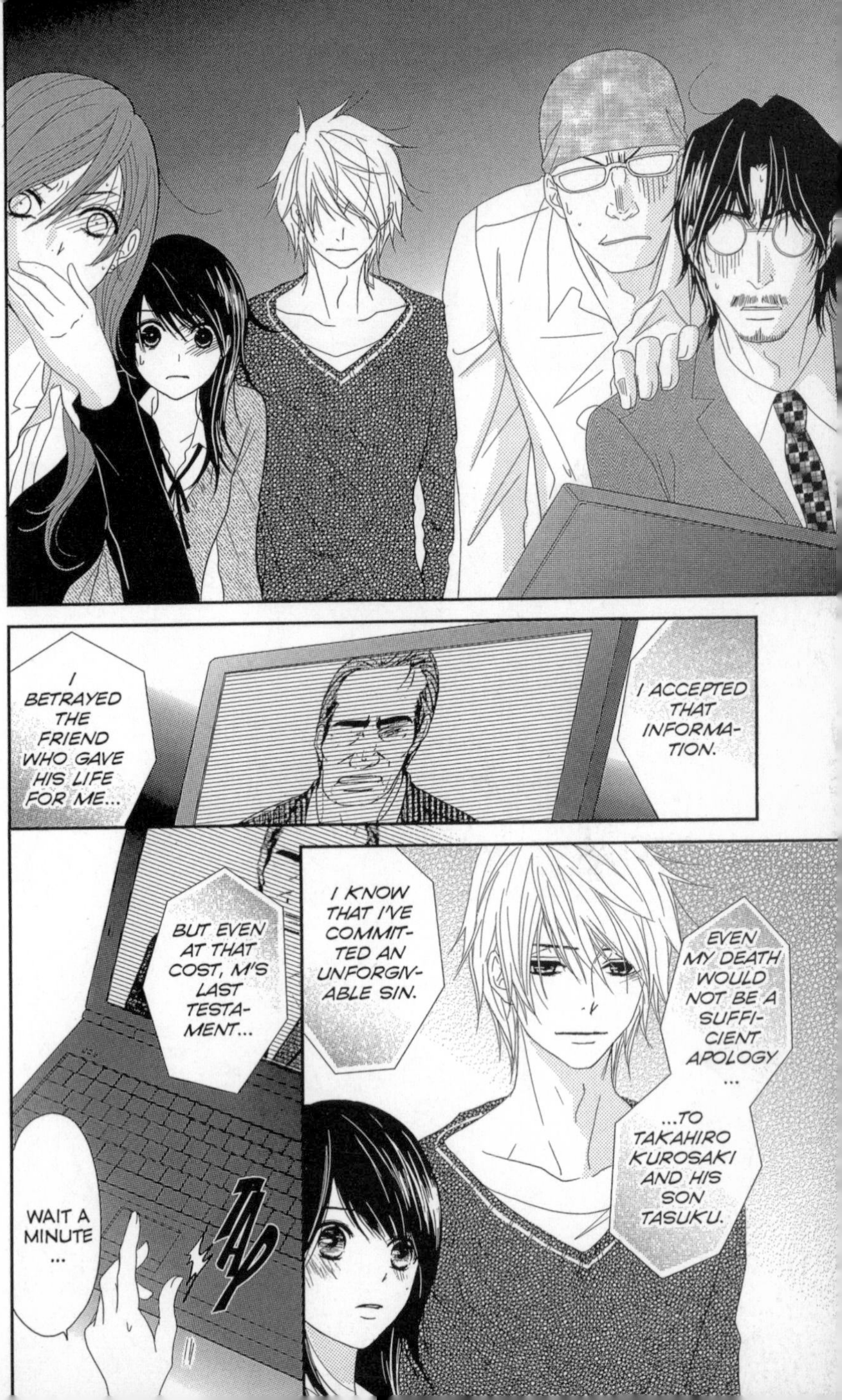
I ACCEPTED THAT INFORMATION.
I BETRAYED THE FRIEND WHO GAVE HIS LIFE FOR ME...
EVEN MY DEATH WOULD NOT BE A SUFFICIENT APOLOGY...
...TO TAKAHIRO KUROSAKI AND HIS SON TASUKU.
I KNOW THAT I'VE COMMITTED AN UNFORGIVABLE SIN.
BUT EVEN AT THAT COST, M'S LAST TESTAMENT...
TAP
WAIT A MINUTE...

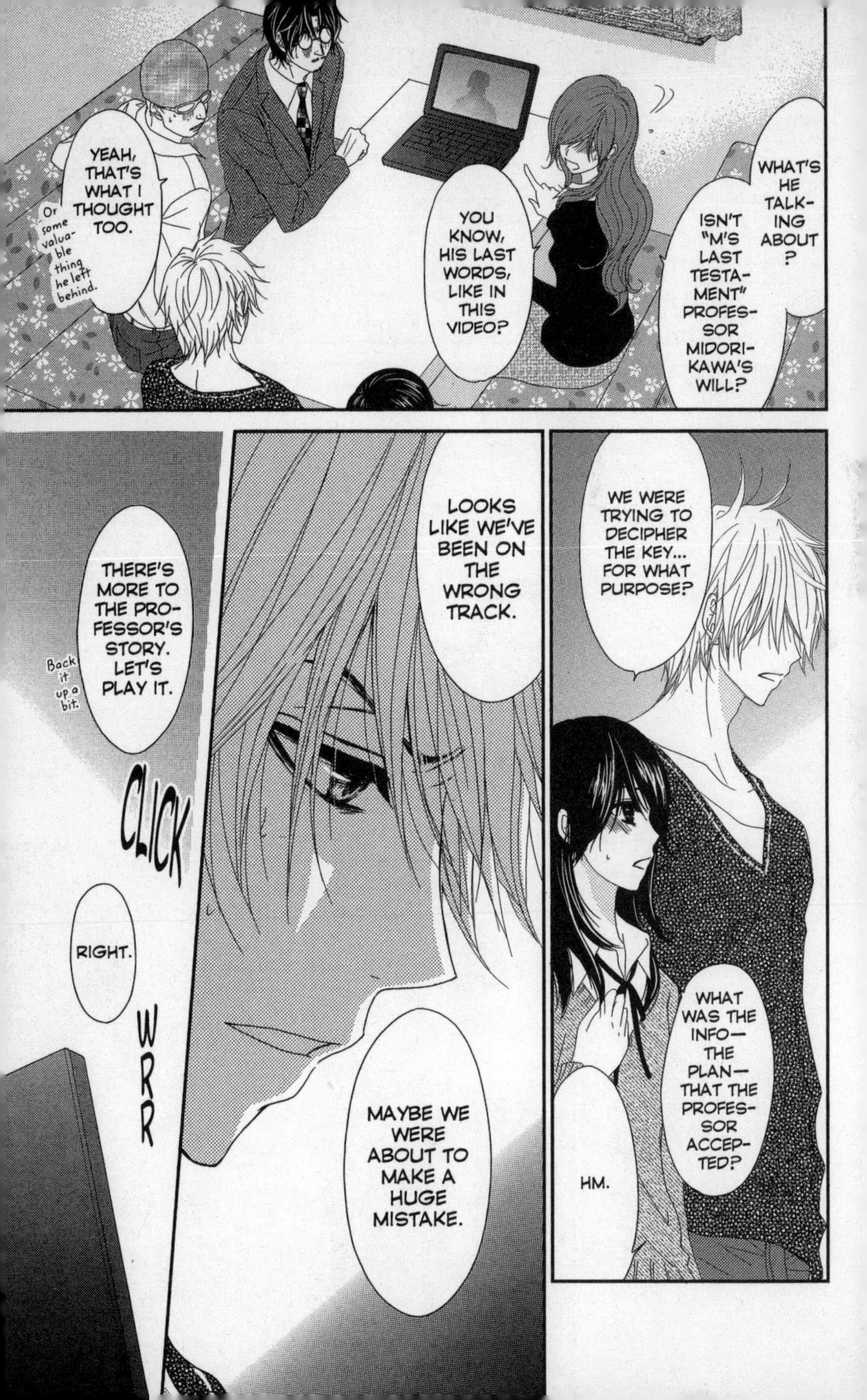
WHAT'S HE TALKING ABOUT?
ISN'T "M'S LAST TESTAMENT" PROFESSOR MIDORIKAWA'S WILL?
YOU KNOW, HIS LAST WORDS, LIKE IN THIS VIDEO?
YEAH, THAT'S WHAT I THOUGHT TOO.
Or some valuable thing he left behind.
WE WERE TRYING TO DECIPHER THE KEY... FOR WHAT PURPOSE?
WHAT WAS THE INFO—THE PLAN—THAT THE PROFESSOR ACCEPTED?
HM.
LOOKS LIKE WE'VE BEEN ON THE WRONG TRACK.
MAYBE WE WERE ABOUT TO MAKE A HUGE MISTAKE.
THERE'S MORE TO THE PROFESSOR'S STORY. LET'S PLAY IT.
Back it up a bit.
CLICK
RIGHT.
WRR

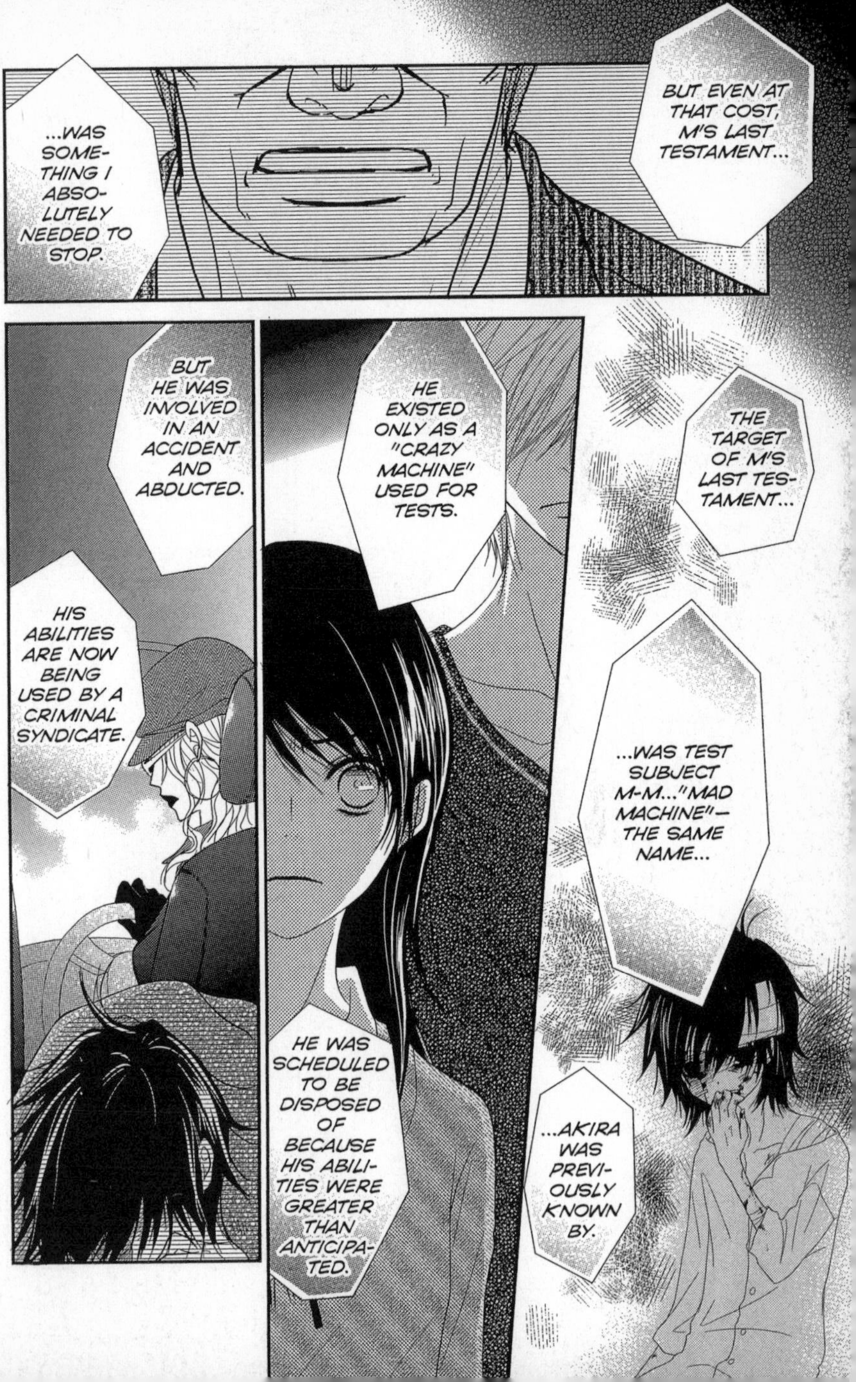
BUT EVEN AT THAT COST, M'S LAST TESTAMENT...
...WAS SOMETHING I ABSOLUTELY NEEDED TO STOP.
THE TARGET OF M'S LAST TESTAMENT...
...WAS TEST SUBJECT M-M..."MAD MACHINE"—THE SAME NAME...
...AKIRA WAS PREVIOUSLY KNOWN BY.
HE EXISTED ONLY AS A "CRAZY MACHINE" USED FOR TESTS.
HE WAS SCHEDULED TO BE DISPOSED OF BECAUSE HIS ABILITIES WERE GREATER THAN ANTICIPATED.
BUT HE WAS INVOLVED IN AN ACCIDENT AND ABDUCTED.
HIS ABILITIES ARE NOW BEING USED BY A CRIMINAL SYNDICATE.

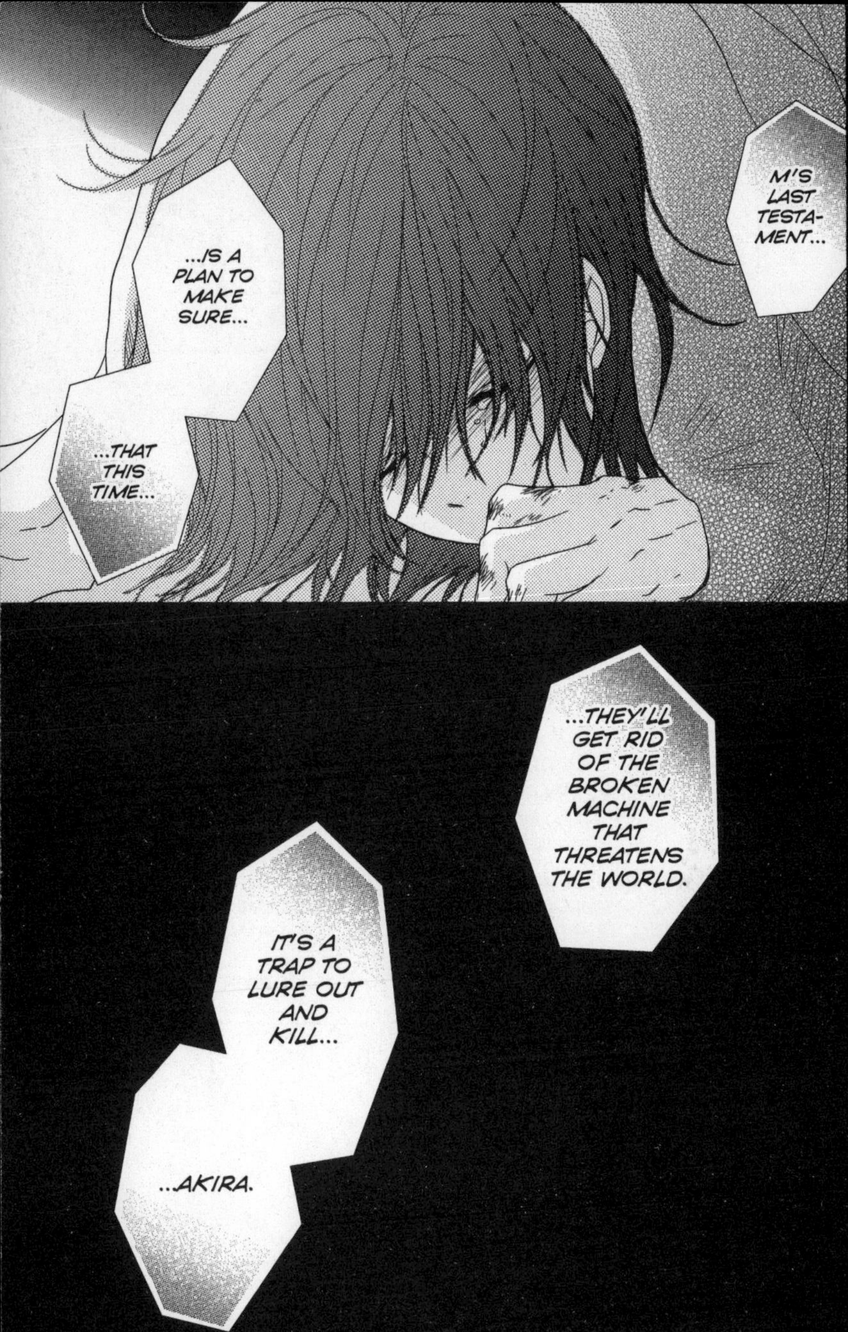
M'S LAST TESTAMENT...
...IS A PLAN TO MAKE SURE...
...THAT THIS TIME...
...THEY'LL GET RID OF THE BROKEN MACHINE THAT THREATENS THE WORLD.
IT'S A TRAP TO LURE OUT AND KILL...
...AKIRA.

DENGEKI DAISY QUESTION CORNER

RELOCATED

BALDLY ASK!!! ①

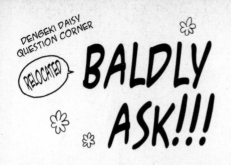

NOW THEN!! "BALDLY ASK" SEEMS TO ONLY DO "RELOCATED" EDITIONS, BUT HERE WE GO AGAIN!! SORRY IT'S TEXT ONLY!!!

HOW DO YOU DO? I'LL COME RIGHT OUT AND ASK. WHEN I START WONDERING ABOUT SOMETHING, I CAN'T STOP, SO I'LL BALDLY ASK. HOW POPULAR IS AKIRA RIGHT NOW? FOR THE RECORD, I LIKE HIM, THOUGH I'M RELUCTANT TO ADMIT IT...

(TWELVE-YEAR-OLD BORN IN THE YEAR OF THE DRAGON, OSAKA PREFECTURE)

YOU KNOW, HE'S ACTUALLY QUITE POPULAR. SURPRISINGLY SO... THERE MIGHT EVEN BE MORE PEOPLE WHO LIKE HIM THAN THOSE WHO LIKE SOICHIRO... IF KUROSAKI DOESN'T WATCH OUT, AKIRA MIGHT PULL (NOT KUROSAKI'S HAIR) RIGHT PAST HIM IN POPULARITY. COME TO THINK OF IT, A FRIEND OF MINE TOLD ME THAT THERE'S A GENRE KNOWN AS "PITIFUL MOE." MAYBE THERE IS. AS I WROTE HERE BEFORE, I'M PRETTY FOND OF DRAWING HIM. RECENTLY, THOUGH, HE'S GONE THROUGH NOTHING BUT HARD TIMES AND HASN'T DONE THAT CREEPY LAUGH OF HIS. I FIND THAT A BIT LACKING.

IN VOLUME 13, A DRUNK KUROSAKI IS DRINKING AN OOLONG HIGHBALL. TERU IS SUPPOSED TO HAVE CLEARED THE TABLE, BUT THE HIGHBALL IS STILL THERE... COULD TERU HAVE BEEN TRYING TO SEND A SIGNAL?

(FOOLISH, FUKUSHIMA PREFECTURE)

WELL, MAYBE. I THINK TERU PROBABLY THOUGHT IT WAS AN ORDINARY OOLONG TEA THAT HADN'T BEEN DRUNK, SO SHE LEFT IT ON THE TABLE... HOWEVER, TERU SEEMS TO ENJOY SEEING KUROSAKI DRUNK (BECAUSE HE BECOMES A KID AND TURNS AGGRESSIVE), SO IT'S POSSIBLE THAT SHE USED HER GRADE C WOMANLY WILES TO SET A TRAP... WHO KNOWS...

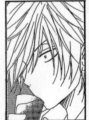

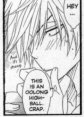

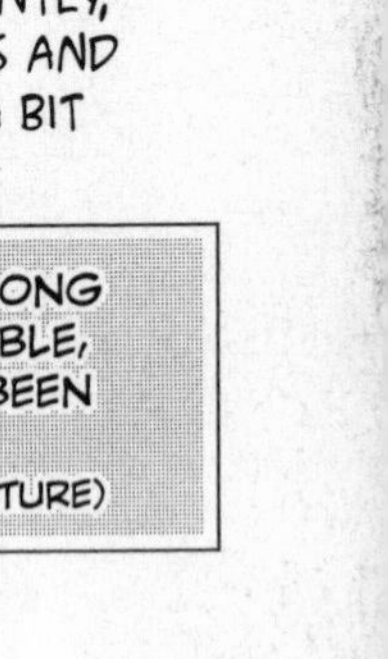

HEY ...
And it's strong.
THIS IS AN OOLONG HIGH-BALL. CRAP.

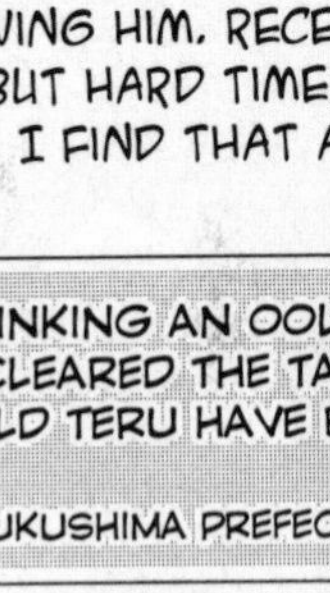

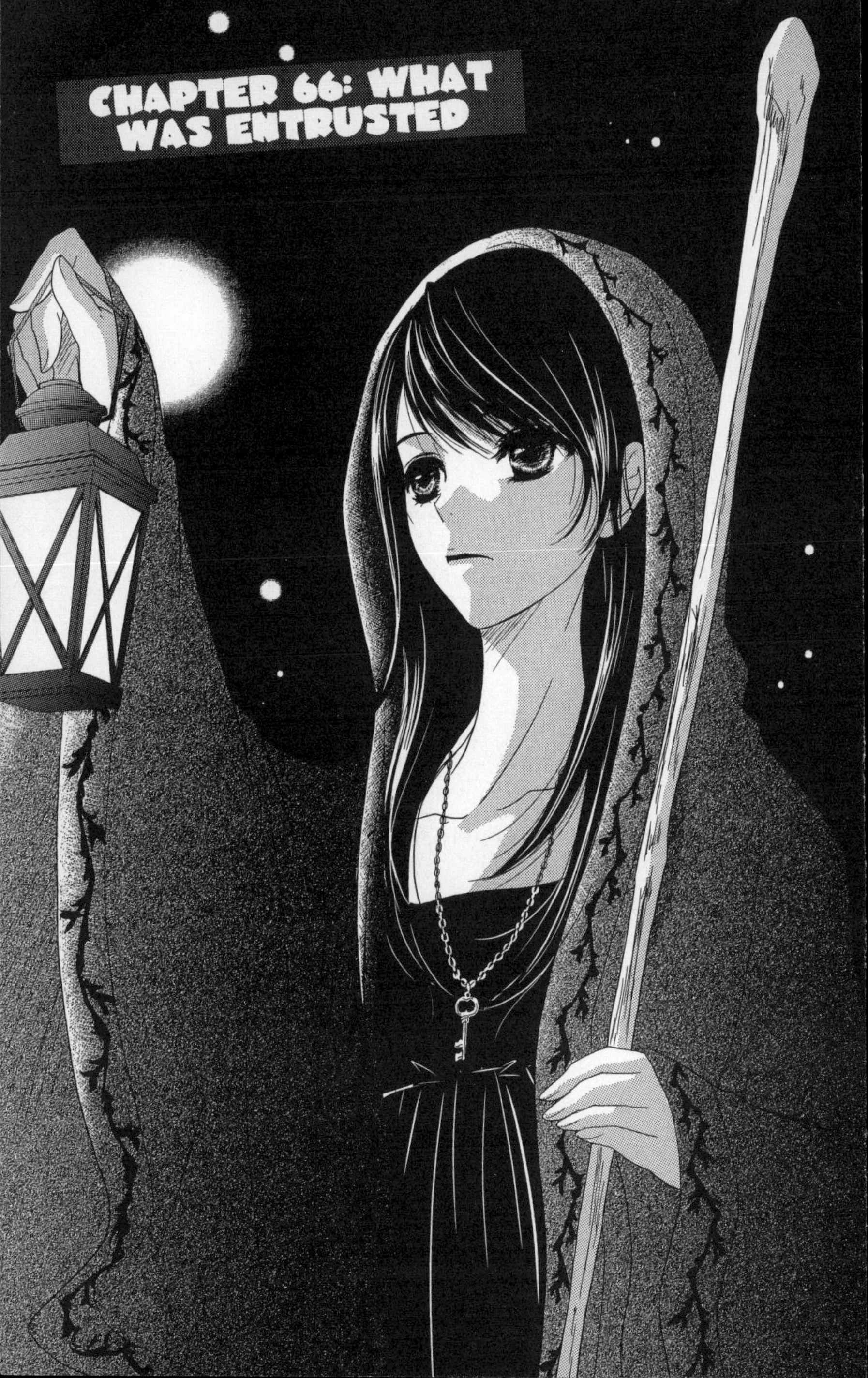
CHAPTER 66: WHAT WAS ENTRUSTED

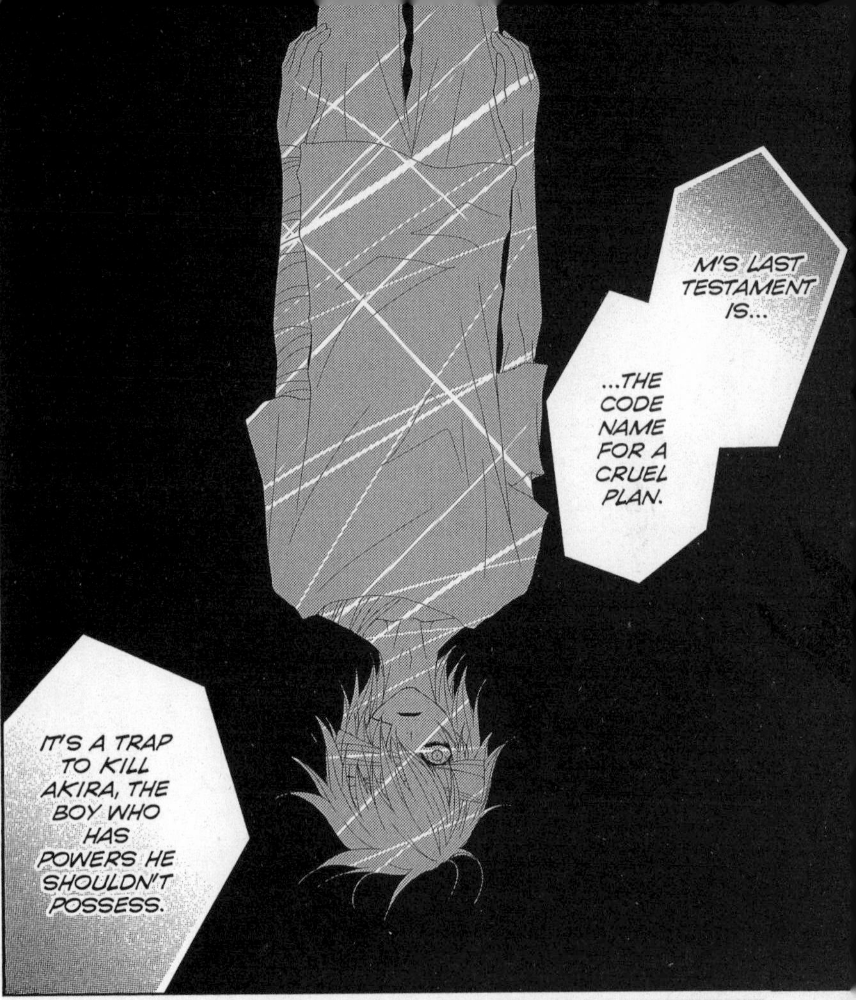
M'S LAST TESTAMENT IS...
...THE CODE NAME FOR A CRUEL PLAN.
IT'S A TRAP TO KILL AKIRA, THE BOY WHO HAS POWERS HE SHOULDN'T POSSESS.

OH, NO... I DREW THE PART ON KUROSAKI'S FATHER'S HEAD IN CHAPTER 65 ON THE OPPOSITE SIDE... BUT HEY, PEOPLE DON'T PART THEIR HAIR ON THE SAME SIDE ALL THEIR LIVES. ORDINARILY, THEY CHANGE IT NOW AND THEN, RIGHT? ...HIS SON CHANGES HIS PART AN AWFUL LOT. MAYBE ONCE EVERY PANEL... I'M SO SORRY...

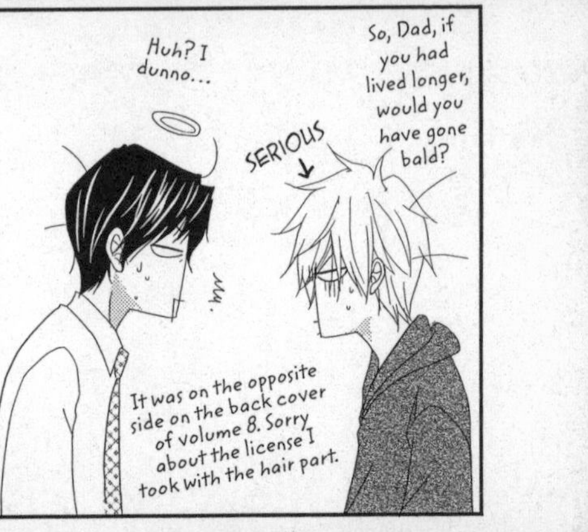
So, Dad, if you had lived longer, would you have gone bald?
SERIOUS
Huh? I dunno...
It was on the opposite side on the back cover of volume 8. Sorry about the license I took with the hair part.

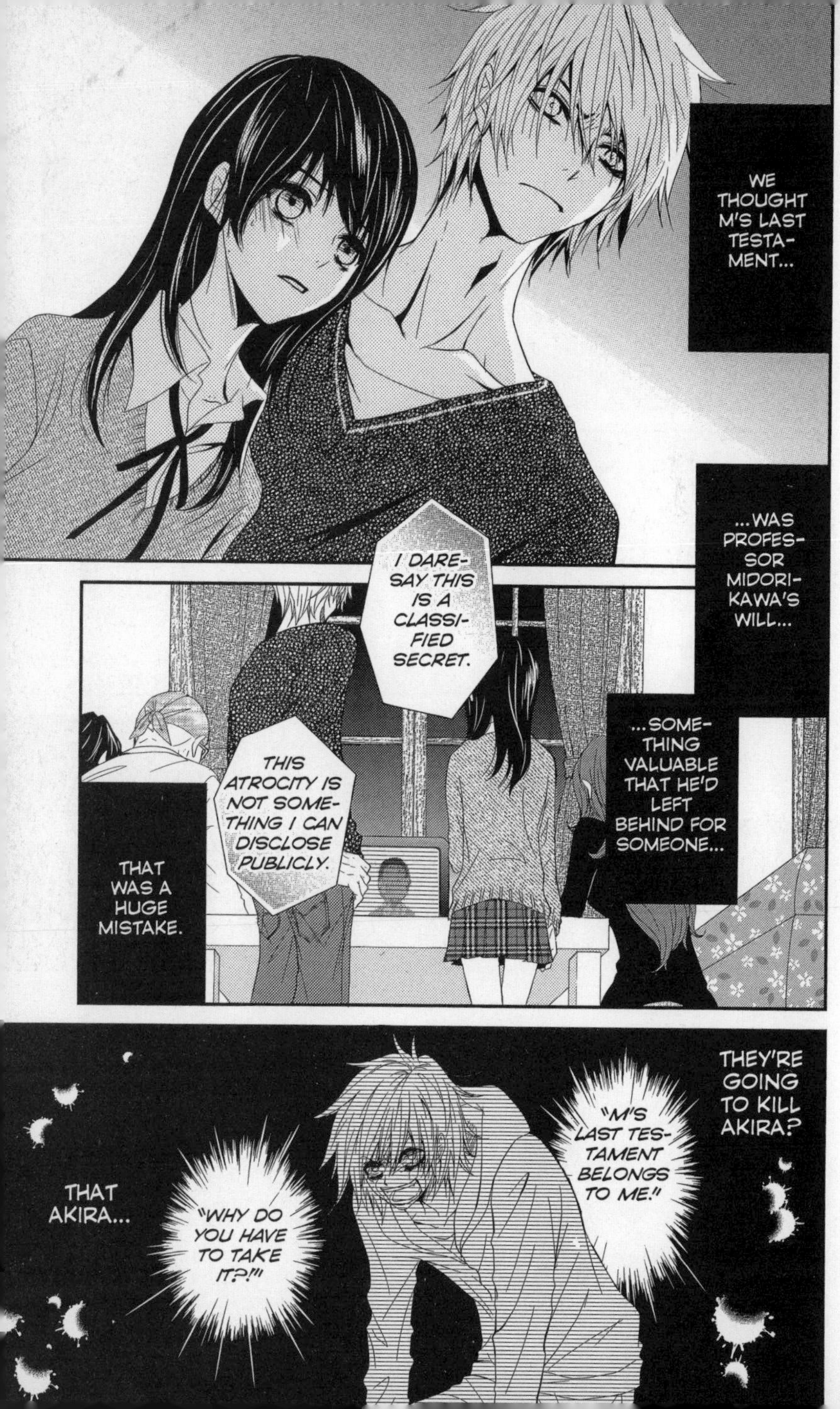
WE THOUGHT M'S LAST TESTAMENT...
...WAS PROFESSOR MIDORIKAWA'S WILL...
...SOMETHING VALUABLE THAT HE'D LEFT BEHIND FOR SOMEONE...
I DARESAY THIS IS A CLASSIFIED SECRET.
THIS ATROCITY IS NOT SOMETHING I CAN DISCLOSE PUBLICLY.
THAT WAS A HUGE MISTAKE.
THEY'RE GOING TO KILL AKIRA?
"M'S LAST TESTAMENT BELONGS TO ME."
"WHY DO YOU HAVE TO TAKE IT?!"
THAT AKIRA...

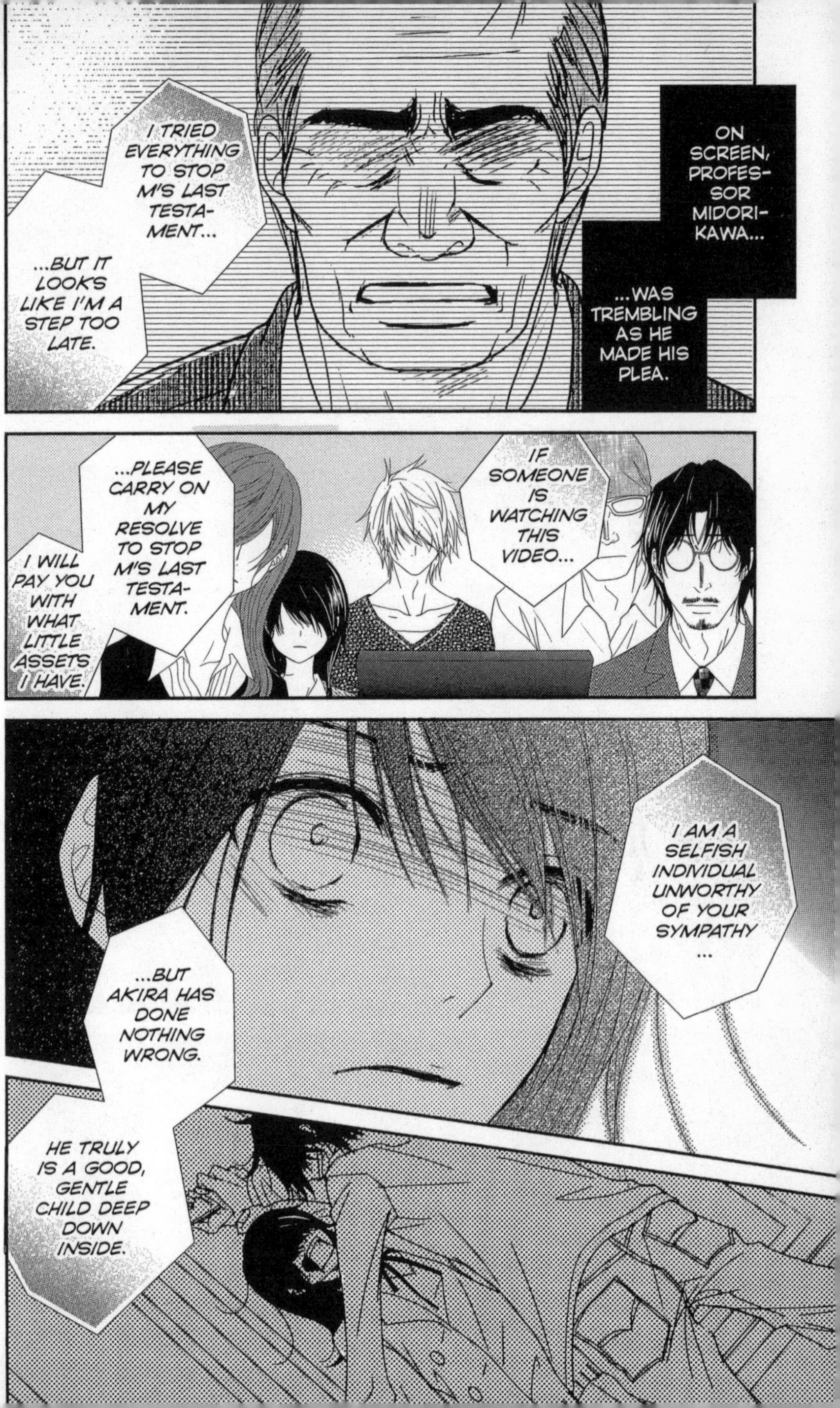
ON SCREEN, PROFESSOR MIDORIKAWA...
...WAS TREMBLING AS HE MADE HIS PLEA.
I TRIED EVERYTHING TO STOP M'S LAST TESTAMENT...
...BUT IT LOOKS LIKE I'M A STEP TOO LATE.
IF SOMEONE IS WATCHING THIS VIDEO...
...PLEASE CARRY ON MY RESOLVE TO STOP M'S LAST TESTAMENT.
I WILL PAY YOU WITH WHAT LITTLE ASSETS I HAVE.
I AM A SELFISH INDIVIDUAL UNWORTHY OF YOUR SYMPATHY...
...BUT AKIRA HAS DONE NOTHING WRONG.
HE TRULY IS A GOOD, GENTLE CHILD DEEP DOWN INSIDE.

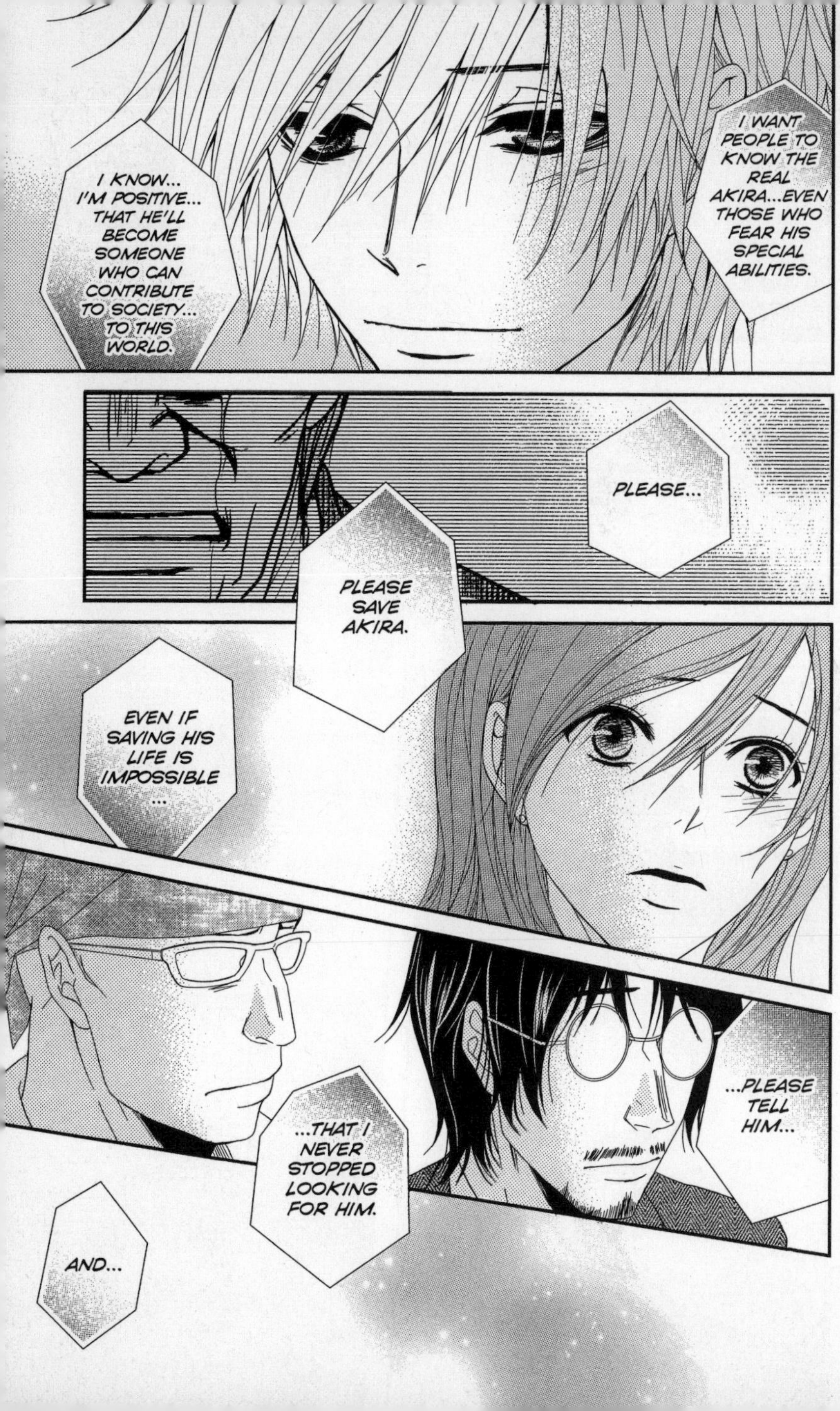
I WANT PEOPLE TO KNOW THE REAL AKIRA...EVEN THOSE WHO FEAR HIS SPECIAL ABILITIES.
I KNOW... I'M POSITIVE... THAT HE'LL BECOME SOMEONE WHO CAN CONTRIBUTE TO SOCIETY... TO THIS WORLD.
PLEASE...
PLEASE SAVE AKIRA.
EVEN IF SAVING HIS LIFE IS IMPOSSIBLE...
...PLEASE TELL HIM...
...THAT I NEVER STOPPED LOOKING FOR HIM.
AND...

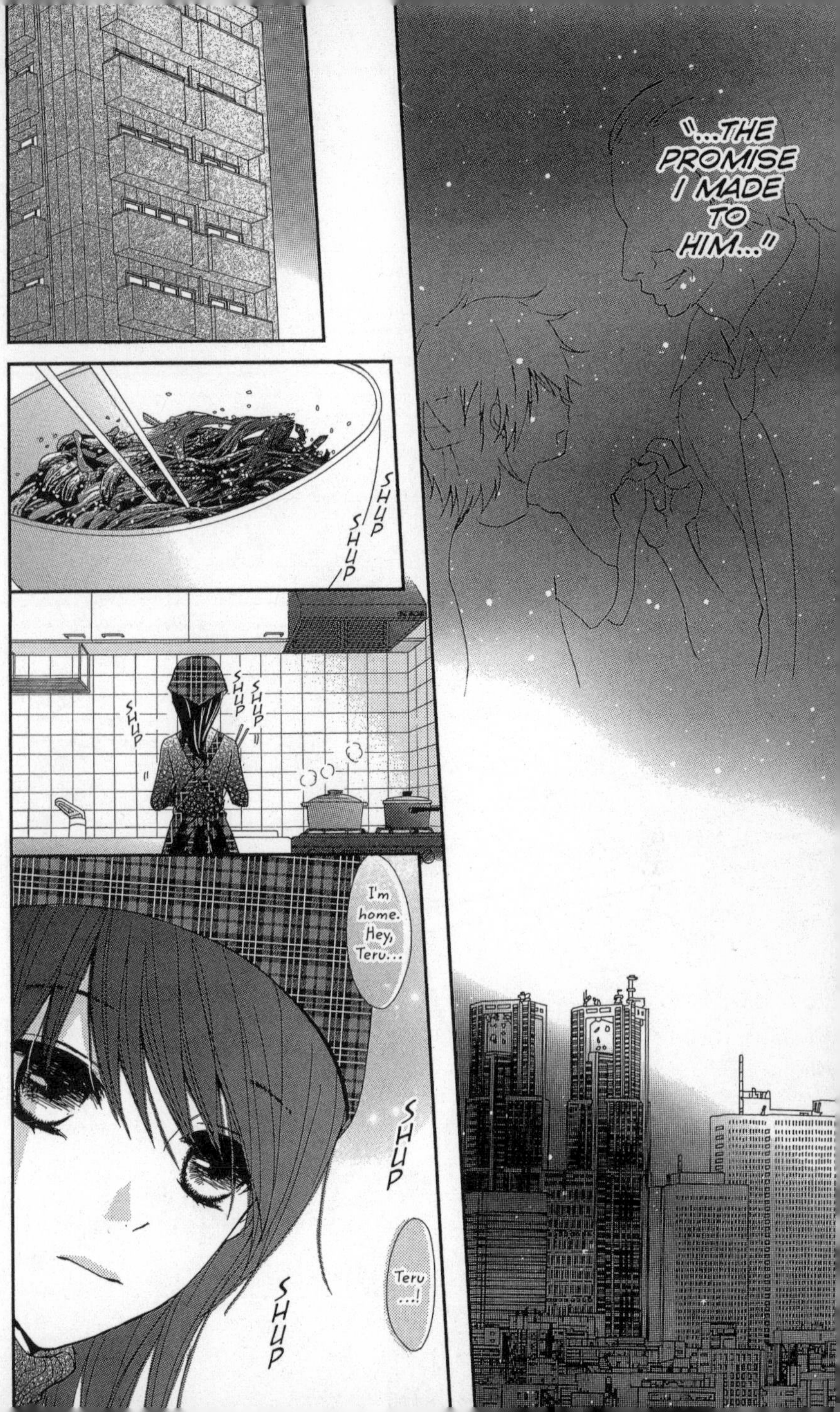
"...THE PROMISE I MADE TO HIM..."
SHUP
SHUP
SHUP
SHUP
SHUP
SHUP
SHUP
I'm home. Hey, Teru...
SHUP
Teru ...!
SHUP

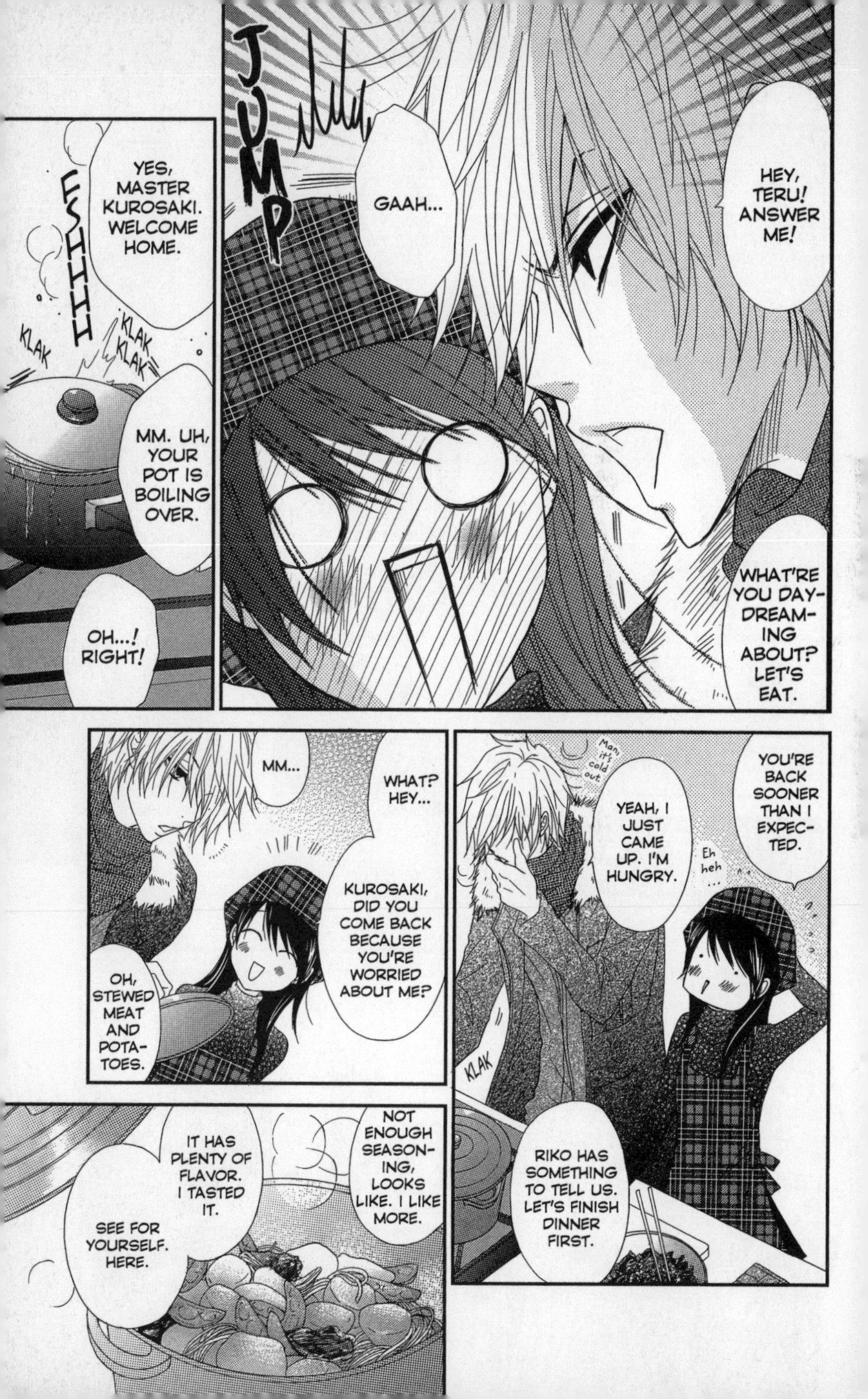
HEY, TERU! ANSWER ME!
WHAT'RE YOU DAY-DREAMING ABOUT? LET'S EAT.
JUMP
GAAH...
YES, MASTER KUROSAKI. WELCOME HOME.
FSHHHH
KLAK
KLAK KLAK KLAK
MM. UH, YOUR POT IS BOILING OVER.
OH...! RIGHT!
YOU'RE BACK SOONER THAN I EXPECTED.
Eh heh...
Man, it's cold out.
YEAH, I JUST CAME UP. I'M HUNGRY.
KLAK
RIKO HAS SOMETHING TO TELL US. LET'S FINISH DINNER FIRST.
MM...
WHAT? HEY...
KUROSAKI, DID YOU COME BACK BECAUSE YOU'RE WORRIED ABOUT ME?
OH, STEWED MEAT AND POTATOES.
NOT ENOUGH SEASONING, LOOKS LIKE. I LIKE MORE.
IT HAS PLENTY OF FLAVOR. I TASTED IT.
SEE FOR YOURSELF. HERE.

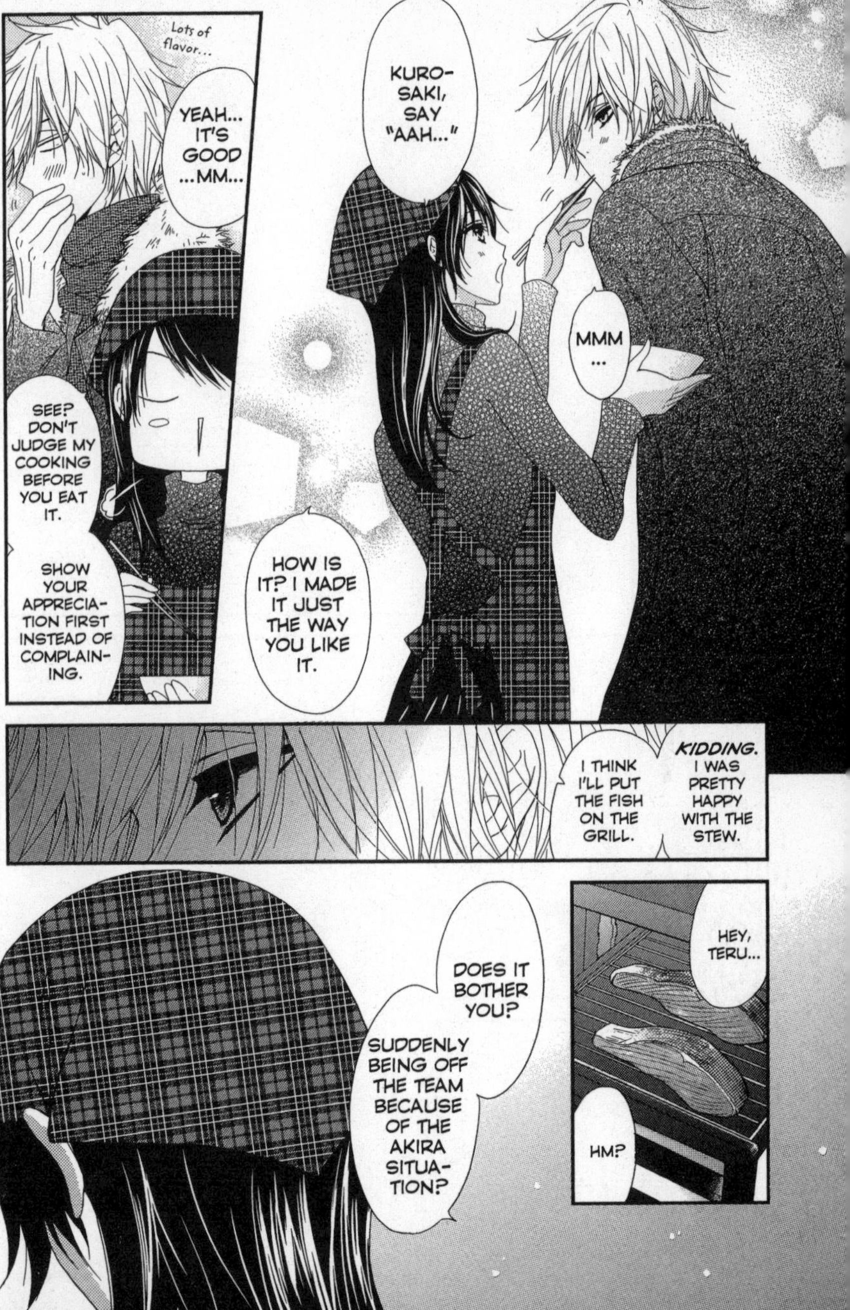
KURO-SAKI, SAY "AAH..."
MMM...
HOW IS IT? I MADE IT JUST THE WAY YOU LIKE IT.
Lots of flavor...
YEAH... IT'S GOOD ...MM...
SEE? DON'T JUDGE MY COOKING BEFORE YOU EAT IT.
SHOW YOUR APPRECIATION FIRST INSTEAD OF COMPLAINING.
KIDDING. I WAS PRETTY HAPPY WITH THE STEW.
I THINK I'LL PUT THE FISH ON THE GRILL.
HEY, TERU...
HM?
DOES IT BOTHER YOU?
SUDDENLY BEING OFF THE TEAM BECAUSE OF THE AKIRA SITUATION?

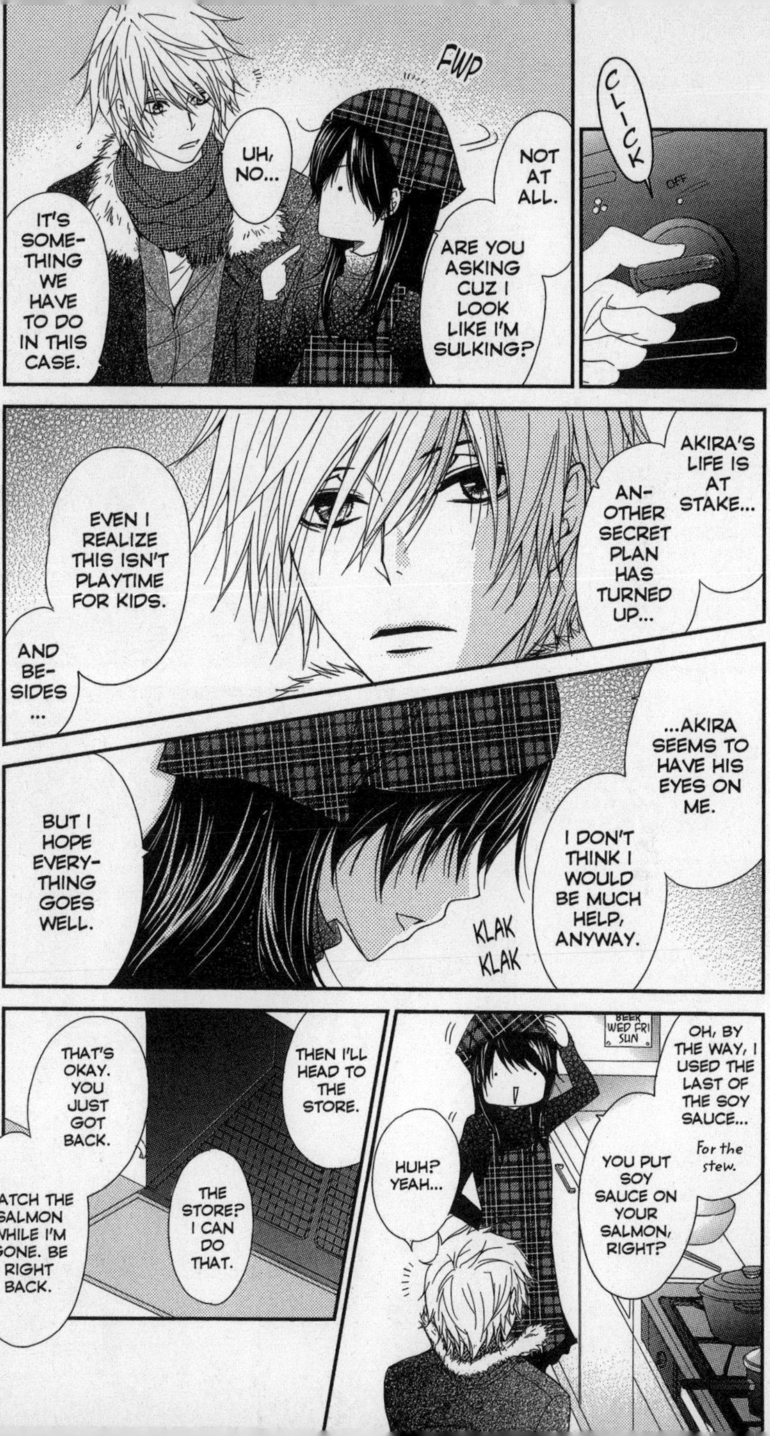
CLICK
OFF
FWP
NOT AT ALL.
ARE YOU ASKING CUZ I LOOK LIKE I'M SULKING?
UH, NO...
IT'S SOMETHING WE HAVE TO DO IN THIS CASE.
AKIRA'S LIFE IS AT STAKE...
ANOTHER SECRET PLAN HAS TURNED UP...
EVEN I REALIZE THIS ISN'T PLAYTIME FOR KIDS.
AND BESIDES...
...AKIRA SEEMS TO HAVE HIS EYES ON ME.
I DON'T THINK I WOULD BE MUCH HELP, ANYWAY.
KLAK KLAK
BUT I HOPE EVERYTHING GOES WELL.
BEER WED FRI SUN
OH, BY THE WAY, I USED THE LAST OF THE SOY SAUCE...
For the stew.
YOU PUT SOY SAUCE ON YOUR SALMON, RIGHT?
HUH? YEAH...
THEN I'LL HEAD TO THE STORE.
THE STORE? I CAN DO THAT.
THAT'S OKAY. YOU JUST GOT BACK.
WATCH THE SALMON WHILE I'M GONE. BE RIGHT BACK.

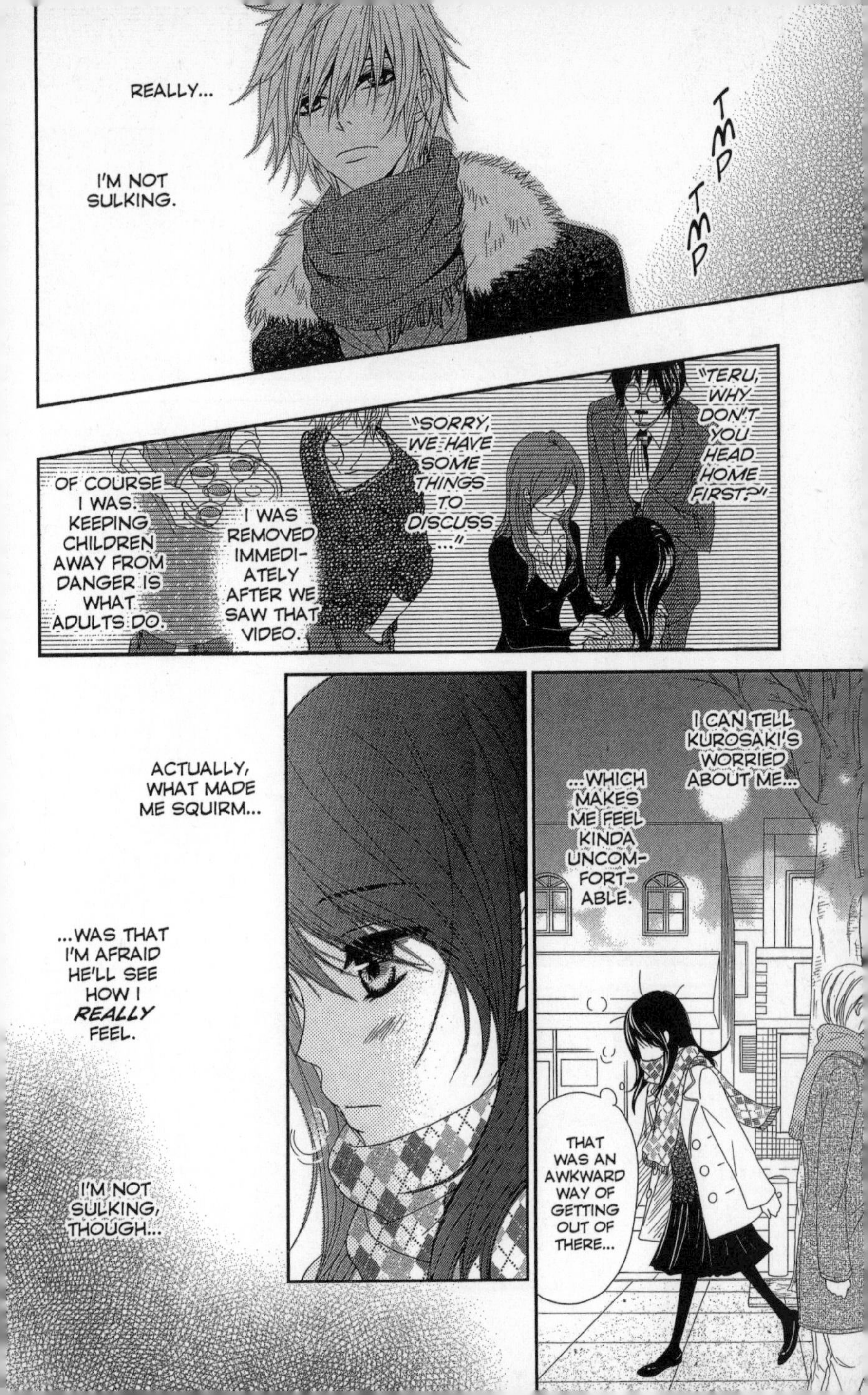
TMP TMP
REALLY...
I'M NOT SULKING.
"TERU, WHY DON'T YOU HEAD HOME FIRST?"
"SORRY, WE HAVE SOME THINGS TO DISCUSS..."
I WAS REMOVED IMMEDI-ATELY AFTER WE SAW THAT VIDEO.
OF COURSE I WAS. KEEPING CHILDREN AWAY FROM DANGER IS WHAT ADULTS DO.
I CAN TELL KUROSAKI'S WORRIED ABOUT ME...
...WHICH MAKES ME FEEL KINDA UNCOM-FORT-ABLE.
THAT WAS AN AWKWARD WAY OF GETTING OUT OF THERE...
ACTUALLY, WHAT MADE ME SQUIRM...
...WAS THAT I'M AFRAID HE'LL SEE HOW I *REALLY* FEEL.
I'M NOT SULKING, THOUGH...

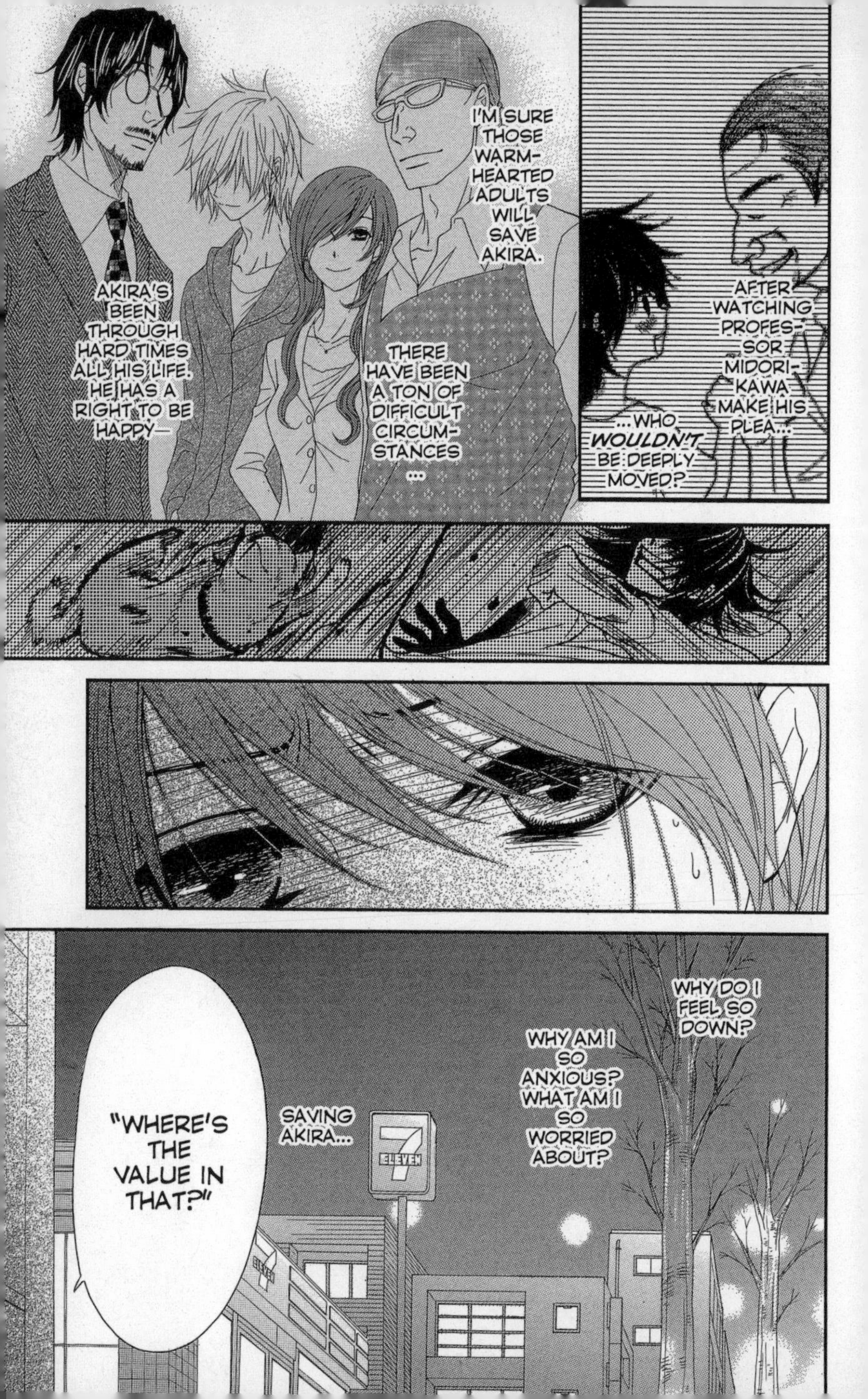
AFTER WATCHING PROFES-SOR MIDORI-KAWA MAKE HIS PLEA...
...WHO **WOULDN'T** BE DEEPLY MOVED?
I'M SURE THOSE WARM-HEARTED ADULTS WILL SAVE AKIRA.
THERE HAVE BEEN A TON OF DIFFICULT CIRCUM-STANCES...
AKIRA'S BEEN THROUGH HARD TIMES ALL HIS LIFE. HE HAS A RIGHT TO BE HAPPY—
WHY DO I FEEL SO DOWN?
WHY AM I SO ANXIOUS? WHAT AM I SO WORRIED ABOUT?
SAVING AKIRA...
"WHERE'S THE VALUE IN THAT?"
7 ELEVEN

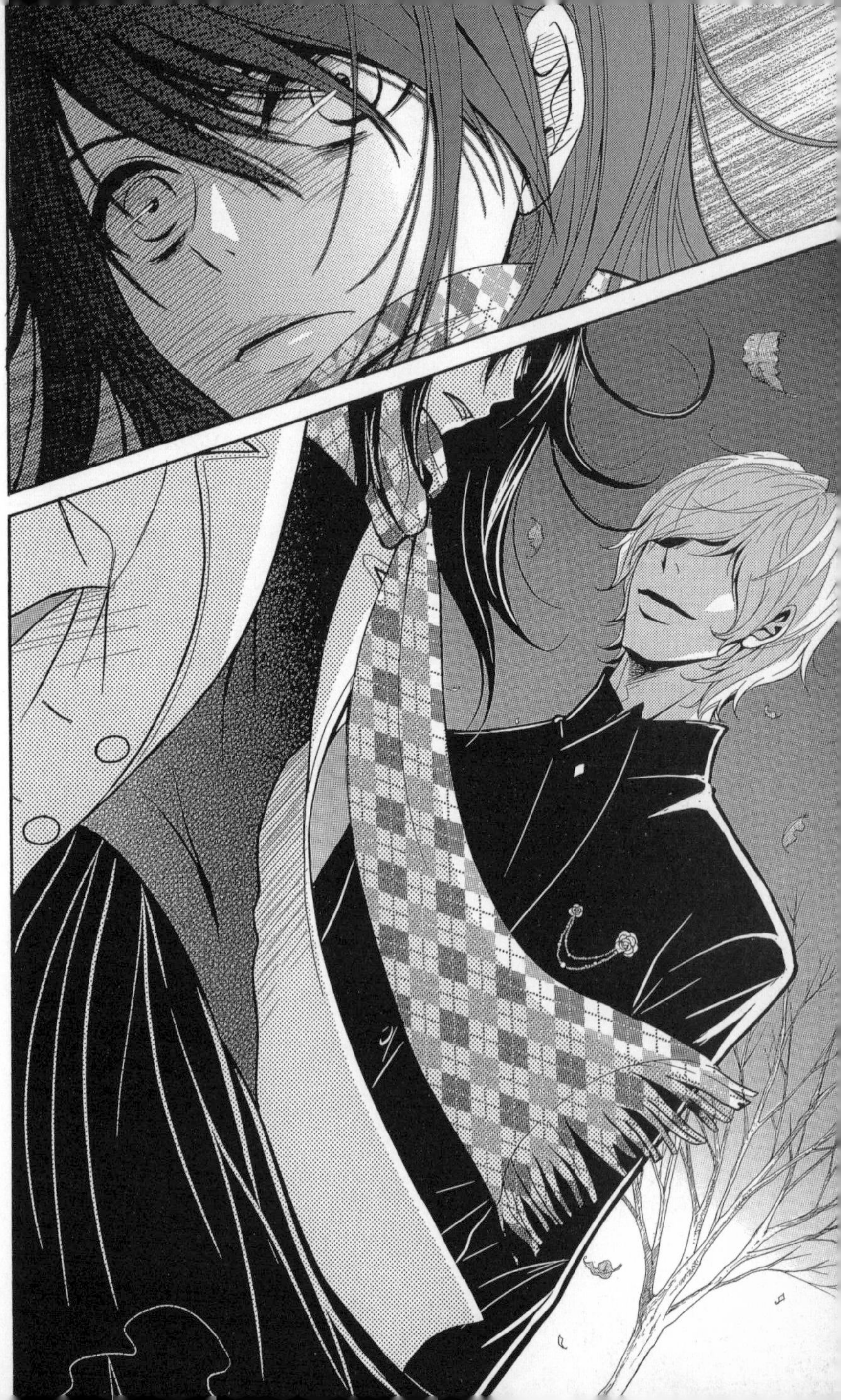

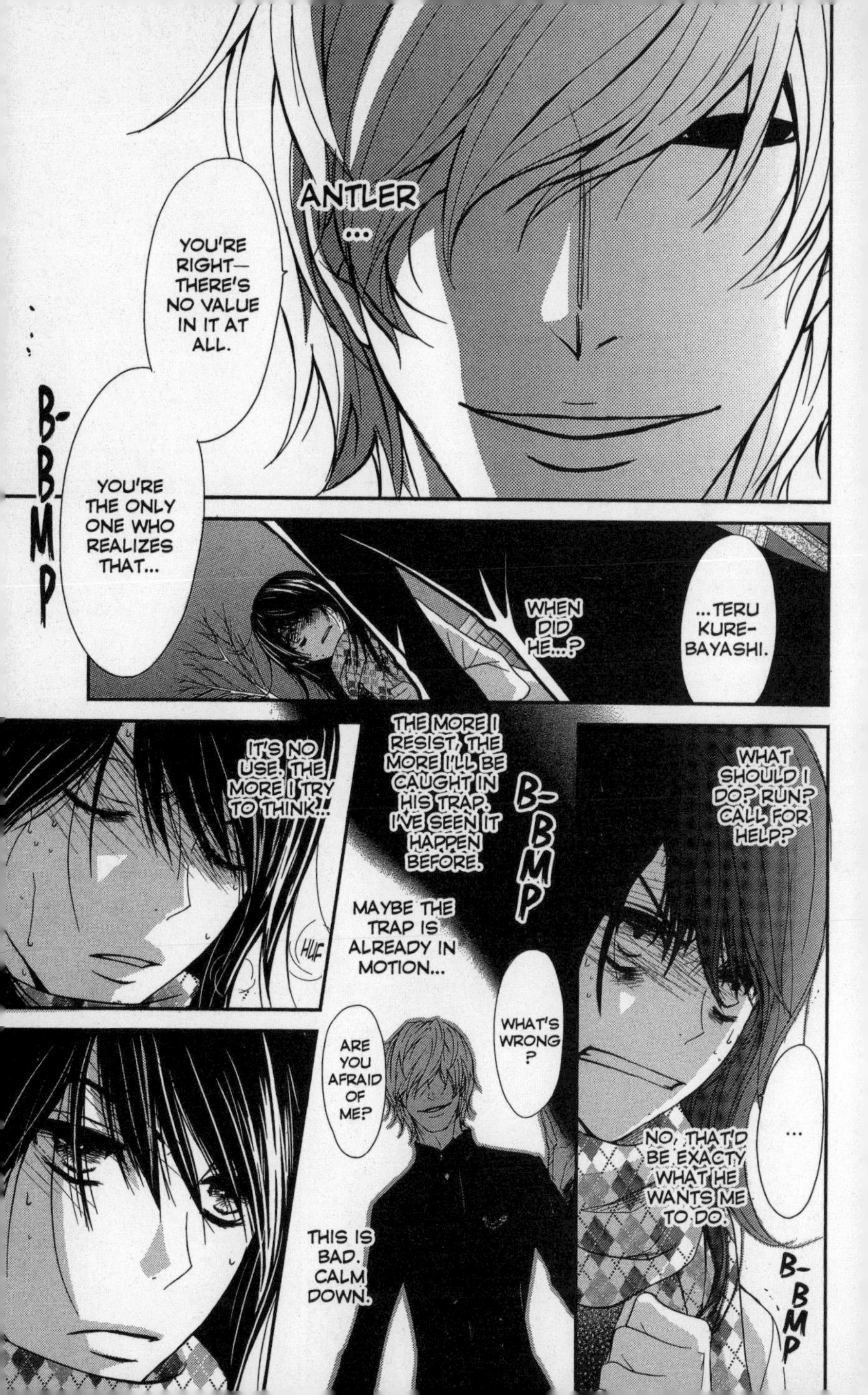
ANTLER...
YOU'RE RIGHT—THERE'S NO VALUE IN IT AT ALL.
YOU'RE THE ONLY ONE WHO REALIZES THAT...
B-BMP
...TERU KURE-BAYASHI.
WHEN DID HE...?
WHAT SHOULD I DO? RUN? CALL FOR HELP?
B-BMP
THE MORE I RESIST, THE MORE I'LL BE CAUGHT IN HIS TRAP. I'VE SEEN IT HAPPEN BEFORE.
MAYBE THE TRAP IS ALREADY IN MOTION...
IT'S NO USE. THE MORE I TRY TO THINK...
HUF
...
NO, THAT'D BE EXACTY WHAT HE WANTS ME TO DO.
B-BMP
WHAT'S WRONG?
ARE YOU AFRAID OF ME?
THIS IS BAD. CALM DOWN.

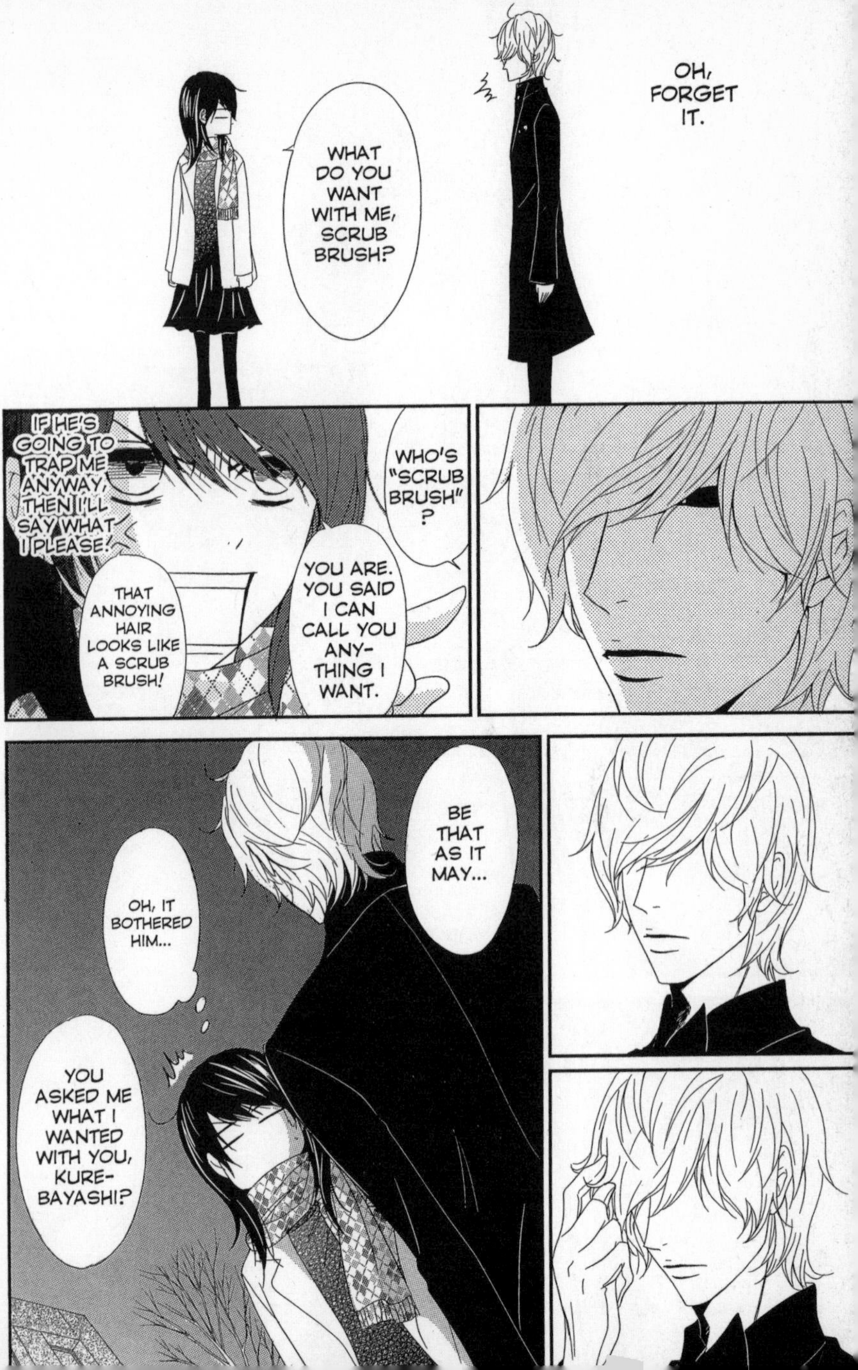
OH, FORGET IT.
WHAT DO YOU WANT WITH ME, SCRUB BRUSH?
WHO'S "SCRUB BRUSH"?
IF HE'S GOING TO TRAP ME ANYWAY, THEN I'LL SAY WHAT I PLEASE!
YOU ARE. YOU SAID I CAN CALL YOU ANY-THING I WANT.
THAT ANNOYING HAIR LOOKS LIKE A SCRUB BRUSH!
BE THAT AS IT MAY...
OH, IT BOTHERED HIM...
YOU ASKED ME WHAT I WANTED WITH YOU, KURE-BAYASHI?

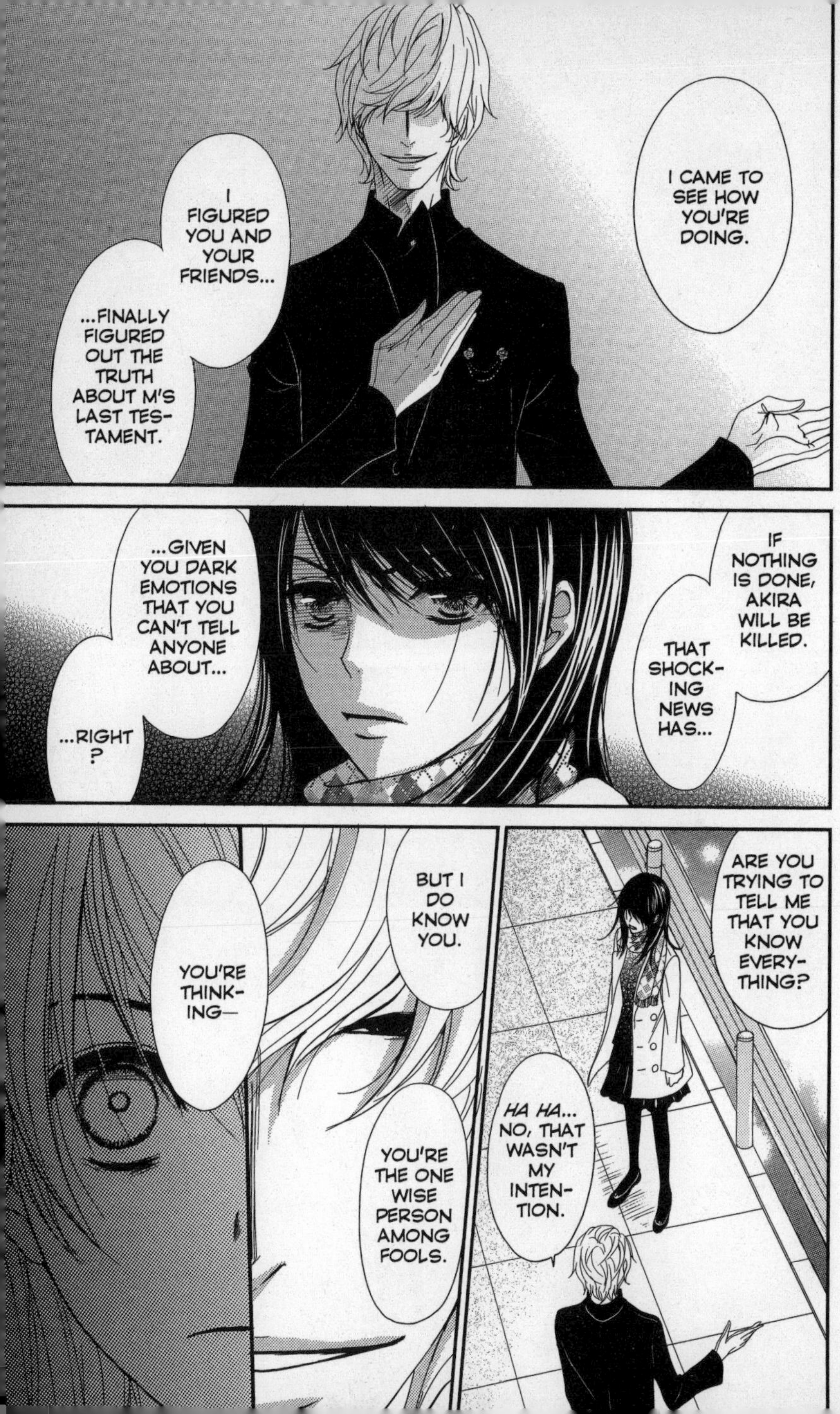
I CAME TO SEE HOW YOU'RE DOING.
I FIGURED YOU AND YOUR FRIENDS...
...FINALLY FIGURED OUT THE TRUTH ABOUT M'S LAST TESTAMENT.
IF NOTHING IS DONE, AKIRA WILL BE KILLED.
THAT SHOCKING NEWS HAS...
...GIVEN YOU DARK EMOTIONS THAT YOU CAN'T TELL ANYONE ABOUT...
...RIGHT?
ARE YOU TRYING TO TELL ME THAT YOU KNOW EVERYTHING?
HA HA... NO, THAT WASN'T MY INTENTION.
BUT I DO KNOW YOU.
YOU'RE THINKING—
YOU'RE THE ONE WISE PERSON AMONG FOOLS.

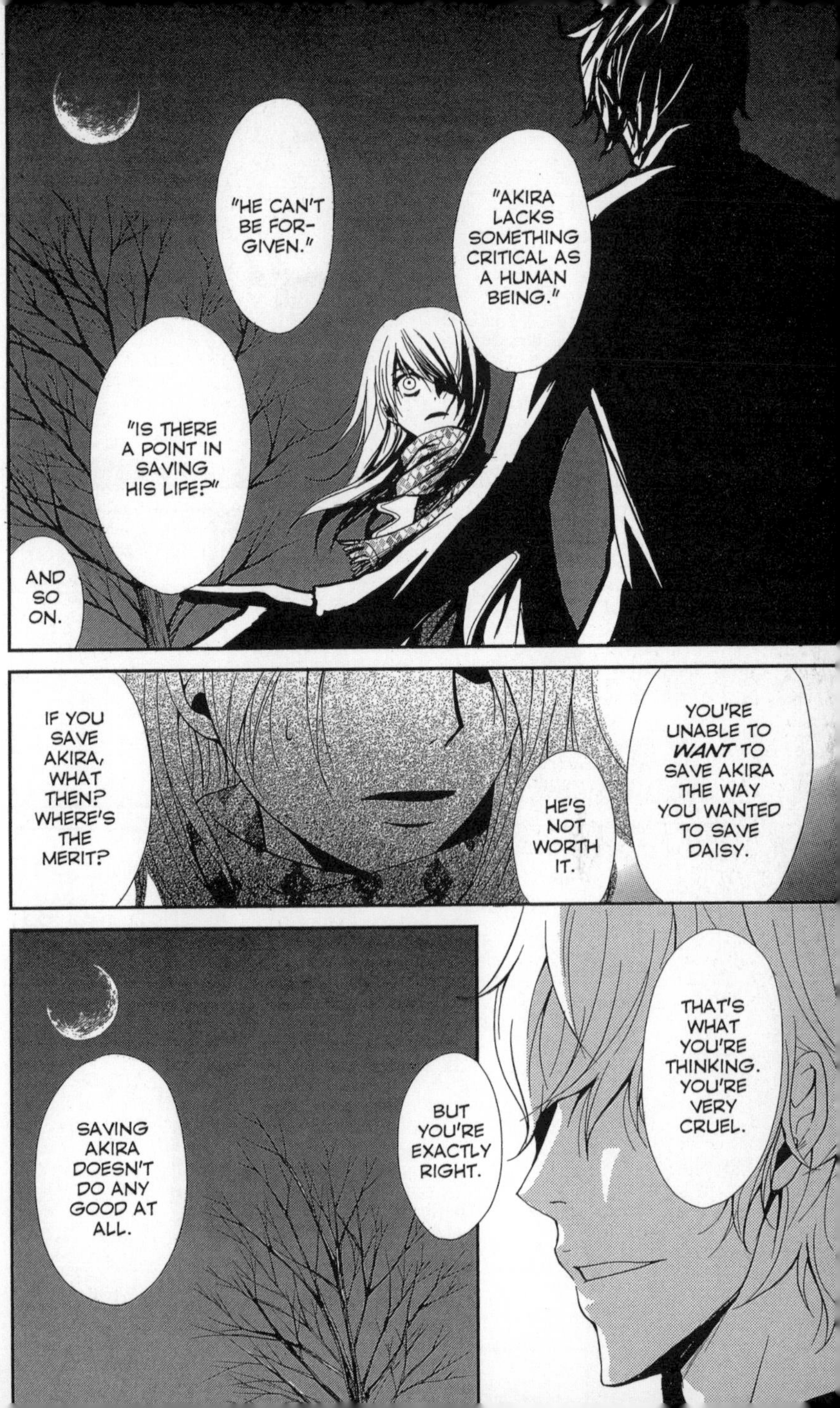
"AKIRA LACKS SOMETHING CRITICAL AS A HUMAN BEING."
"HE CAN'T BE FOR-GIVEN."
"IS THERE A POINT IN SAVING HIS LIFE?"
AND SO ON.
YOU'RE UNABLE TO *WANT* TO SAVE AKIRA THE WAY YOU WANTED TO SAVE DAISY.
HE'S NOT WORTH IT.
IF YOU SAVE AKIRA, WHAT THEN? WHERE'S THE MERIT?
THAT'S WHAT YOU'RE THINKING. YOU'RE VERY CRUEL.
BUT YOU'RE EXACTLY RIGHT.
SAVING AKIRA DOESN'T DO ANY GOOD AT ALL.

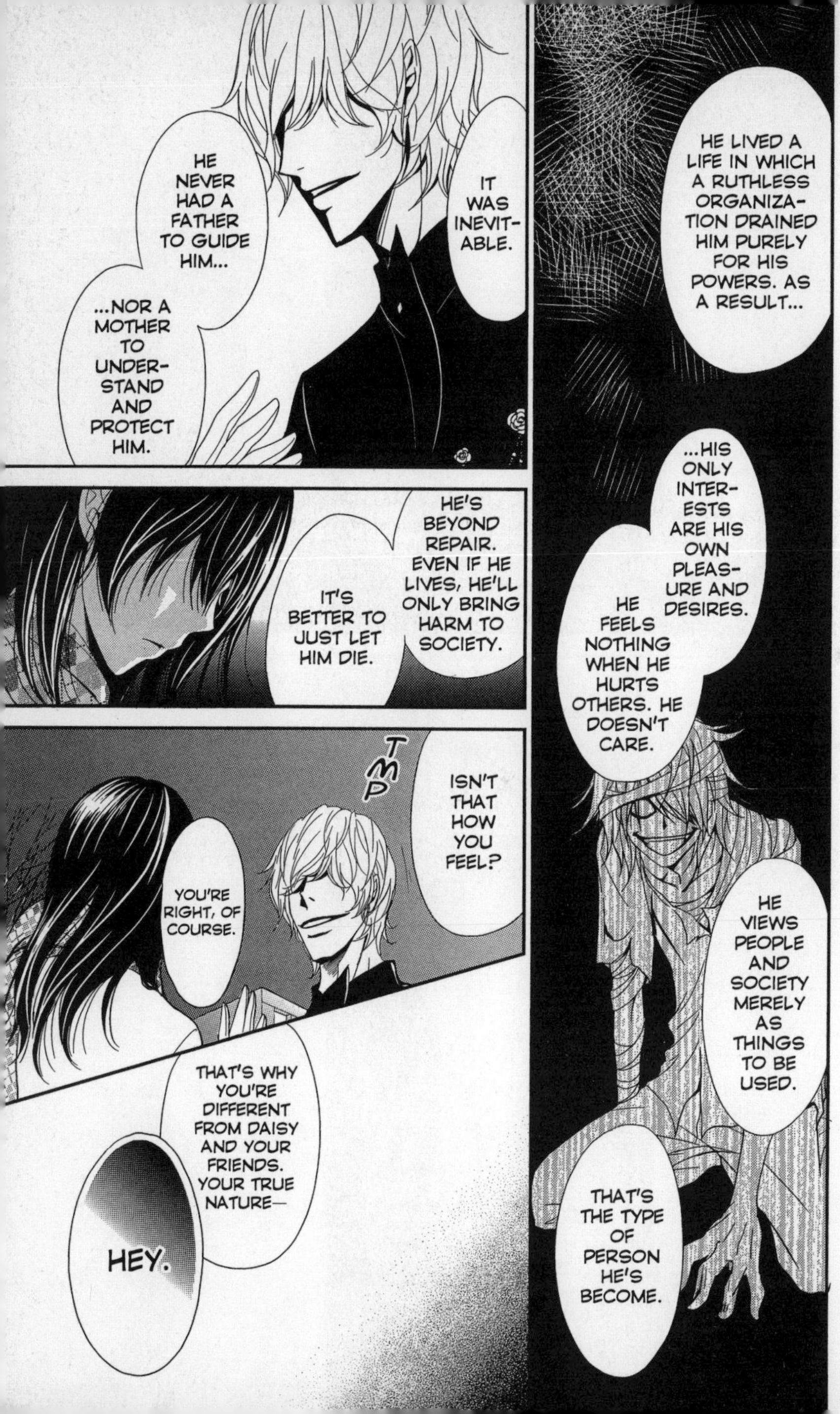
IT WAS INEVIT-ABLE.
HE NEVER HAD A FATHER TO GUIDE HIM...
...NOR A MOTHER TO UNDER-STAND AND PROTECT HIM.
HE LIVED A LIFE IN WHICH A RUTHLESS ORGANIZA-TION DRAINED HIM PURELY FOR HIS POWERS. AS A RESULT...
...HIS ONLY INTER-ESTS ARE HIS OWN PLEAS-URE AND DESIRES.
HE FEELS NOTHING WHEN HE HURTS OTHERS. HE DOESN'T CARE.
HE VIEWS PEOPLE AND SOCIETY MERELY AS THINGS TO BE USED.
THAT'S THE TYPE OF PERSON HE'S BECOME.
HE'S BEYOND REPAIR. EVEN IF HE LIVES, HE'LL ONLY BRING HARM TO SOCIETY.
IT'S BETTER TO JUST LET HIM DIE.
TMP
ISN'T THAT HOW YOU FEEL?
YOU'RE RIGHT, OF COURSE.
THAT'S WHY YOU'RE DIFFERENT FROM DAISY AND YOUR FRIENDS. YOUR TRUE NATURE—
HEY.

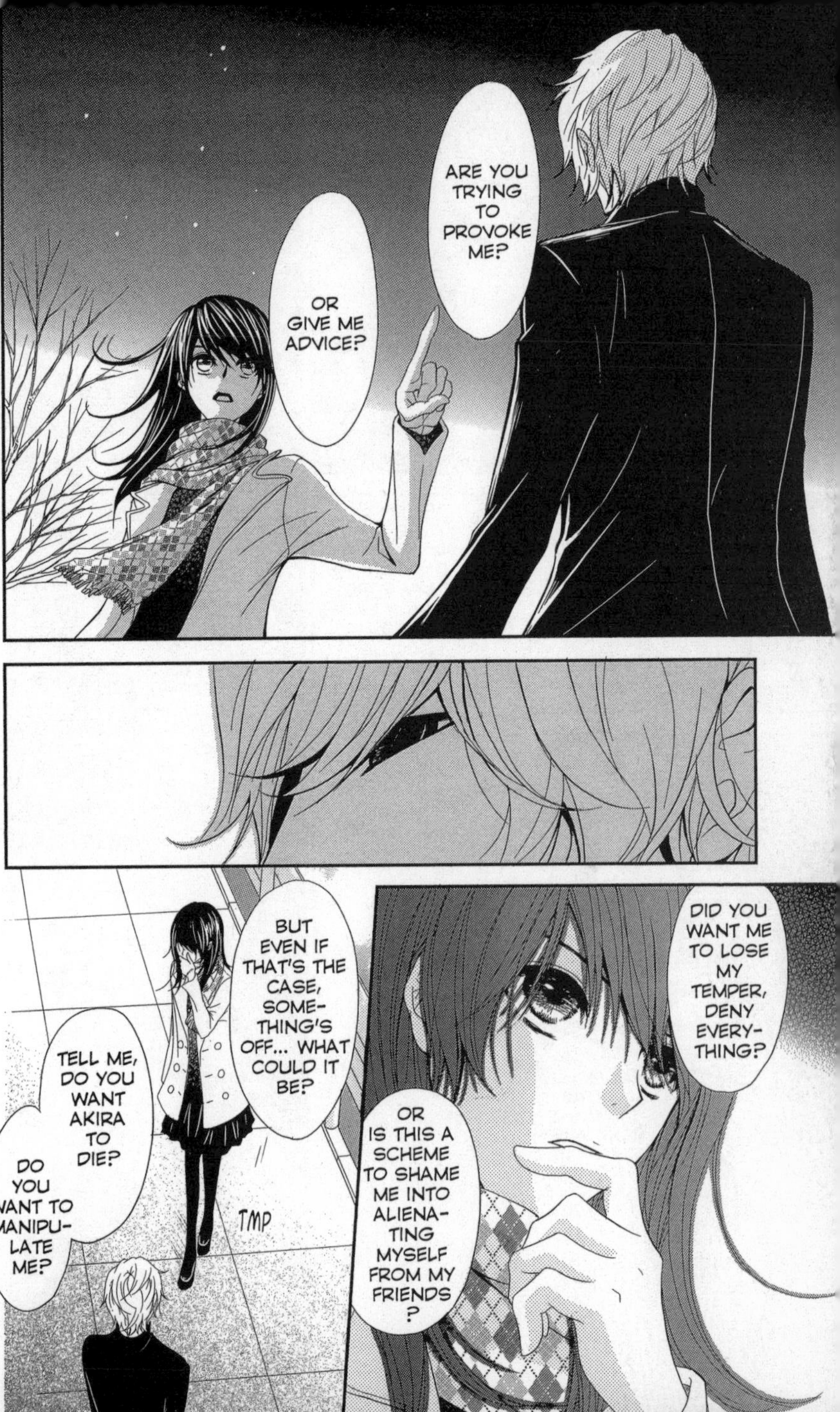
ARE YOU TRYING TO PROVOKE ME?
OR GIVE ME ADVICE?
DID YOU WANT ME TO LOSE MY TEMPER, DENY EVERYTHING?
OR IS THIS A SCHEME TO SHAME ME INTO ALIENATING MYSELF FROM MY FRIENDS?
BUT EVEN IF THAT'S THE CASE, SOMETHING'S OFF... WHAT COULD IT BE?
TMP
TELL ME, DO YOU WANT AKIRA TO DIE?
DO YOU WANT TO MANIPULATE ME?

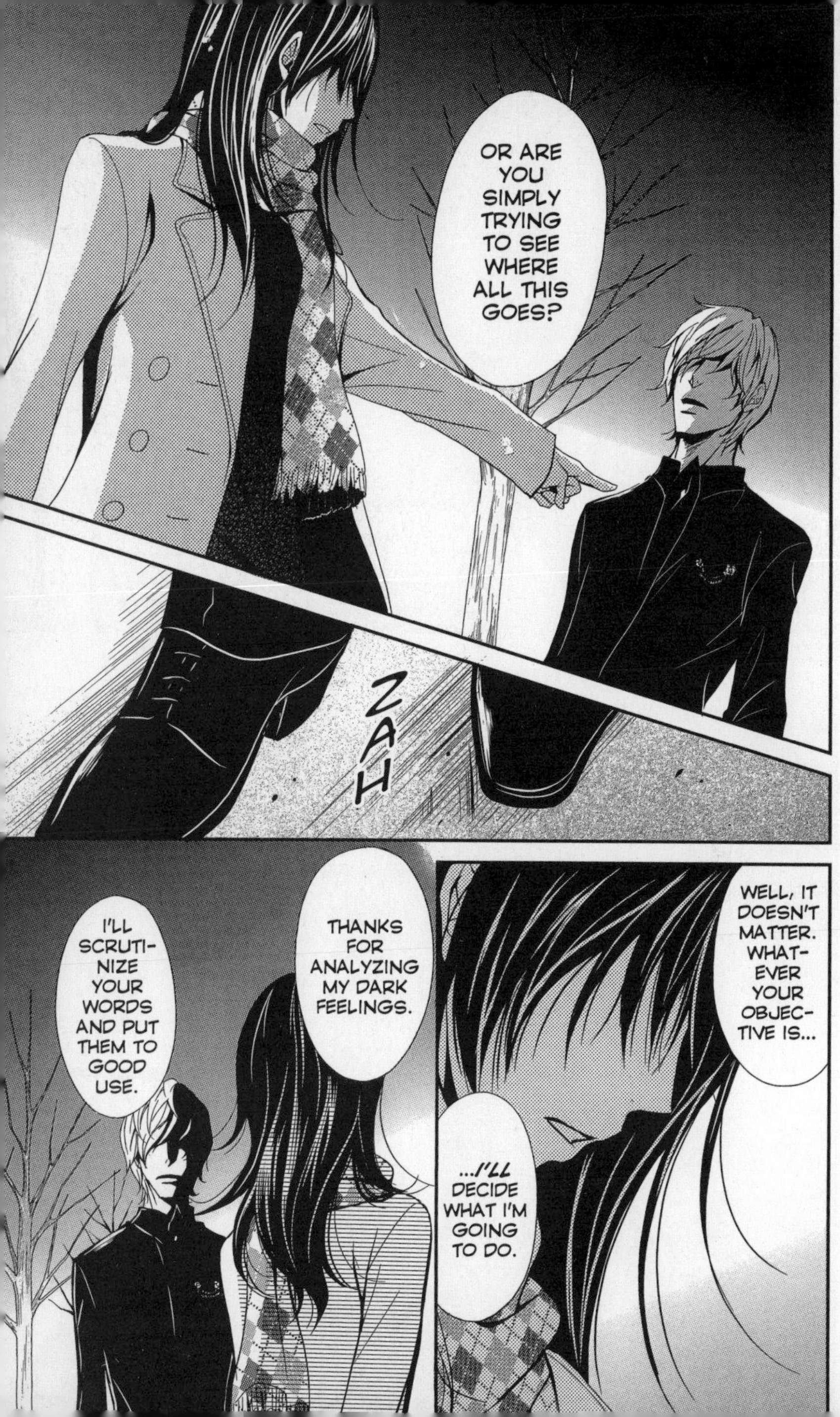
OR ARE YOU SIMPLY TRYING TO SEE WHERE ALL THIS GOES?
ZAH
WELL, IT DOESN'T MATTER. WHAT-EVER YOUR OBJEC-TIVE IS...
...I'LL DECIDE WHAT I'M GOING TO DO.
THANKS FOR ANALYZING MY DARK FEELINGS.
I'LL SCRUTI-NIZE YOUR WORDS AND PUT THEM TO GOOD USE.

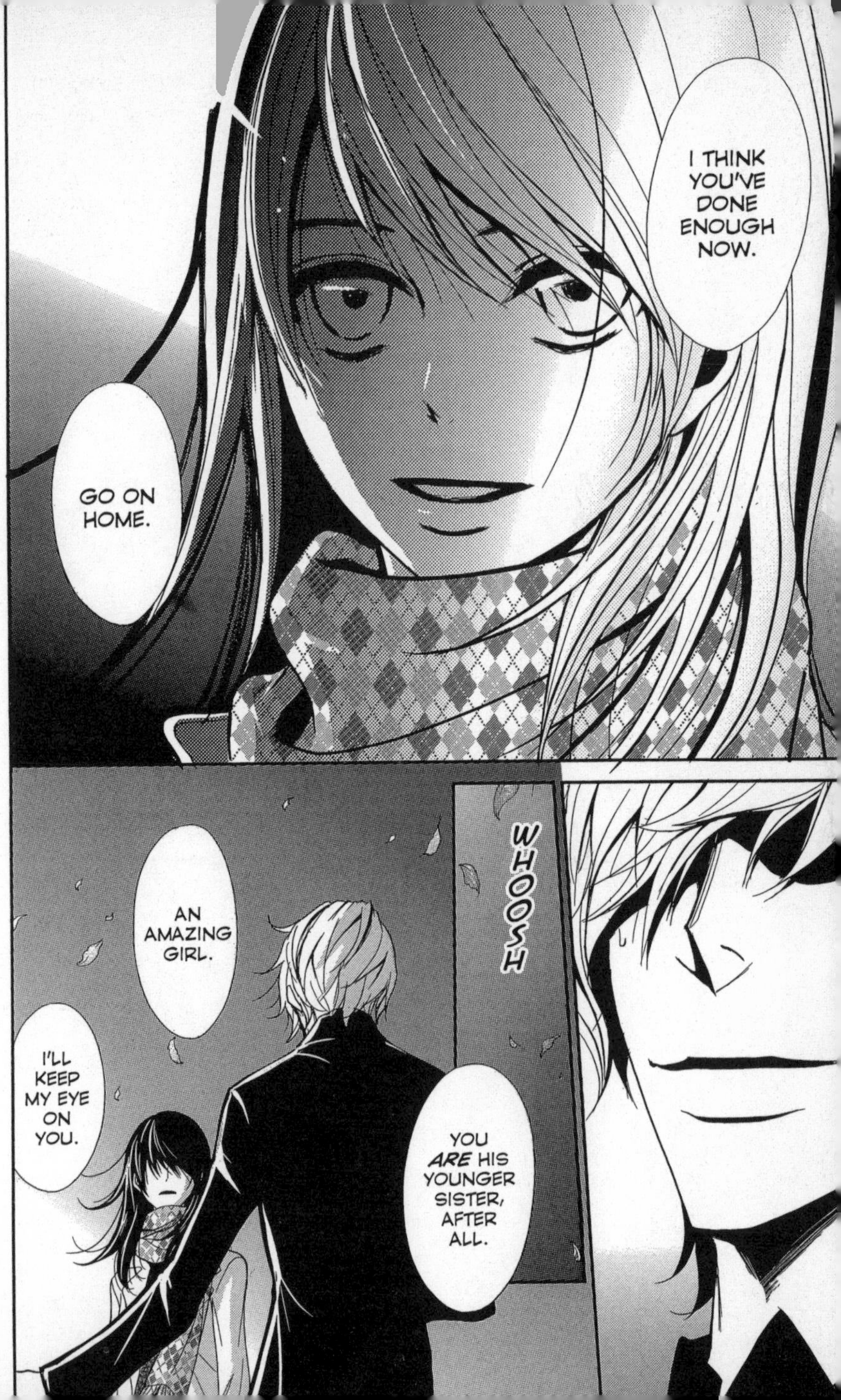
I THINK YOU'VE DONE ENOUGH NOW.
GO ON HOME.
WHOOSH
YOU ***ARE*** HIS YOUNGER SISTER, AFTER ALL.
AN AMAZING GIRL.
I'LL KEEP MY EYE ON YOU.

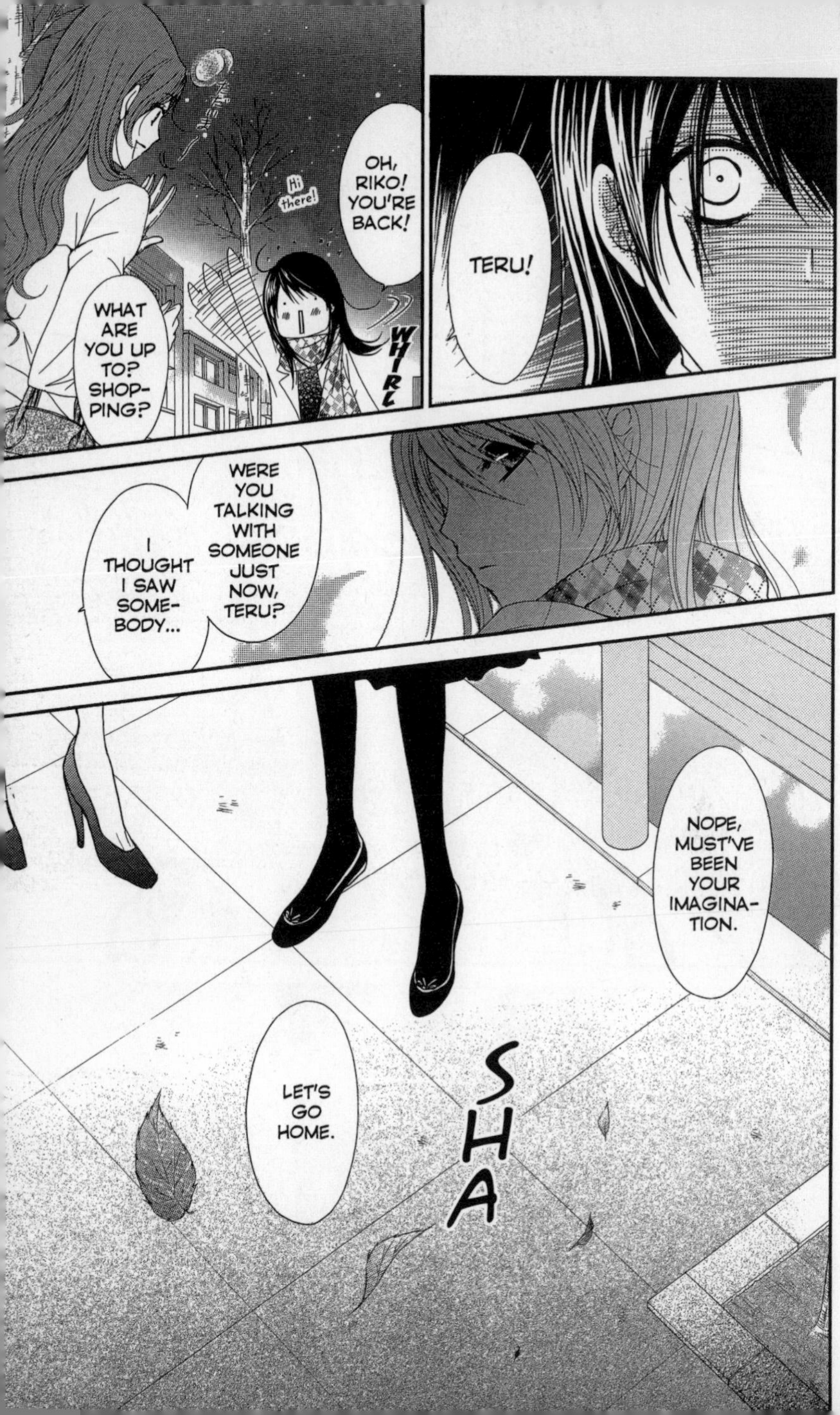
TERU!
OH, RIKO! YOU'RE BACK!
Hi there!
WHIRL
WHAT ARE YOU UP TO? SHOPPING?
WERE YOU TALKING WITH SOMEONE JUST NOW, TERU?
I THOUGHT I SAW SOMEBODY...
NOPE, MUST'VE BEEN YOUR IMAGINATION.
SHA
LET'S GO HOME.

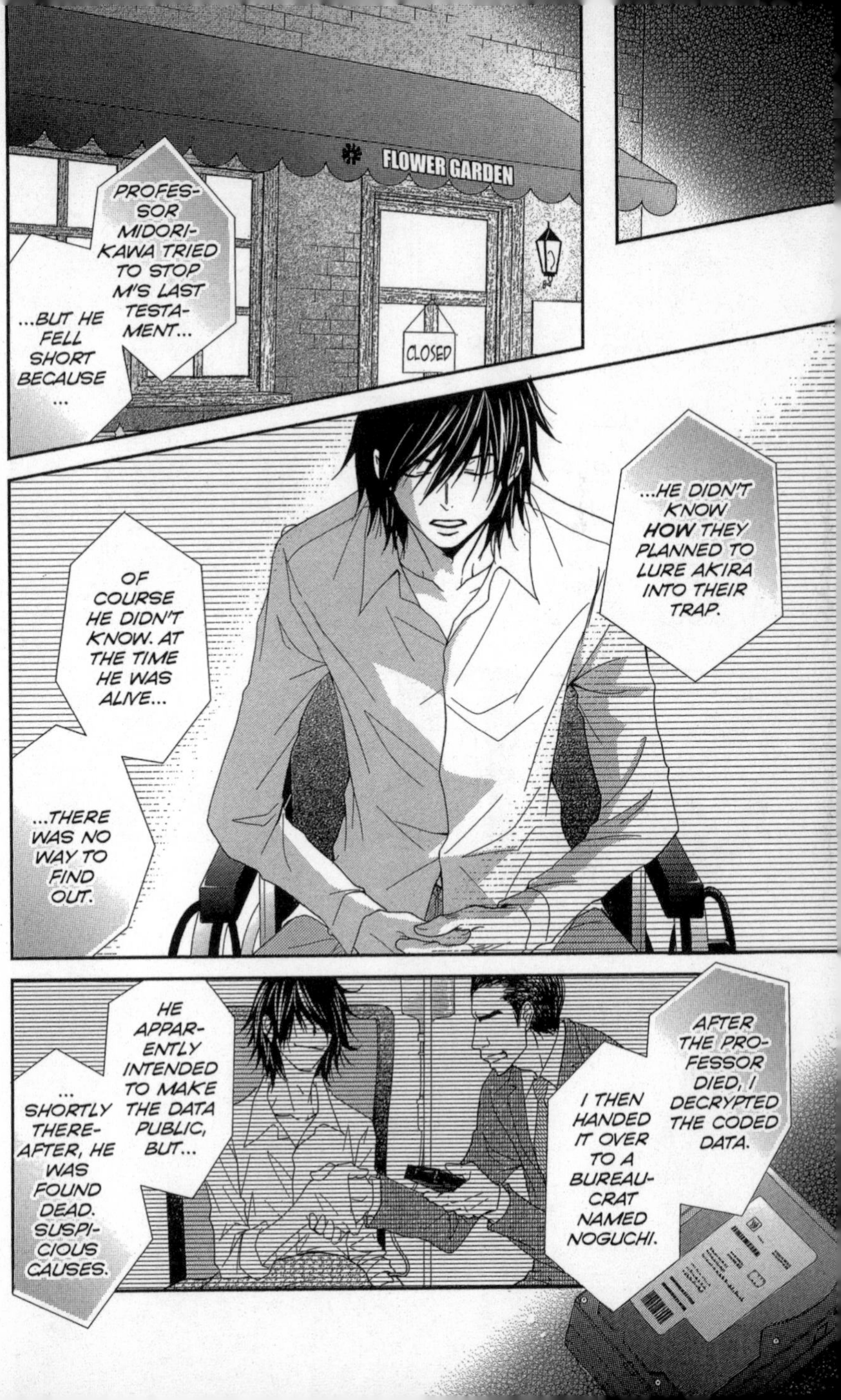
FLOWER GARDEN
CLOSED
PROFESSOR MIDORIKAWA TRIED TO STOP M'S LAST TESTAMENT...
...BUT HE FELL SHORT BECAUSE...
...HE DIDN'T KNOW **HOW** THEY PLANNED TO LURE AKIRA INTO THEIR TRAP.
OF COURSE HE DIDN'T KNOW. AT THE TIME HE WAS ALIVE...
...THERE WAS NO WAY TO FIND OUT.
AFTER THE PROFESSOR DIED, I DECRYPTED THE CODED DATA.
I THEN HANDED IT OVER TO A BUREAUCRAT NAMED NOGUCHI.
HE APPARENTLY INTENDED TO MAKE THE DATA PUBLIC, BUT...
...SHORTLY THEREAFTER, HE WAS FOUND DEAD. SUSPICIOUS CAUSES.

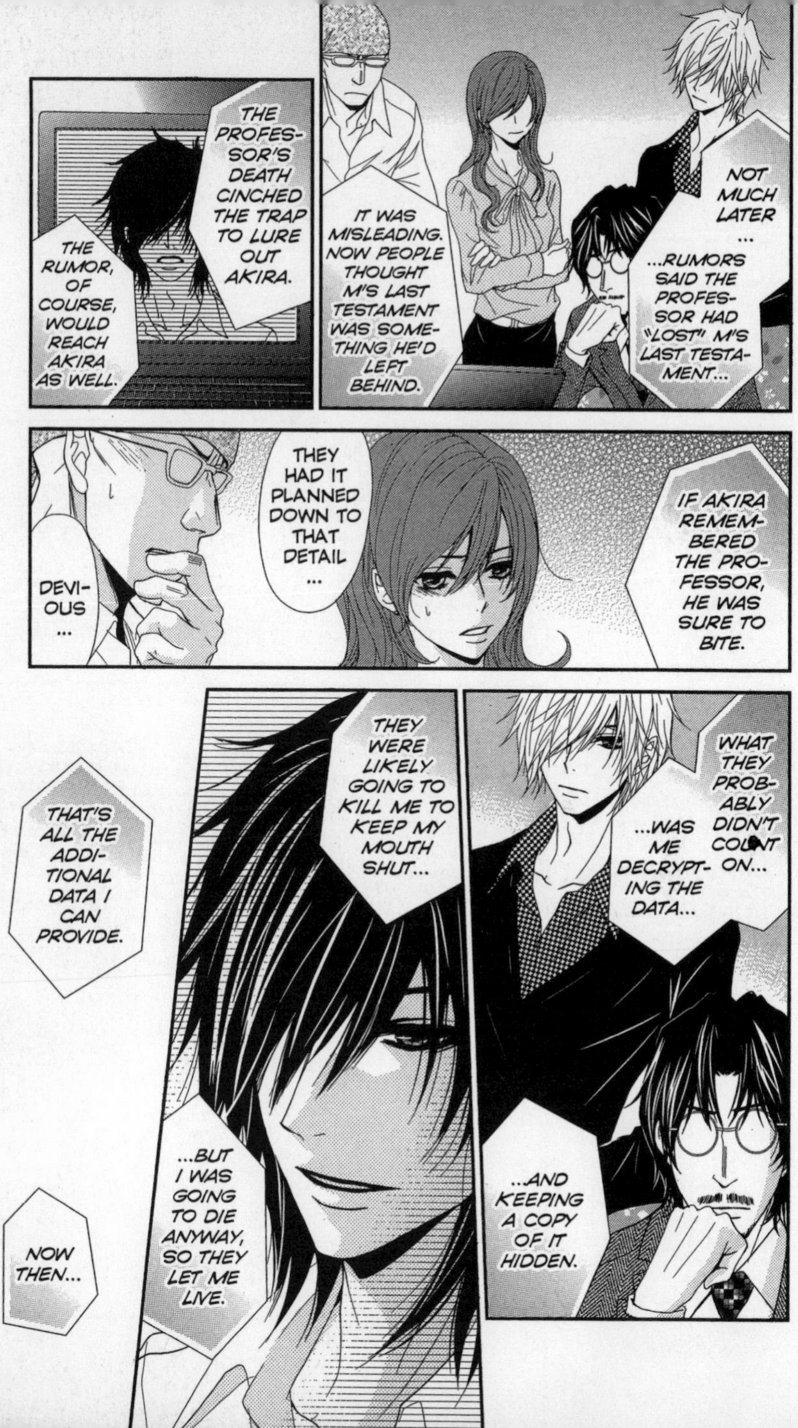
NOT MUCH LATER ...
...RUMORS SAID THE PROFESSOR HAD "LOST" M'S LAST TESTAMENT...
IT WAS MISLEADING. NOW PEOPLE THOUGHT M'S LAST TESTAMENT WAS SOMETHING HE'D LEFT BEHIND.
THE PROFESSOR'S DEATH CINCHED THE TRAP TO LURE OUT AKIRA.
THE RUMOR, OF COURSE, WOULD REACH AKIRA AS WELL.
IF AKIRA REMEMBERED THE PROFESSOR, HE WAS SURE TO BITE.
THEY HAD IT PLANNED DOWN TO THAT DETAIL ...
DEVIOUS ...
WHAT THEY PROBABLY DIDN'T COUNT ON...
...WAS ME DECRYPTING THE DATA...
...AND KEEPING A COPY OF IT HIDDEN.
THEY WERE LIKELY GOING TO KILL ME TO KEEP MY MOUTH SHUT...
...BUT I WAS GOING TO DIE ANYWAY, SO THEY LET ME LIVE.
THAT'S ALL THE ADDITIONAL DATA I CAN PROVIDE.
NOW THEN...

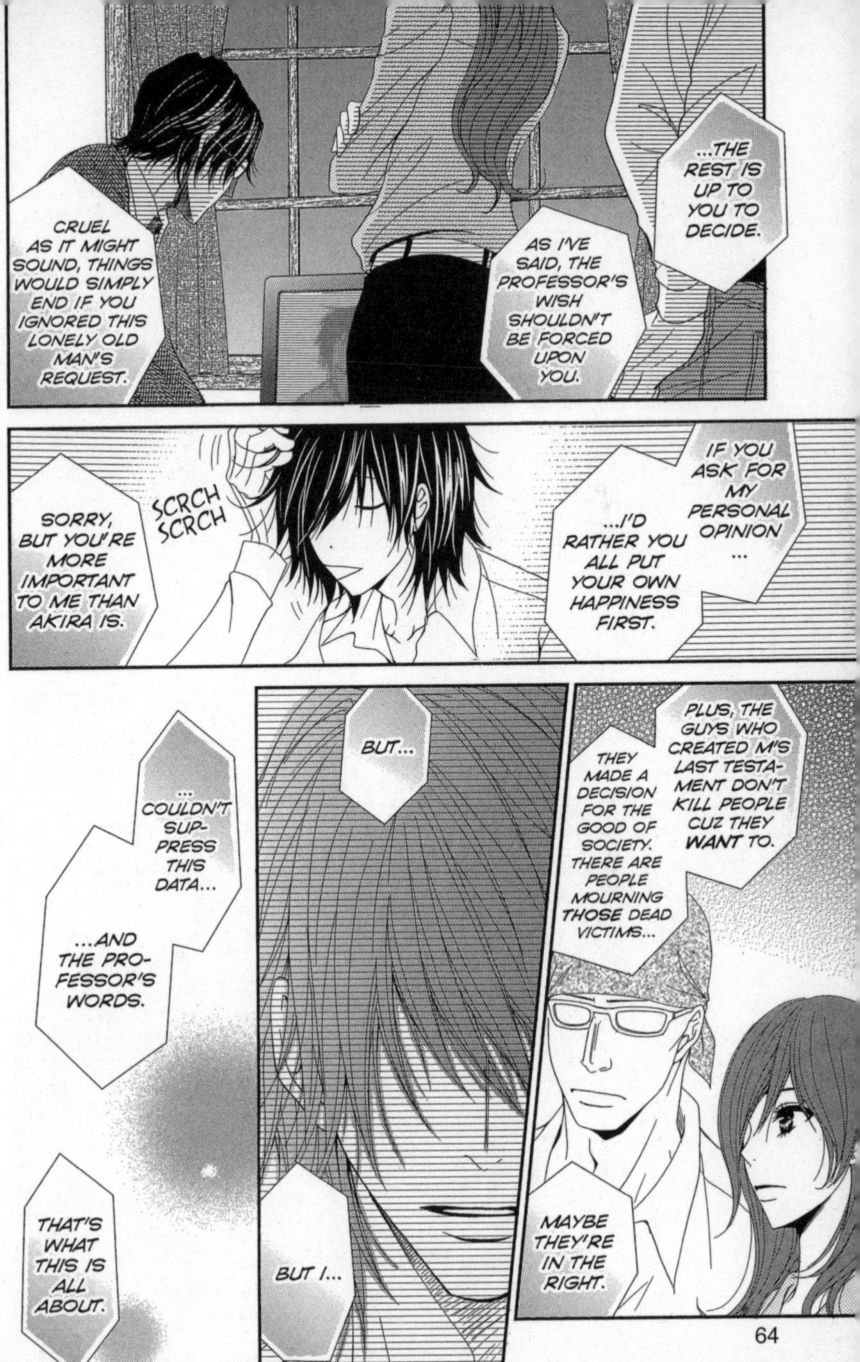
...THE REST IS UP TO YOU TO DECIDE.
AS I'VE SAID, THE PROFESSOR'S WISH SHOULDN'T BE FORCED UPON YOU.
CRUEL AS IT MIGHT SOUND, THINGS WOULD SIMPLY END IF YOU IGNORED THIS LONELY OLD MAN'S REQUEST.
IF YOU ASK FOR MY PERSONAL OPINION...
...I'D RATHER YOU ALL PUT YOUR OWN HAPPINESS FIRST.
SCRCH SCRCH
SORRY, BUT YOU'RE MORE IMPORTANT TO ME THAN AKIRA IS.
PLUS, THE GUYS WHO CREATED M'S LAST TESTAMENT DON'T KILL PEOPLE CUZ THEY WANT TO.
THEY MADE A DECISION FOR THE GOOD OF SOCIETY. THERE ARE PEOPLE MOURNING THOSE DEAD VICTIMS...
MAYBE THEY'RE IN THE RIGHT.
BUT...
BUT I...
...COULDN'T SUPPRESS THIS DATA...
...AND THE PROFESSOR'S WORDS.
THAT'S WHAT THIS IS ALL ABOUT.

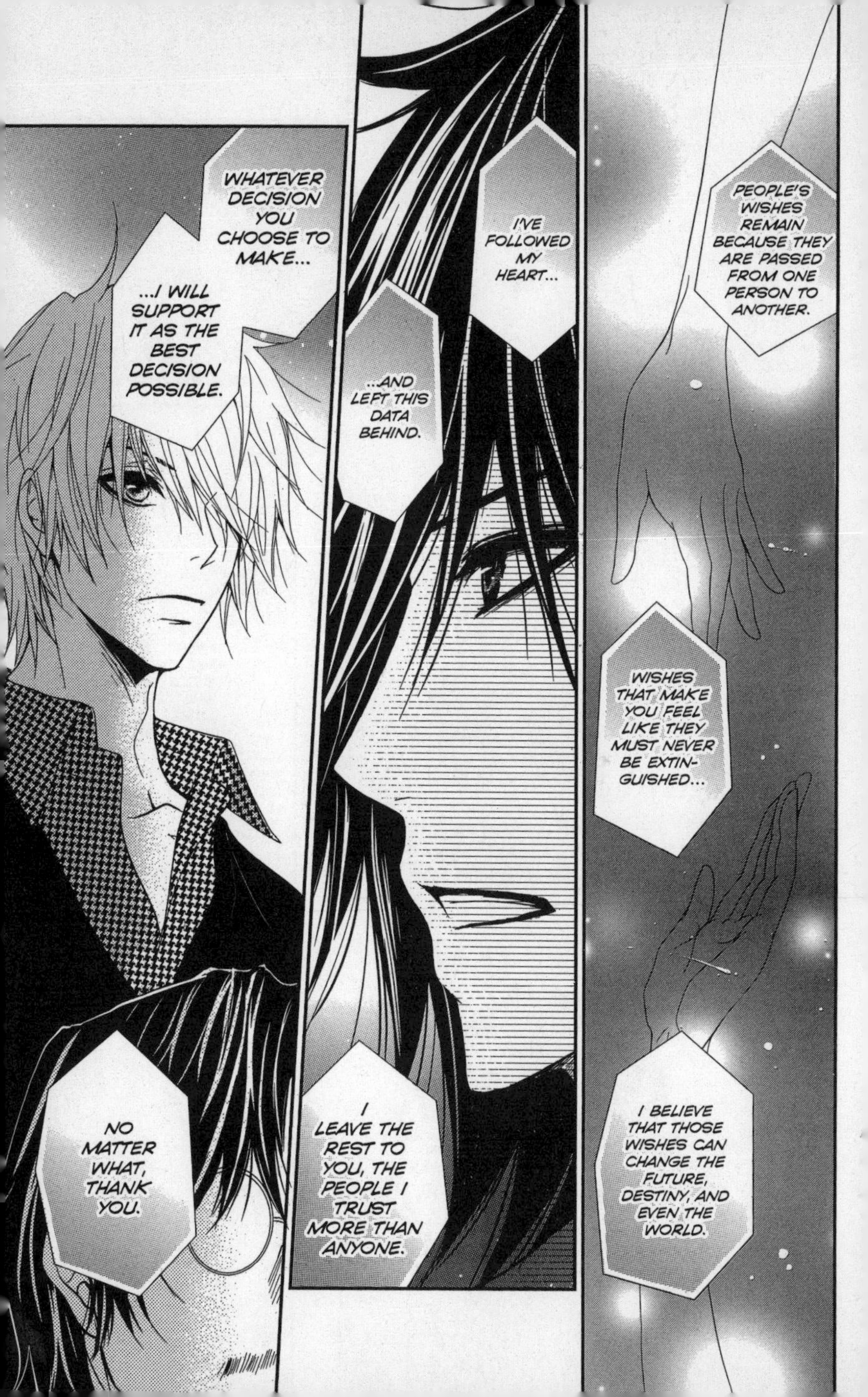
PEOPLE'S WISHES REMAIN BECAUSE THEY ARE PASSED FROM ONE PERSON TO ANOTHER.
WISHES THAT MAKE YOU FEEL LIKE THEY MUST NEVER BE EXTIN-GUISHED...
I BELIEVE THAT THOSE WISHES CAN CHANGE THE FUTURE, DESTINY, AND EVEN THE WORLD.
I'VE FOLLOWED MY HEART...
...AND LEFT THIS DATA BEHIND.
I LEAVE THE REST TO YOU, THE PEOPLE I TRUST MORE THAN ANYONE.
WHATEVER DECISION YOU CHOOSE TO MAKE...
...I WILL SUPPORT IT AS THE BEST DECISION POSSIBLE.
NO MATTER WHAT, THANK YOU.

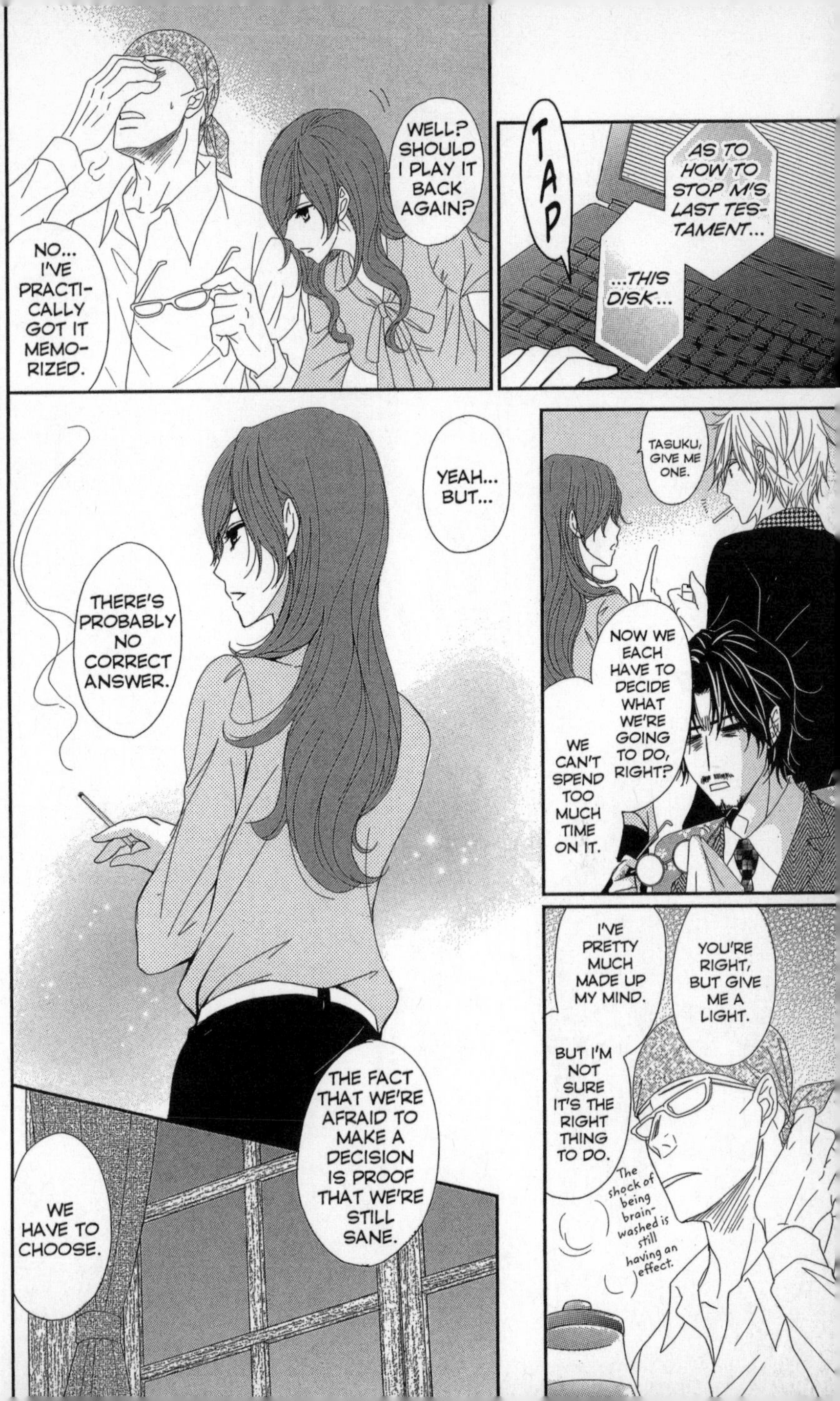
TAP
AS TO HOW TO STOP M'S LAST TES-TAMENT...
...THIS DISK...
WELL? SHOULD I PLAY IT BACK AGAIN?
NO... I'VE PRACTI-CALLY GOT IT MEMO-RIZED.
TASUKU, GIVE ME ONE.
NOW WE EACH HAVE TO DECIDE WHAT WE'RE GOING TO DO, RIGHT?
WE CAN'T SPEND TOO MUCH TIME ON IT.
YOU'RE RIGHT, BUT GIVE ME A LIGHT.
I'VE PRETTY MUCH MADE UP MY MIND.
BUT I'M NOT SURE IT'S THE RIGHT THING TO DO.
The shock of being brain-washed is still having an effect.
YEAH... BUT...
THERE'S PROBABLY NO CORRECT ANSWER.
THE FACT THAT WE'RE AFRAID TO MAKE A DECISION IS PROOF THAT WE'RE STILL SANE.
WE HAVE TO CHOOSE.

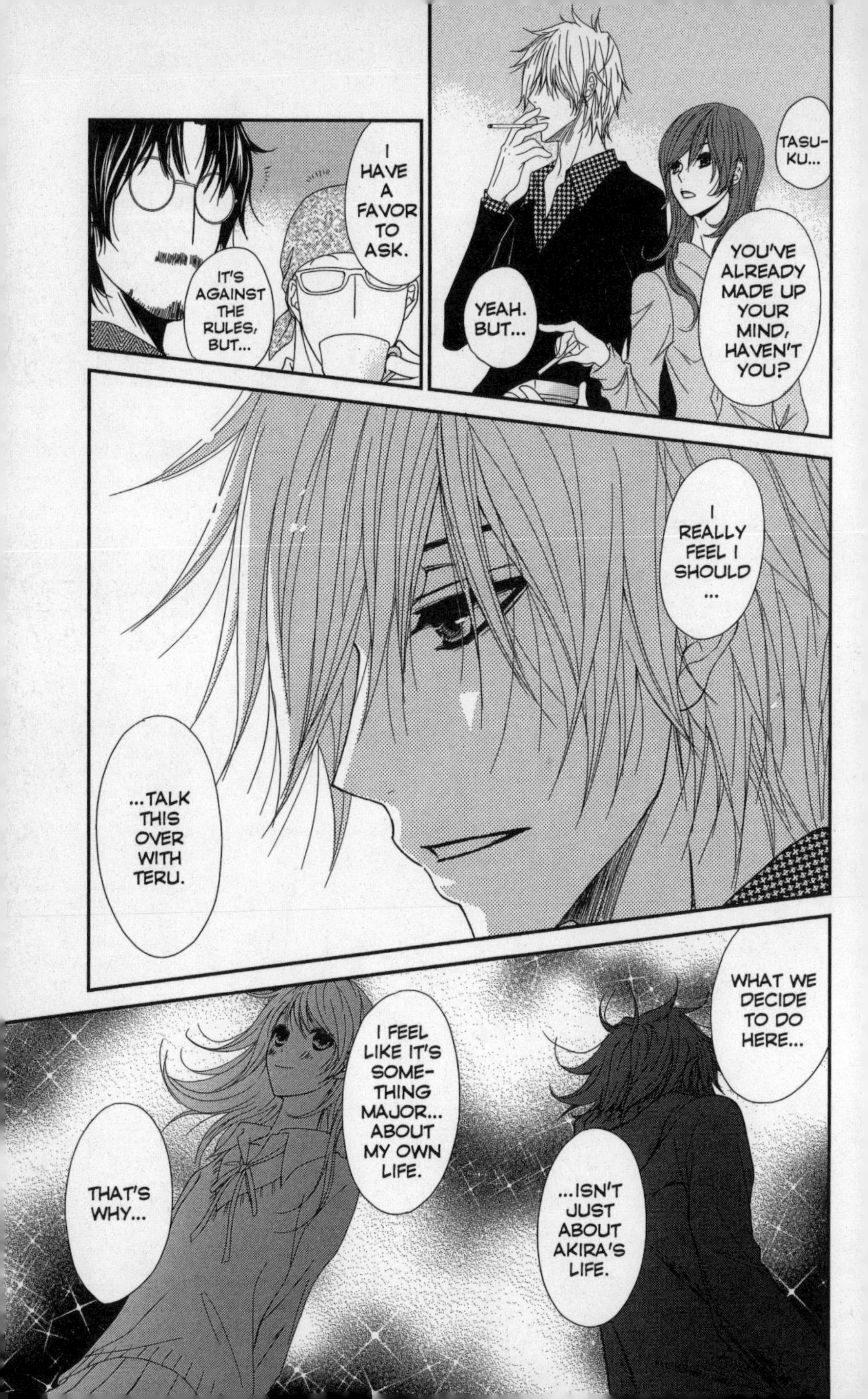
TASU-KU...
YOU'VE ALREADY MADE UP YOUR MIND, HAVEN'T YOU?
YEAH. BUT...
I HAVE A FAVOR TO ASK.
IT'S AGAINST THE RULES, BUT...
I REALLY FEEL I SHOULD ...
...TALK THIS OVER WITH TERU.
WHAT WE DECIDE TO DO HERE...
...ISN'T JUST ABOUT AKIRA'S LIFE.
I FEEL LIKE IT'S SOME-THING MAJOR... ABOUT MY OWN LIFE.
THAT'S WHY...

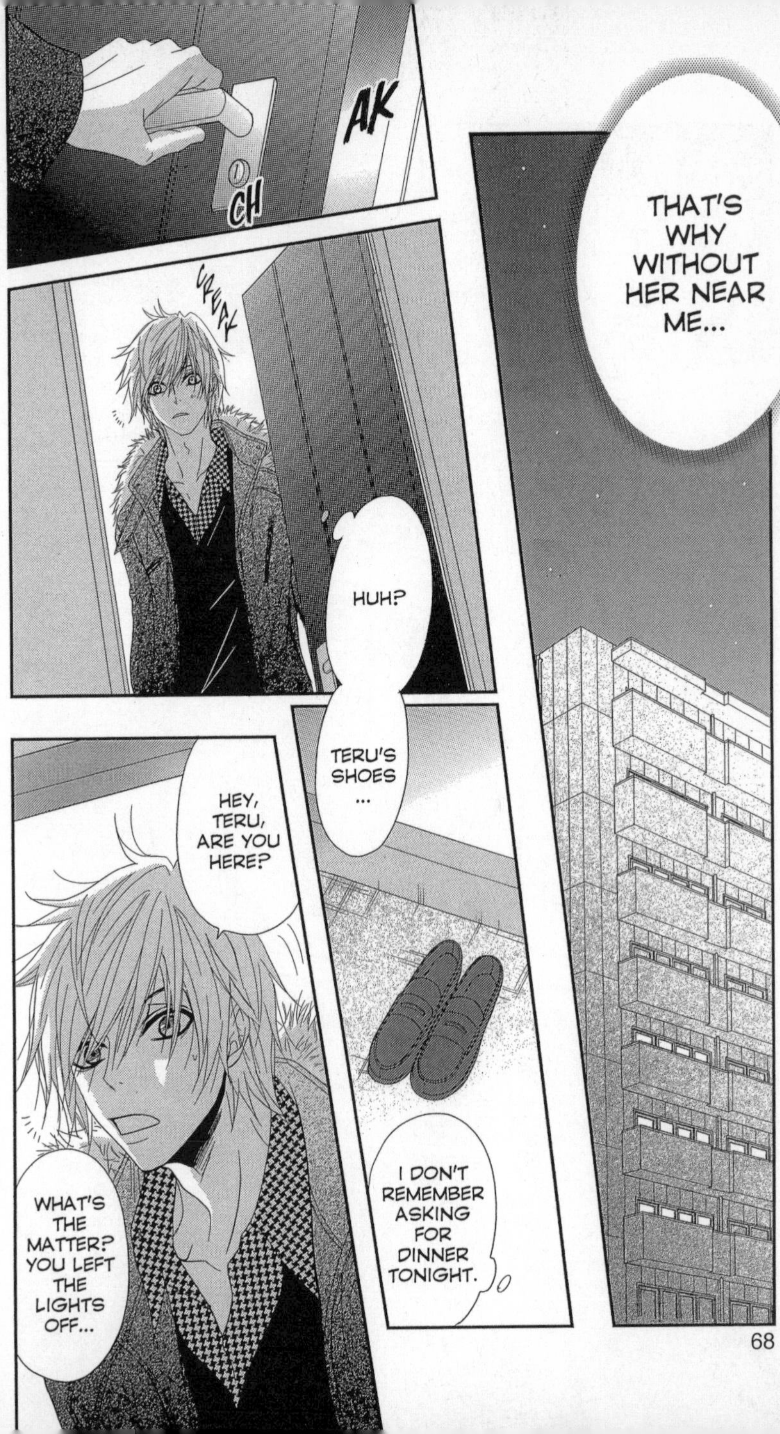
THAT'S WHY WITHOUT HER NEAR ME...
CH
AK
CREAK
HUH?
TERU'S SHOES ...
I DON'T REMEMBER ASKING FOR DINNER TONIGHT.
HEY, TERU, ARE YOU HERE?
WHAT'S THE MATTER? YOU LEFT THE LIGHTS OFF...

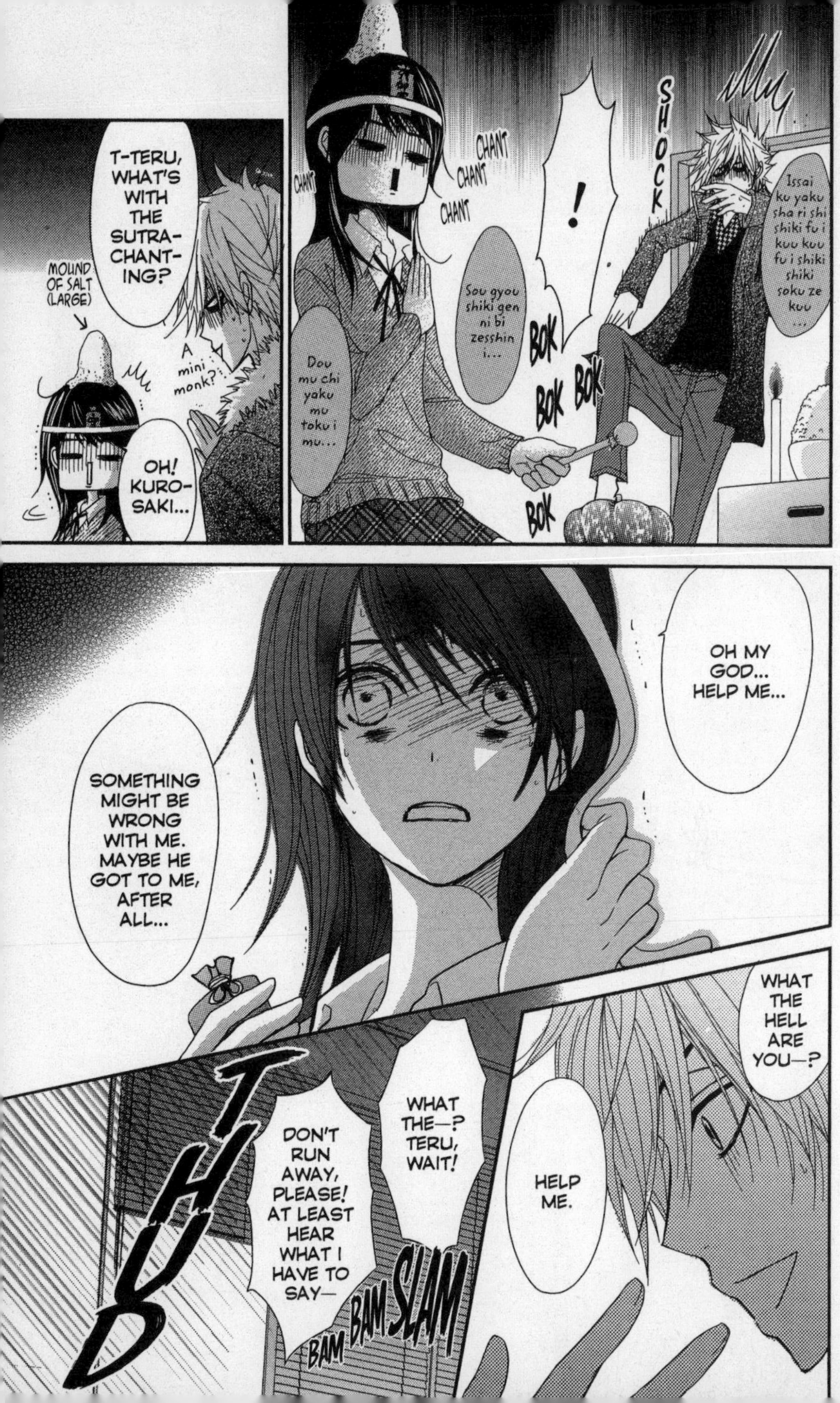
Issai ku yaku sha ri shi shiki fu i kuu kuu fu i shiki shiki soku ze kuu ...
SHOCK
!
CHANT
CHANT
CHANT
CHANT
Sou gyou shiki gen ni bi zesshin i...
BOK
BOK BOK
BOK
Dou mu chi yaku mu toku i mu...
BOK
T-TERU, WHAT'S WITH THE SUTRA-CHANTING?
A mini monk?
MOUND OF SALT (LARGE)
OH! KUROSAKI...
OH MY GOD... HELP ME...
SOMETHING MIGHT BE WRONG WITH ME. MAYBE HE GOT TO ME, AFTER ALL...
WHAT THE HELL ARE YOU—?
HELP ME.
WHAT THE—? TERU, WAIT!
DON'T RUN AWAY, PLEASE! AT LEAST HEAR WHAT I HAVE TO SAY—
SLAM
BAM
BAM
THUD

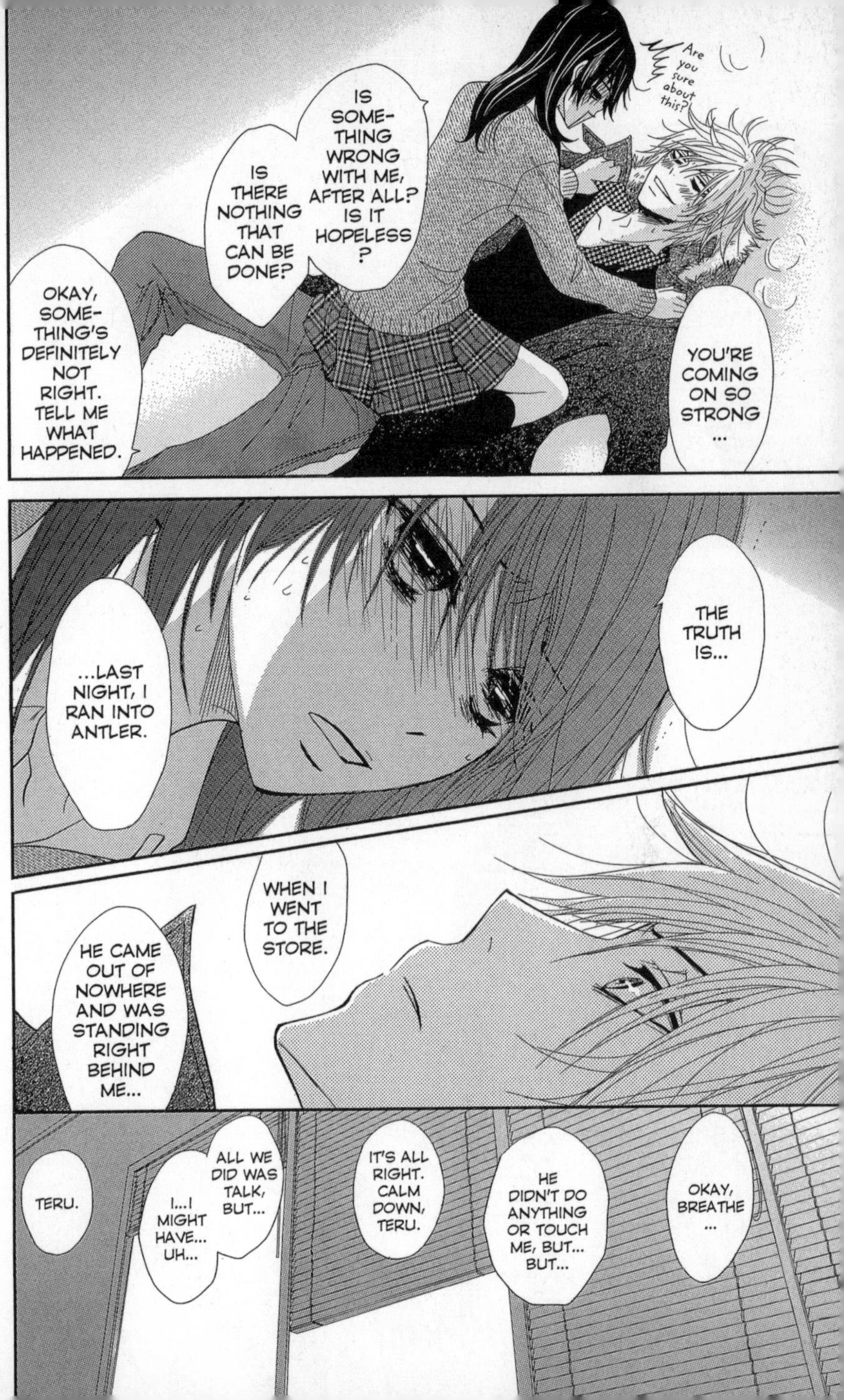
Are you sure about this?
YOU'RE COMING ON SO STRONG...
IS SOMETHING WRONG WITH ME, AFTER ALL? IS IT HOPELESS?
IS THERE NOTHING THAT CAN BE DONE?
OKAY, SOMETHING'S DEFINITELY NOT RIGHT. TELL ME WHAT HAPPENED.
THE TRUTH IS...
...LAST NIGHT, I RAN INTO ANTLER.
WHEN I WENT TO THE STORE.
HE CAME OUT OF NOWHERE AND WAS STANDING RIGHT BEHIND ME...
OKAY, BREATHE...
HE DIDN'T DO ANYTHING OR TOUCH ME, BUT... BUT...
IT'S ALL RIGHT. CALM DOWN, TERU.
ALL WE DID WAS TALK, BUT...
I...I MIGHT HAVE... UH...
TERU.

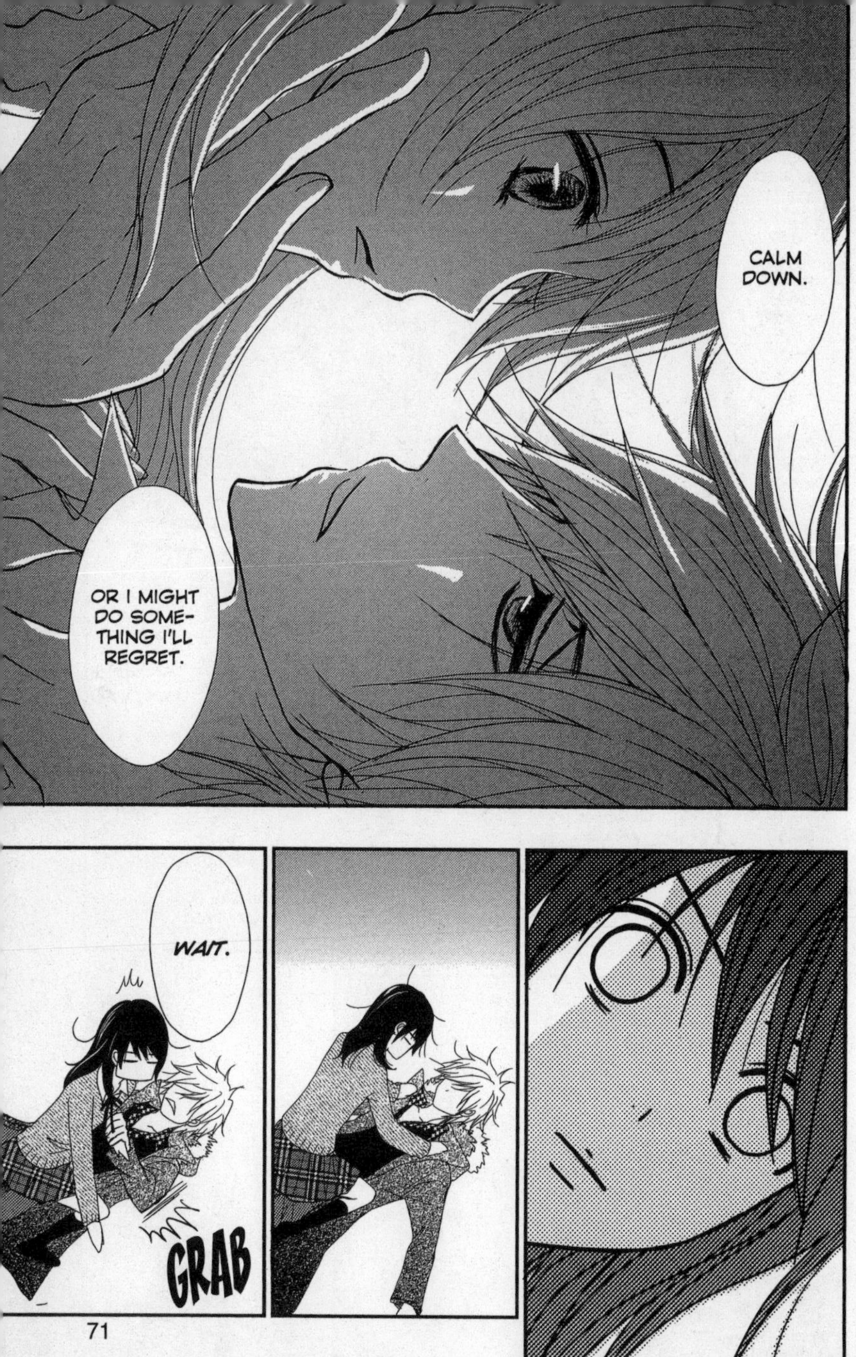
CALM DOWN.
OR I MIGHT DO SOME-THING I'LL REGRET.
WAIT.
GRAB

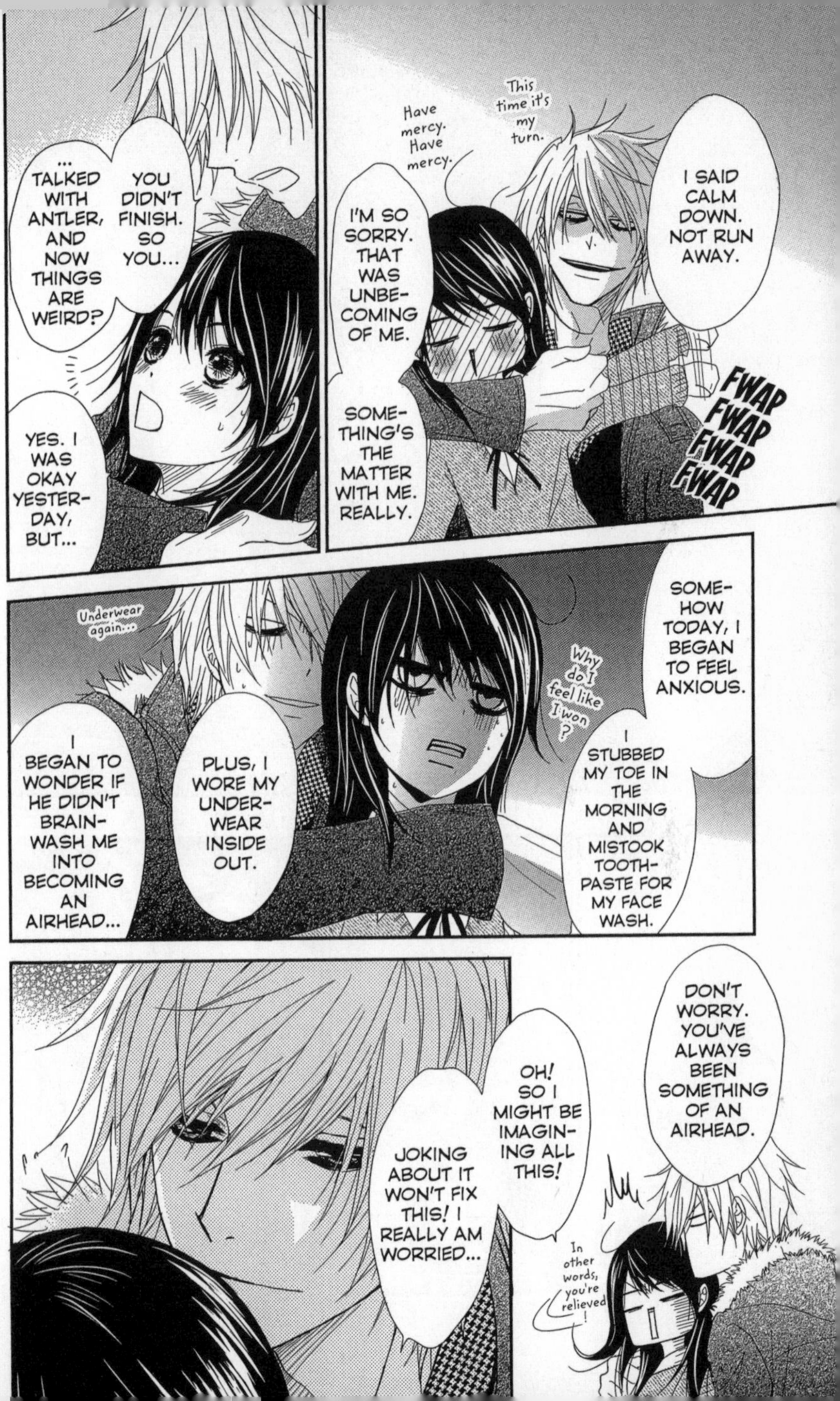
I SAID CALM DOWN. NOT RUN AWAY.
This time it's my turn.
Have mercy. Have mercy.
I'M SO SORRY. THAT WAS UNBECOMING OF ME.
FWAP FWAP FWAP FWAP
SOMETHING'S THE MATTER WITH ME. REALLY.
YOU DIDN'T FINISH. SO YOU...
...TALKED WITH ANTLER, AND NOW THINGS ARE WEIRD?
YES. I WAS OKAY YESTERDAY, BUT...
SOMEHOW TODAY, I BEGAN TO FEEL ANXIOUS.
Why do I feel like I won?
I STUBBED MY TOE IN THE MORNING AND MISTOOK TOOTHPASTE FOR MY FACE WASH.
Underwear again...
PLUS, I WORE MY UNDERWEAR INSIDE OUT.
I BEGAN TO WONDER IF HE DIDN'T BRAINWASH ME INTO BECOMING AN AIRHEAD...
DON'T WORRY. YOU'VE ALWAYS BEEN SOMETHING OF AN AIRHEAD.
OH! SO I MIGHT BE IMAGINING ALL THIS!
JOKING ABOUT IT WON'T FIX THIS! I REALLY AM WORRIED...
In other words, you're relieved!

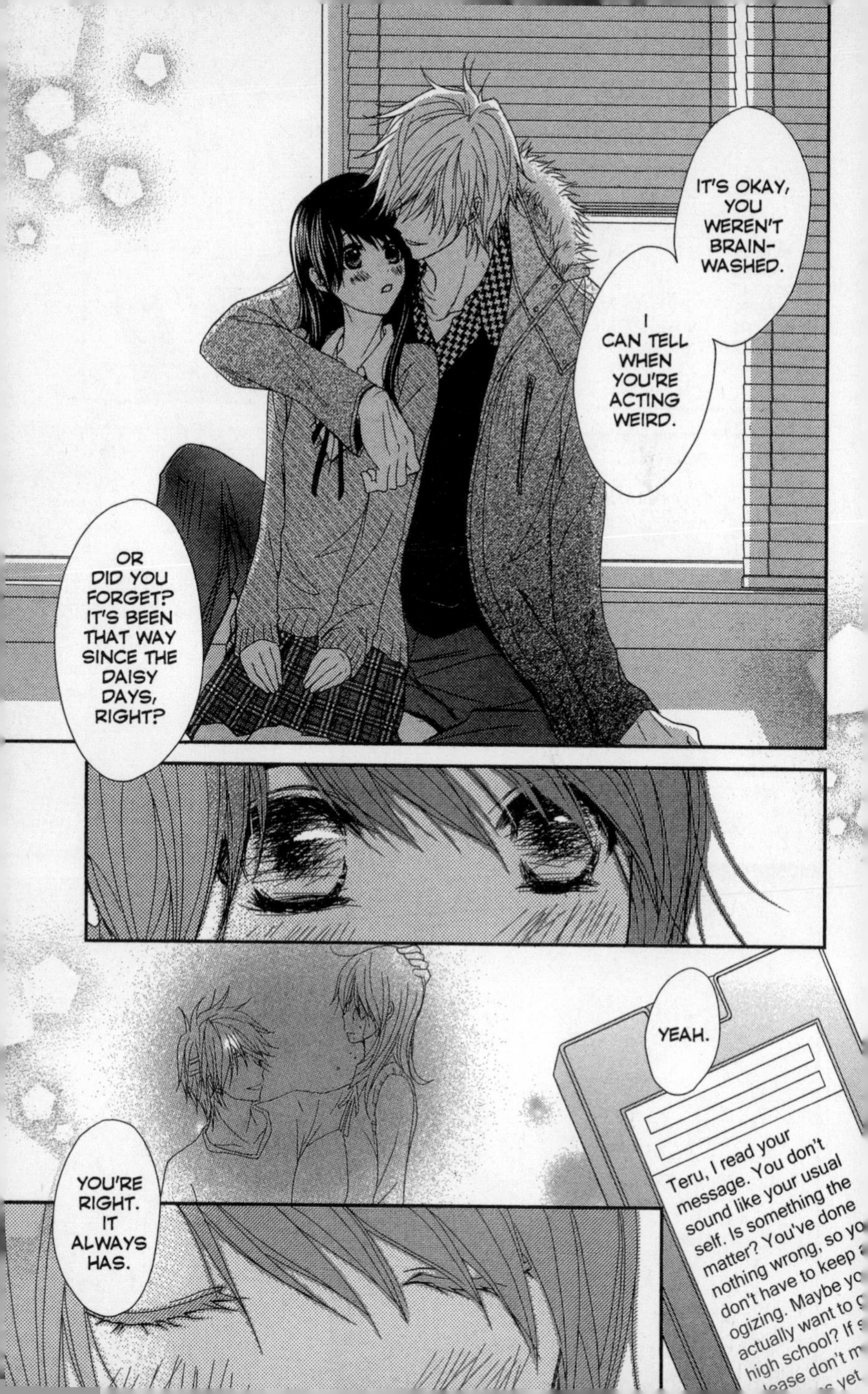

IT'S OKAY, YOU WEREN'T BRAIN-WASHED.
I CAN TELL WHEN YOU'RE ACTING WEIRD.
OR DID YOU FORGET? IT'S BEEN THAT WAY SINCE THE DAISY DAYS, RIGHT?
YEAH.
Teru, I read your message. You don't sound like your usual self. Is something the matter? You've done nothing wrong, so yo don't have to keep ogizing. Maybe yo actually want to high school? If
YOU'RE RIGHT. IT ALWAYS HAS.

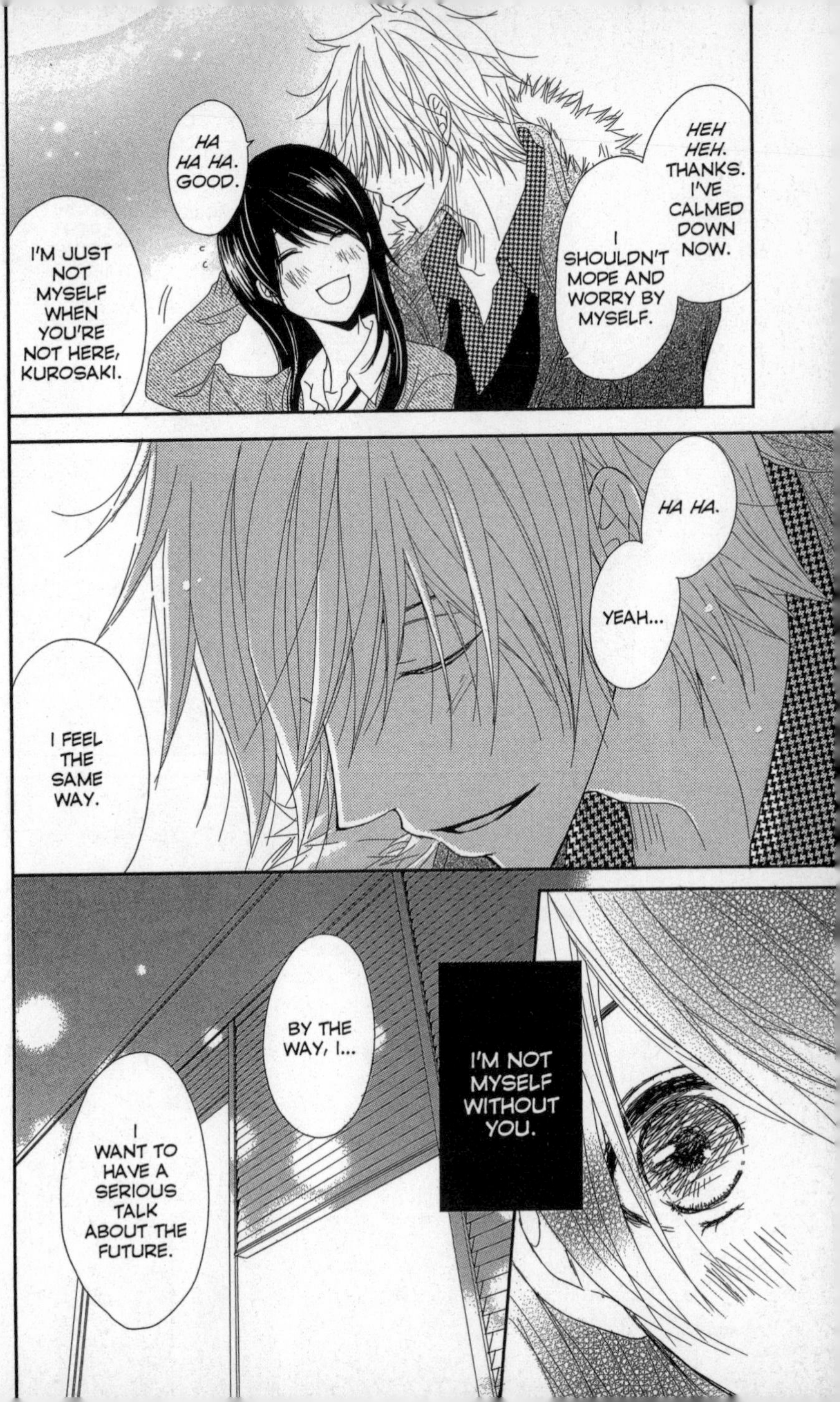
HEH HEH. THANKS. I'VE CALMED DOWN NOW.
I SHOULDN'T MOPE AND WORRY BY MYSELF.
HA HA HA. GOOD.
I'M JUST NOT MYSELF WHEN YOU'RE NOT HERE, KUROSAKI.
HA HA.
YEAH...
I FEEL THE SAME WAY.
I'M NOT MYSELF WITHOUT YOU.
BY THE WAY, I...
I WANT TO HAVE A SERIOUS TALK ABOUT THE FUTURE.

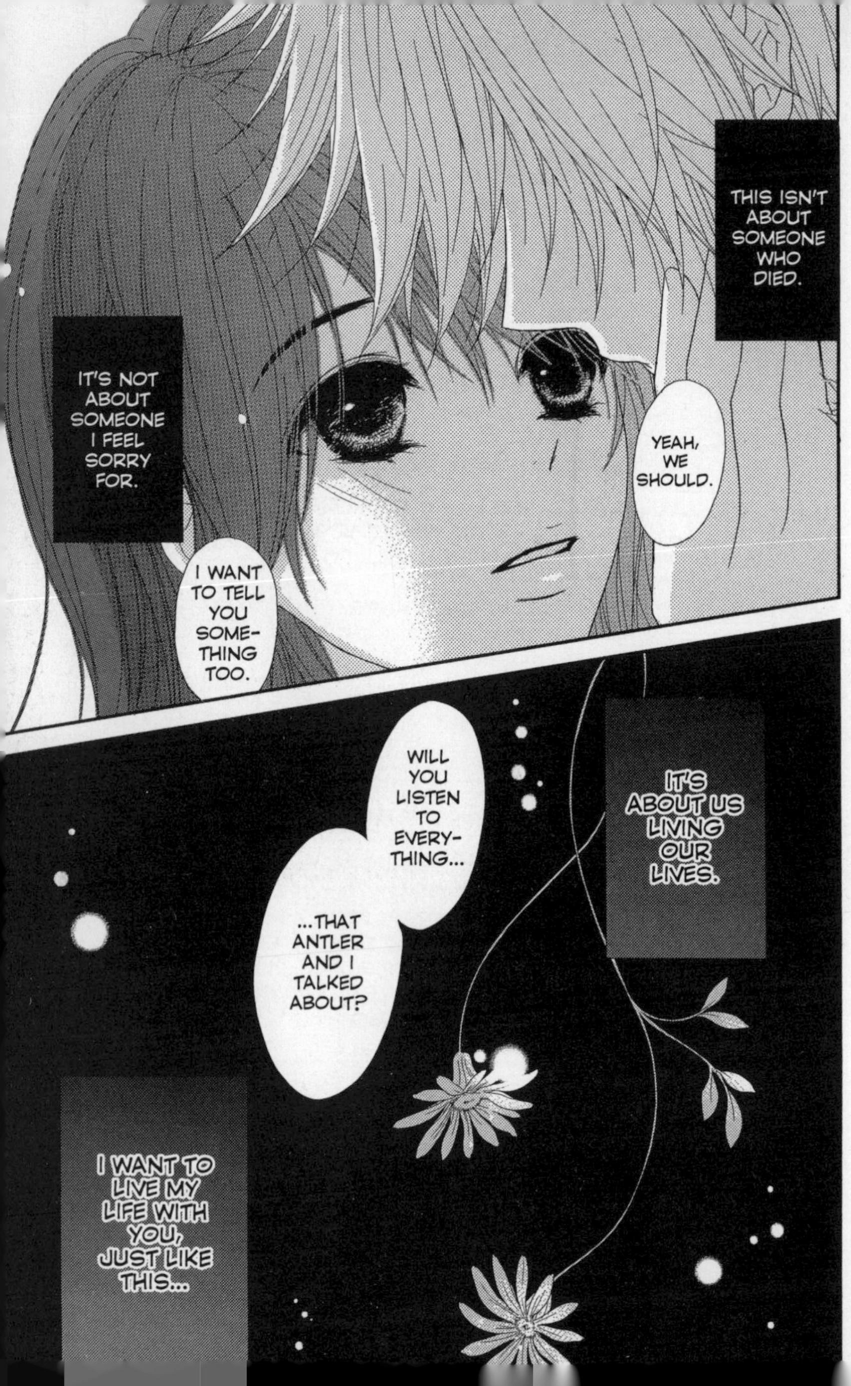
THIS ISN'T ABOUT SOMEONE WHO DIED.
YEAH, WE SHOULD.
IT'S NOT ABOUT SOMEONE I FEEL SORRY FOR.
I WANT TO TELL YOU SOME-THING TOO.
IT'S ABOUT US LIVING OUR LIVES.
WILL YOU LISTEN TO EVERY-THING...
...THAT ANTLER AND I TALKED ABOUT?
I WANT TO LIVE MY LIFE WITH YOU, JUST LIKE THIS...

DENGEKI DAISY QUESTION CORNER

RELOCATED

BALDLY ASK!!! ②

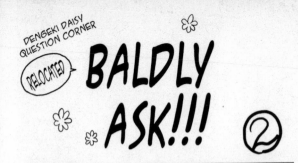

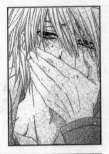

PEOPLE WITH BLOOD TYPE AB ARE SAID TO BE RESISTANT TO BALDING, BUT IS KUROSAKI AN EXCEPTION? ALSO, IF DAISY BECAME INVISIBLE FOR A DAY, WHAT WOULD HE DO?
(MOKKORO KIRIZO, AICHI PREFECTURE)

ARE YOU SERIOUS?! KUROSAKI WOULD CRY TEARS OF JOY. PROBABLY AS MUCH AS THAT TIME IN VOLUME 9. HM, IF KUROSAKI WERE INVISIBLE, HE'D PROBABLY DO SOMETHING OBVIOUS. BETTER SCATTER SOME CALTROPS AROUND THE BATHTUB IN TERU'S HOME.

IN VOLUME 1, KUROSAKI HIT HIS HEAD ON A FOOTREST BUT DIDN'T GO DOWN. SO WHY IS IT THAT IN VOLUME 4, WHEN HE GOT HIS HEAD HIT BY A DESK AND CHAIR (IT WASN'T EVEN A DIRECT IMPACT), HE COLLAPSED? ISN'T A HEAVY FOOTREST MORE DANGEROUS? OR ARE YOU TRYING TO SAY THAT KUROSAKI ISN'T NORMAL?
(KUROTERU, OSAKA PREFECTURE)

~~KUROSAKI WAS OKAY EVEN THOUGH HE WAS BLEEDING BECAUSE IT'S A COMIC.~~

WELL, LET ME SEE... I HAVEN'T STUDIED PHYSICS OF THE PAST 300 YEARS, SO I ONLY HAVE ABOUT A MICRON OF PHYSICS MEMORY LEFT IN ME. I SEEM TO REMEMBER THAT WHEN AN OBJECT DROPS FROM A HIGH PLACE, THERE'S POTENTIAL ENERGY AND ACCELERATION, AND THINGS LIKE THAT MAKE IT DANGEROUS. ASK YOUR SCHOOLTEACHER FOR DETAILS. BUT DON'T GO MENTIONING THIS MANGA. YOUR TEACHER WILL SCOLD YOU AND TELL YOU NOT TO READ A BOOK DONE BY A STUPID PERSON.

IT OCCURRED TO ME WHEN I SAW KUROSAKI'S SALARYMAN SOCKS IN CHAPTER 68—WHO HAS THE STINKIER FEET: SOICHIRO OR KUROSAKI?
(A.U., KAGOSHIMA PREFECTURE)

THAT'D PROBABLY BE SOICHIRO. HE COLLECTS 3-4 DAYS OF STINK IN NO TIME AT ALL. BUT IF KUROSAKI WORKS LATE INTO THE NIGHT ON A TOUGH JOB WITH HIS SHOES ON, HIS FEET WOULD GET PRETTY SMELLY, TOO. I DON'T THINK TERU WOULD MIND VERY MUCH, THOUGH. I THINK SHE'D MATTER-OF-FACTLY TELL HIM, JUST LIKE SHE TOLD SOICHIRO, "IT STINKS, WASH YOUR FEET."

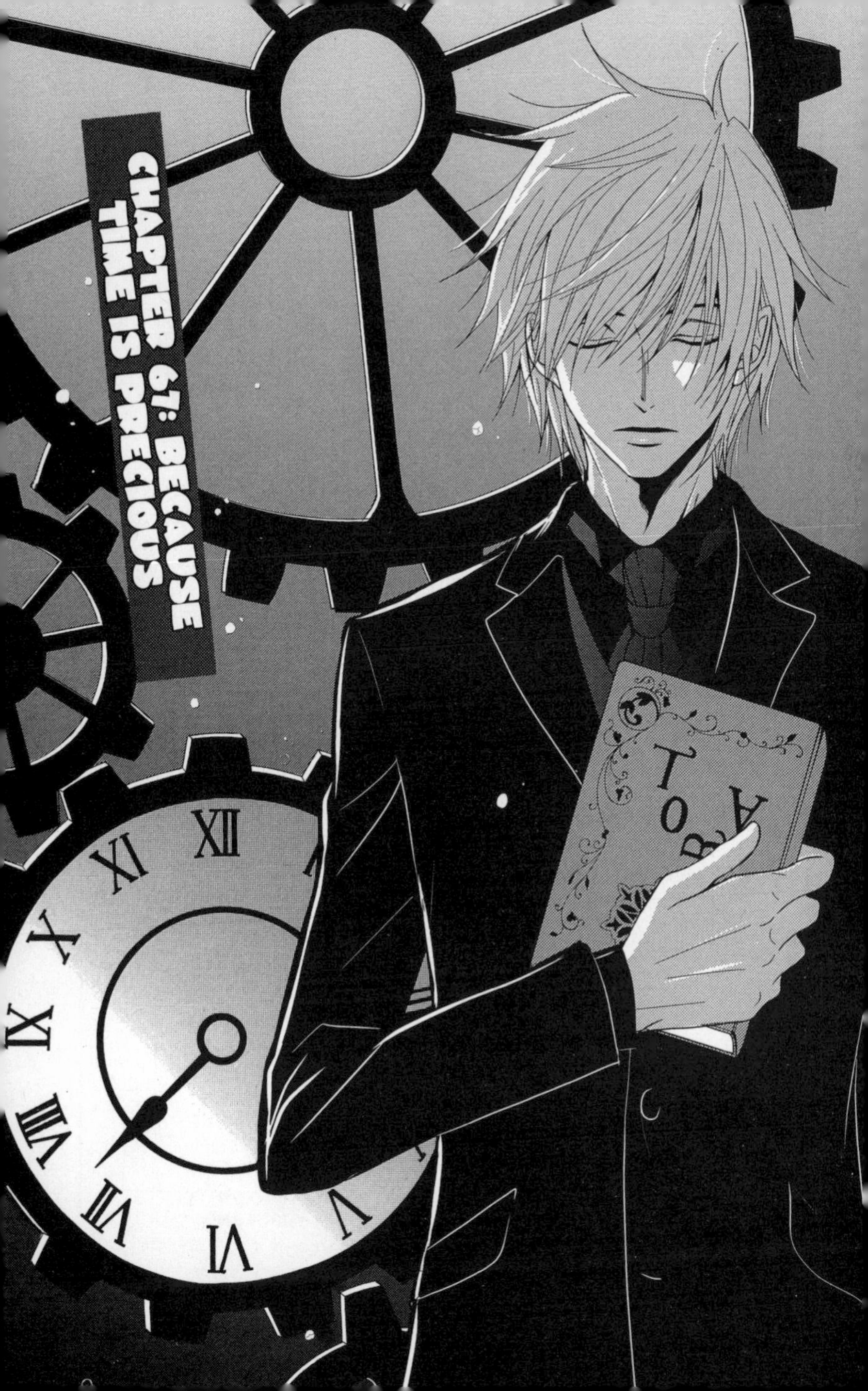
CHAPTER 67: BECAUSE
TIME IS PRECIOUS

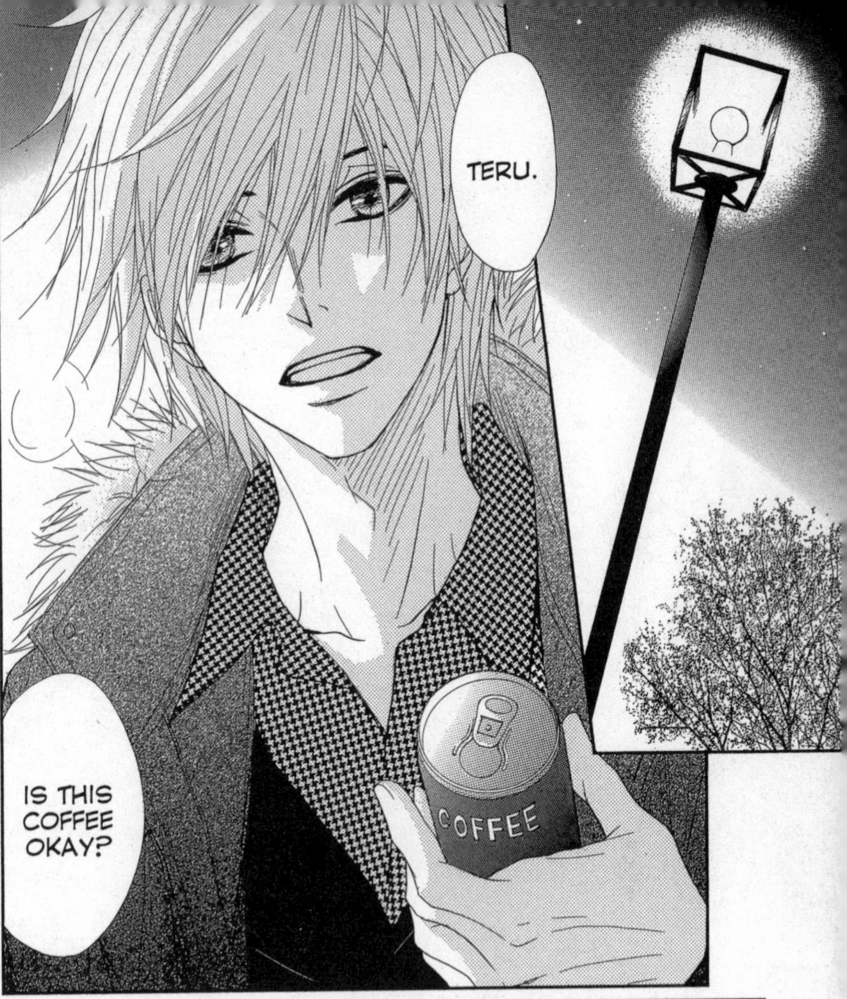
TERU.
IS THIS COFFEE OKAY?
COFFEE

THE CHANT THAT TERU IS MUTTERING IN CHAPTER 66 IS THE HANNYA SHINGYO. YOU ALREADY KNOW THAT IT IS A SHORT AND VERY POPULAR SUTRA. I THINK LEARNING IT MIGHT BE HELPFUL IN A LOT OF WAYS. HEY, YOU NEVER KNOW WHEN YOU MIGHT HAVE TO BATTLE DANGEROUS SPIRIT PEOPLE. I AM A BUDDHIST MYSELF (AT LEAST TO THE EXTENT THAT A LOT OF JAPANESE PEOPLE ARE), SO WHEN I FINISH THIS MANUSCRIPT, I THOUGHT I MIGHT TAKE ON THE CHALLENGE OF MEMORIZING IT. (GET BACK TO YOUR STORYBOARD!)

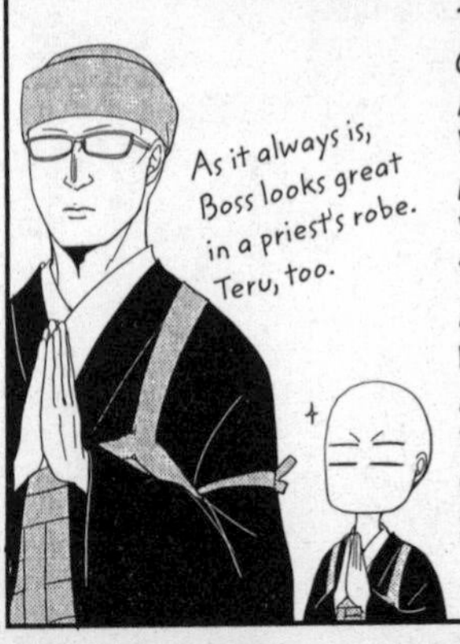
As it always is,
Boss looks great
in a priest's robe.
Teru, too.

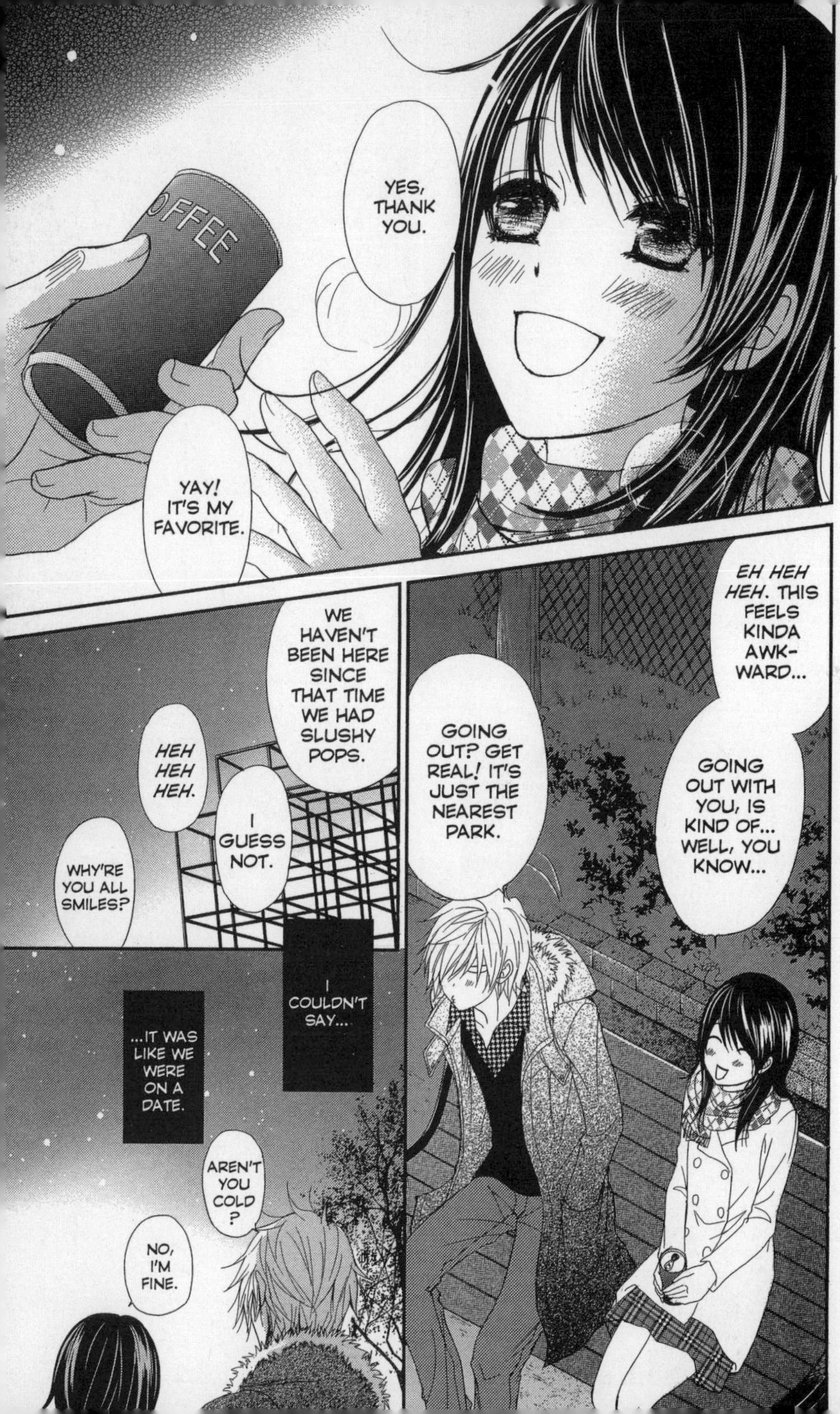
YES, THANK YOU.
YAY! IT'S MY FAVORITE.
EH HEH HEH. THIS FEELS KINDA AWK-WARD...
GOING OUT WITH YOU, IS KIND OF... WELL, YOU KNOW...
GOING OUT? GET REAL! IT'S JUST THE NEAREST PARK.
WE HAVEN'T BEEN HERE SINCE THAT TIME WE HAD SLUSHY POPS.
HEH HEH HEH.
I GUESS NOT.
WHY'RE YOU ALL SMILES?
I COULDN'T SAY...
...IT WAS LIKE WE WERE ON A DATE.
AREN'T YOU COLD?
NO, I'M FINE.

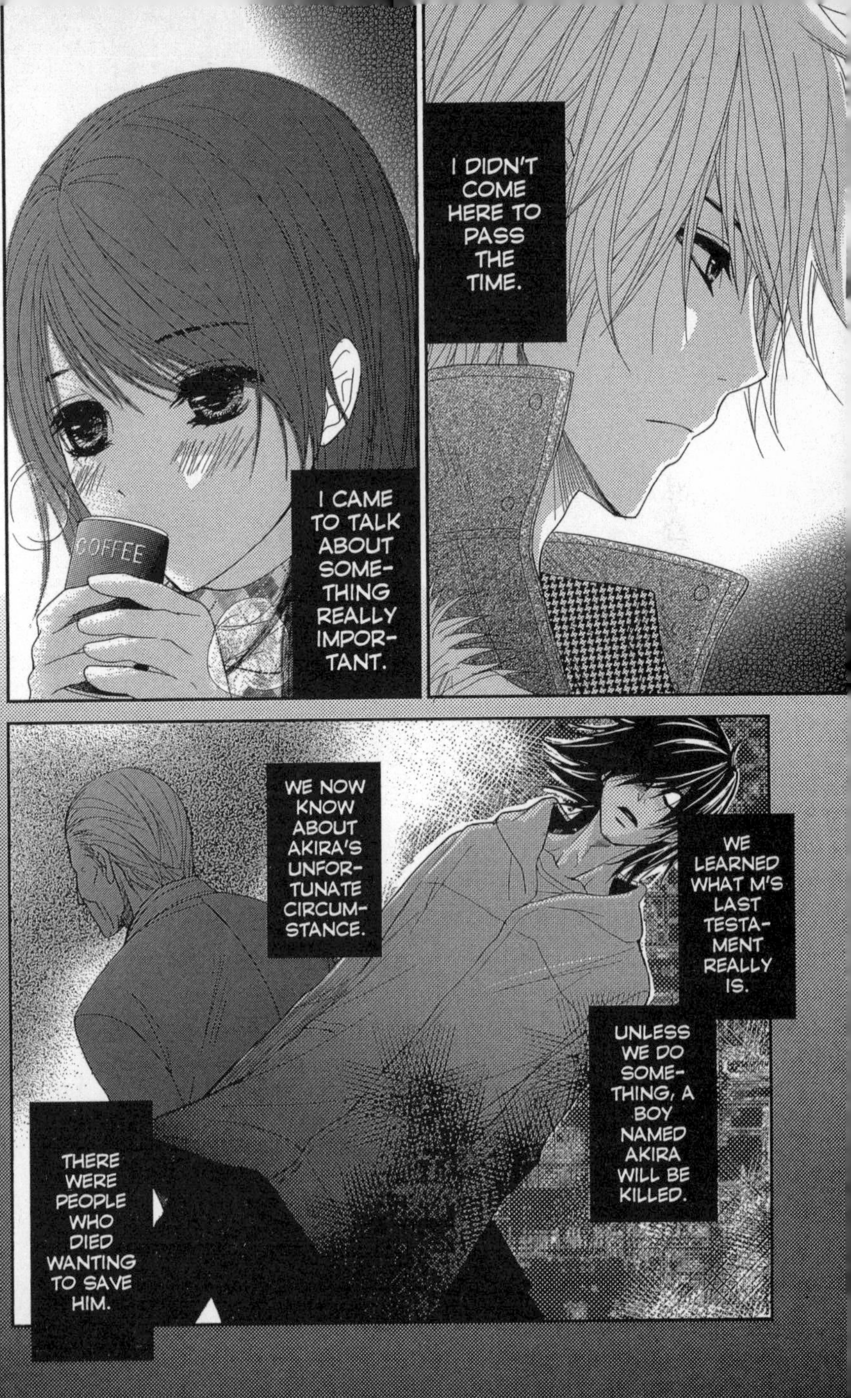
I DIDN'T COME HERE TO PASS THE TIME.
COFFEE
I CAME TO TALK ABOUT SOME-THING REALLY IMPOR-TANT.
WE LEARNED WHAT M'S LAST TESTA-MENT REALLY IS.
WE NOW KNOW ABOUT AKIRA'S UNFOR-TUNATE CIRCUM-STANCE.
UNLESS WE DO SOME-THING, A BOY NAMED AKIRA WILL BE KILLED.
THERE WERE PEOPLE WHO DIED WANTING TO SAVE HIM.

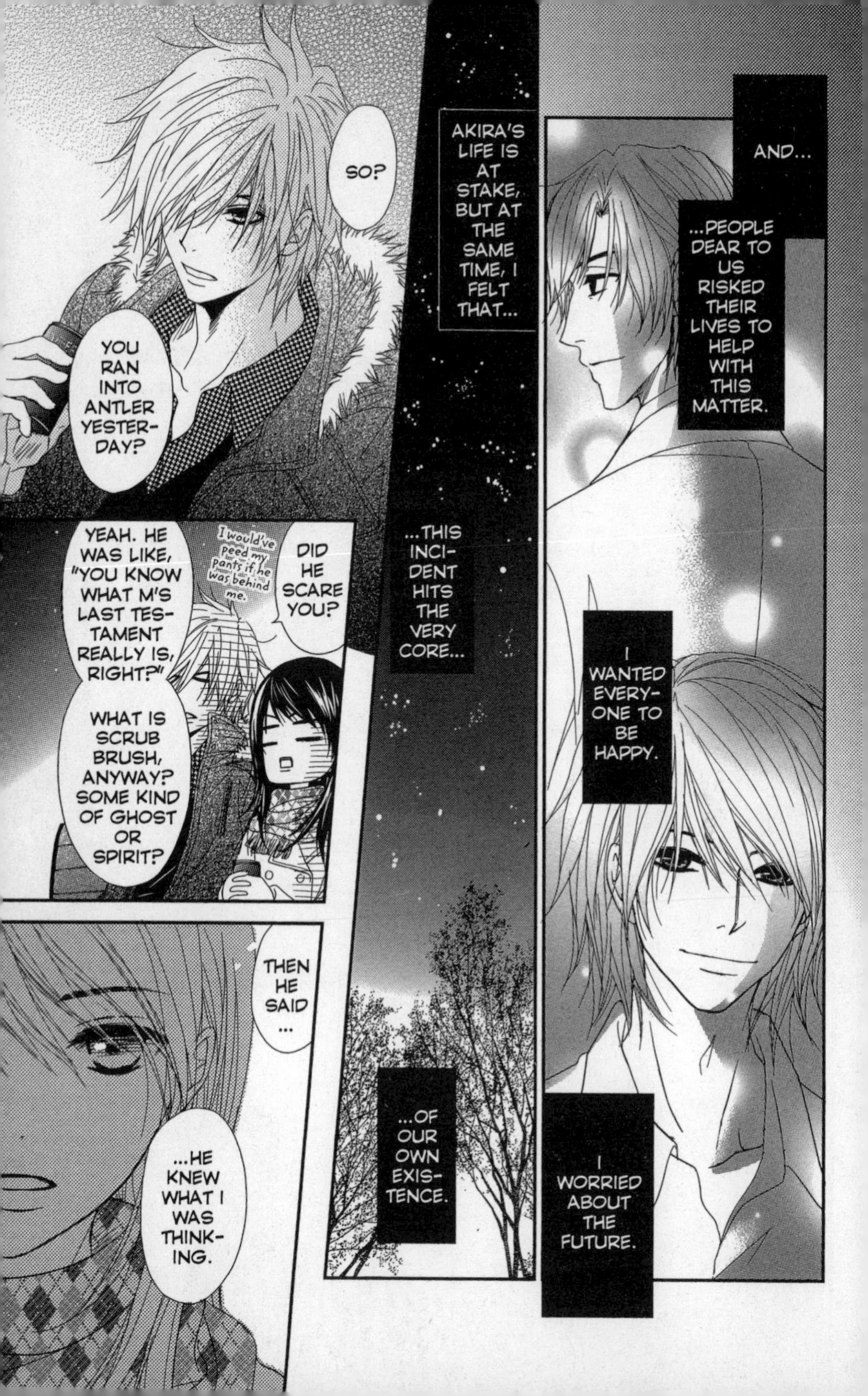
AND...
...PEOPLE DEAR TO US RISKED THEIR LIVES TO HELP WITH THIS MATTER.
I WANTED EVERYONE TO BE HAPPY.
I WORRIED ABOUT THE FUTURE.
AKIRA'S LIFE IS AT STAKE, BUT AT THE SAME TIME, I FELT THAT...
...THIS INCIDENT HITS THE VERY CORE...
...OF OUR OWN EXISTENCE.
SO?
YOU RAN INTO ANTLER YESTERDAY?
DID HE SCARE YOU?
I would've peed my pants if he was behind me.
YEAH. HE WAS LIKE, "YOU KNOW WHAT M'S LAST TESTAMENT REALLY IS, RIGHT?"
WHAT IS SCRUB BRUSH, ANYWAY? SOME KIND OF GHOST OR SPIRIT?
THEN HE SAID...
...HE KNEW WHAT I WAS THINKING.

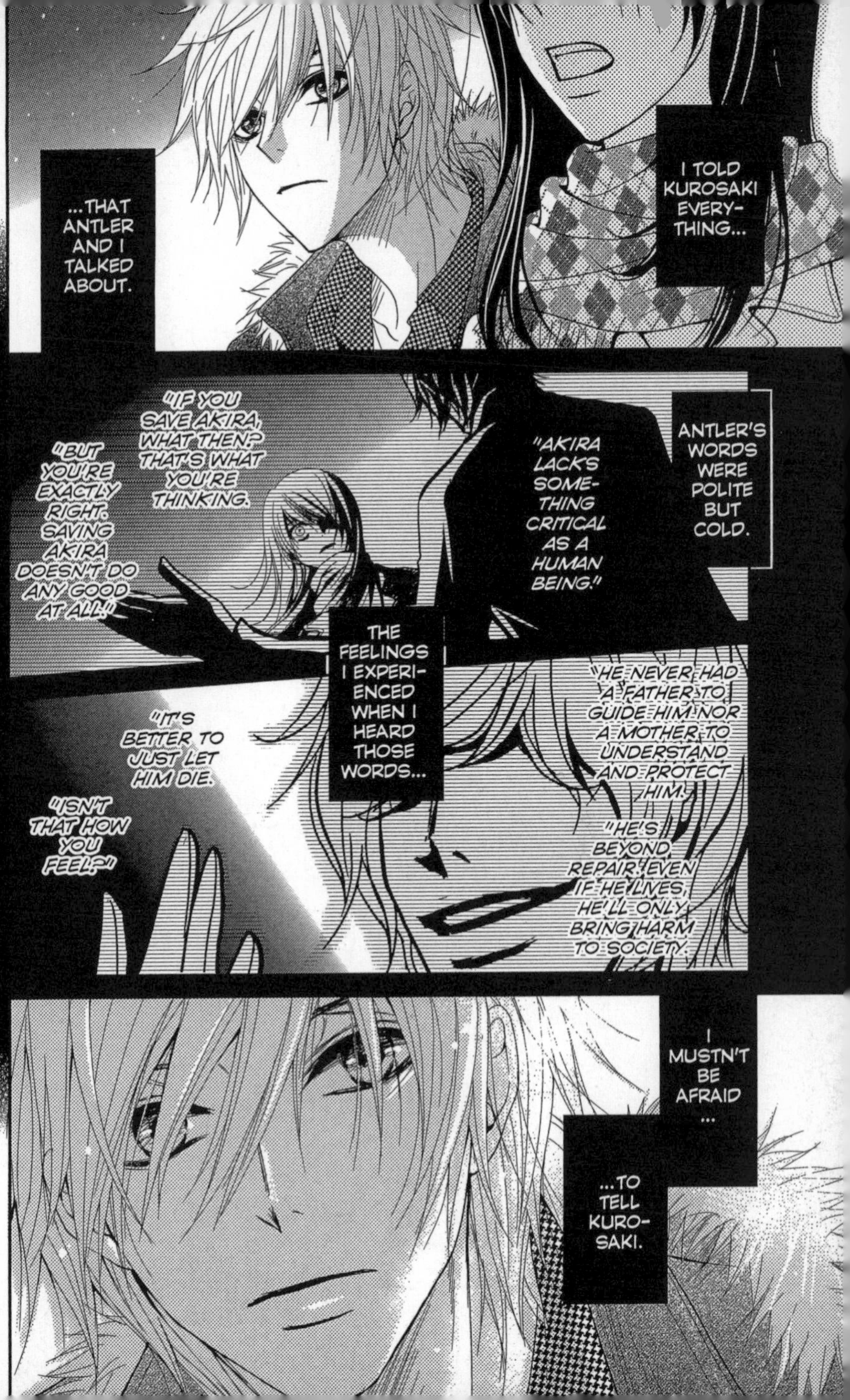
I TOLD KUROSAKI EVERYTHING...
...THAT ANTLER AND I TALKED ABOUT.
ANTLER'S WORDS WERE POLITE BUT COLD.
"AKIRA LACKS SOMETHING CRITICAL AS A HUMAN BEING."
"IF YOU SAVE AKIRA, WHAT THEN? THAT'S WHAT YOU'RE THINKING.
"BUT YOU'RE EXACTLY RIGHT. SAVING AKIRA DOESN'T DO ANY GOOD AT ALL."
"HE NEVER HAD A FATHER TO GUIDE HIM NOR A MOTHER TO UNDERSTAND AND PROTECT HIM.
"HE'S BEYOND REPAIR. EVEN IF HE LIVES, HE'LL ONLY BRING HARM TO SOCIETY.
THE FEELINGS I EXPERIENCED WHEN I HEARD THOSE WORDS...
"IT'S BETTER TO JUST LET HIM DIE.
"ISN'T THAT HOW YOU FEEL?"
I MUSTN'T BE AFRAID...
...TO TELL KUROSAKI.

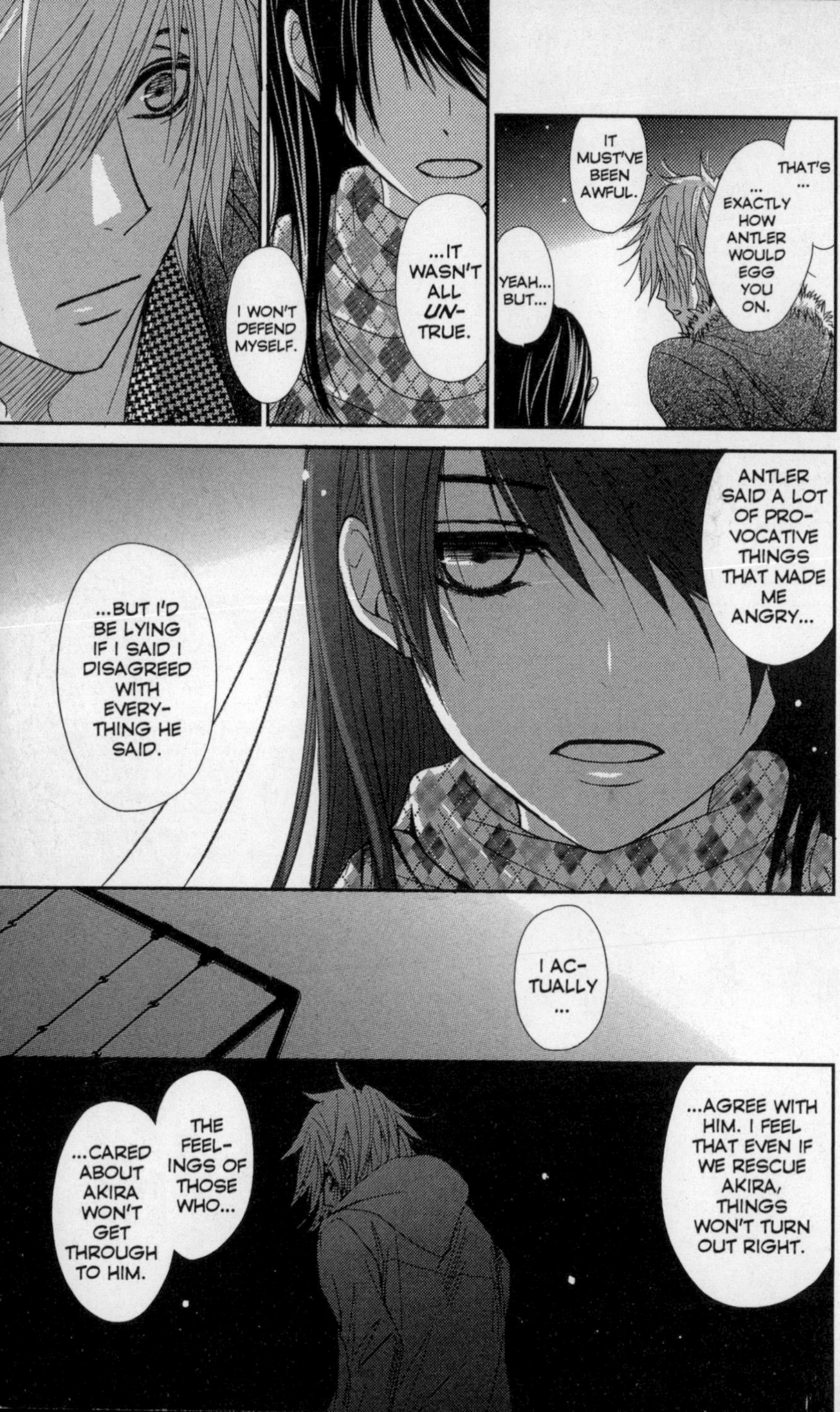
THAT'S ... ... EXACTLY HOW ANTLER WOULD EGG YOU ON.
IT MUST'VE BEEN AWFUL.
YEAH... BUT...
...IT WASN'T ALL *UN*-TRUE.
I WON'T DEFEND MYSELF.
ANTLER SAID A LOT OF PRO-VOCATIVE THINGS THAT MADE ME ANGRY...
...BUT I'D BE LYING IF I SAID I DISAGREED WITH EVERY-THING HE SAID.
I AC-TUALLY ...
...AGREE WITH HIM. I FEEL THAT EVEN IF WE RESCUE AKIRA, THINGS WON'T TURN OUT RIGHT.
THE FEEL-INGS OF THOSE WHO...
...CARED ABOUT AKIRA WON'T GET THROUGH TO HIM.

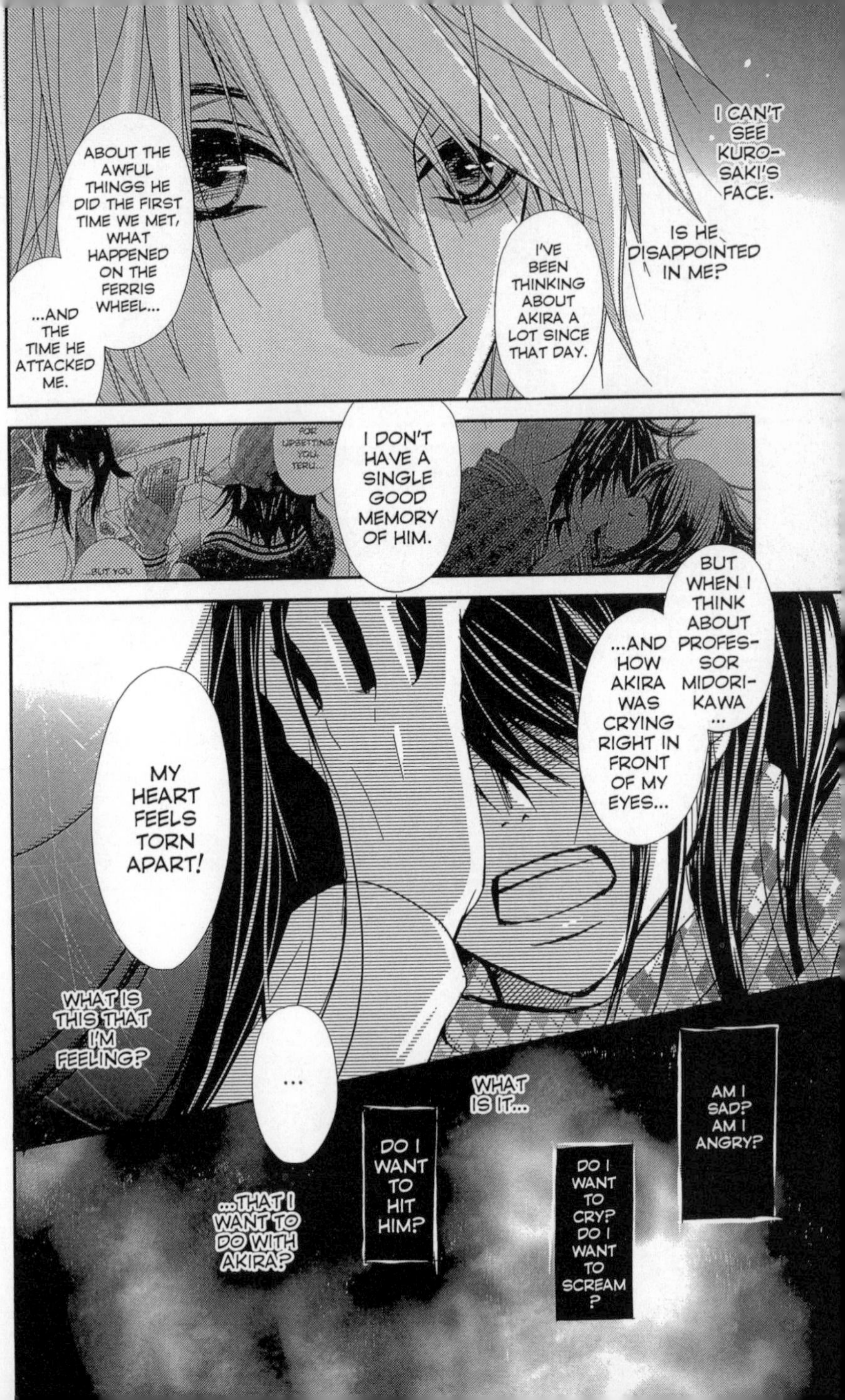

I CAN'T SEE KURO-SAKI'S FACE.
IS HE DISAPPOINTED IN ME?
I'VE BEEN THINKING ABOUT AKIRA A LOT SINCE THAT DAY.
ABOUT THE AWFUL THINGS HE DID THE FIRST TIME WE MET, WHAT HAPPENED ON THE FERRIS WHEEL...
...AND THE TIME HE ATTACKED ME.
I DON'T HAVE A SINGLE GOOD MEMORY OF HIM.
FOR UPSETTING YOU, TERU...
...BUT YOU
BUT WHEN I THINK ABOUT PROFES-SOR MIDORI-KAWA...
...AND HOW AKIRA WAS CRYING RIGHT IN FRONT OF MY EYES...
MY HEART FEELS TORN APART!
WHAT IS THIS THAT I'M FEELING?
AM I SAD? AM I ANGRY?
DO I WANT TO CRY? DO I WANT TO SCREAM?
WHAT IS IT...
DO I WANT TO HIT HIM?
...
...THAT I WANT TO DO WITH AKIRA?

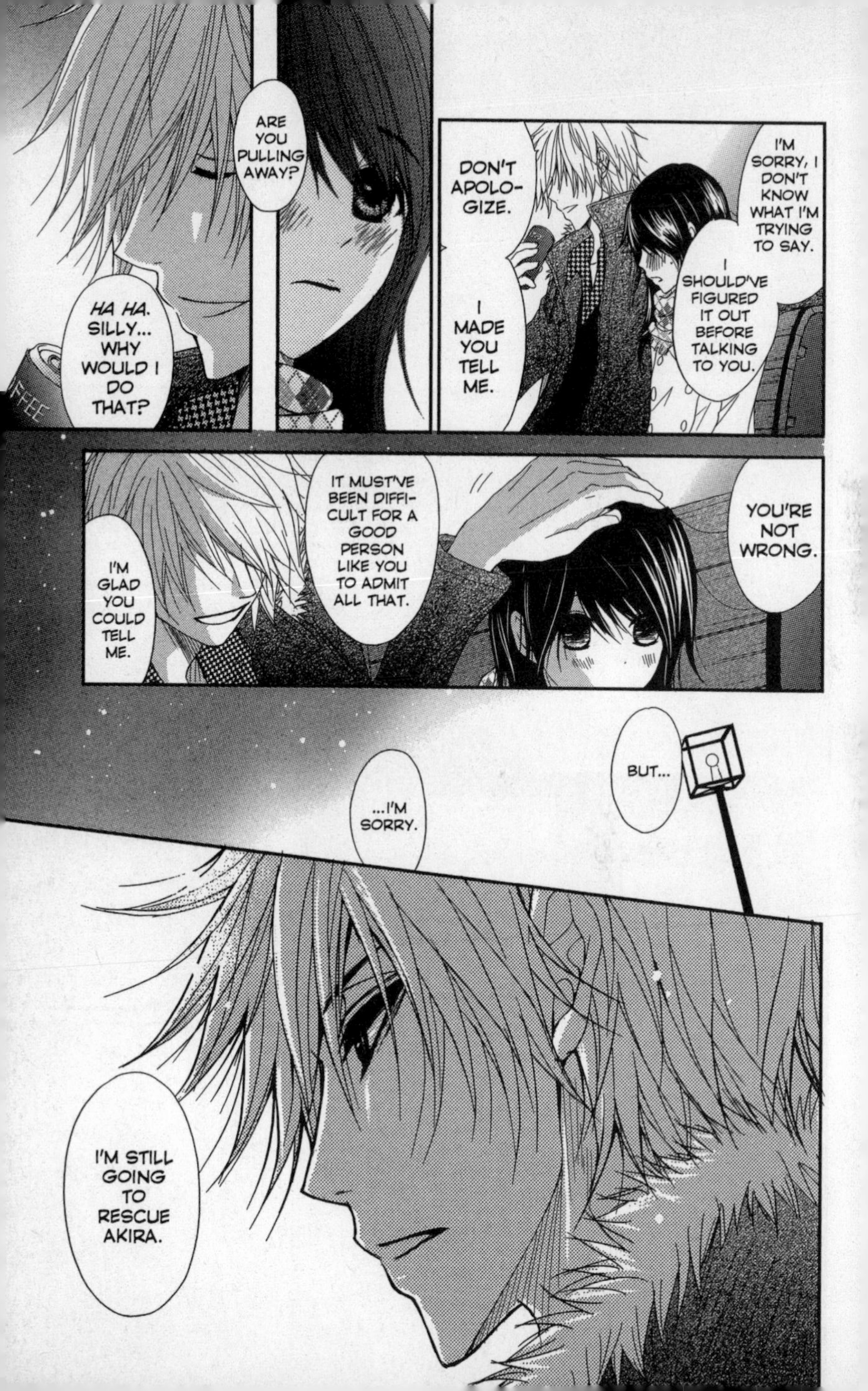
I'M SORRY, I DON'T KNOW WHAT I'M TRYING TO SAY.
I SHOULD'VE FIGURED IT OUT BEFORE TALKING TO YOU.
DON'T APOLOGIZE.
I MADE YOU TELL ME.
ARE YOU PULLING AWAY?
HA HA. SILLY... WHY WOULD I DO THAT?
YOU'RE NOT WRONG.
IT MUST'VE BEEN DIFFICULT FOR A GOOD PERSON LIKE YOU TO ADMIT ALL THAT.
I'M GLAD YOU COULD TELL ME.
BUT...
...I'M SORRY.
I'M STILL GOING TO RESCUE AKIRA.

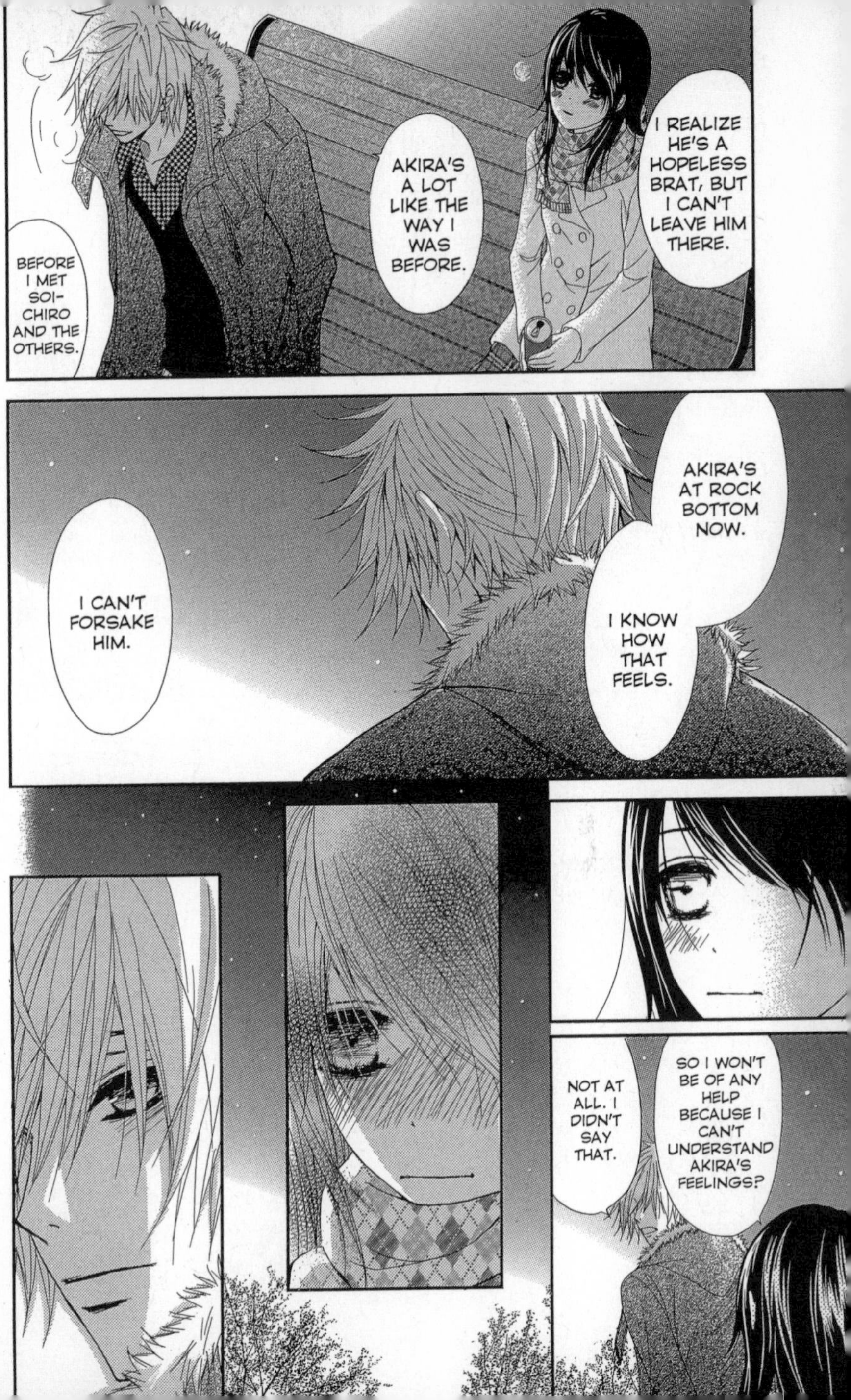
I REALIZE HE'S A HOPELESS BRAT, BUT I CAN'T LEAVE HIM THERE.
AKIRA'S A LOT LIKE THE WAY I WAS BEFORE.
BEFORE I MET SOI-CHIRO AND THE OTHERS.
AKIRA'S AT ROCK BOTTOM NOW.
I KNOW HOW THAT FEELS.
I CAN'T FORSAKE HIM.
SO I WON'T BE OF ANY HELP BECAUSE I CAN'T UNDERSTAND AKIRA'S FEELINGS?
NOT AT ALL. I DIDN'T SAY THAT.

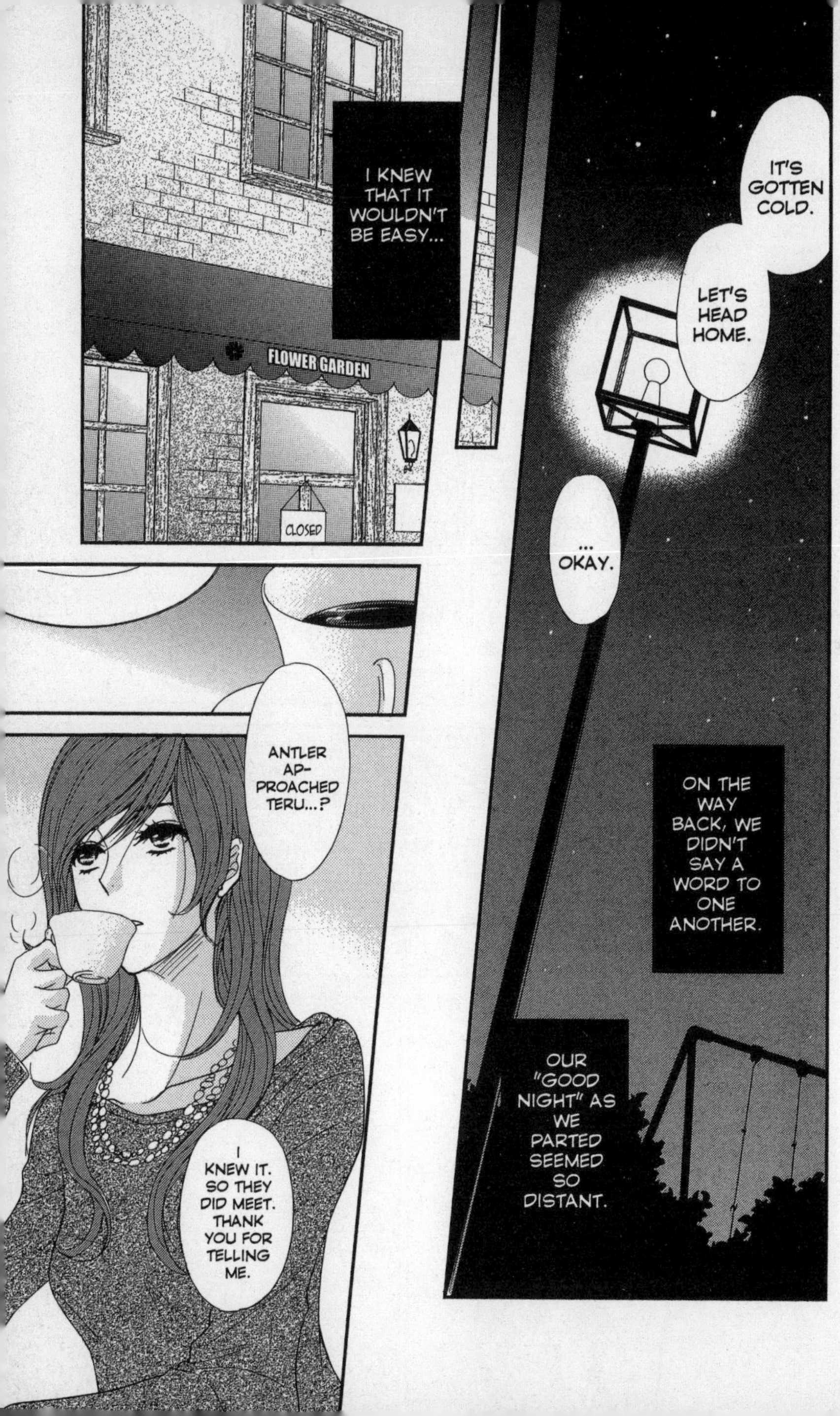
IT'S GOTTEN COLD.
LET'S HEAD HOME.
... OKAY.
ON THE WAY BACK, WE DIDN'T SAY A WORD TO ONE ANOTHER.
OUR "GOOD NIGHT" AS WE PARTED SEEMED SO DISTANT.
I KNEW THAT IT WOULDN'T BE EASY...
FLOWER GARDEN
CLOSED
ANTLER AP-PROACHED TERU...?
I KNEW IT. SO THEY DID MEET. THANK YOU FOR TELLING ME.

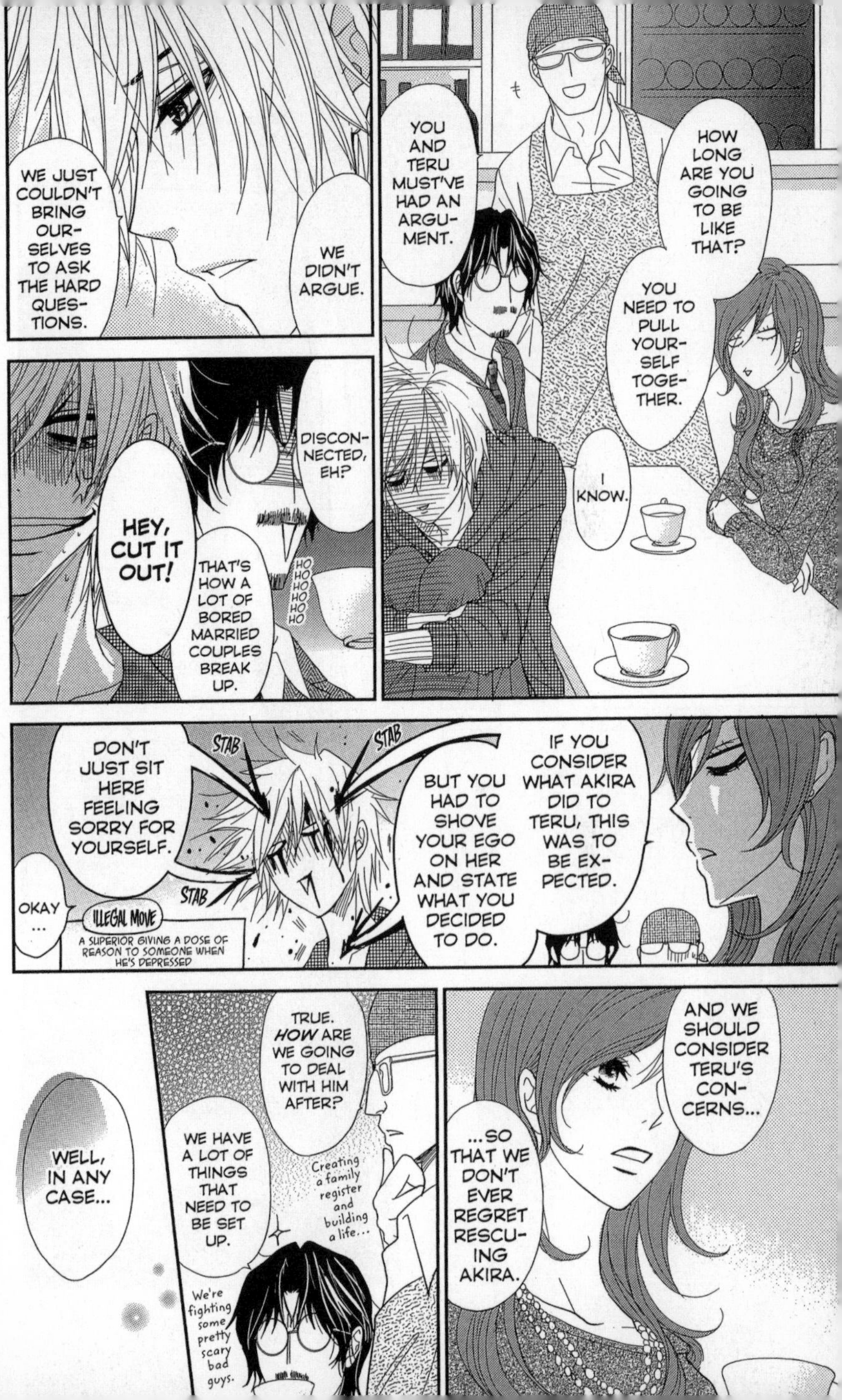
HOW LONG ARE YOU GOING TO BE LIKE THAT?
YOU AND TERU MUST'VE HAD AN ARGUMENT.
YOU NEED TO PULL YOURSELF TOGETHER.
I KNOW.
WE DIDN'T ARGUE.
WE JUST COULDN'T BRING OURSELVES TO ASK THE HARD QUESTIONS.
DISCONNECTED, EH?
THAT'S HOW A LOT OF BORED MARRIED COUPLES BREAK UP.
HO HO HO HO HO HO
HEY, CUT IT OUT!
IF YOU CONSIDER WHAT AKIRA DID TO TERU, THIS WAS TO BE EXPECTED.
BUT YOU HAD TO SHOVE YOUR EGO ON HER AND STATE WHAT YOU DECIDED TO DO.
STAB
STAB
DON'T JUST SIT HERE FEELING SORRY FOR YOURSELF.
STAB
ILLEGAL MOVE
A SUPERIOR GIVING A DOSE OF REASON TO SOMEONE WHEN HE'S DEPRESSED
OKAY...
AND WE SHOULD CONSIDER TERU'S CONCERNS...
...SO THAT WE DON'T EVER REGRET RESCUING AKIRA.
TRUE. *HOW* ARE WE GOING TO DEAL WITH HIM AFTER?
Creating a family register and building a life...
WE HAVE A LOT OF THINGS THAT NEED TO BE SET UP.
WELL, IN ANY CASE...
We're fighting some pretty scary bad guys.

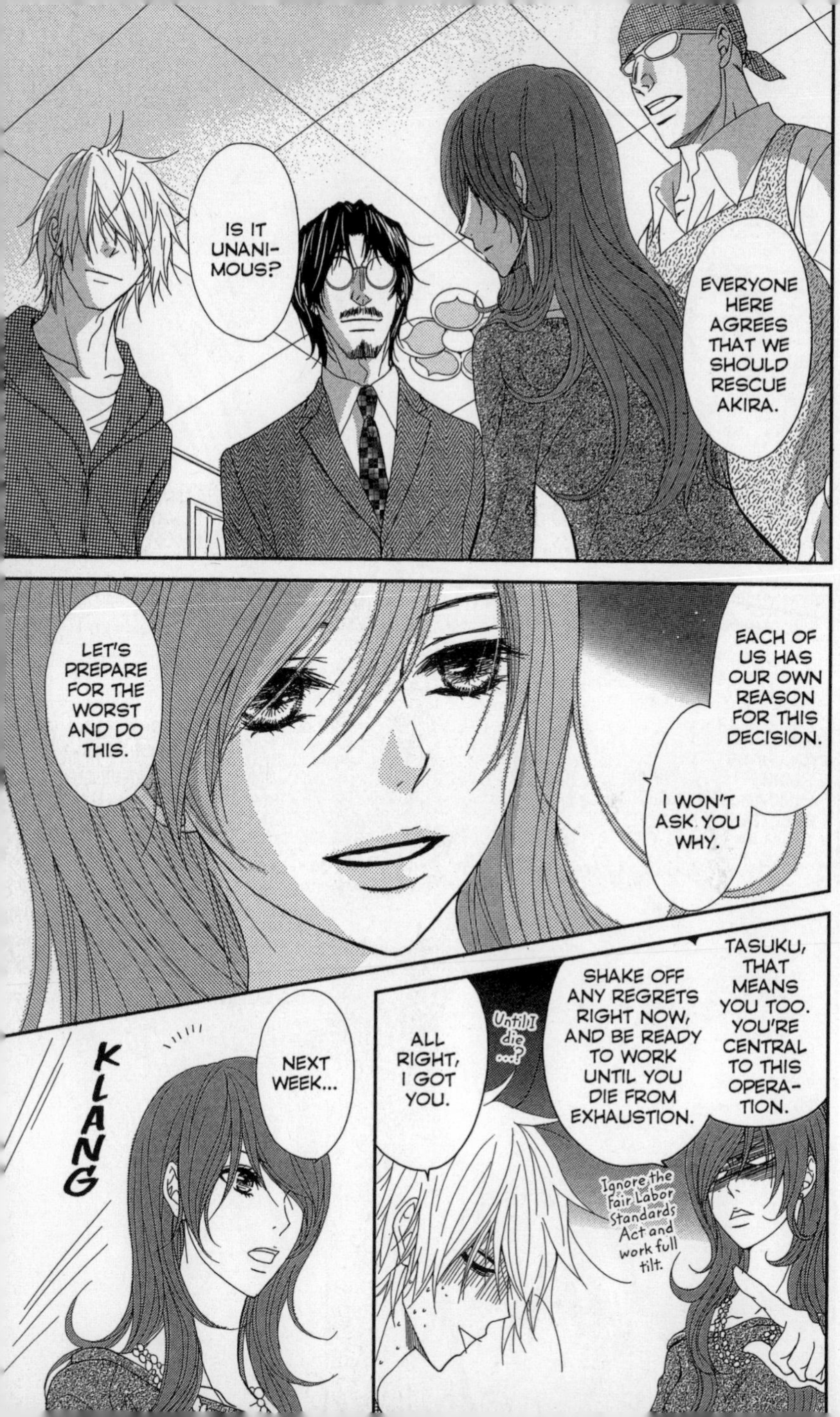
EVERYONE HERE AGREES THAT WE SHOULD RESCUE AKIRA.
IS IT UNANIMOUS?
EACH OF US HAS OUR OWN REASON FOR THIS DECISION.
I WON'T ASK YOU WHY.
LET'S PREPARE FOR THE WORST AND DO THIS.
TASUKU, THAT MEANS YOU TOO. YOU'RE CENTRAL TO THIS OPERATION.
SHAKE OFF ANY REGRETS RIGHT NOW, AND BE READY TO WORK UNTIL YOU DIE FROM EXHAUSTION.
Ignore the Fair Labor Standards Act and work full tilt.
Until I die...?
ALL RIGHT, I GOT YOU.
NEXT WEEK...
KLANG

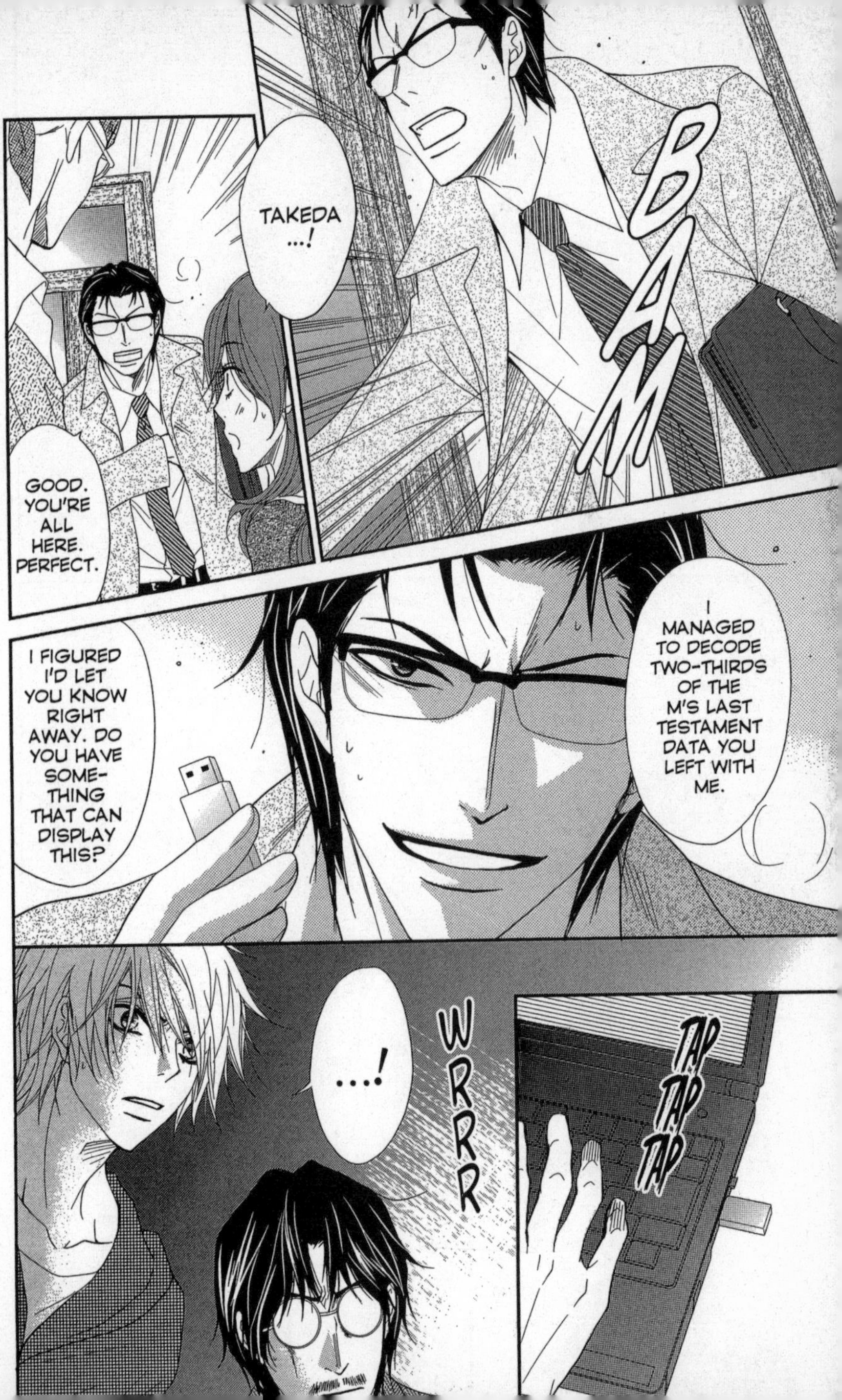
BAM
TAKEDA ...!
GOOD. YOU'RE ALL HERE. PERFECT.
I MANAGED TO DECODE TWO-THIRDS OF THE M'S LAST TESTAMENT DATA YOU LEFT WITH ME.
I FIGURED I'D LET YOU KNOW RIGHT AWAY. DO YOU HAVE SOME-THING THAT CAN DISPLAY THIS?
TAP TAP TAP
WRRR
...!

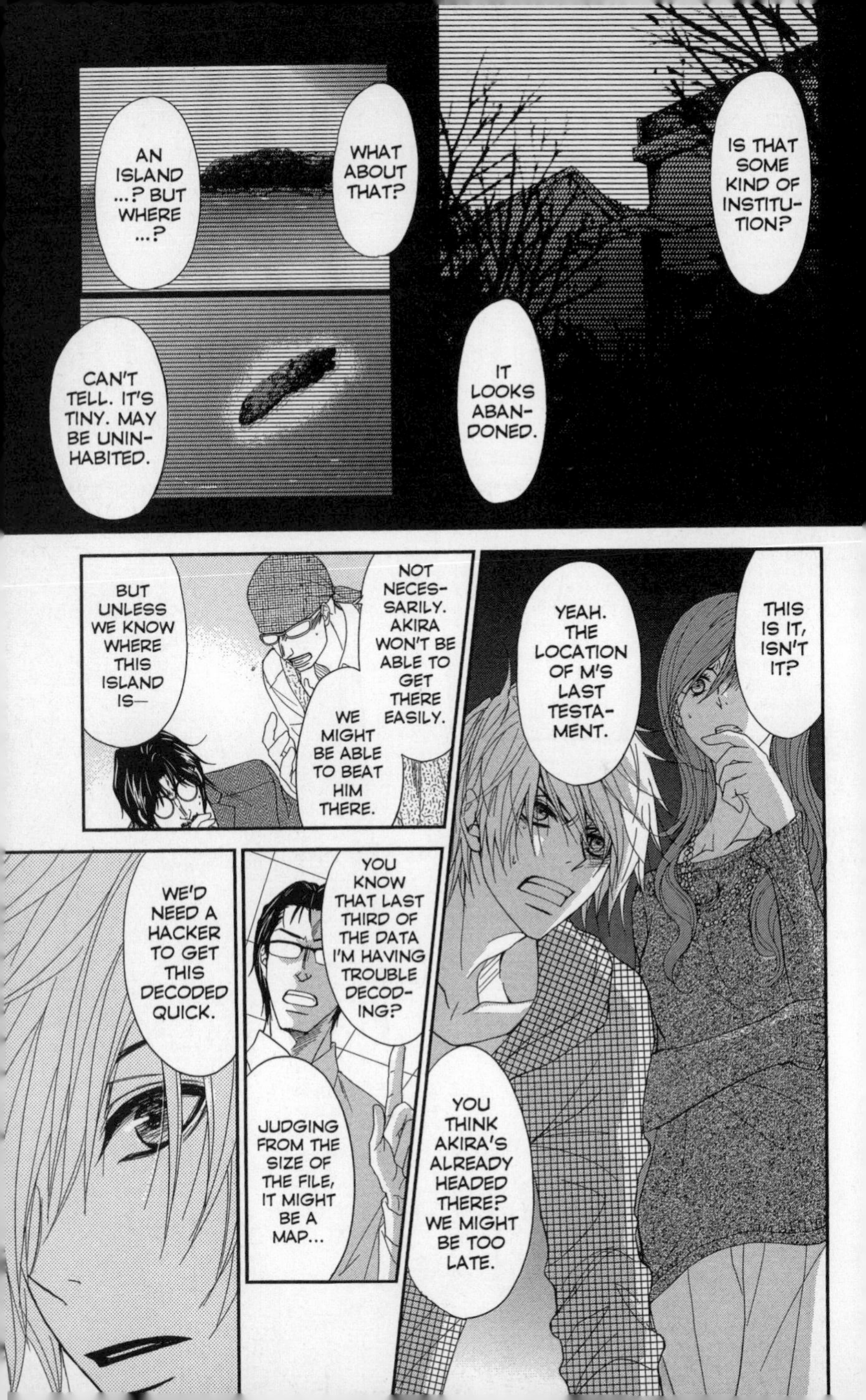
IS THAT SOME KIND OF INSTITUTION?
IT LOOKS ABANDONED.
WHAT ABOUT THAT?
AN ISLAND ...? BUT WHERE ...?
CAN'T TELL. IT'S TINY. MAY BE UNINHABITED.
THIS IS IT, ISN'T IT?
YEAH. THE LOCATION OF M'S LAST TESTAMENT.
YOU THINK AKIRA'S ALREADY HEADED THERE? WE MIGHT BE TOO LATE.
NOT NECESSARILY. AKIRA WON'T BE ABLE TO GET THERE EASILY.
WE MIGHT BE ABLE TO BEAT HIM THERE.
BUT UNLESS WE KNOW WHERE THIS ISLAND IS—
YOU KNOW THAT LAST THIRD OF THE DATA I'M HAVING TROUBLE DECODING?
JUDGING FROM THE SIZE OF THE FILE, IT MIGHT BE A MAP...
WE'D NEED A HACKER TO GET THIS DECODED QUICK.

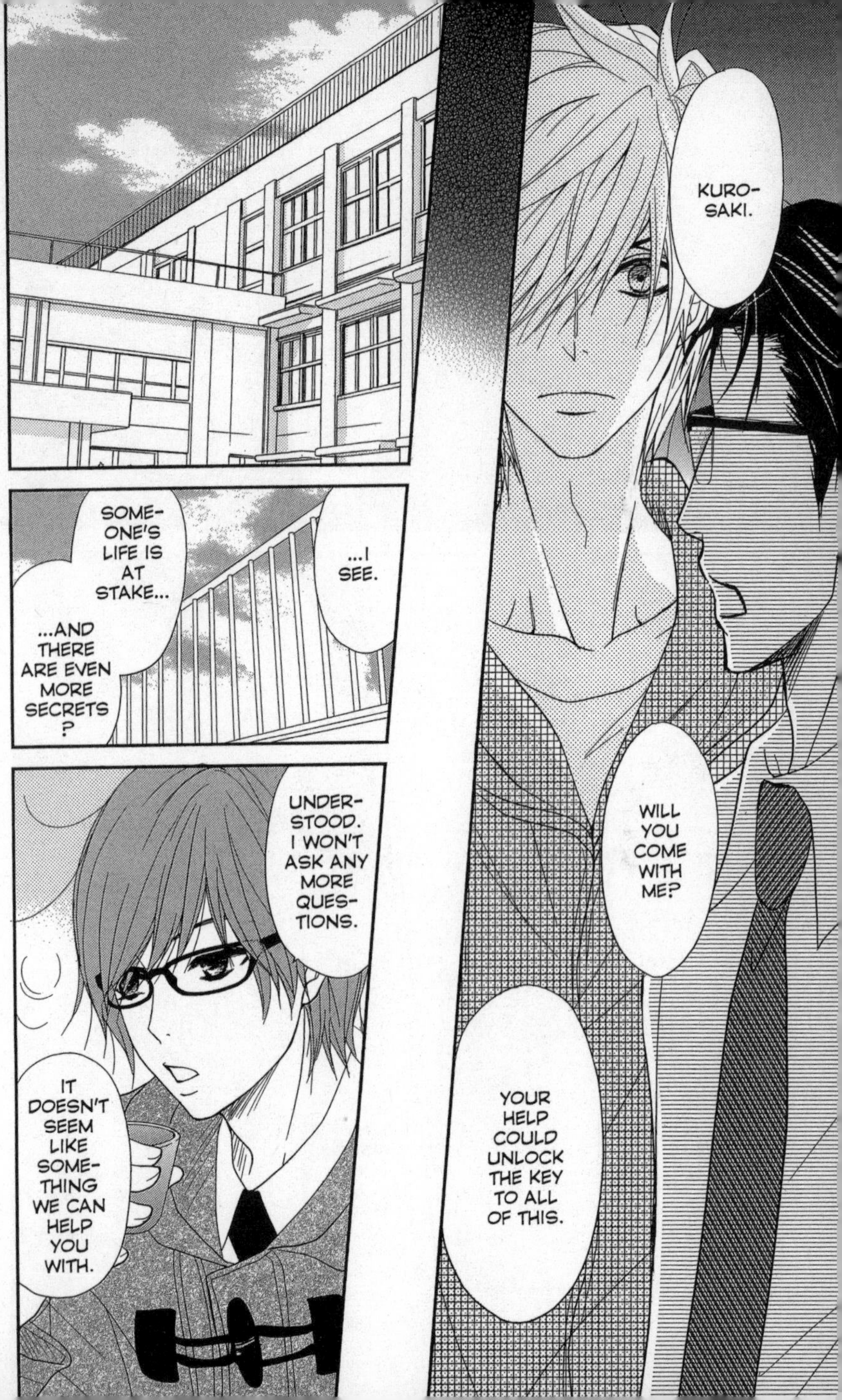
KURO-SAKI.
WILL YOU COME WITH ME?
YOUR HELP COULD UNLOCK THE KEY TO ALL OF THIS.
...I SEE.
SOME-ONE'S LIFE IS AT STAKE...
...AND THERE ARE EVEN MORE SECRETS?
UNDER-STOOD. I WON'T ASK ANY MORE QUES-TIONS.
IT DOESN'T SEEM LIKE SOME-THING WE CAN HELP YOU WITH.

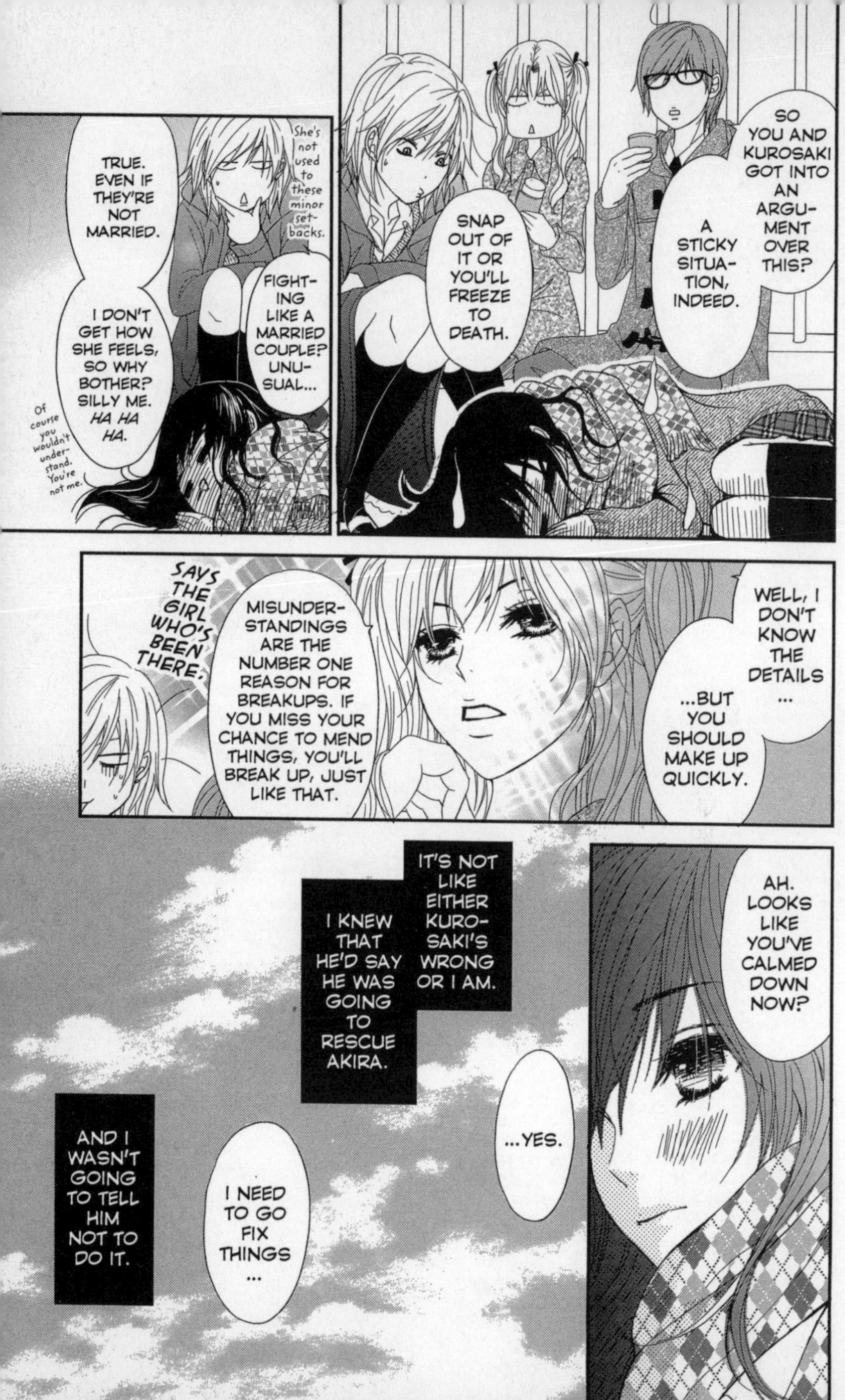
SO YOU AND KUROSAKI GOT INTO AN ARGUMENT OVER THIS?
A STICKY SITUATION, INDEED.
SNAP OUT OF IT OR YOU'LL FREEZE TO DEATH.
She's not used to these minor setbacks.
TRUE. EVEN IF THEY'RE NOT MARRIED.
FIGHTING LIKE A MARRIED COUPLE? UNUSUAL...
I DON'T GET HOW SHE FEELS, SO WHY BOTHER? SILLY ME. *HA HA HA.*
Of course you wouldn't understand. You're not me.
WELL, I DON'T KNOW THE DETAILS...
...BUT YOU SHOULD MAKE UP QUICKLY.
MISUNDERSTANDINGS ARE THE NUMBER ONE REASON FOR BREAKUPS. IF YOU MISS YOUR CHANCE TO MEND THINGS, YOU'LL BREAK UP, JUST LIKE THAT.
SAYS THE GIRL WHO'S BEEN THERE.
AH. LOOKS LIKE YOU'VE CALMED DOWN NOW?
...YES.
IT'S NOT LIKE EITHER KUROSAKI'S WRONG OR I AM.
I KNEW THAT HE'D SAY HE WAS GOING TO RESCUE AKIRA.
I NEED TO GO FIX THINGS...
AND I WASN'T GOING TO TELL HIM NOT TO DO IT.

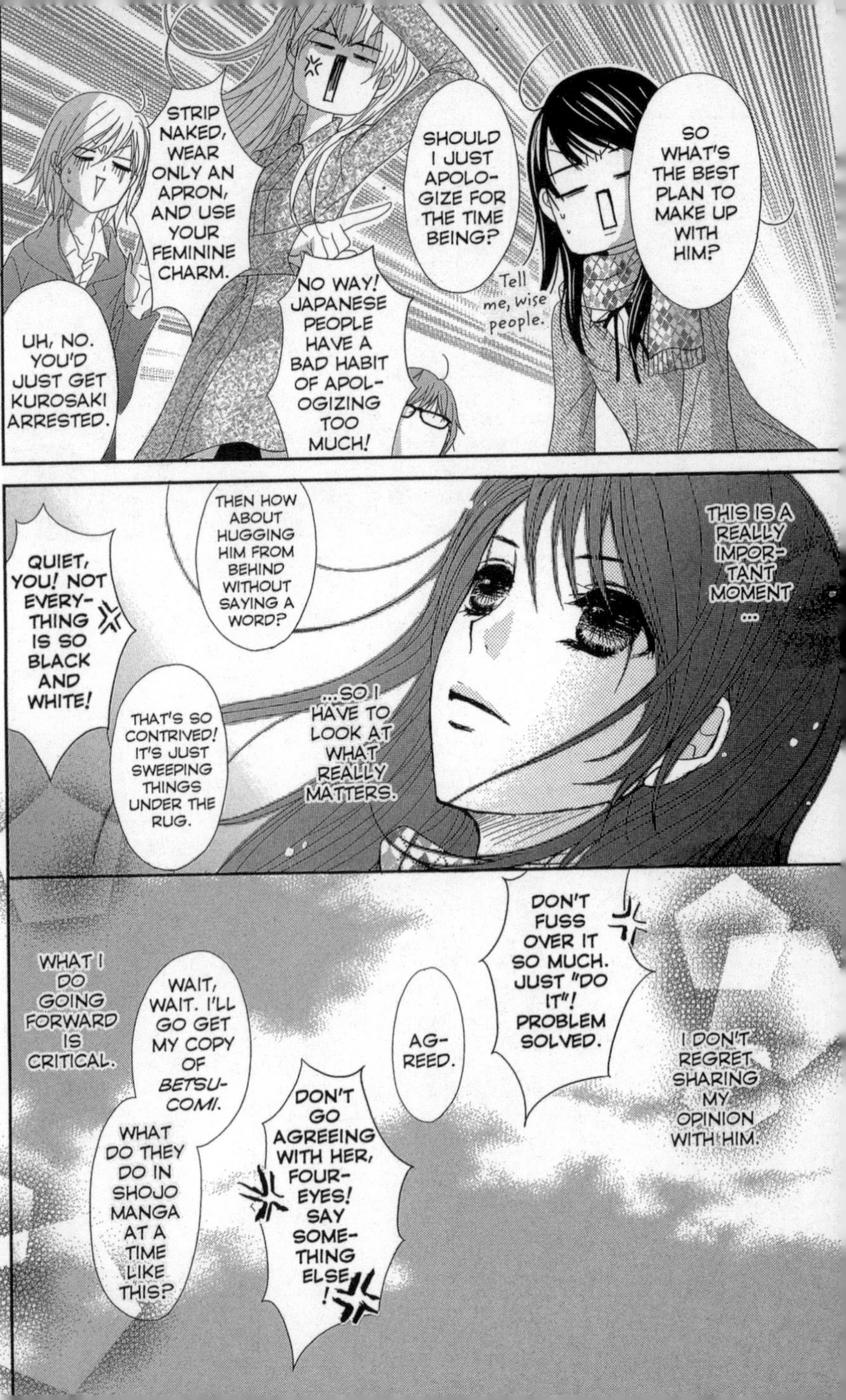
SO WHAT'S THE BEST PLAN TO MAKE UP WITH HIM?
Tell me, wise people.
SHOULD I JUST APOLOGIZE FOR THE TIME BEING?
NO WAY! JAPANESE PEOPLE HAVE A BAD HABIT OF APOLOGIZING TOO MUCH!
STRIP NAKED, WEAR ONLY AN APRON, AND USE YOUR FEMININE CHARM.
UH, NO. YOU'D JUST GET KUROSAKI ARRESTED.
THIS IS A REALLY IMPORTANT MOMENT...
THEN HOW ABOUT HUGGING HIM FROM BEHIND WITHOUT SAYING A WORD?
QUIET, YOU! NOT EVERYTHING IS SO BLACK AND WHITE!
...SO I HAVE TO LOOK AT WHAT REALLY MATTERS.
THAT'S SO CONTRIVED! IT'S JUST SWEEPING THINGS UNDER THE RUG.
I DON'T REGRET SHARING MY OPINION WITH HIM.
DON'T FUSS OVER IT SO MUCH. JUST "DO IT"! PROBLEM SOLVED.
AGREED.
DON'T GO AGREEING WITH HER, FOUR-EYES! SAY SOMETHING ELSE!
WAIT, WAIT. I'LL GO GET MY COPY OF *BETSUCOMI*.
WHAT I DO GOING FORWARD IS CRITICAL.
WHAT DO THEY DO IN SHOJO MANGA AT A TIME LIKE THIS?

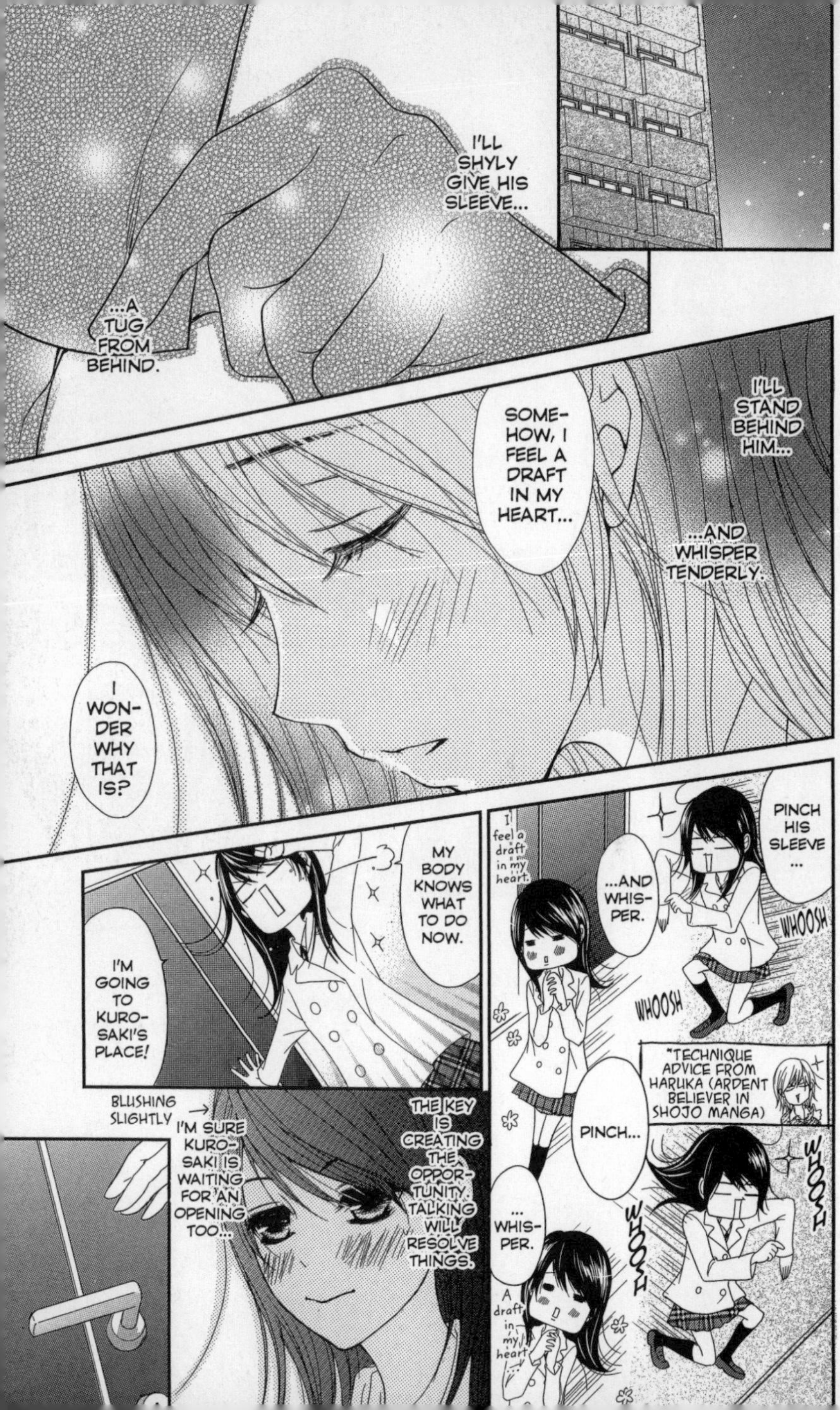
I'LL SHYLY GIVE HIS SLEEVE...
...A TUG FROM BEHIND.
I'LL STAND BEHIND HIM...
...AND WHISPER TENDERLY.
SOMEHOW, I FEEL A DRAFT IN MY HEART...
I WONDER WHY THAT IS?
PINCH HIS SLEEVE...
...AND WHISPER.
I feel a draft in my heart.
WHOOSH
WHOOSH
*TECHNIQUE ADVICE FROM HARUKA (ARDENT BELIEVER IN SHOJO MANGA)
PINCH...
WHOOSH
WHOOSH
...WHISPER.
A draft in my heart...
MY BODY KNOWS WHAT TO DO NOW.
I'M GOING TO KUROSAKI'S PLACE!
BLUSHING SLIGHTLY
THE KEY IS CREATING THE OPPORTUNITY. TALKING WILL RESOLVE THINGS.
I'M SURE KUROSAKI IS WAITING FOR AN OPENING TOO...

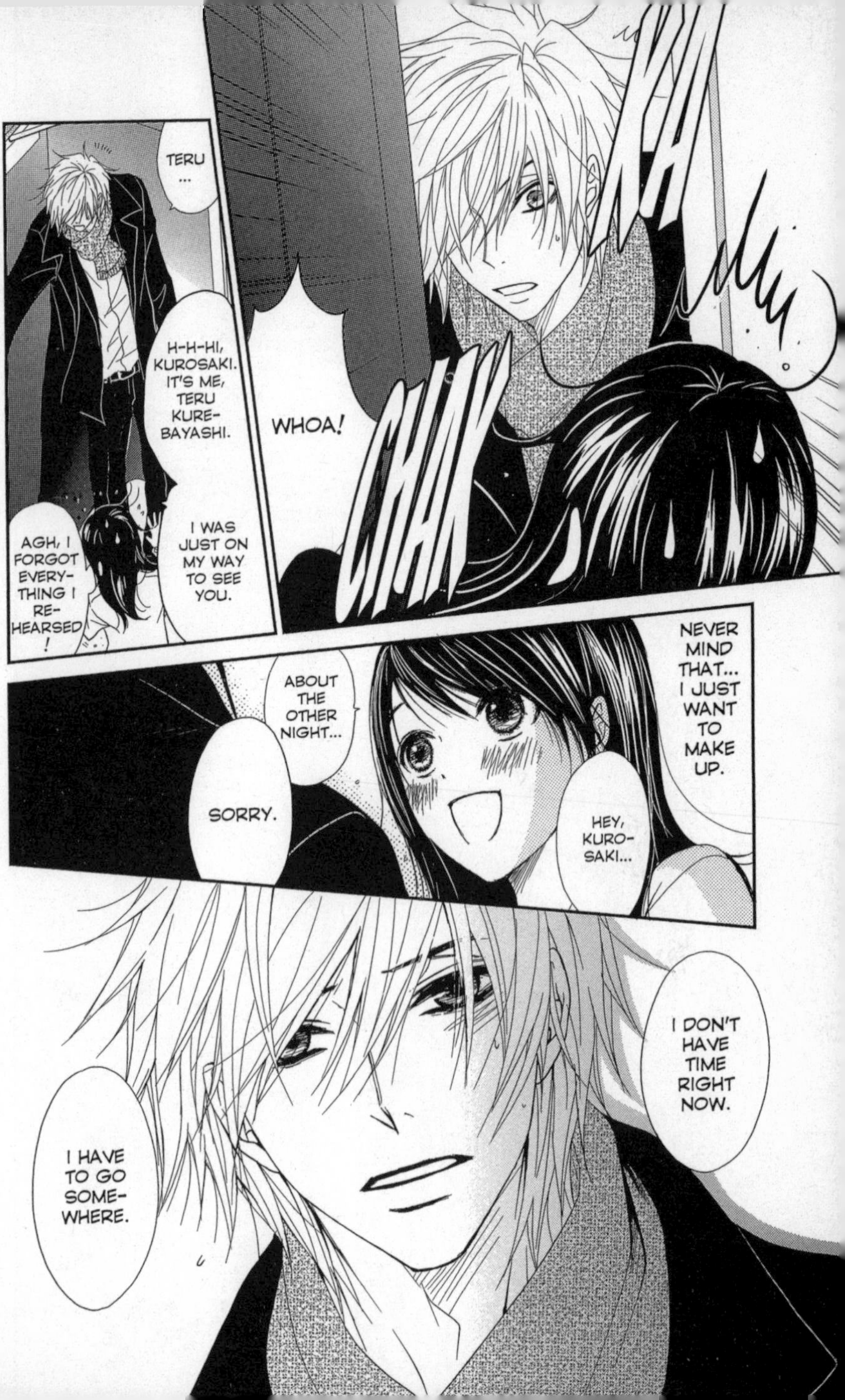
WHOA!
TERU ...
H-H-HI, KUROSAKI. IT'S ME, TERU KURE-BAYASHI.
I WAS JUST ON MY WAY TO SEE YOU.
AGH, I FORGOT EVERY-THING I RE-HEARSED!
NEVER MIND THAT... I JUST WANT TO MAKE UP.
HEY, KURO-SAKI...
ABOUT THE OTHER NIGHT...
SORRY.
I DON'T HAVE TIME RIGHT NOW.
I HAVE TO GO SOME-WHERE.

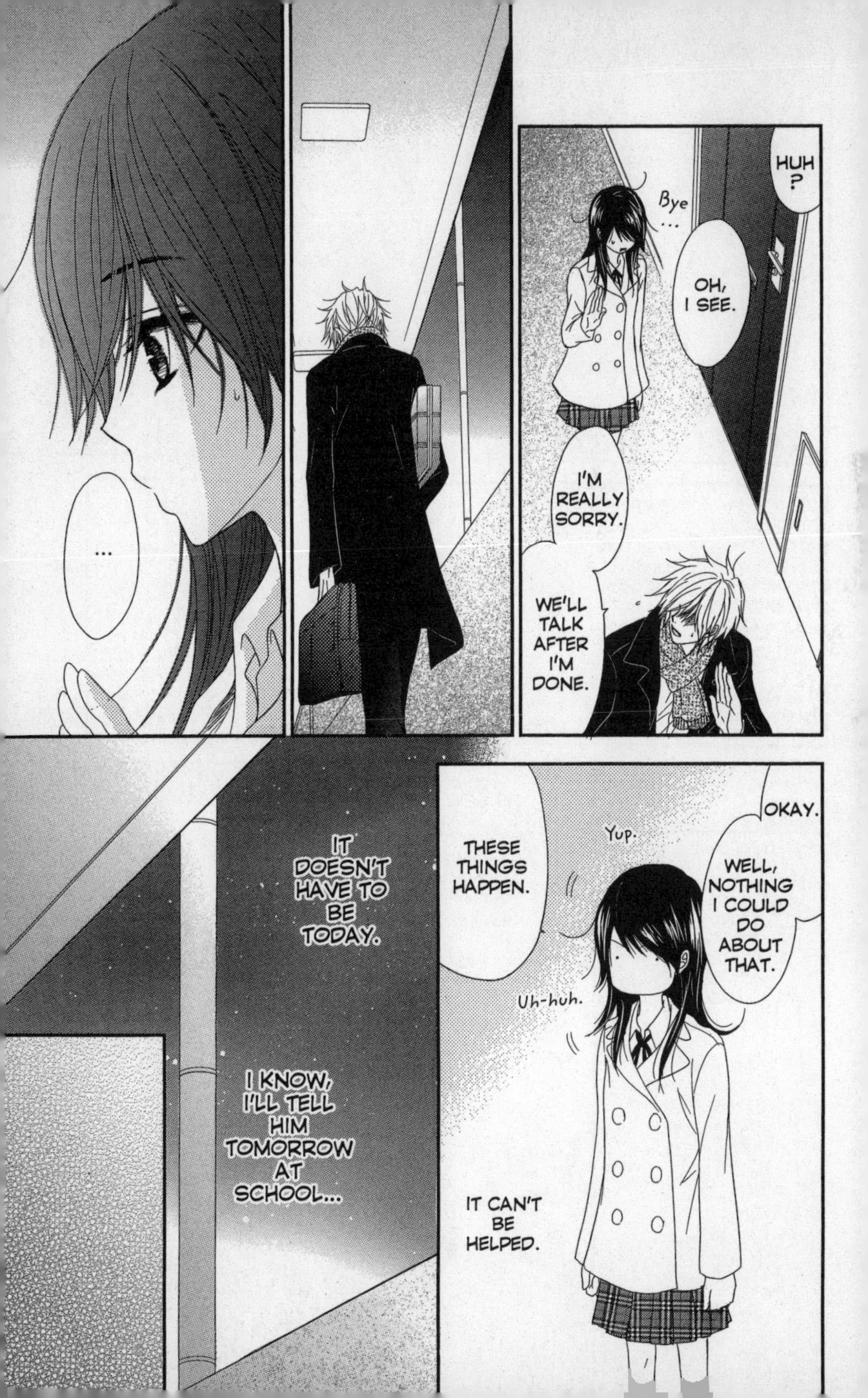
HUH?
Bye...
OH, I SEE.
I'M REALLY SORRY.
WE'LL TALK AFTER I'M DONE.
...
OKAY.
WELL, NOTHING I COULD DO ABOUT THAT.
Yup.
THESE THINGS HAPPEN.
Uh-huh.
IT CAN'T BE HELPED.
IT DOESN'T HAVE TO BE TODAY.
I KNOW, I'LL TELL HIM TOMORROW AT SCHOOL...

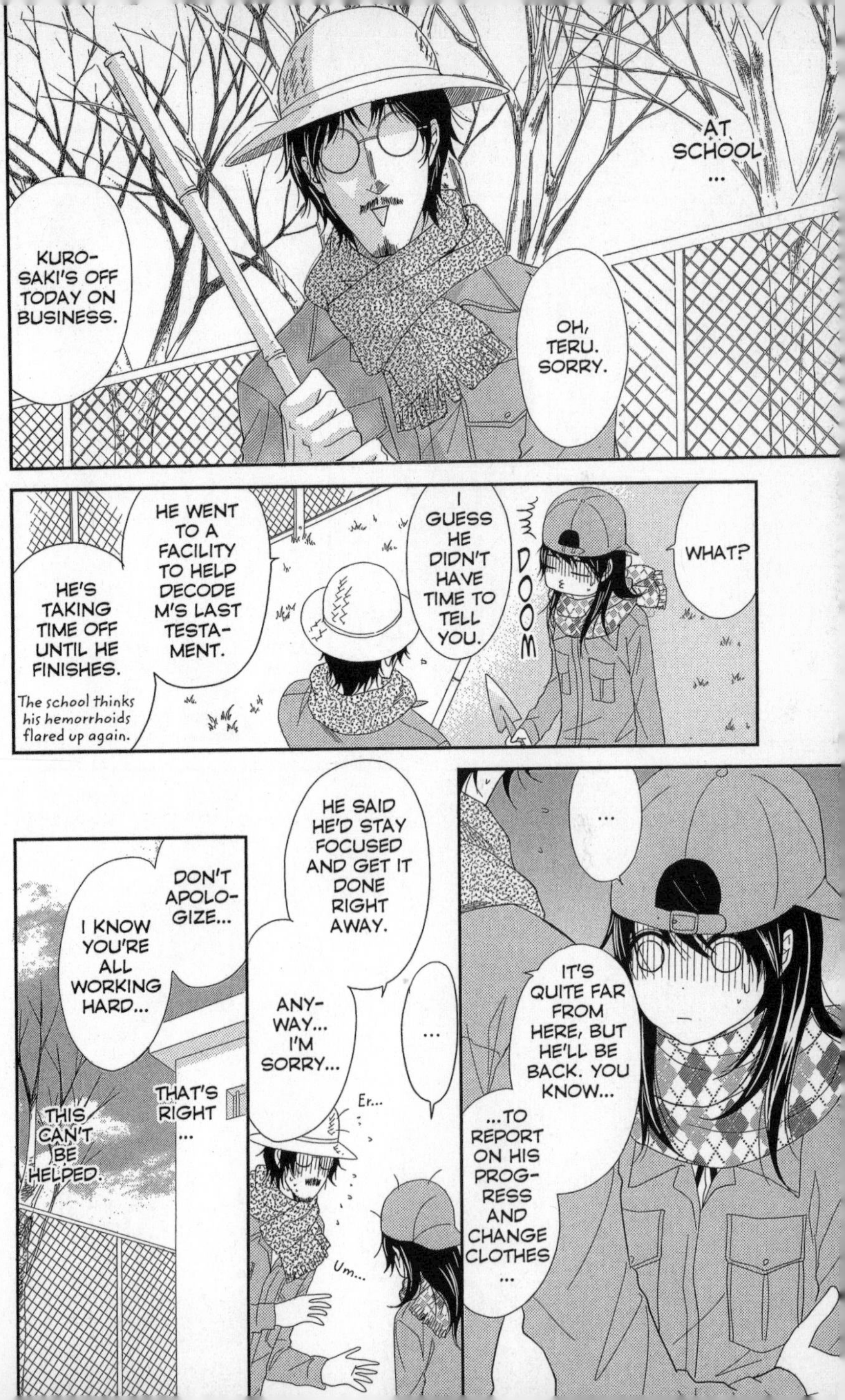
AT SCHOOL ...
OH, TERU. SORRY.
KURO-SAKI'S OFF TODAY ON BUSINESS.
WHAT?
DOOM
I GUESS HE DIDN'T HAVE TIME TO TELL YOU.
HE WENT TO A FACILITY TO HELP DECODE M'S LAST TESTA-MENT.
HE'S TAKING TIME OFF UNTIL HE FINISHES.
The school thinks his hemorrhoids flared up again.
...
IT'S QUITE FAR FROM HERE, BUT HE'LL BE BACK. YOU KNOW...
...TO REPORT ON HIS PROG-RESS AND CHANGE CLOTHES ...
HE SAID HE'D STAY FOCUSED AND GET IT DONE RIGHT AWAY.
...
ANY-WAY... I'M SORRY...
Er...
Um...
DON'T APOLO-GIZE...
I KNOW YOU'RE ALL WORKING HARD...
THAT'S RIGHT ...
THIS CAN'T BE HELPED.

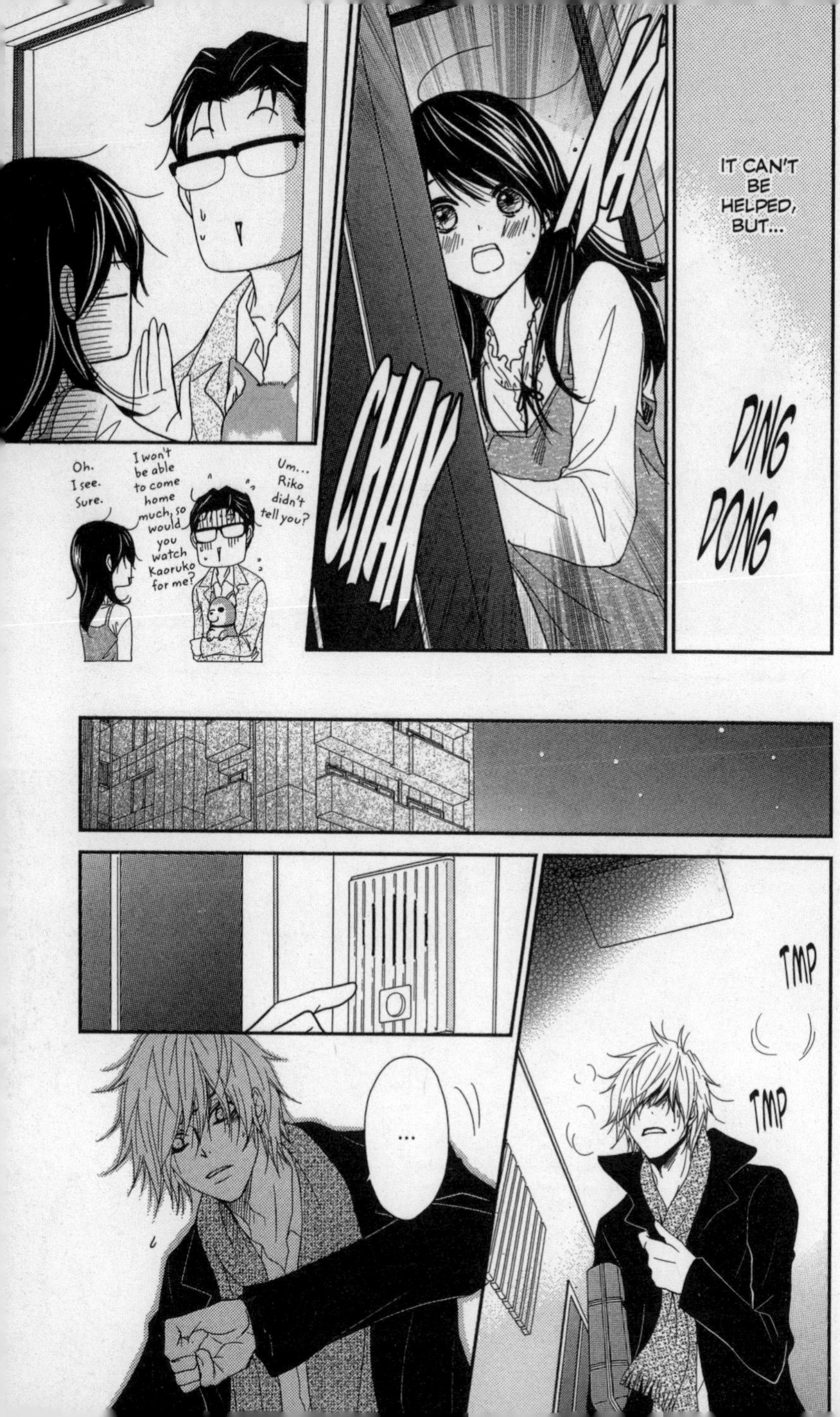
IT CAN'T BE HELPED, BUT...
DING DONG
CHAK
Um... Riko didn't tell you?
I won't be able to come home much, so would you watch Kaoruko for me?
Oh. I see. Sure.
TMP
TMP
...

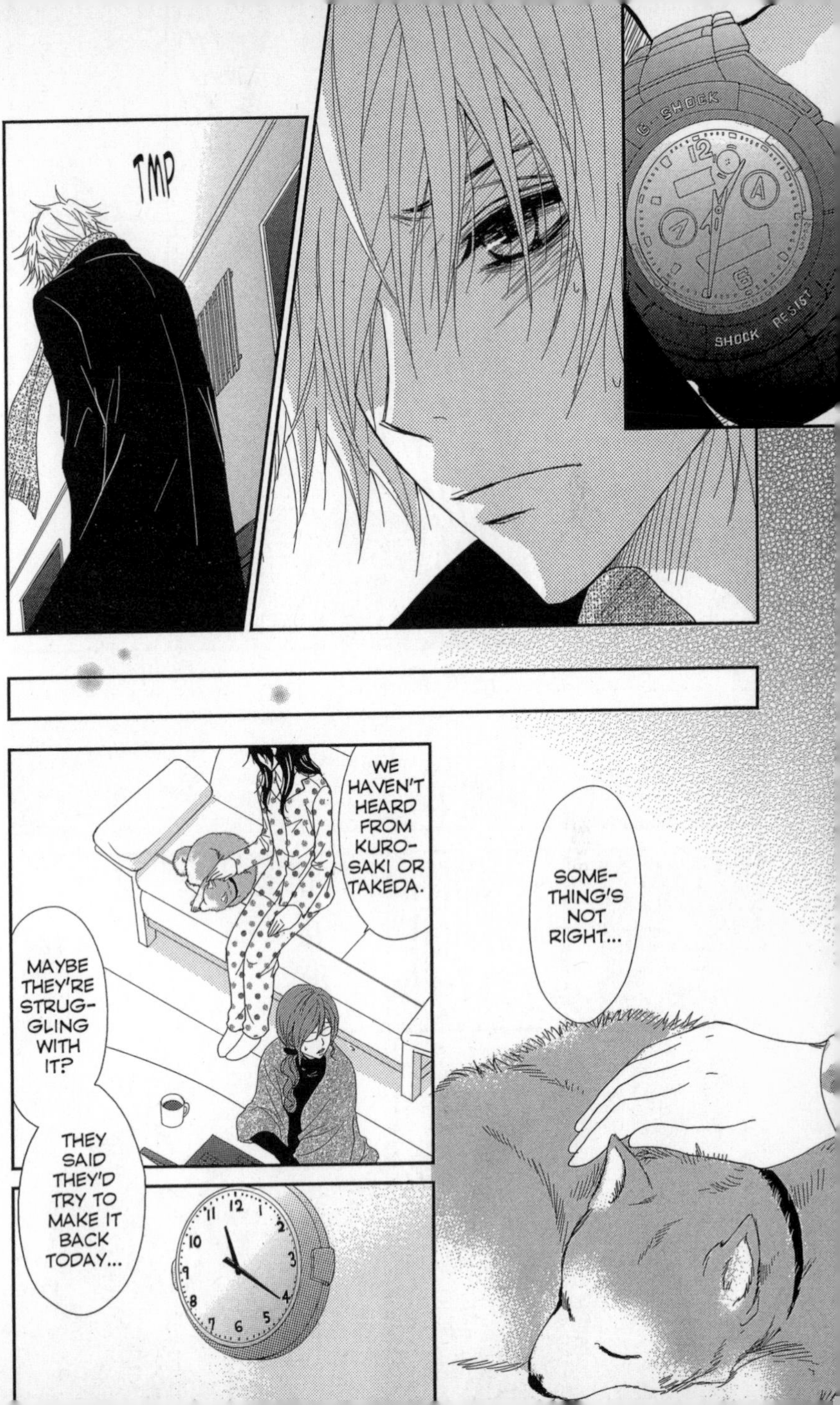
G-SHOCK
SHOCK RESIST
TMP
SOMETHING'S NOT RIGHT...
WE HAVEN'T HEARD FROM KUROSAKI OR TAKEDA.
MAYBE THEY'RE STRUGGLING WITH IT?
THEY SAID THEY'D TRY TO MAKE IT BACK TODAY...

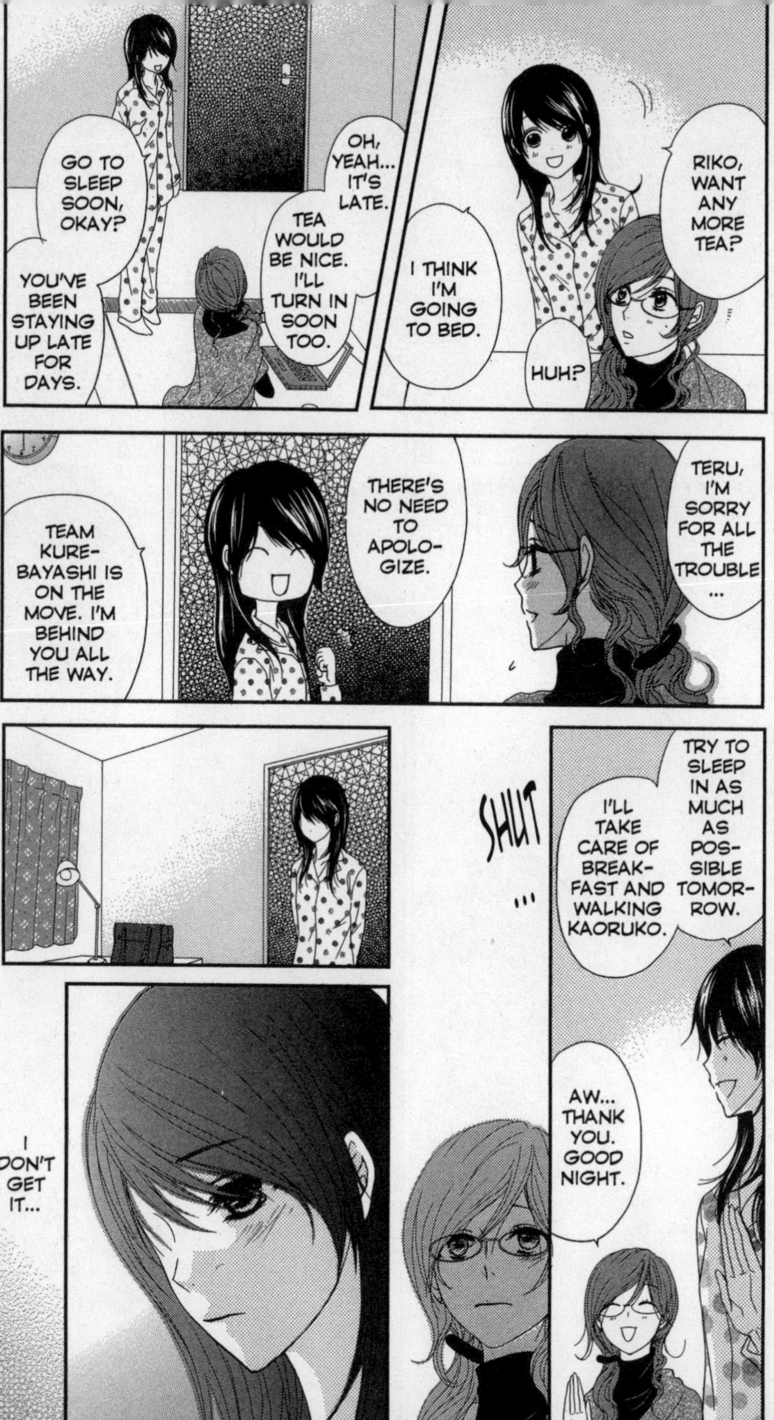
RIKO, WANT ANY MORE TEA?
HUH?
I THINK I'M GOING TO BED.
OH, YEAH... IT'S LATE.
TEA WOULD BE NICE. I'LL TURN IN SOON TOO.
GO TO SLEEP SOON, OKAY?
YOU'VE BEEN STAYING UP LATE FOR DAYS.
TERU, I'M SORRY FOR ALL THE TROUBLE...
THERE'S NO NEED TO APOLO-GIZE.
TEAM KURE-BAYASHI IS ON THE MOVE. I'M BEHIND YOU ALL THE WAY.
TRY TO SLEEP IN AS MUCH AS POS-SIBLE TOMOR-ROW.
I'LL TAKE CARE OF BREAK-FAST AND WALKING KAORUKO.
AW... THANK YOU. GOOD NIGHT.
SHUT
...
I DON'T GET IT...

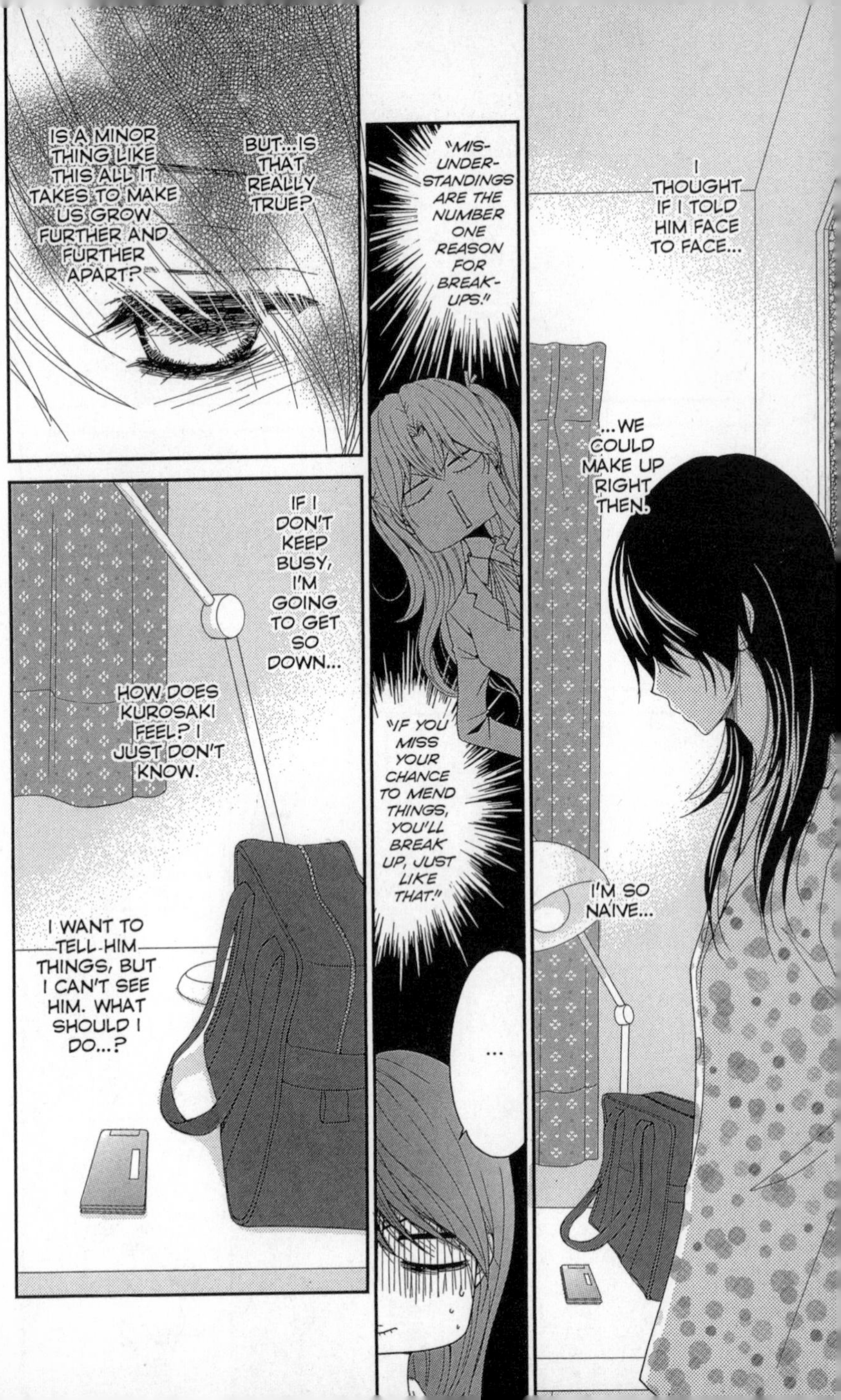
I THOUGHT IF I TOLD HIM FACE TO FACE...
...WE COULD MAKE UP RIGHT THEN.
I'M SO NAÏVE...
"MIS-UNDERSTANDINGS ARE THE NUMBER ONE REASON FOR BREAK-UPS."
"IF YOU MISS YOUR CHANCE TO MEND THINGS, YOU'LL BREAK UP, JUST LIKE THAT."
...
BUT...IS THAT REALLY TRUE?
IS A MINOR THING LIKE THIS ALL IT TAKES TO MAKE US GROW FURTHER AND FURTHER APART?
IF I DON'T KEEP BUSY, I'M GOING TO GET SO DOWN...
HOW DOES KUROSAKI FEEL? I JUST DON'T KNOW.
I WANT TO TELL HIM THINGS, BUT I CAN'T SEE HIM. WHAT SHOULD I DO...?

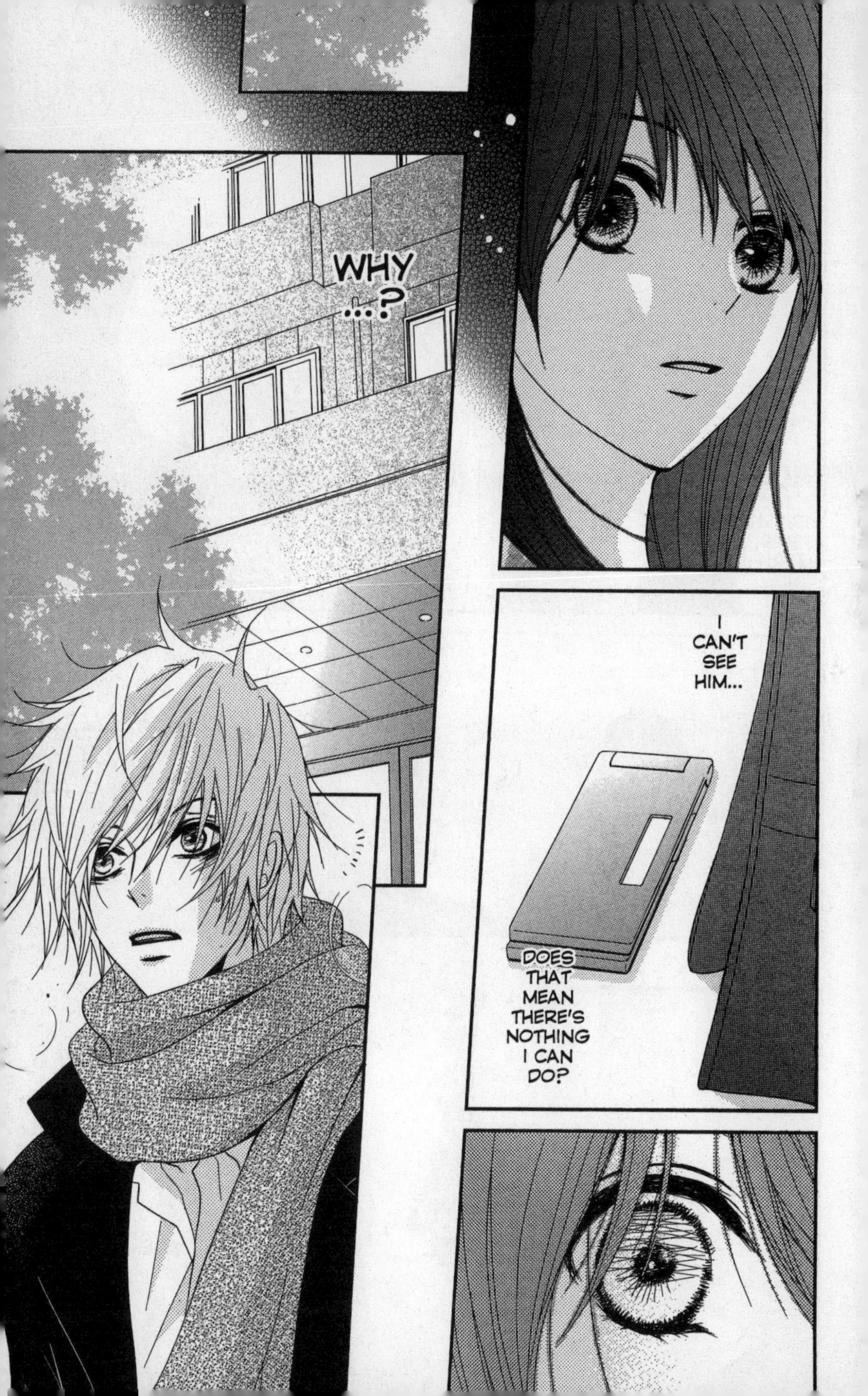
I CAN'T SEE HIM...
DOES THAT MEAN THERE'S NOTHING I CAN DO?
WHY ...?

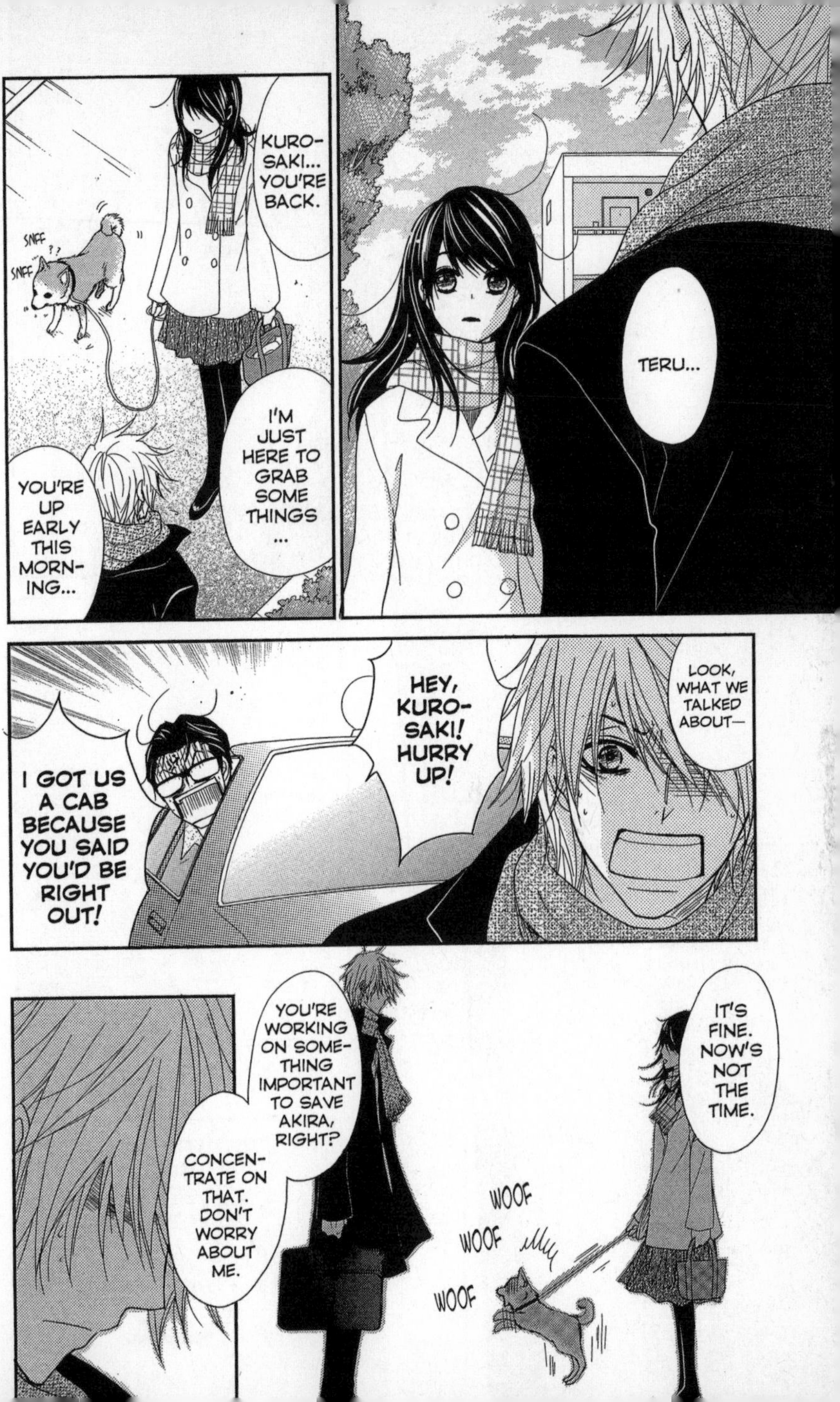
TERU...
KURO-SAKI... YOU'RE BACK.
SNFF
SNFF
I'M JUST HERE TO GRAB SOME THINGS...
YOU'RE UP EARLY THIS MORN-ING...
LOOK, WHAT WE TALKED ABOUT—
HEY, KURO-SAKI! HURRY UP!
I GOT US A CAB BECAUSE YOU SAID YOU'D BE RIGHT OUT!
IT'S FINE. NOW'S NOT THE TIME.
YOU'RE WORKING ON SOME-THING IMPORTANT TO SAVE AKIRA, RIGHT?
CONCEN-TRATE ON THAT. DON'T WORRY ABOUT ME.
WOOF
WOOF
WOOF

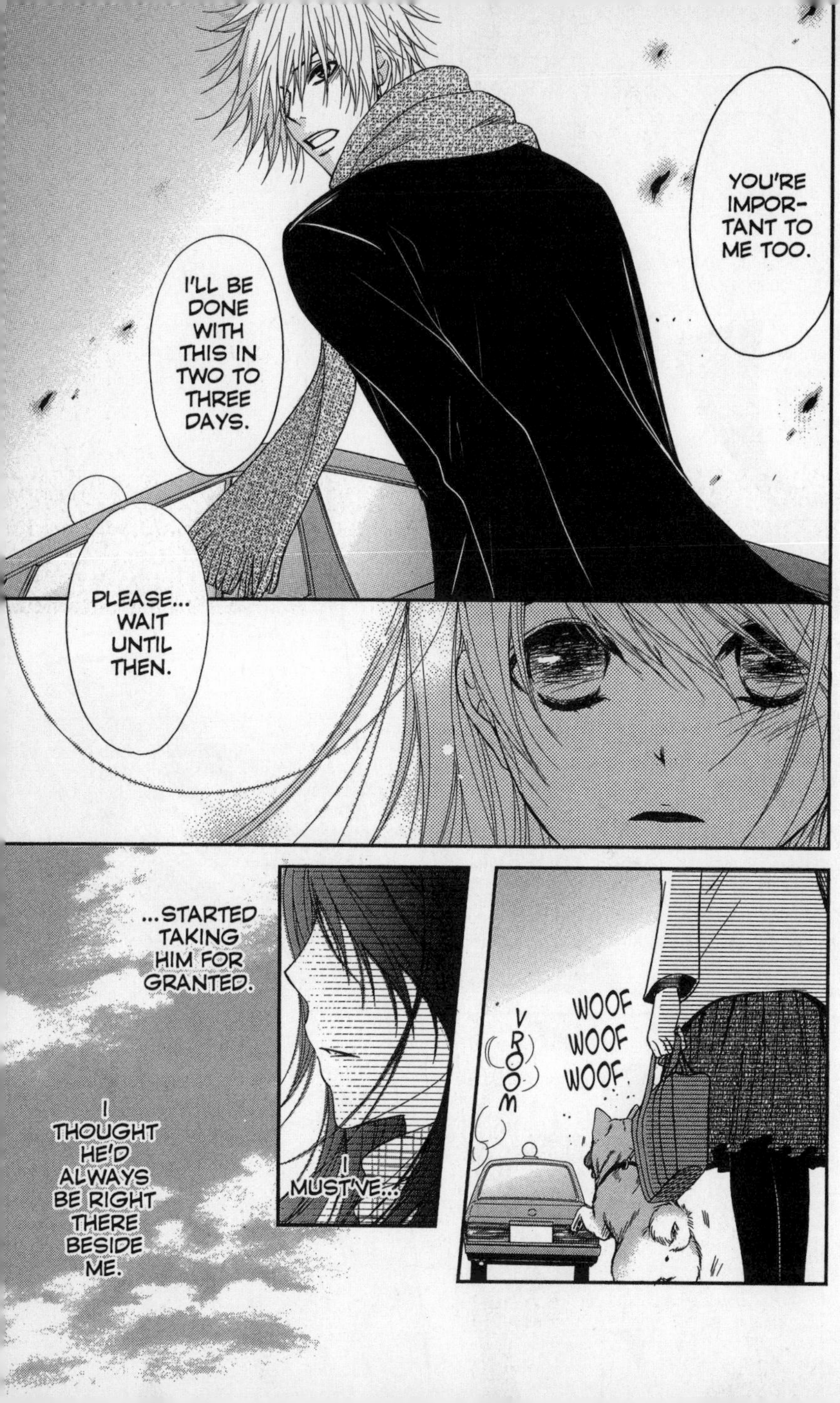
YOU'RE IMPORTANT TO ME TOO.
I'LL BE DONE WITH THIS IN TWO TO THREE DAYS.
PLEASE... WAIT UNTIL THEN.
WOOF WOOF WOOF
VROOM
I MUST'VE...
...STARTED TAKING HIM FOR GRANTED.
I THOUGHT HE'D ALWAYS BE RIGHT THERE BESIDE ME.

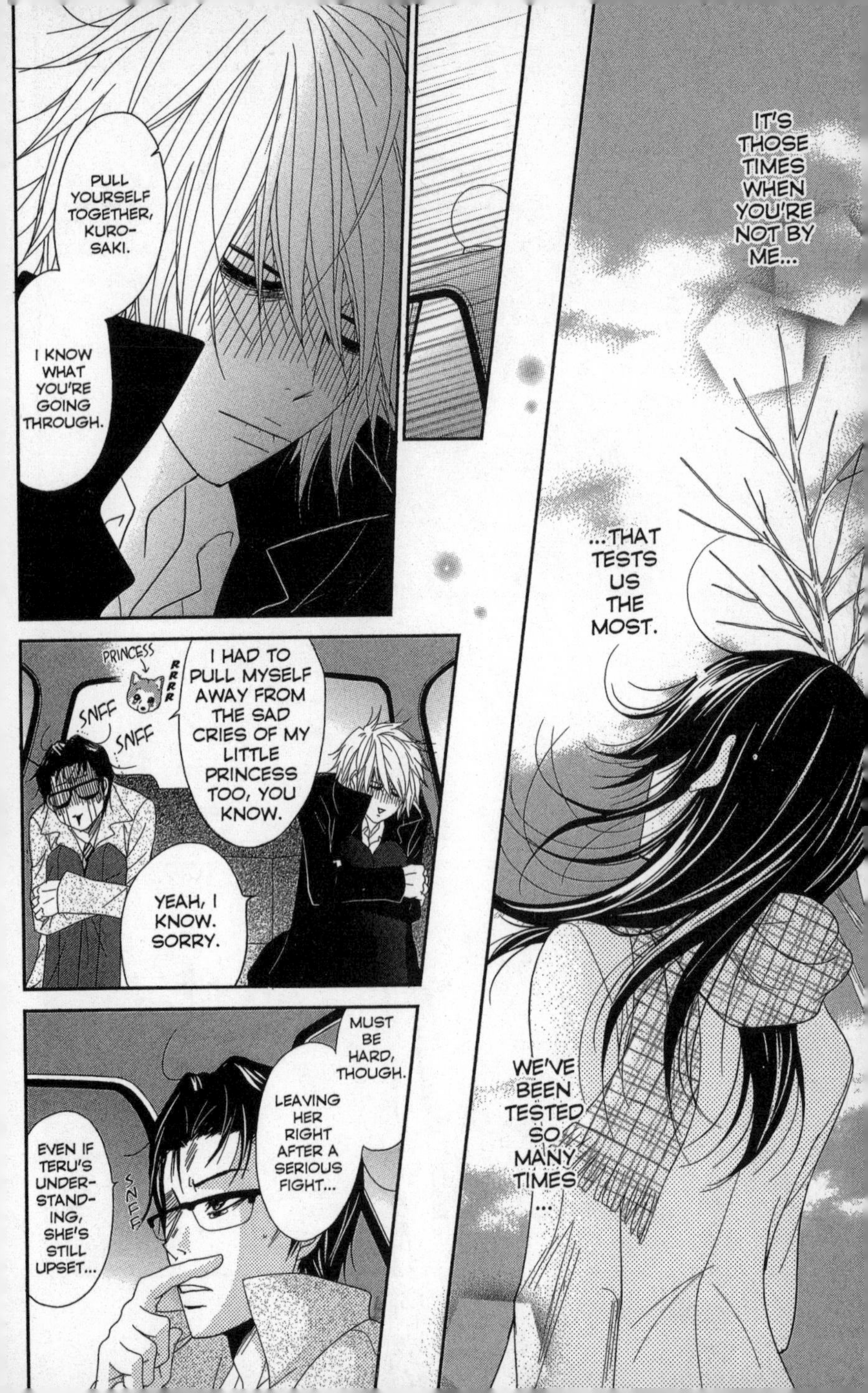
IT'S THOSE TIMES WHEN YOU'RE NOT BY ME...
...THAT TESTS US THE MOST.
WE'VE BEEN TESTED SO MANY TIMES...
PULL YOURSELF TOGETHER, KURO-SAKI.
I KNOW WHAT YOU'RE GOING THROUGH.
I HAD TO PULL MYSELF AWAY FROM THE SAD CRIES OF MY LITTLE PRINCESS TOO, YOU KNOW.
PRINCESS
RRRR
SNFF
SNFF
YEAH, I KNOW. SORRY.
MUST BE HARD, THOUGH.
LEAVING HER RIGHT AFTER A SERIOUS FIGHT...
SNFF
EVEN IF TERU'S UNDER-STAND-ING, SHE'S STILL UPSET...

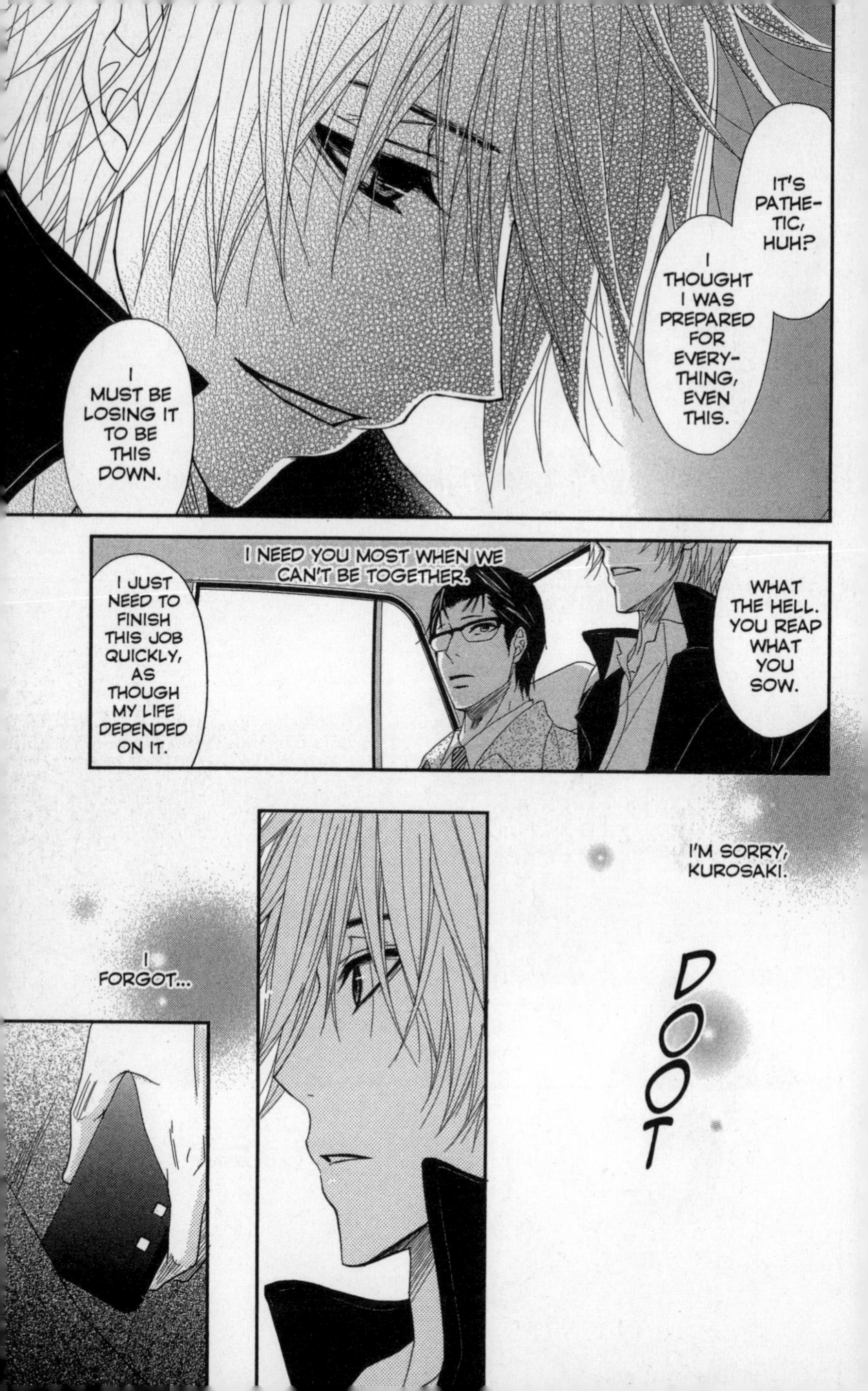
IT'S PATHETIC, HUH?
I THOUGHT I WAS PREPARED FOR EVERYTHING, EVEN THIS.
I MUST BE LOSING IT TO BE THIS DOWN.
WHAT THE HELL. YOU REAP WHAT YOU SOW.
I NEED YOU MOST WHEN WE CAN'T BE TOGETHER.
I JUST NEED TO FINISH THIS JOB QUICKLY, AS THOUGH MY LIFE DEPENDED ON IT.
I'M SORRY, KUROSAKI.
DOOOT
I FORGOT...

EVEN IF WE CAN'T SEE EACH OTHER...

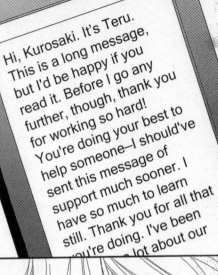

Hi, Kurosaki. It's Teru. This is a long message, but I'd be happy if you read it. Before I go any further, though, thank you for working so hard! You're doing your best to help someone—I should've sent this message of support much sooner. I have so much to learn still. Thank you for all that you're doing. I've been [...] a lot about our

EVEN IF WE CAN'T TALK FACE-TO-FACE...

...I CAN STILL COMMUNICATE WHAT'S IMPORTANT.

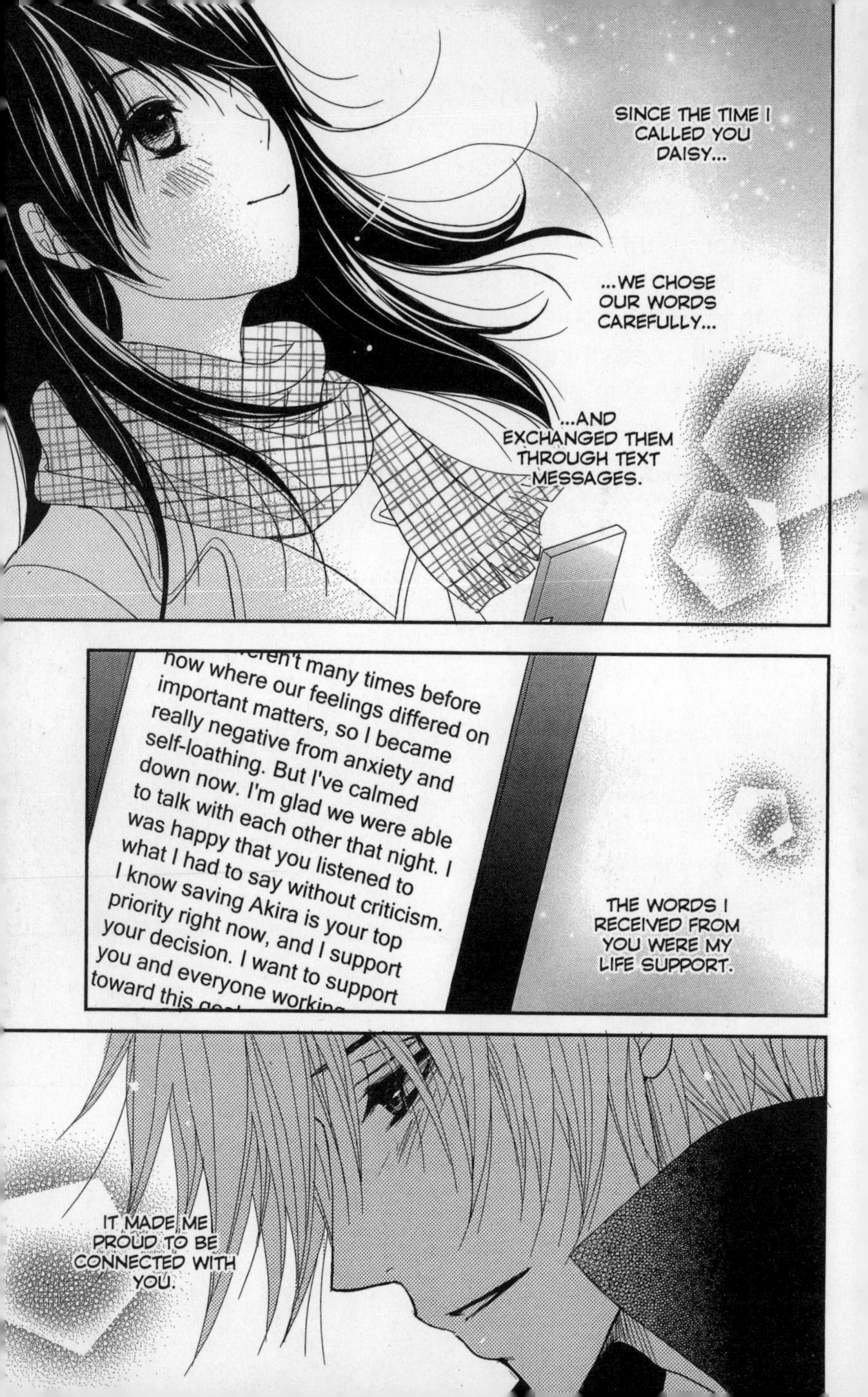
SINCE THE TIME I CALLED YOU DAISY...
...WE CHOSE OUR WORDS CAREFULLY...
...AND EXCHANGED THEM THROUGH TEXT MESSAGES.
ren't many times before
now where our feelings differed on
important matters, so I became
really negative from anxiety and
self-loathing. But I've calmed
down now. I'm glad we were able
to talk with each other that night. I
was happy that you listened to
what I had to say without criticism.
I know saving Akira is your top
priority right now, and I support
your decision. I want to support
you and everyone working
toward this
THE WORDS I RECEIVED FROM YOU WERE MY LIFE SUPPORT.
IT MADE ME PROUD TO BE CONNECTED WITH YOU.

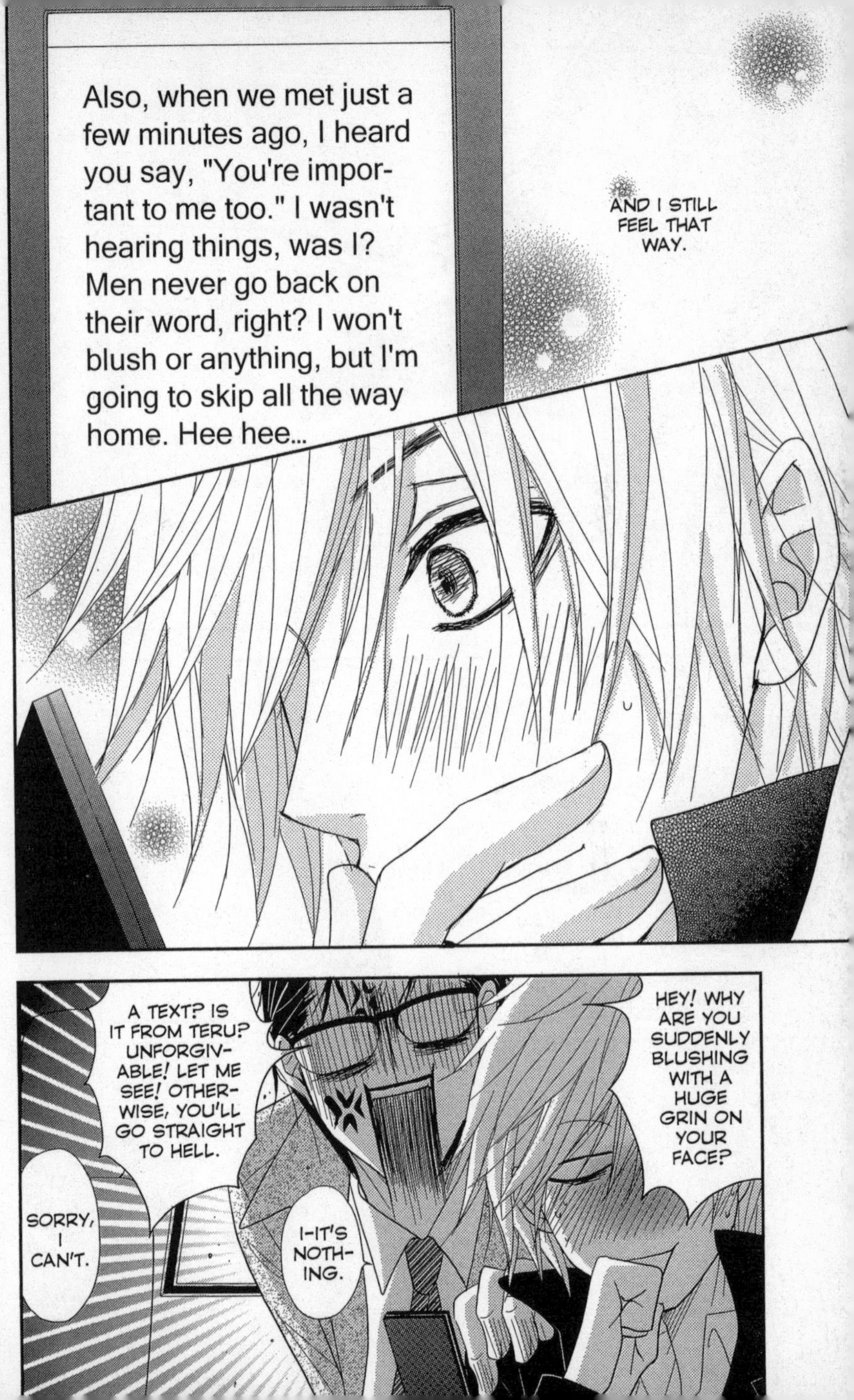
Also, when we met just a few minutes ago, I heard you say, "You're important to me too." I wasn't hearing things, was I? Men never go back on their word, right? I won't blush or anything, but I'm going to skip all the way home. Hee hee...
AND I STILL FEEL THAT WAY.
HEY! WHY ARE YOU SUDDENLY BLUSHING WITH A HUGE GRIN ON YOUR FACE?
A TEXT? IS IT FROM TERU? UNFORGIVABLE! LET ME SEE! OTHERWISE, YOU'LL GO STRAIGHT TO HELL.
I-IT'S NOTHING.
SORRY, I CAN'T.

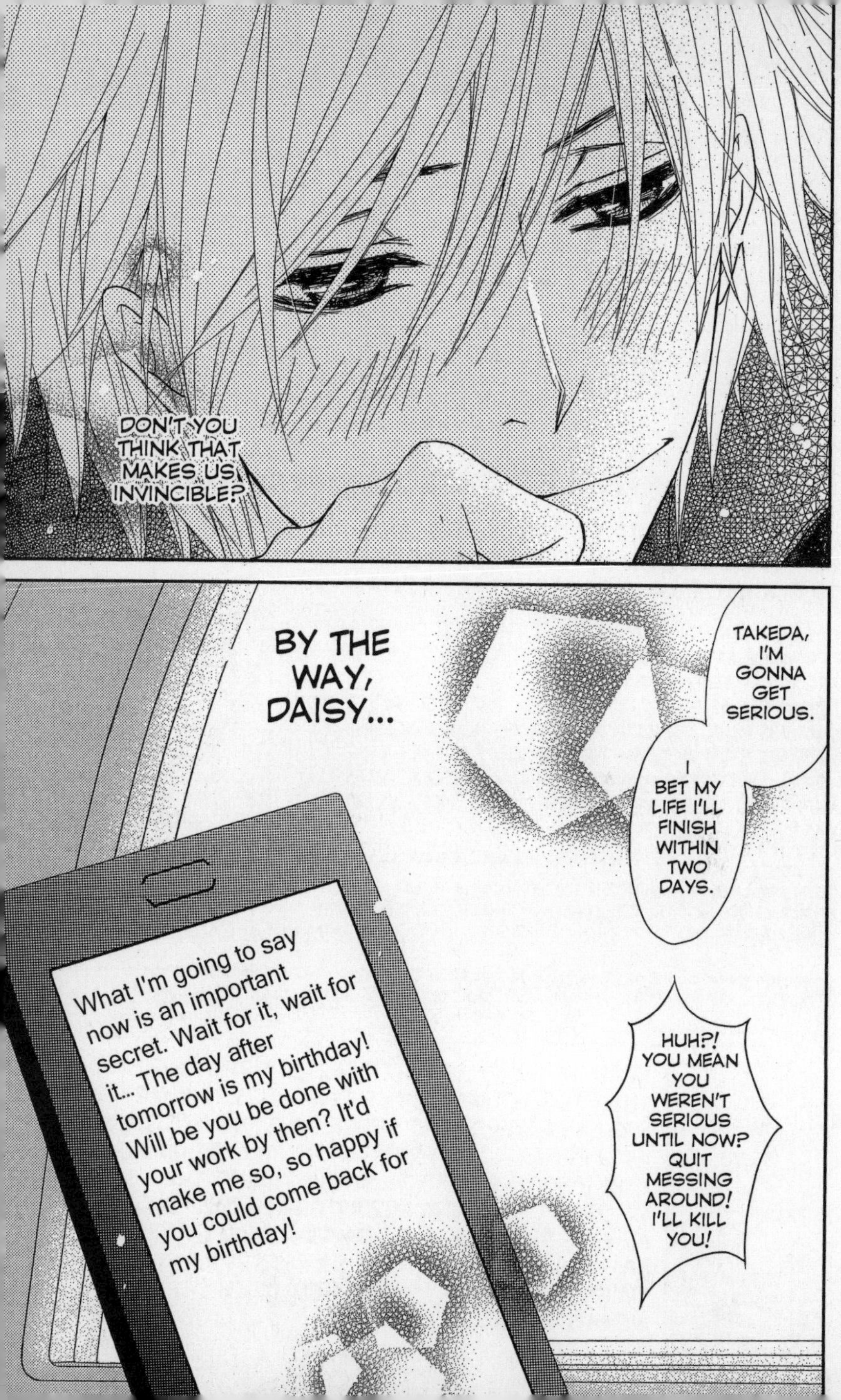
DON'T YOU THINK THAT MAKES US INVINCIBLE?
TAKEDA, I'M GONNA GET SERIOUS.
I BET MY LIFE I'LL FINISH WITHIN TWO DAYS.
BY THE WAY, DAISY...
What I'm going to say now is an important secret. Wait for it, wait for it.. The day after tomorrow is my birthday! Will be you be done with your work by then? It'd make me so, so happy if you could come back for my birthday!
HUH?! YOU MEAN YOU WEREN'T SERIOUS UNTIL NOW? QUIT MESSING AROUND! I'LL KILL YOU!

DENGEKI DAISY QUESTION CORNER

RELOCATED

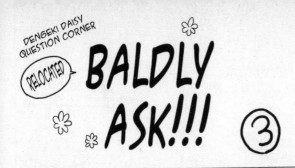

BALDLY ASK!!! ③

WHAT IS THE REASON THAT TAKEDA NAMED HIS DOG KAORUKO?

(TERUTERUKO)

TAKEDA LOOKS TOO DIFFERENT IN VOLUME 13, CHAPTER 61! I THOUGHT HIS HAIR JUST AFTER HE SHOWERED WAS REALLY NICE, SO WHY IS IT THAT HE'S ALWAYS GOT A HO-HUM SALARYMAN HAIRSTYLE?

(DICE, KANAGAWA PREFECTURE)

PROBABLY BECAUSE TO TAKEDA, THE NAME "KAORUKO" CONJURED UP AN IMAGE OF A LOVELY WOMAN. IT'S SORT OF LIKE THE WAY ●YA KI● OF S●AP NAMED HIS PET DOG "BONITA." OR NOT.

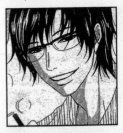

AS FOR TAKEDA'S HAIRSTYLE, I THINK HE CHOOSES IT BECAUSE AS A BASIC RULE OF THUMB, HE'D RATHER PORTRAY HIMSELF AS SOMEONE WHO LOOKS COMPETENT AT HIS JOB RATHER THAN SOMEONE WHO IS POPULAR WITH WOMEN. AS IT IS, SINCE HE APPARENTLY WORKS AT A JOB THAT PEOPLE FIND EASY TO DESPISE HIM FOR, HE WANTS TO AT LEAST APPEAR CONSERVATIVE. ANYWAY, IT'S OKAY AS LONG AS KAORUKO LOVES TAKEDA.

IN VOLUME 10, CHAPTER 49, KUROSAKI SAID SOMETHING ABOUT KNOWING ROUGHLY HOW MUCH TERU WEIGHED, RIGHT? WHY IS THAT? CAN PERVERTS TELL A PERSON'S WEIGHT JUST BY LOOKING AT THEM?

ALSO, IN VOLUME 3, CHAPTER 10, KUROSAKI SAYS, "HOW PERVERTED DO YOU THINK I AM?" HOW FAR WOULD YOU HAVE ALLOWED HIM TO GO?

(C.I., AICHI PREFECTURE)

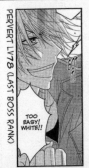

GOT IT!
TOO EASY! WHITE!!
PERVERT LV78 (LAST BOSS RANK)

YEAH, HE'S GONE PRETTY FAR. IT'S BEEN MORE THAN TEN VOLUMES SINCE THEN. HE'S BECOME SUCH A PERVERT THAT THERE'S NO TURNING BACK. WITH REGARD TO TERU'S WEIGHT, MAYBE HE GOT IT BY ASKING RIKO? YOU KNOW, BUYING THE INFORMATION FROM HER WITH EXPENSIVE SAKE, MAYBE? BUT, WELL, HE'S CARRIED TERU ON HIS BACK AND PUT HER ON HIS SHOULDERS MANY TIMES, SO HE MIGHT KNOW HOW MUCH SHE WEIGHS.

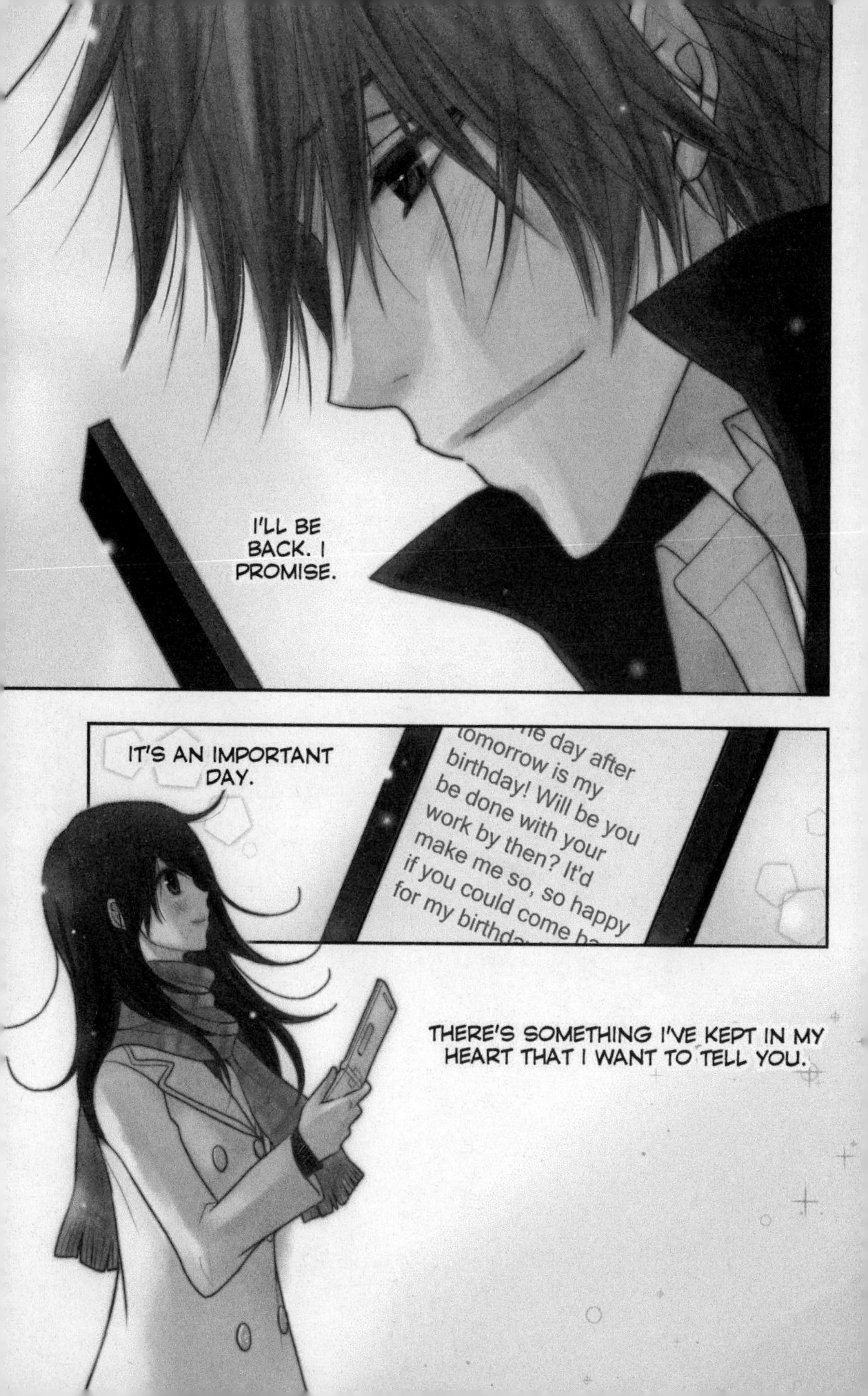
I'LL BE BACK. I PROMISE.
day after tomorrow is my birthday! Will be you be done with your work by then? It'd make me so, so happy if you could come
for my
IT'S AN IMPORTANT DAY.
THERE'S SOMETHING I'VE KEPT IN MY HEART THAT I WANT TO TELL YOU.

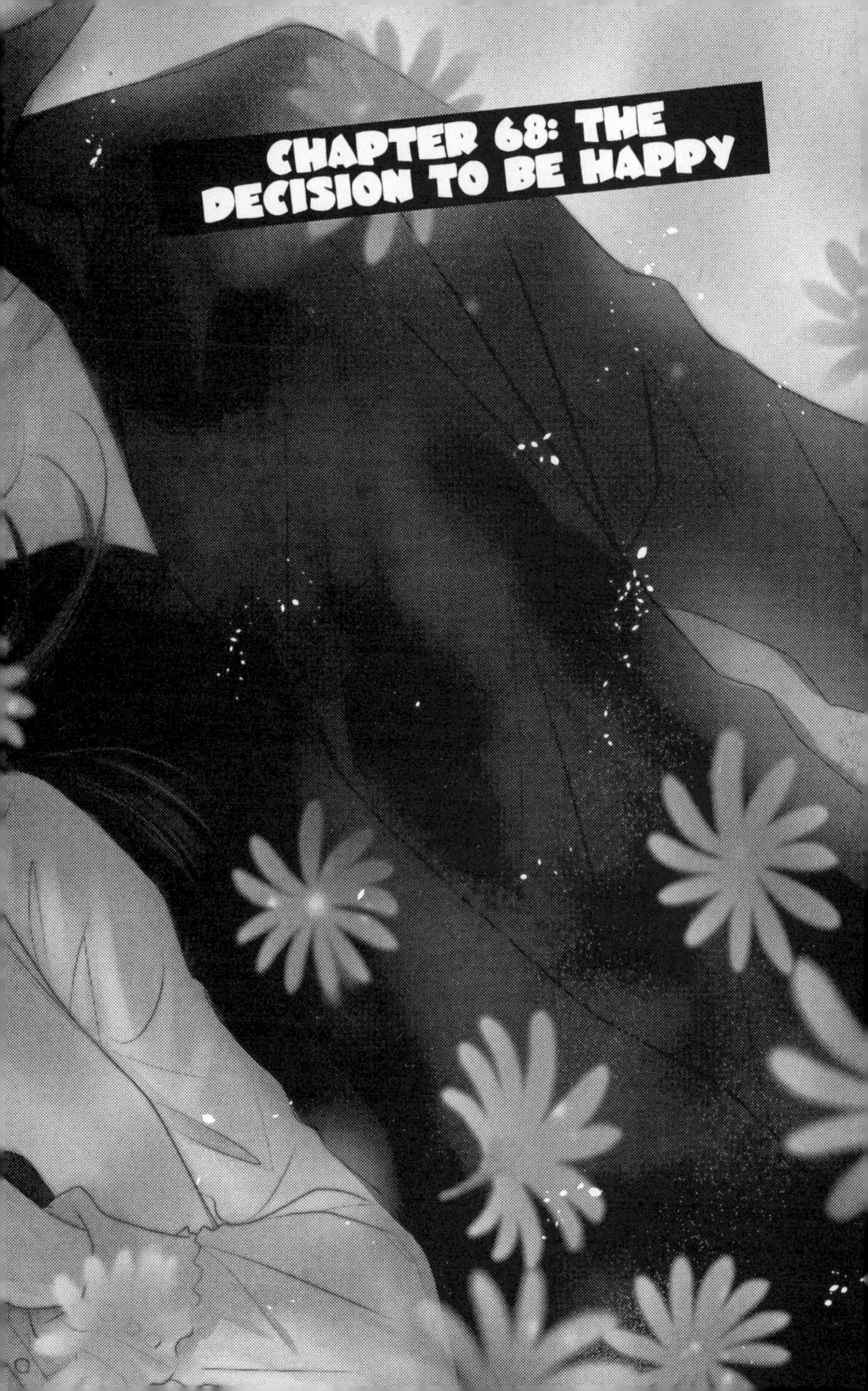
CHAPTER 68: THE DECISION TO BE HAPPY

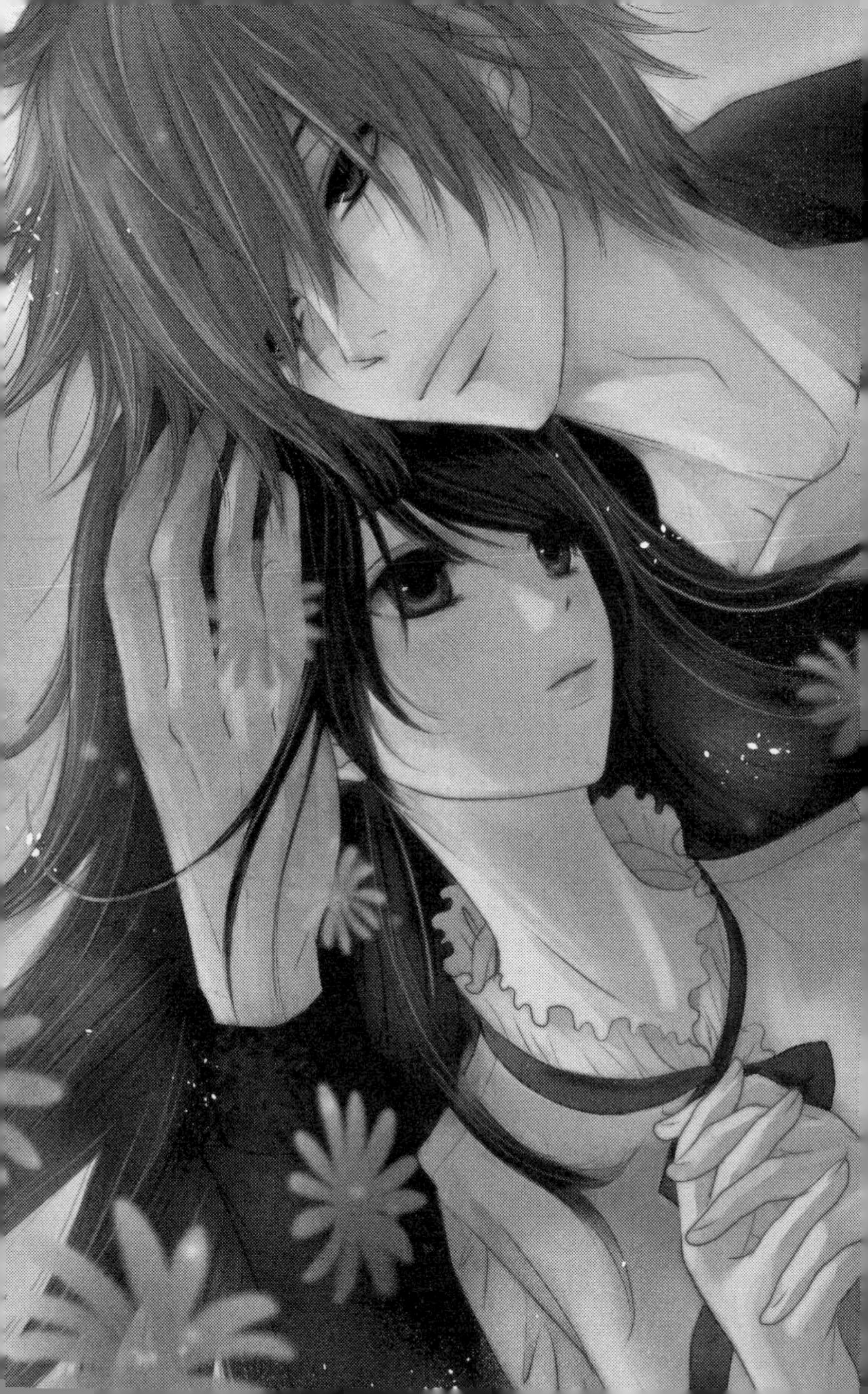

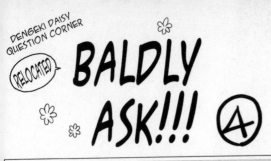

DENGEKI DAISY QUESTION CORNER

RELOCATED

BALDLY ASK!!! ④

WHAT ARE THE FAVORITE KARAOKE SONGS THAT TERU AND HER FRIENDS LIKE TO SING? I ALREADY KNOW WHAT KIYOSHI'S FAVORITE IS.

(KONOHA KUREKAZE ET AL., SAPPORO CITY)

TERU: CAT'S EYE (ANRI)
KUROSAKI: BASKET CASE (GREEN DAY)
RIKO: UFO (PINK LADY)
BOSS: A MAN'S GOTTA DO WHAT A MAN'S GOTTA DO (CRAZY KEN BAND)
ANDY: MASQUERADE BALL (SHONENTAI)
HARUKA (LATELY): THESE TEARS AREN'T FOR SHOW (AKINA NAKAMORI)
RENA (LATELY): GONNA KILL THE EX BOYFRIEND (GOLDEN BOMBER)
KIYOSHI (LATELY): ROCKET DIVE (HIDE)
YOSHI & KEN: END OF SUMMER HARMONY (KOJI TAMAKI AND YOSUI INOUE)
KAKO & MEI: LONELY TROPICAL FISH (WINK)
TAKEDA: MARCH 9 (REMIOROMEN)
SOICHIRO: SPACE SHERIFF GAVAN (AKIRA KUSHIDA)

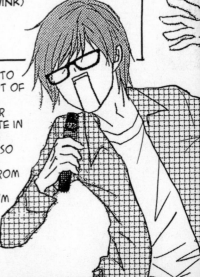

I REALLY PUT A LOT OF SERIOUS THOUGHT INTO THIS—ABOUT THREE HOURS. I ALSO GET A LOT OF QUESTIONS LIKE, "WHAT KIND OF MUSIC DOES EACH CHARACTER LIKE?" AND "WHO ARE THEIR FAVORITE ARTISTS?" AS THE AUTHOR, MY TASTE IN MUSIC IS QUITE BIASED, SO I DON'T HAVE THE CONFIDENCE TO ANSWER THOSE QUESTIONS. SO PLEASE LET ME OFF THE HOOK WITH THESE ANSWERS. I RECEIVED LOTS OF COMMENTS FROM EVERYONE THAT KUROSAKI'S FAVORITE SONG LACKED CONNECTION WITH THE STORY, SO I'M TEACHING HIM TO SING A NEW SONG, "MELODY OF MEN," BY SHOGUN.

AND THAT'S ALL FOR THIS TIME!! WE'LL CONTINUE IN THE NEXT VOLUME!!!

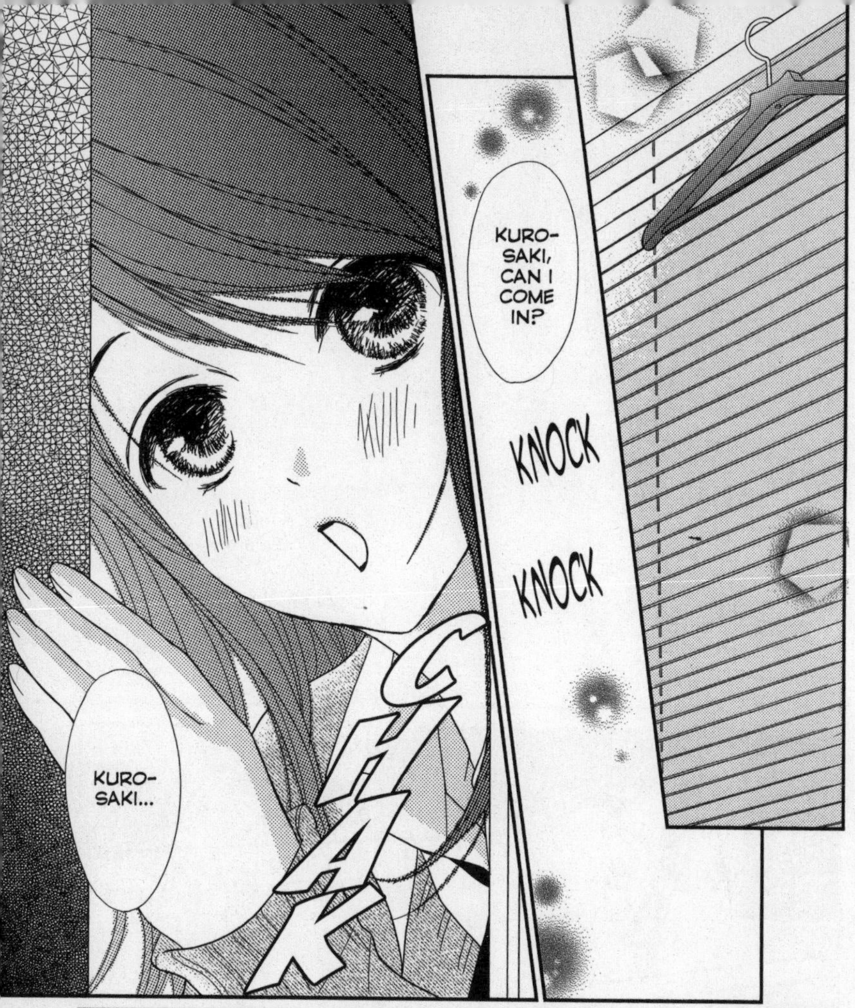
KURO-SAKI, CAN I COME IN?
KNOCK
KNOCK
CHAK
KURO-SAKI...

REGARDING THAT LINE I WROTE IN CHAPTER 67 WHERE TERU SAYS, "I FEEL A DRAFT IN MY HEART..." MY ASSISTANTS TOLD ME THEY DIDN'T GET IT AT ALL. THEY WEREN'T THE ONLY ONES. EVEN MY EDITOR THOUGHT SO. "HMM... I DON'T REALLY UNDERSTAND IT, BUT IT SOUNDS INTERESTING, SO I GUESS IT'S OKAY. (*LAUGH*)" ***WHAT'S WRONG WITH IT?!!*** TEN YEARS AGO (ABOUT THE TIME I MADE MY DEBUT), AT *DELUXE BETSUCOMI*, EVERYONE WAS USING IT!!!!

JUST FOR YOUR INFORMATION, IT'S AN EXPRESSION THAT MEANS "A SAD FEELING, LIKE A DRAFT BLOWING THROUGH YOUR HEART WHEN THINGS AREN'T GOING RIGHT WITH THE BOY YOU LIKE." IT'S DEFINITELY AN EXPRESSION YOU NEVER HEAR THESE DAYS, THOUGH. DO I FEEL A DRAFT?

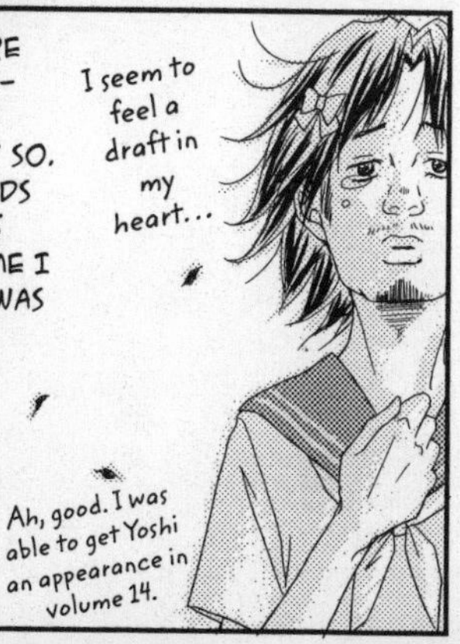
I seem to feel a draft in my heart...
Ah, good. I was able to get Yoshi an appearance in volume 14.

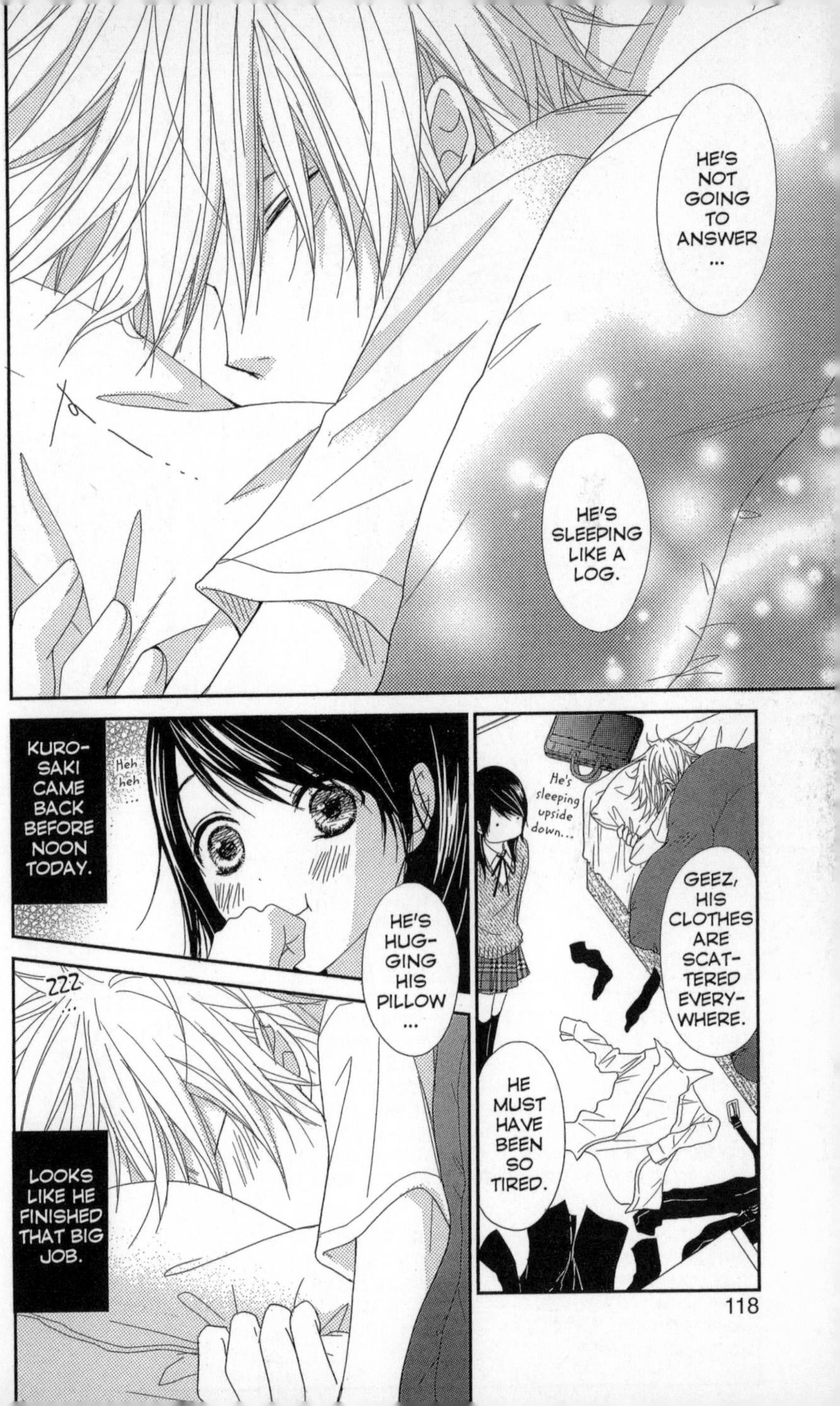
HE'S NOT GOING TO ANSWER ...
HE'S SLEEPING LIKE A LOG.
He's sleeping upside down...
GEEZ, HIS CLOTHES ARE SCAT-TERED EVERY-WHERE.
HE MUST HAVE BEEN SO TIRED.
KURO-SAKI CAME BACK BEFORE NOON TODAY.
Heh heh ...
HE'S HUG-GING HIS PILLOW ...
ZZZ
LOOKS LIKE HE FINISHED THAT BIG JOB.

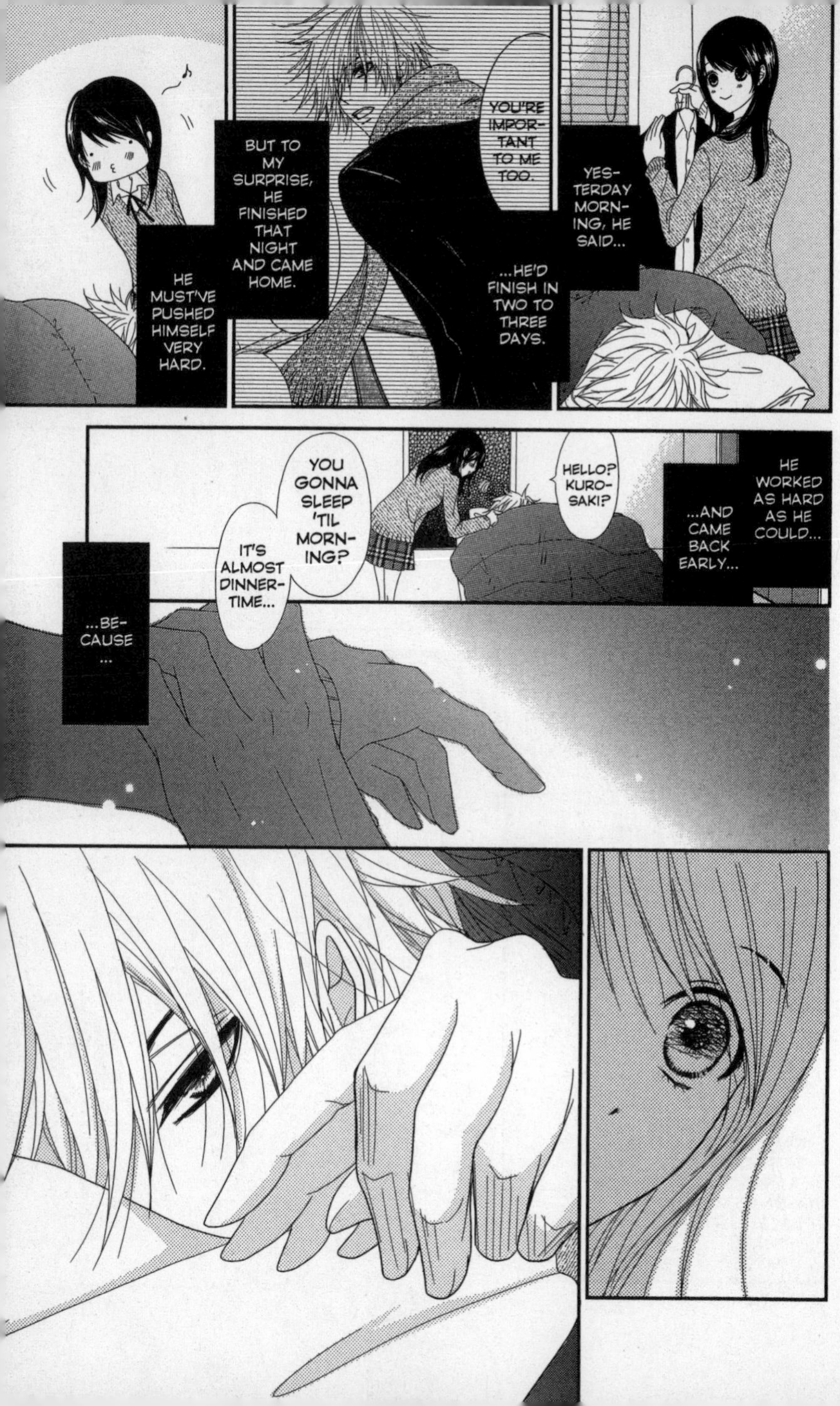
YES-TERDAY MORN-ING, HE SAID...
YOU'RE IMPOR-TANT TO ME TOO.
...HE'D FINISH IN TWO TO THREE DAYS.
BUT TO MY SURPRISE, HE FINISHED THAT NIGHT AND CAME HOME.
HE MUST'VE PUSHED HIMSELF VERY HARD.
HE WORKED AS HARD AS HE COULD...
...AND CAME BACK EARLY...
HELLO? KURO-SAKI?
YOU GONNA SLEEP 'TIL MORN-ING?
IT'S ALMOST DINNER-TIME...
...BE-CAUSE ...

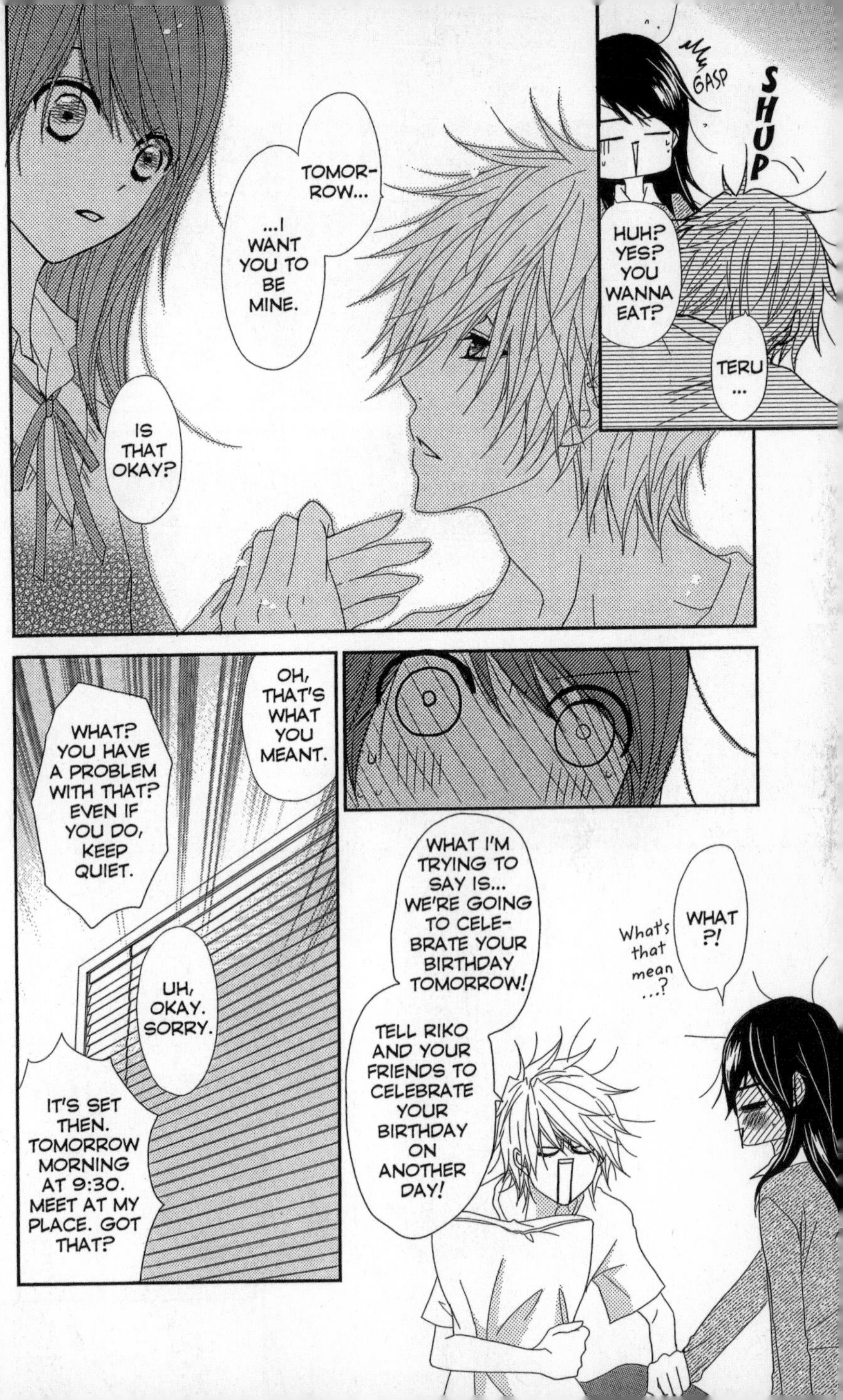
SHUP
GASP
HUH? YES? YOU WANNA EAT?
TERU...
TOMORROW...
...I WANT YOU TO BE MINE.
IS THAT OKAY?
WHAT I'M TRYING TO SAY IS... WE'RE GOING TO CELEBRATE YOUR BIRTHDAY TOMORROW!
WHAT?!
What's that mean...?
TELL RIKO AND YOUR FRIENDS TO CELEBRATE YOUR BIRTHDAY ON ANOTHER DAY!
OH, THAT'S WHAT YOU MEANT.
WHAT? YOU HAVE A PROBLEM WITH THAT? EVEN IF YOU DO, KEEP QUIET.
UH, OKAY. SORRY.
IT'S SET THEN. TOMORROW MORNING AT 9:30. MEET AT MY PLACE. GOT THAT?

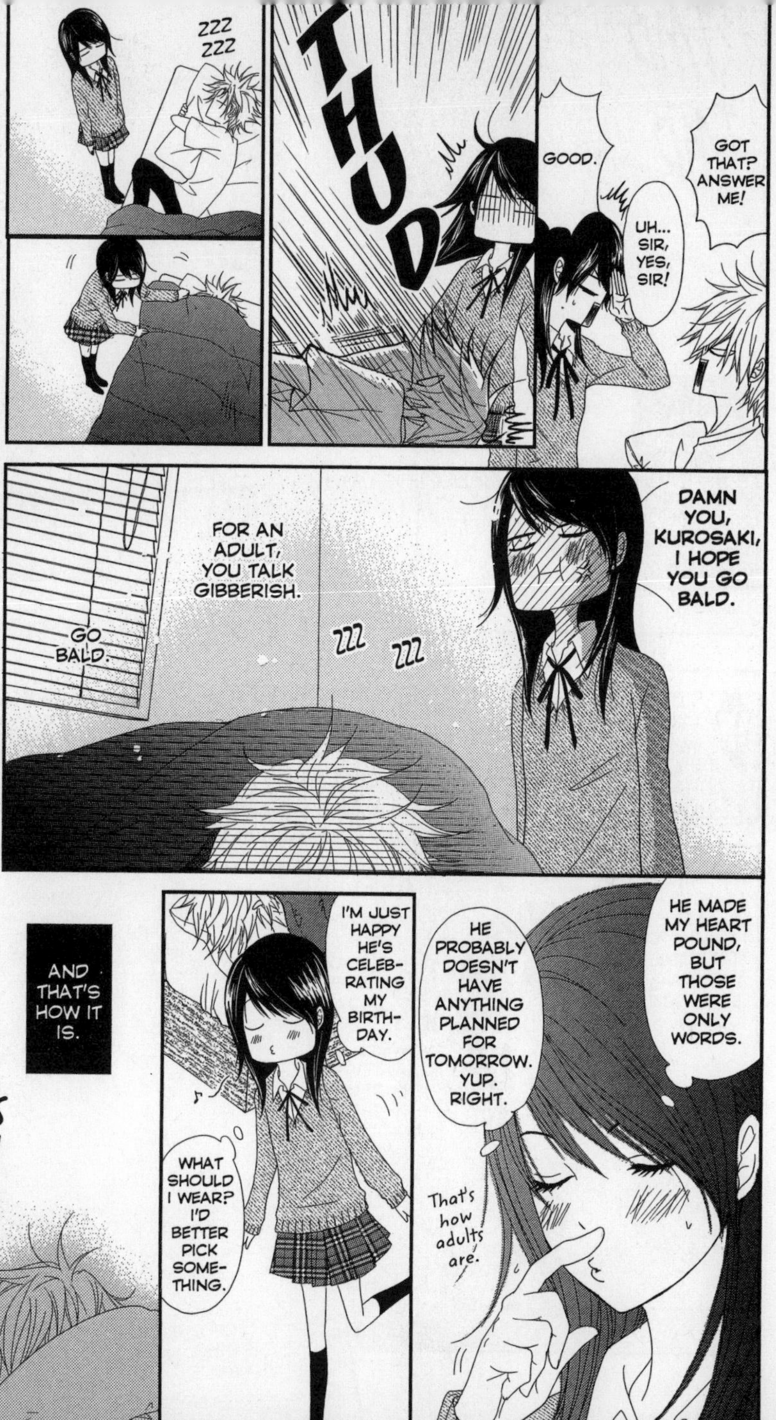
GOT THAT? ANSWER ME!
UH... SIR, YES, SIR!
GOOD.
THUD
ZZZ ZZZ
DAMN YOU, KUROSAKI, I HOPE YOU GO BALD.
ZZZ
ZZZ
FOR AN ADULT, YOU TALK GIBBERISH.
GO BALD.
HE MADE MY HEART POUND, BUT THOSE WERE ONLY WORDS.
HE PROBABLY DOESN'T HAVE ANYTHING PLANNED FOR TOMORROW. YUP. RIGHT.
That's how adults are.
I'M JUST HAPPY HE'S CELEB-RATING MY BIRTH-DAY.
WHAT SHOULD I WEAR? I'D BETTER PICK SOME-THING.
AND THAT'S HOW IT IS.
SHUT

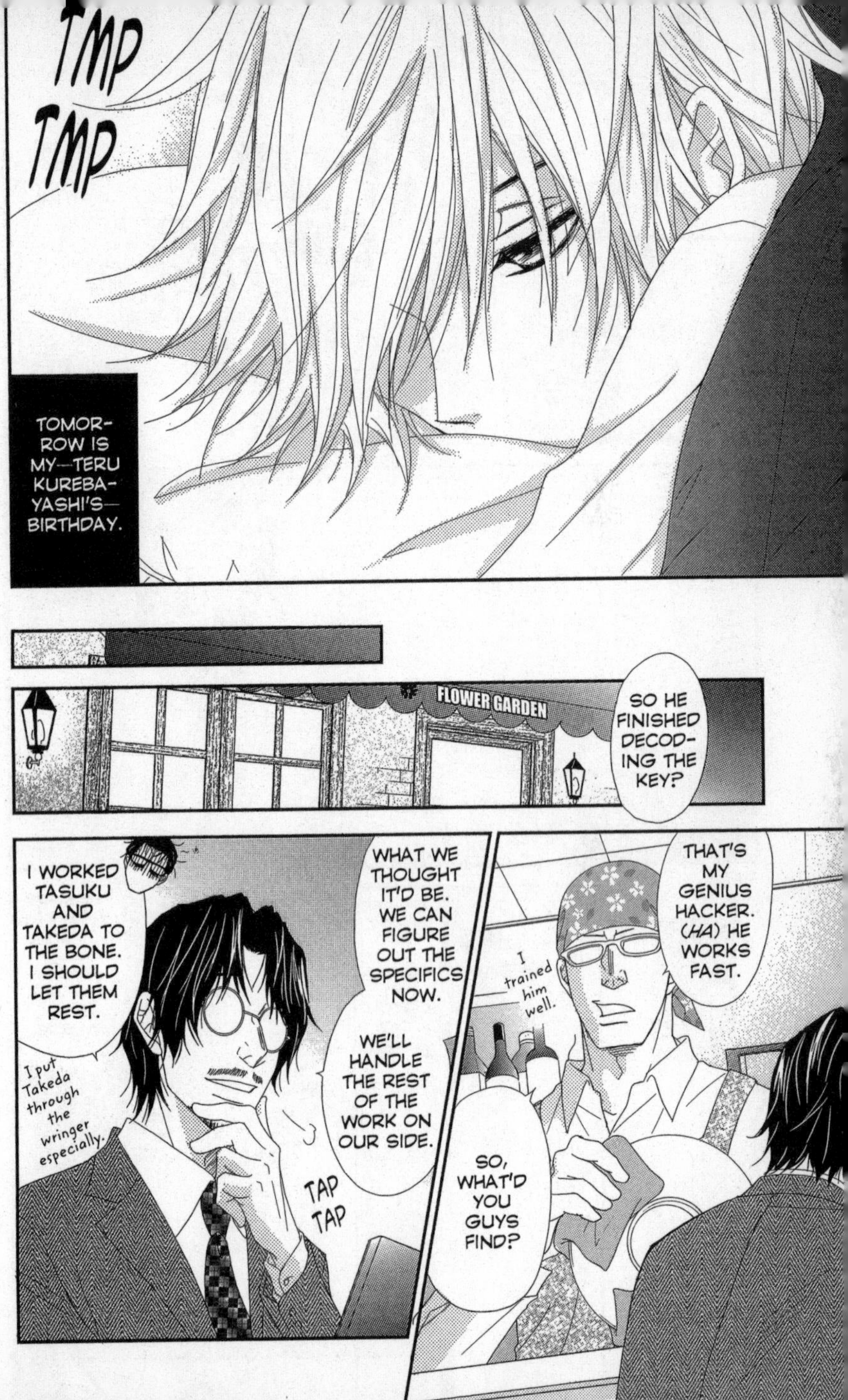
TMP
TMP
TOMORROW IS MY—TERU KUREBAYASHI'S—BIRTHDAY.
FLOWER GARDEN
SO HE FINISHED DECODING THE KEY?
THAT'S MY GENIUS HACKER. (HA) HE WORKS FAST.
I trained him well.
SO, WHAT'D YOU GUYS FIND?
WHAT WE THOUGHT IT'D BE. WE CAN FIGURE OUT THE SPECIFICS NOW.
I WORKED TASUKU AND TAKEDA TO THE BONE. I SHOULD LET THEM REST.
WE'LL HANDLE THE REST OF THE WORK ON OUR SIDE.
I put Takeda through the wringer especially.
TAP
TAP

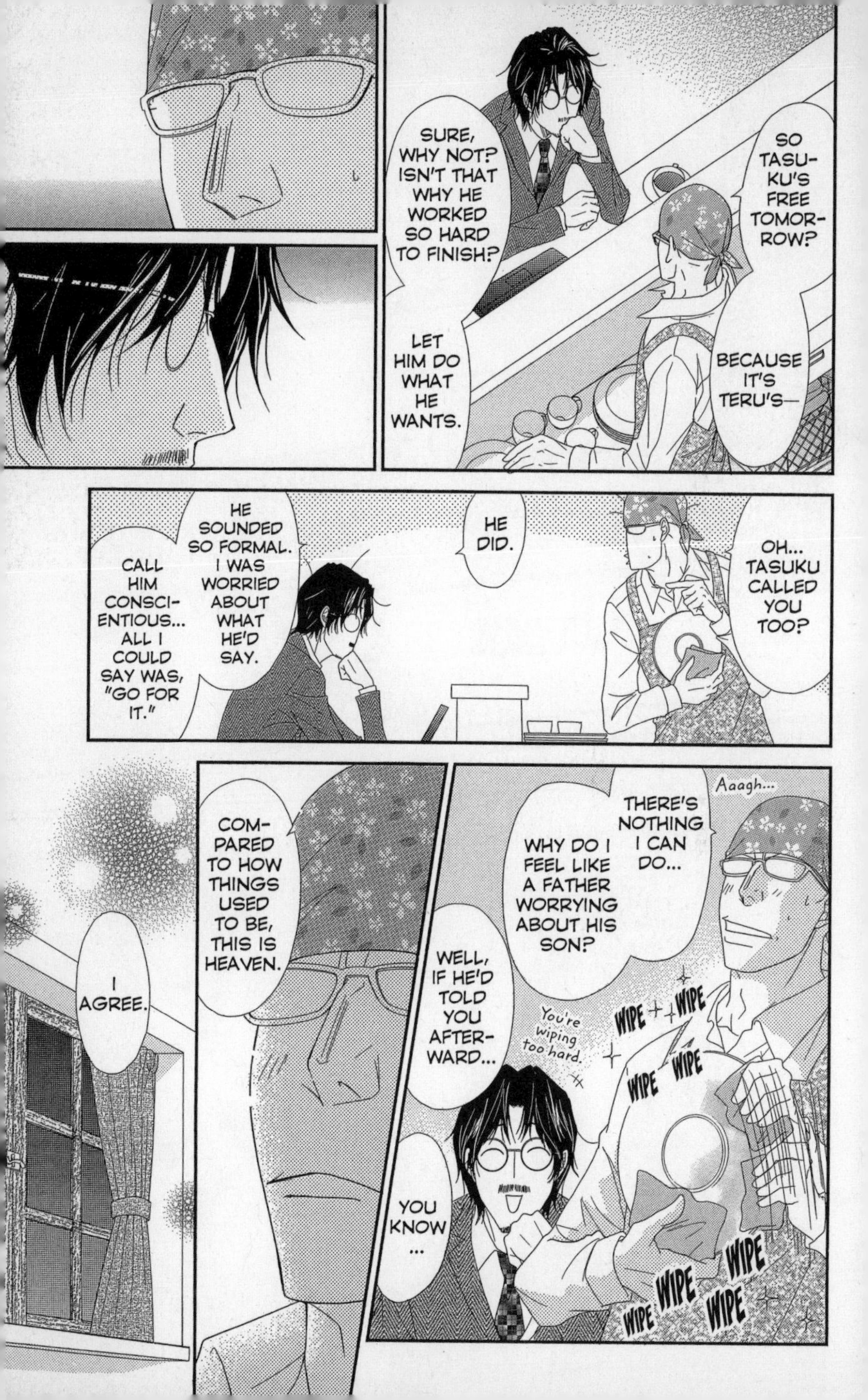
SO TASUKU'S FREE TOMORROW?
SURE, WHY NOT? ISN'T THAT WHY HE WORKED SO HARD TO FINISH?
BECAUSE IT'S TERU'S—
LET HIM DO WHAT HE WANTS.
OH... TASUKU CALLED YOU TOO?
HE DID.
HE SOUNDED SO FORMAL. I WAS WORRIED ABOUT WHAT HE'D SAY.
CALL HIM CONSCIENTIOUS... ALL I COULD SAY WAS, "GO FOR IT."
Aaagh...
THERE'S NOTHING I CAN DO...
WHY DO I FEEL LIKE A FATHER WORRYING ABOUT HIS SON?
WELL, IF HE'D TOLD YOU AFTERWARD...
WIPE WIPE
You're wiping too hard.
WIPE WIPE
YOU KNOW...
WIPE WIPE WIPE WIPE WIPE
COMPARED TO HOW THINGS USED TO BE, THIS IS HEAVEN.
I AGREE.

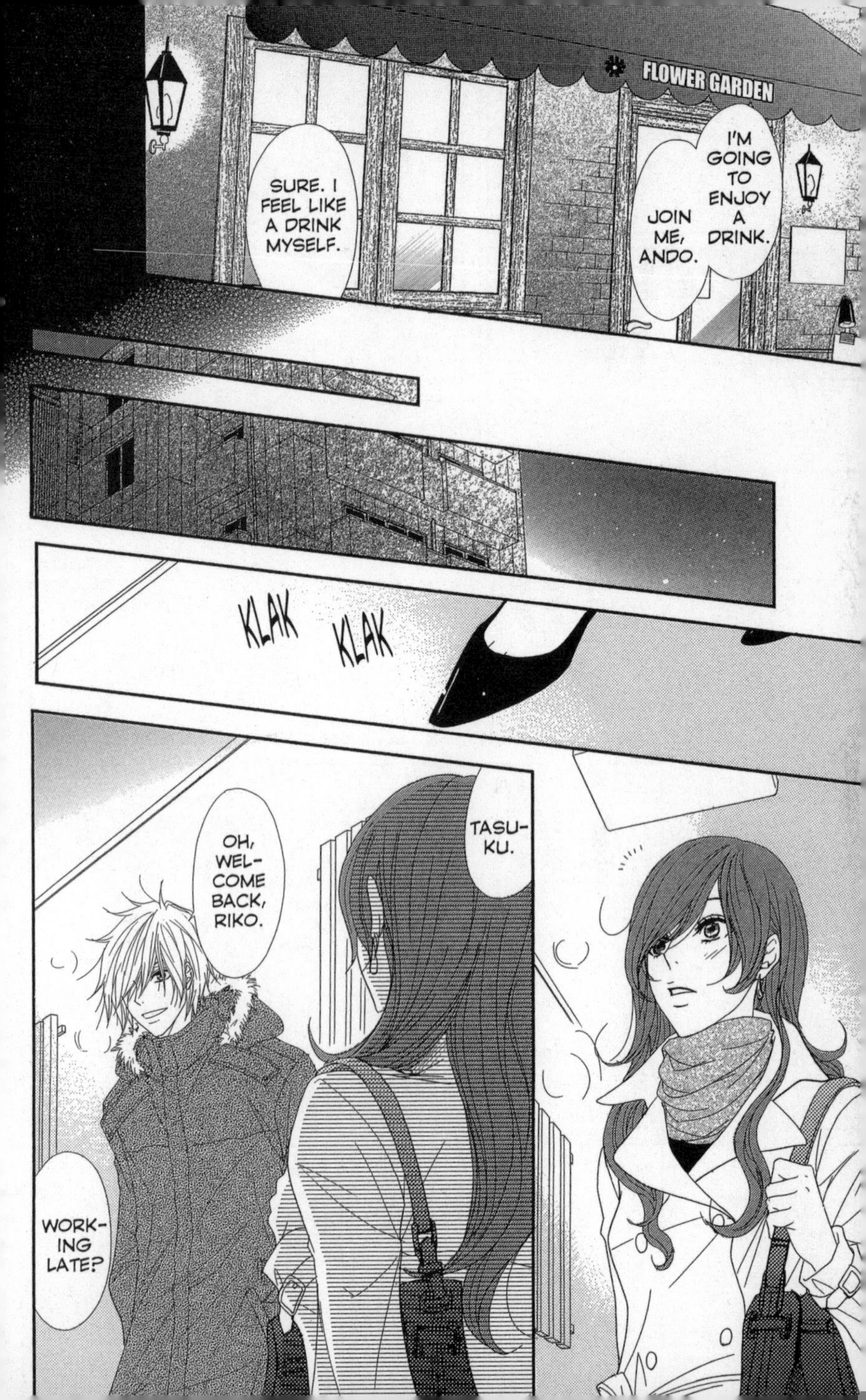
FLOWER GARDEN
I'M GOING TO ENJOY A DRINK.
JOIN ME, ANDO.
SURE. I FEEL LIKE A DRINK MYSELF.
KLAK KLAK
TASU-KU.
OH, WEL-COME BACK, RIKO.
WORK-ING LATE?

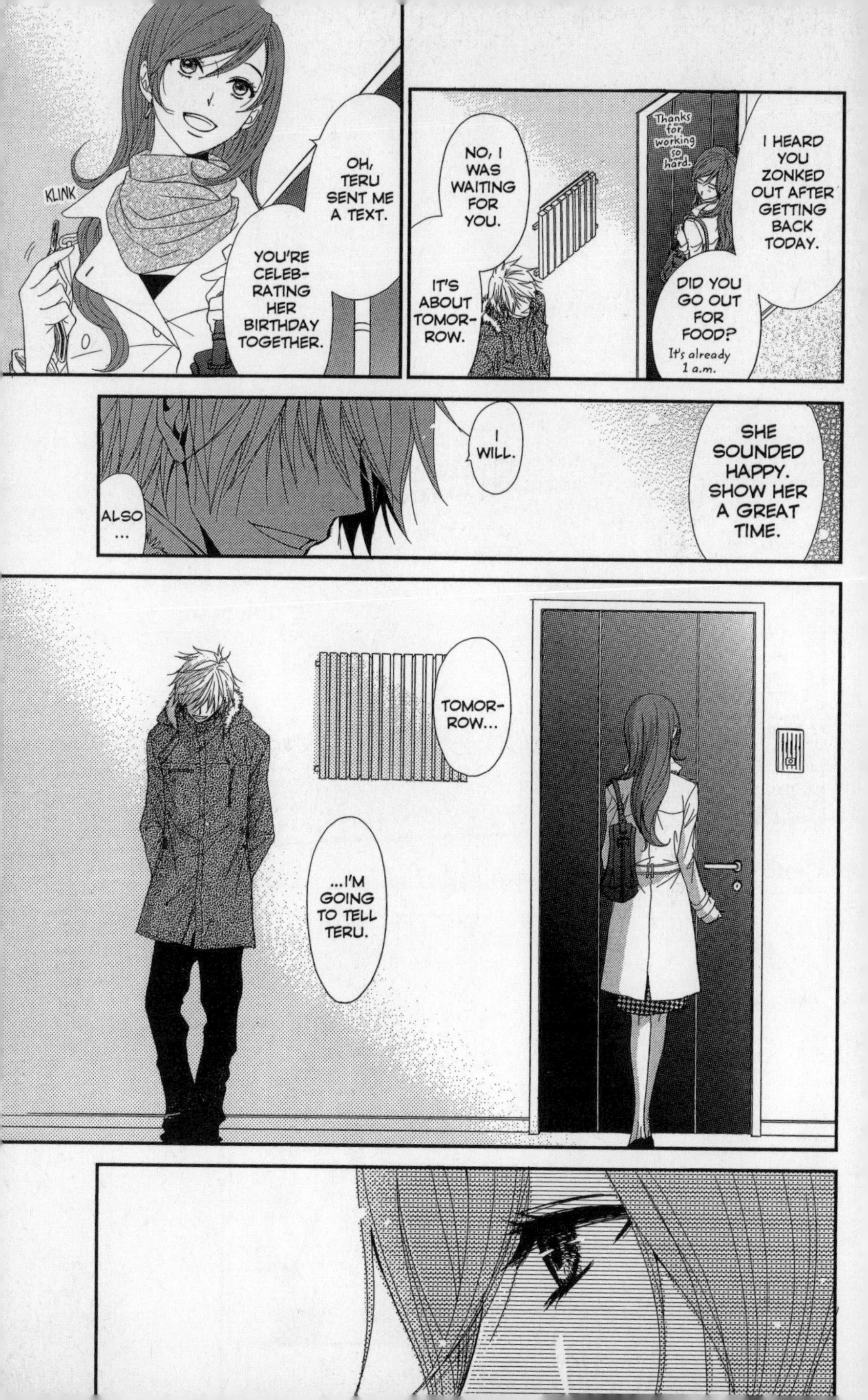
I HEARD YOU ZONKED OUT AFTER GETTING BACK TODAY.
Thanks for working so hard.
DID YOU GO OUT FOR FOOD?
It's already 1 a.m.
NO, I WAS WAITING FOR YOU.
IT'S ABOUT TOMORROW.
OH, TERU SENT ME A TEXT.
YOU'RE CELEB-RATING HER BIRTHDAY TOGETHER.
KLINK
SHE SOUNDED HAPPY. SHOW HER A GREAT TIME.
I WILL.
ALSO ...
TOMOR-ROW...
...I'M GOING TO TELL TERU.

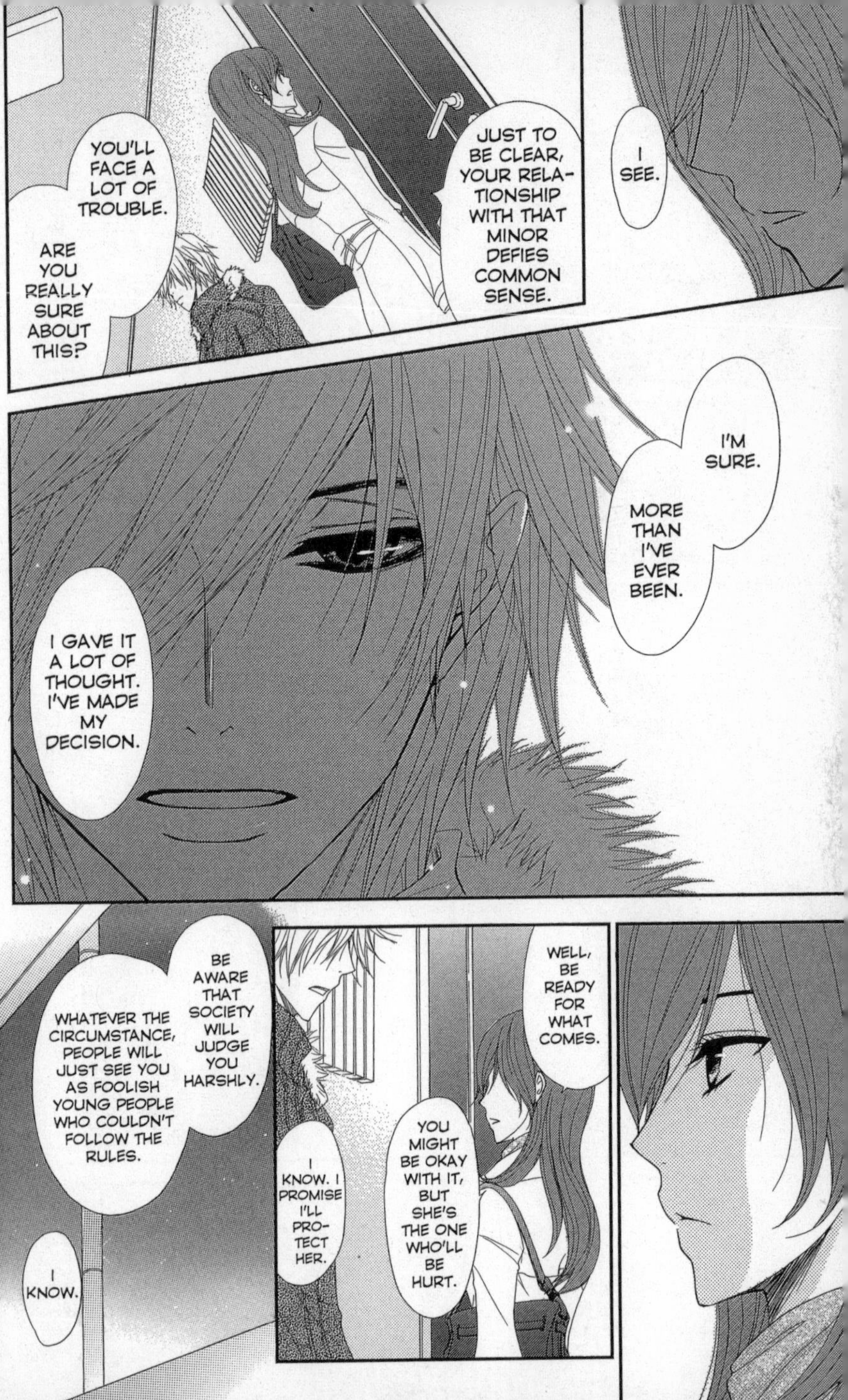
I SEE.
JUST TO BE CLEAR, YOUR RELATIONSHIP WITH THAT MINOR DEFIES COMMON SENSE.
YOU'LL FACE A LOT OF TROUBLE.
ARE YOU REALLY SURE ABOUT THIS?
I'M SURE.
MORE THAN I'VE EVER BEEN.
I GAVE IT A LOT OF THOUGHT. I'VE MADE MY DECISION.
WELL, BE READY FOR WHAT COMES.
YOU MIGHT BE OKAY WITH IT, BUT SHE'S THE ONE WHO'LL BE HURT.
I KNOW. I PROMISE I'LL PROTECT HER.
BE AWARE THAT SOCIETY WILL JUDGE YOU HARSHLY.
WHATEVER THE CIRCUMSTANCE, PEOPLE WILL JUST SEE YOU AS FOOLISH YOUNG PEOPLE WHO COULDN'T FOLLOW THE RULES.
I KNOW.

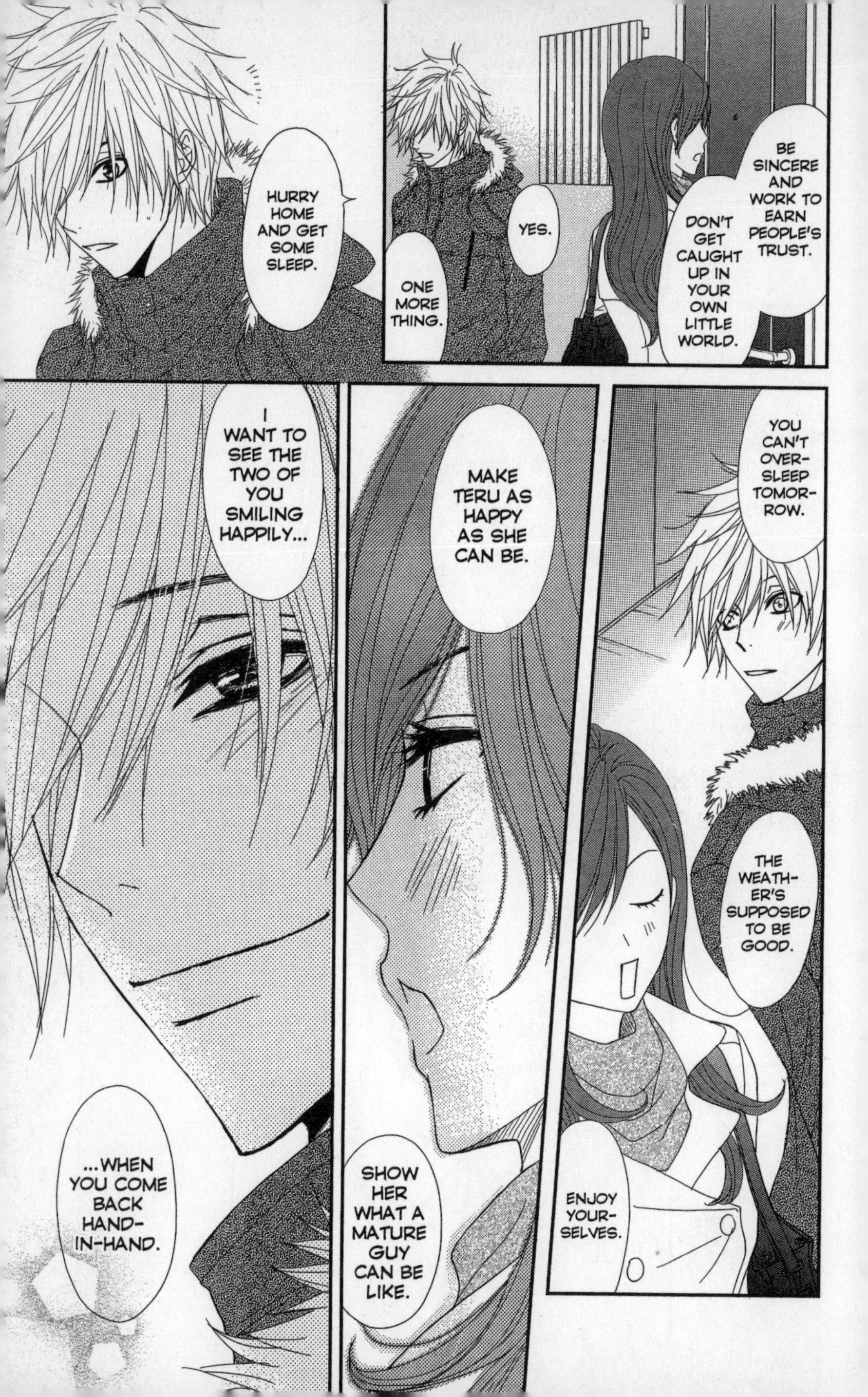
BE SINCERE AND WORK TO EARN PEOPLE'S TRUST.
DON'T GET CAUGHT UP IN YOUR OWN LITTLE WORLD.
YES.
ONE MORE THING.
HURRY HOME AND GET SOME SLEEP.
YOU CAN'T OVERSLEEP TOMORROW.
THE WEATHER'S SUPPOSED TO BE GOOD.
ENJOY YOURSELVES.
MAKE TERU AS HAPPY AS SHE CAN BE.
SHOW HER WHAT A MATURE GUY CAN BE LIKE.
I WANT TO SEE THE TWO OF YOU SMILING HAPPILY...
...WHEN YOU COME BACK HAND-IN-HAND.

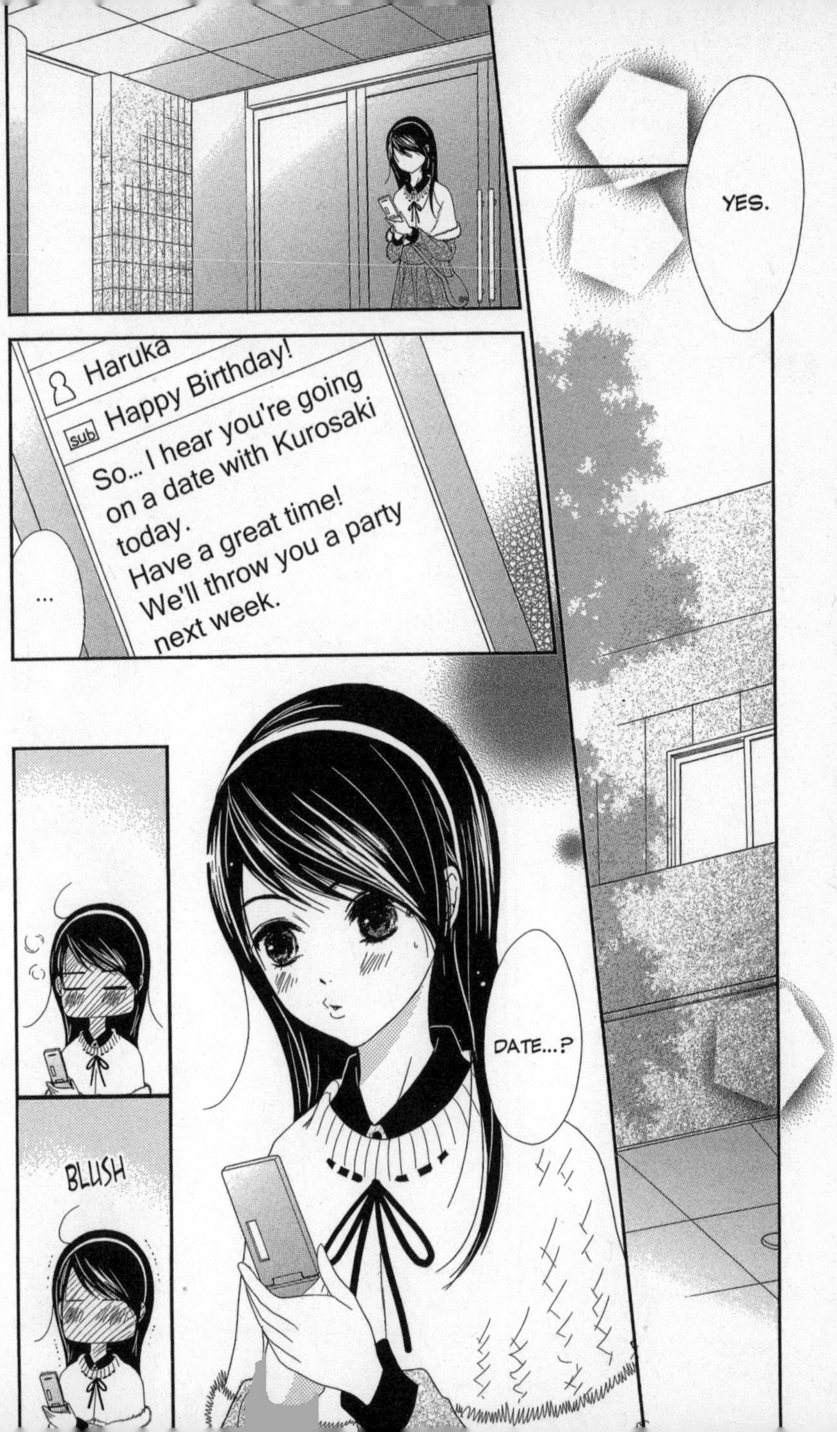
YES.
Haruka
sub Happy Birthday!
So... I hear you're going on a date with Kurosaki today.
Have a great time!
We'll throw you a party next week.
...
DATE...?
BLUSH

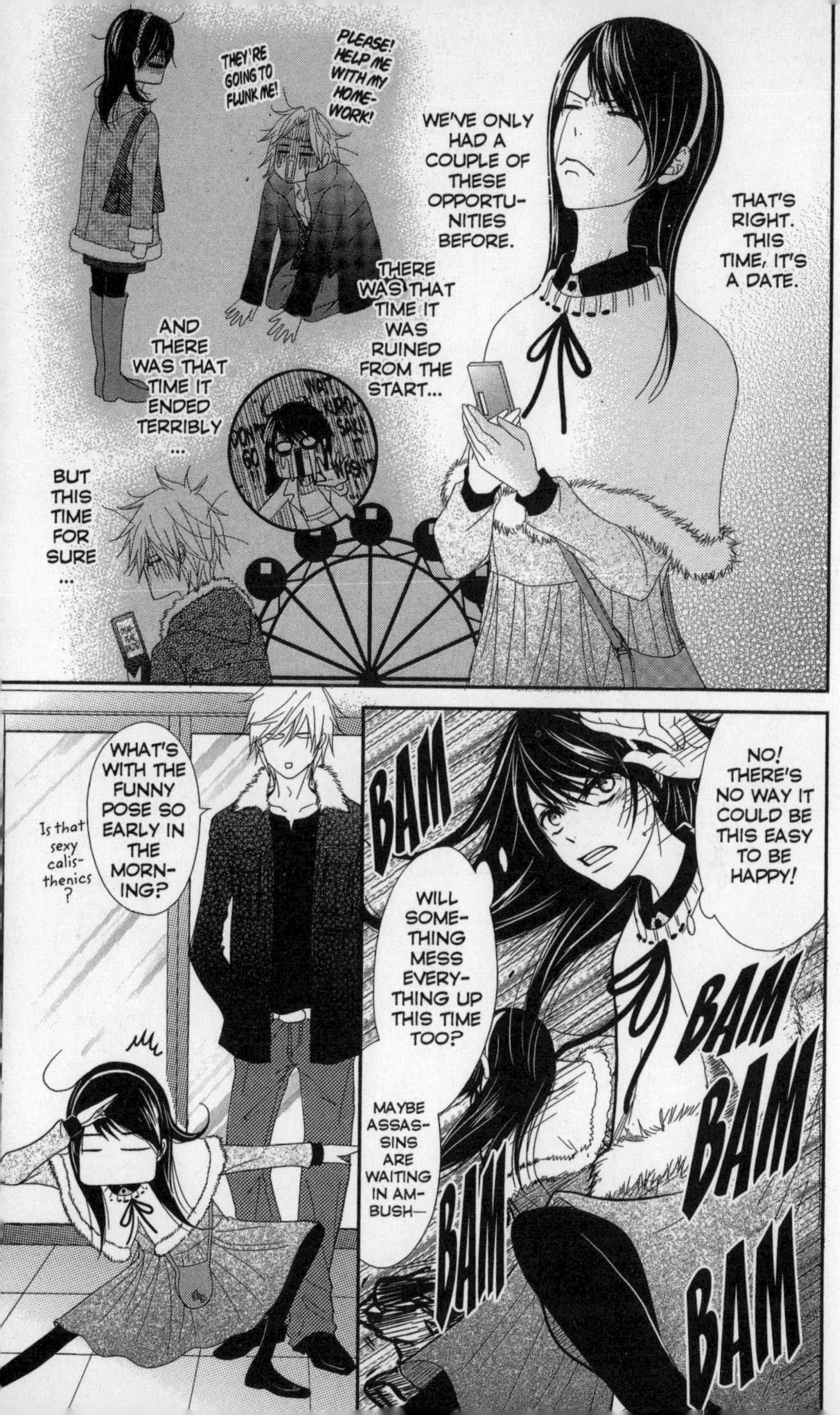
THAT'S RIGHT. THIS TIME, IT'S A DATE.
WE'VE ONLY HAD A COUPLE OF THESE OPPORTU-NITIES BEFORE.
PLEASE! HELP ME WITH MY HOME-WORK!
THEY'RE GOING TO FLUNK ME!
THERE WAS THAT TIME IT WAS RUINED FROM THE START...
AND THERE WAS THAT TIME IT ENDED TERRIBLY...
WAIT KURO-SAKI! IT WASN'T
DON'T GO
BUT THIS TIME FOR SURE...
NO! THERE'S NO WAY IT COULD BE THIS EASY TO BE HAPPY!
BAM
WILL SOME-THING MESS EVERY-THING UP THIS TIME TOO?
BAM BAM BAM BAM
MAYBE ASSAS-SINS ARE WAITING IN AM-BUSH—
BAM
WHAT'S WITH THE FUNNY POSE SO EARLY IN THE MORN-ING?
Is that sexy calis-thenics?

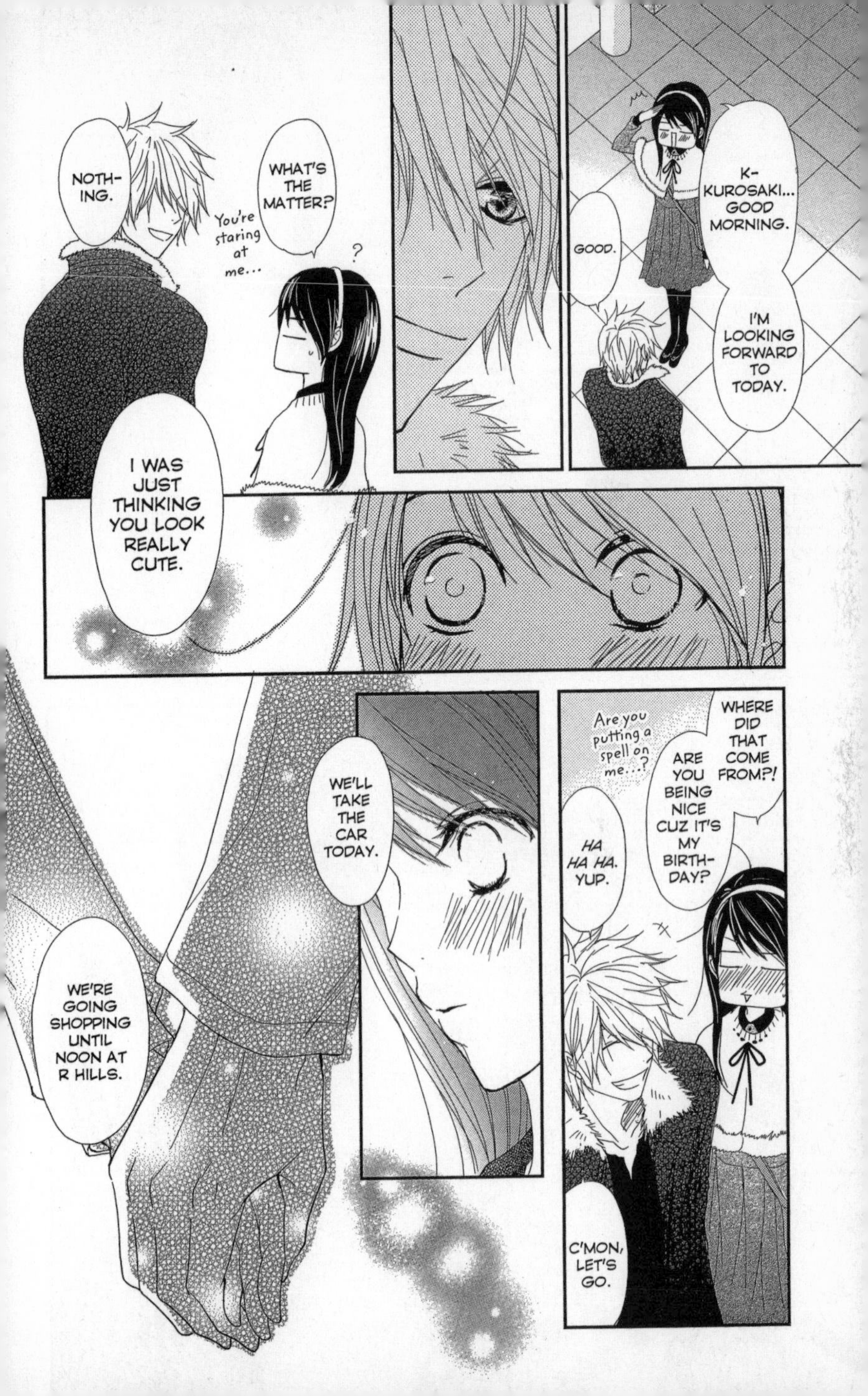
K-KUROSAKI... GOOD MORNING.
GOOD.
I'M LOOKING FORWARD TO TODAY.
WHAT'S THE MATTER?
You're staring at me...
?
NOTH-ING.
I WAS JUST THINKING YOU LOOK REALLY CUTE.
WHERE DID THAT COME FROM?!
Are you putting a spell on me...?
ARE YOU BEING NICE CUZ IT'S MY BIRTH-DAY?
HA HA HA. YUP.
C'MON, LET'S GO.
WE'LL TAKE THE CAR TODAY.
WE'RE GOING SHOPPING UNTIL NOON AT R HILLS.

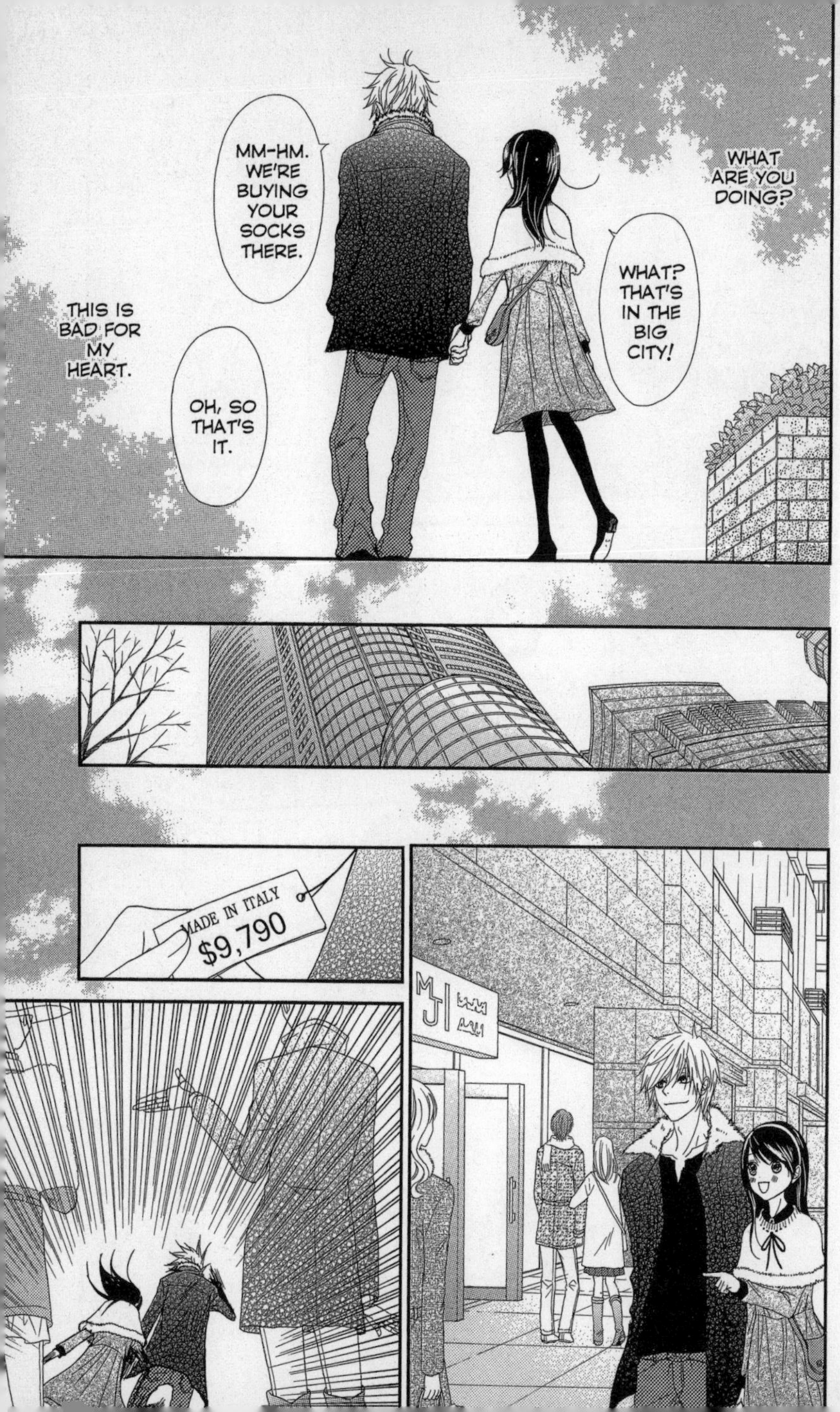
WHAT ARE YOU DOING?
WHAT? THAT'S IN THE BIG CITY!
MM-HM. WE'RE BUYING YOUR SOCKS THERE.
OH, SO THAT'S IT.
THIS IS BAD FOR MY HEART.
MADE IN ITALY
$9,790

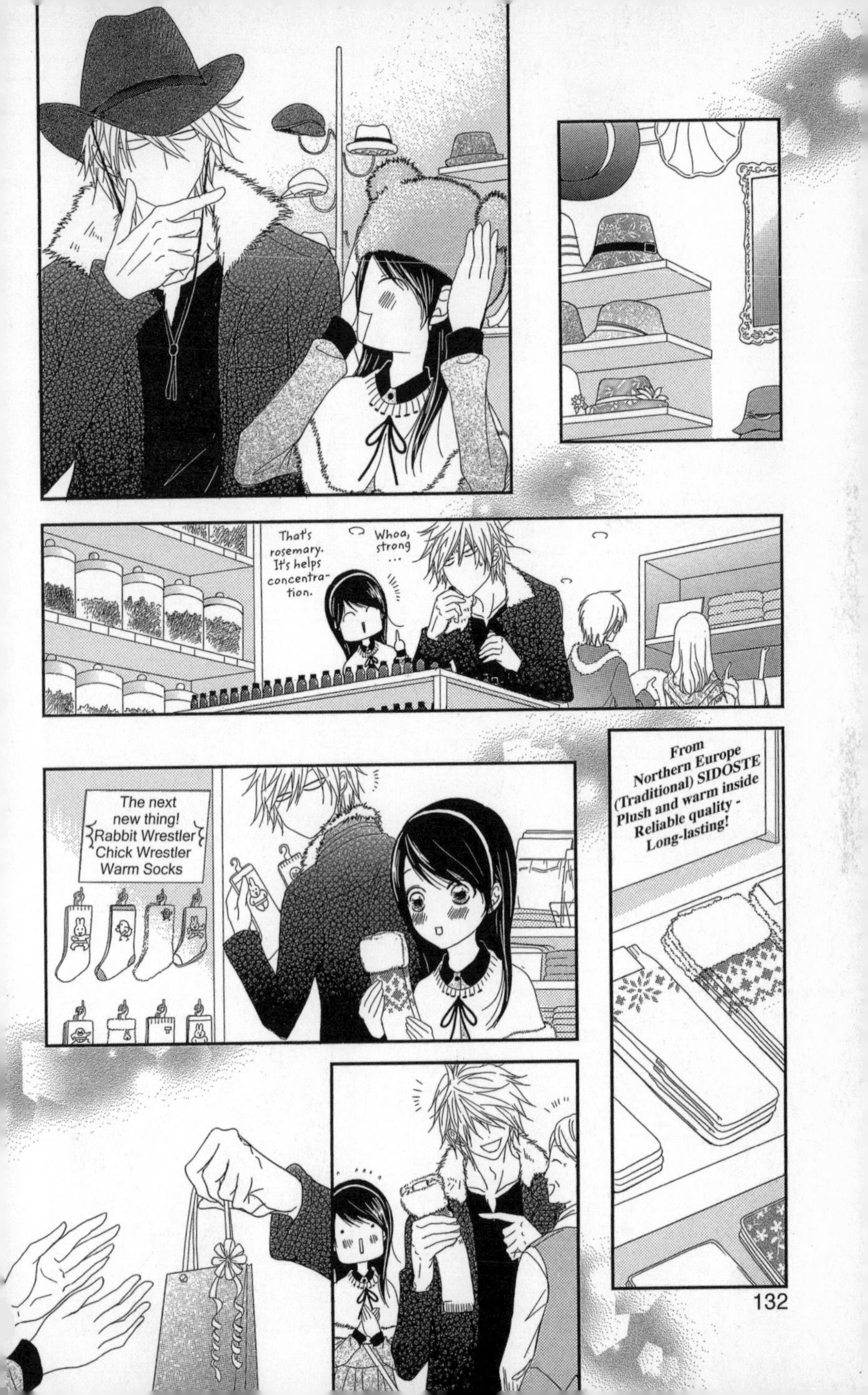

Whoa, strong ...
That's rosemary. It's helps concentration.
From Northern Europe (Traditional) SIDOSTE Plush and warm inside Reliable quality - Long-lasting!
The next new thing! Rabbit Wrestler Chick Wrestler Warm Socks

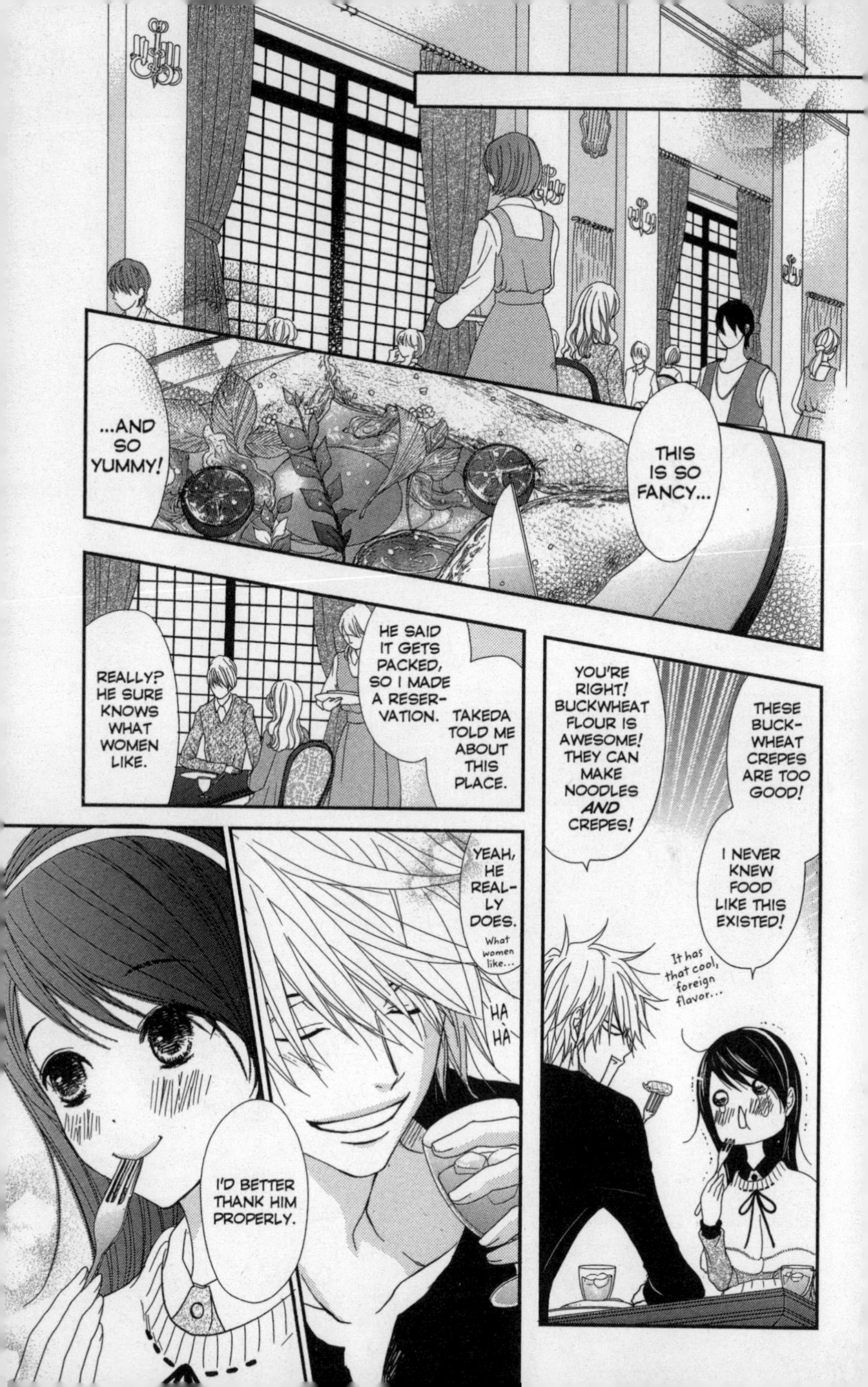
THIS IS SO FANCY...
...AND SO YUMMY!
THESE BUCKWHEAT CREPES ARE TOO GOOD!
YOU'RE RIGHT! BUCKWHEAT FLOUR IS AWESOME! THEY CAN MAKE NOODLES *AND* CREPES!
I NEVER KNEW FOOD LIKE THIS EXISTED!
It has that cool, foreign flavor...
TAKEDA TOLD ME ABOUT THIS PLACE.
HE SAID IT GETS PACKED, SO I MADE A RESERVATION.
REALLY? HE SURE KNOWS WHAT WOMEN LIKE.
YEAH, HE REALLY DOES.
What women like...
HA HA
I'D BETTER THANK HIM PROPERLY.

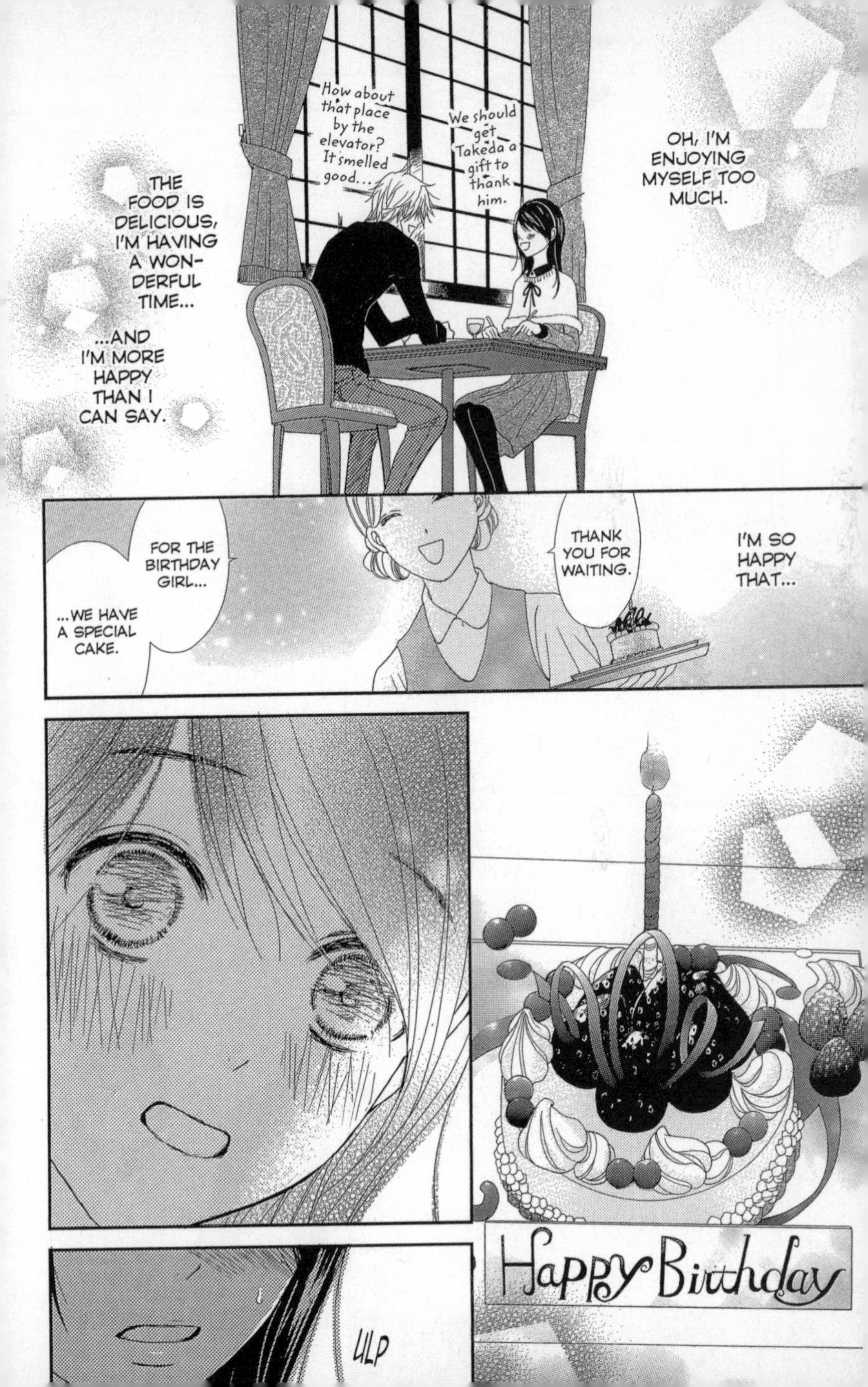
OH, I'M ENJOYING MYSELF TOO MUCH.
We should get Takeda a gift to thank him.
How about that place by the elevator? It smelled good...
THE FOOD IS DELICIOUS, I'M HAVING A WON-DERFUL TIME...
...AND I'M MORE HAPPY THAN I CAN SAY.
I'M SO HAPPY THAT...
THANK YOU FOR WAITING.
FOR THE BIRTHDAY GIRL...
...WE HAVE A SPECIAL CAKE.
Happy Birthday
ULP

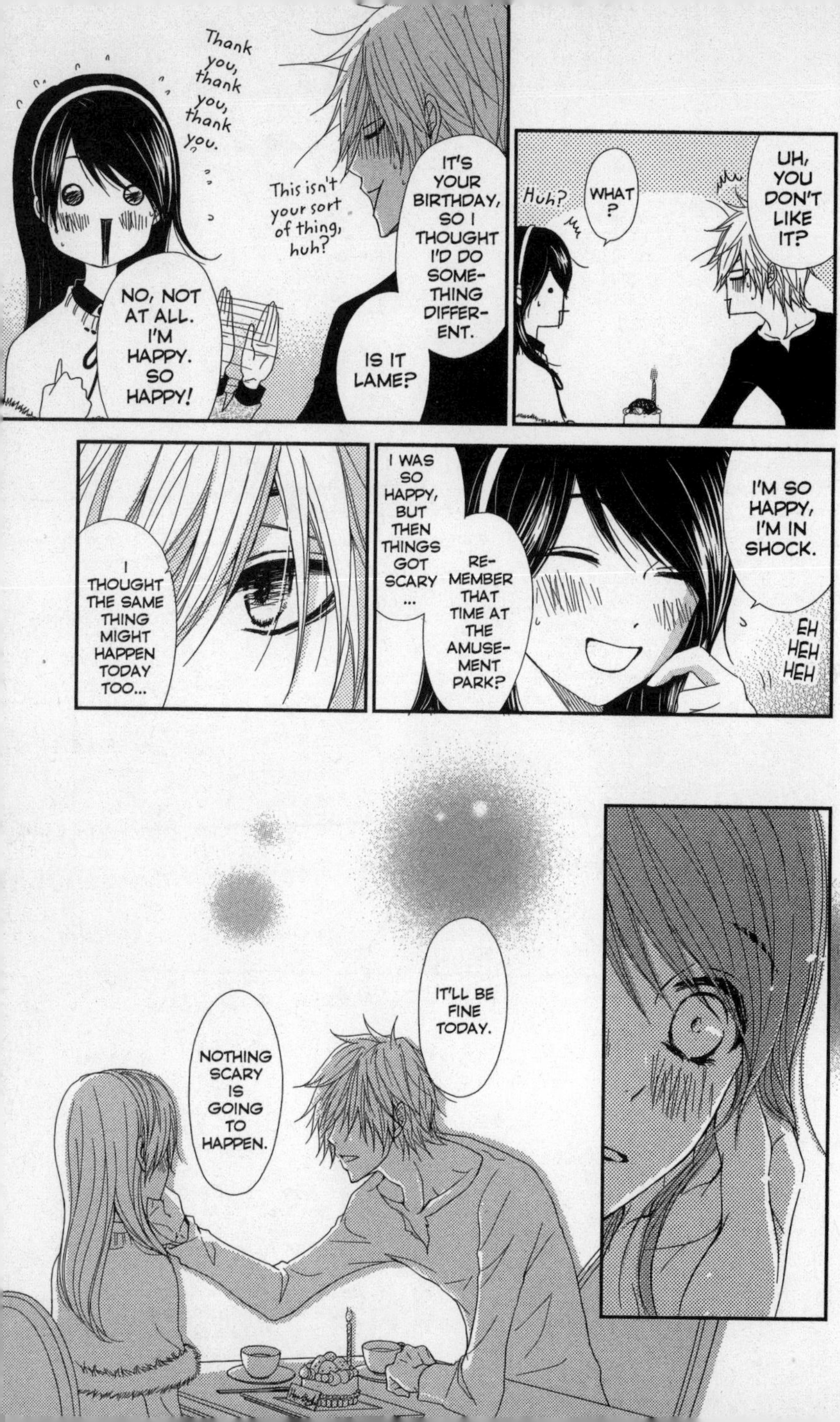
UH, YOU DON'T LIKE IT?
WHAT?
Huh?
IT'S YOUR BIRTHDAY, SO I THOUGHT I'D DO SOME-THING DIFFER-ENT.
IS IT LAME?
This isn't your sort of thing, huh?
Thank you, thank you, thank you.
NO, NOT AT ALL. I'M HAPPY. SO HAPPY!
I'M SO HAPPY, I'M IN SHOCK.
EH HEH HEH
RE-MEMBER THAT TIME AT THE AMUSE-MENT PARK?
I WAS SO HAPPY, BUT THEN THINGS GOT SCARY ...
I THOUGHT THE SAME THING MIGHT HAPPEN TODAY TOO...
IT'LL BE FINE TODAY.
NOTHING SCARY IS GOING TO HAPPEN.

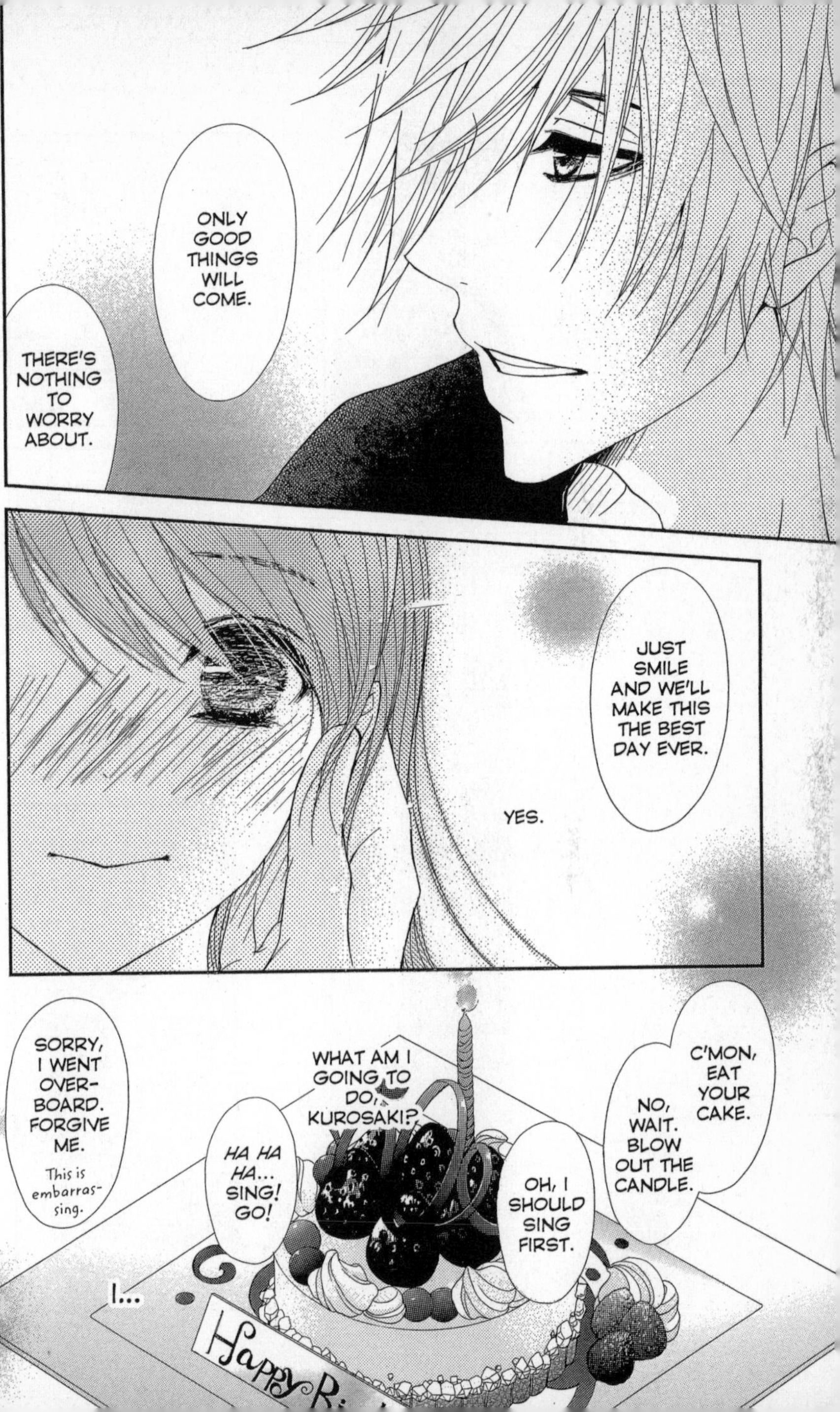
ONLY GOOD THINGS WILL COME.
THERE'S NOTHING TO WORRY ABOUT.
JUST SMILE AND WE'LL MAKE THIS THE BEST DAY EVER.
YES.
C'MON, EAT YOUR CAKE.
NO, WAIT. BLOW OUT THE CANDLE.
OH, I SHOULD SING FIRST.
WHAT AM I GOING TO DO, KUROSAKI!?
HA HA HA... SING! GO!
SORRY, I WENT OVER-BOARD. FORGIVE ME.
This is embarras-sing.
I...
Happy

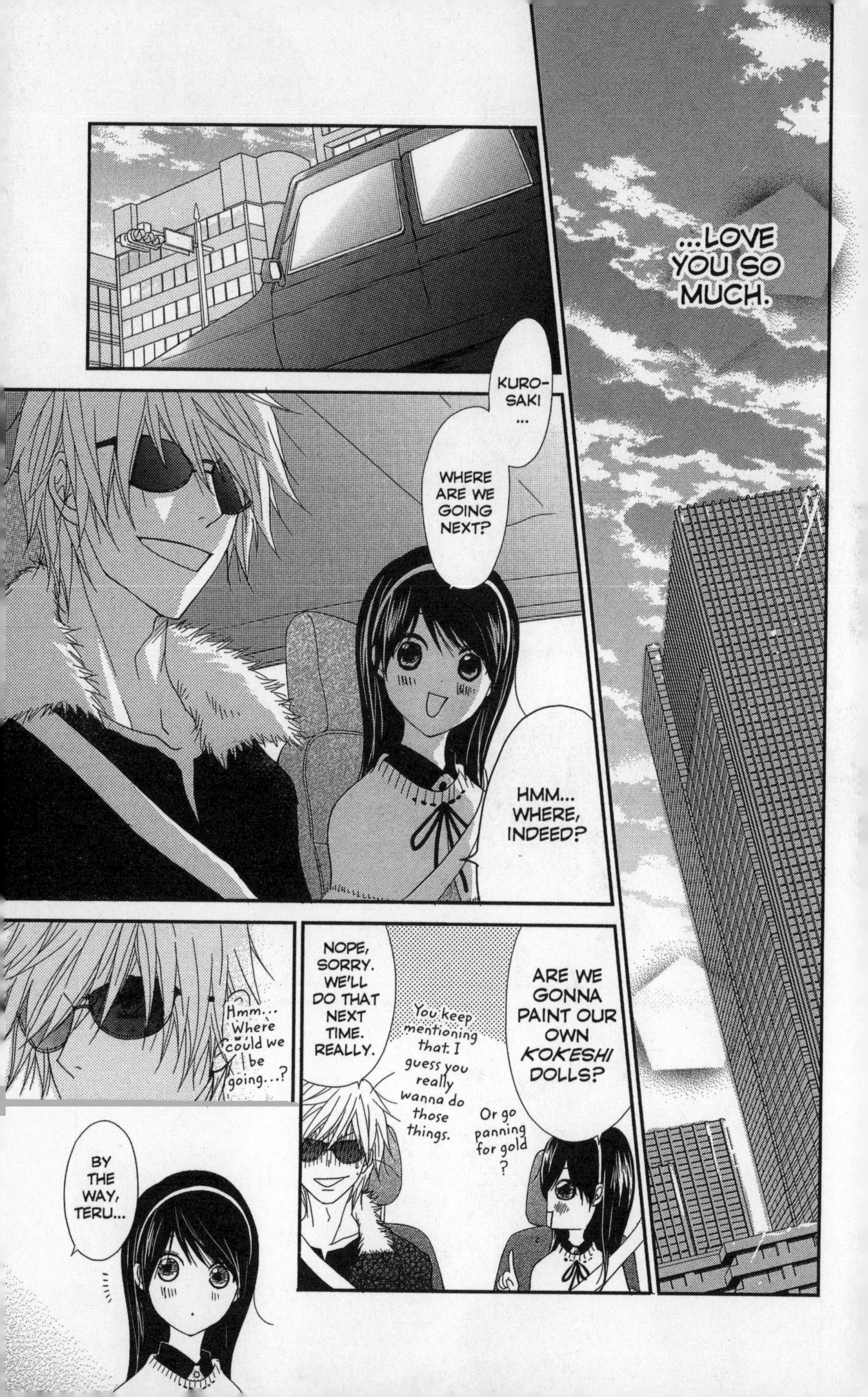
...LOVE YOU SO MUCH.
KURO-SAKI...
WHERE ARE WE GOING NEXT?
HMM... WHERE, INDEED?
ARE WE GONNA PAINT OUR OWN *KOKESHI* DOLLS?
Or go panning for gold?
NOPE, SORRY. WE'LL DO THAT NEXT TIME. REALLY.
You keep mentioning that. I guess you really wanna do those things.
Hmm... Where could we be going...?
BY THE WAY, TERU...

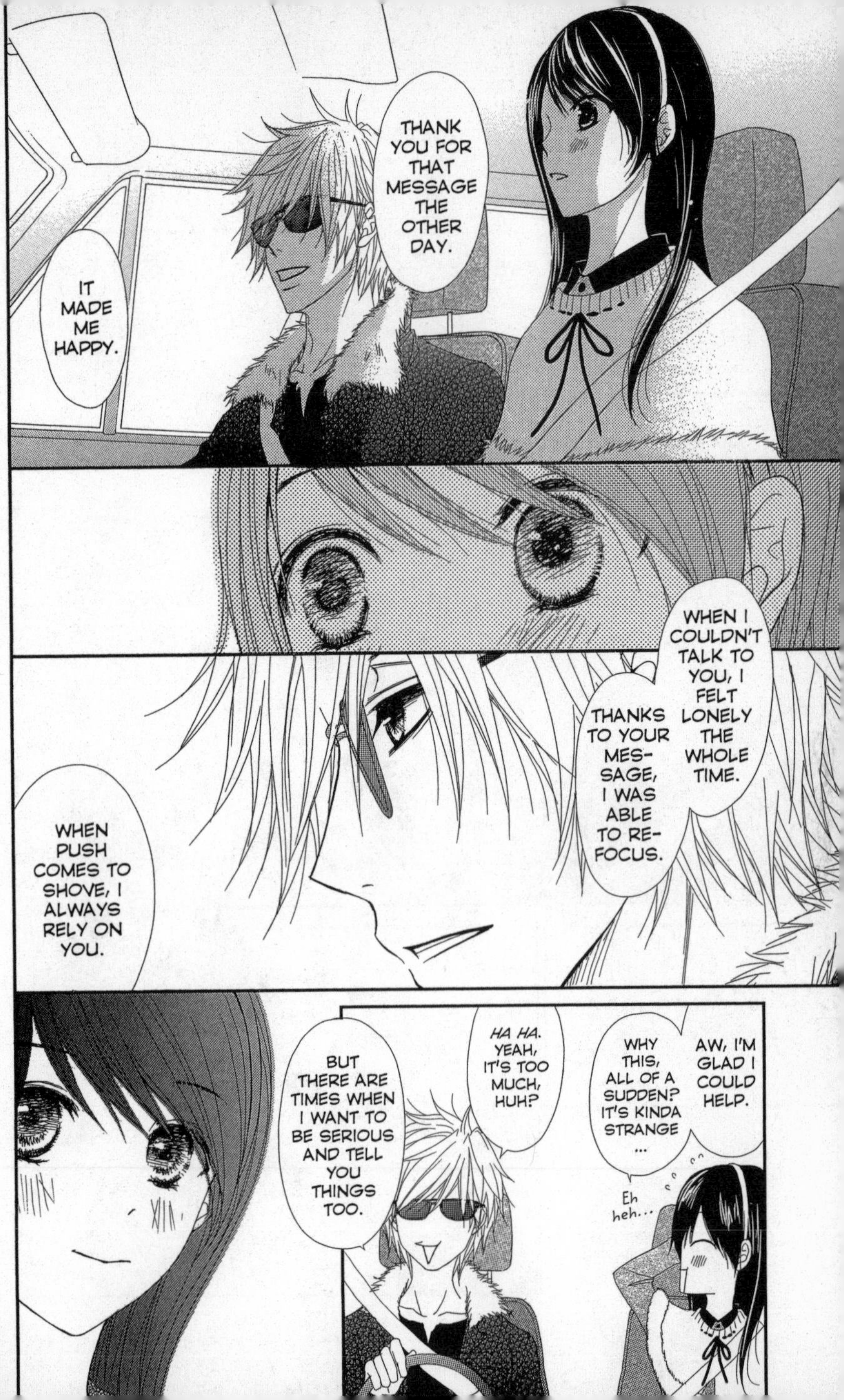
THANK YOU FOR THAT MESSAGE THE OTHER DAY.
IT MADE ME HAPPY.
WHEN I COULDN'T TALK TO YOU, I FELT LONELY THE WHOLE TIME.
THANKS TO YOUR MES-SAGE, I WAS ABLE TO RE-FOCUS.
WHEN PUSH COMES TO SHOVE, I ALWAYS RELY ON YOU.
AW, I'M GLAD I COULD HELP.
WHY THIS, ALL OF A SUDDEN? IT'S KINDA STRANGE ...
Eh heh...
HA HA. YEAH, IT'S TOO MUCH, HUH?
BUT THERE ARE TIMES WHEN I WANT TO BE SERIOUS AND TELL YOU THINGS TOO.

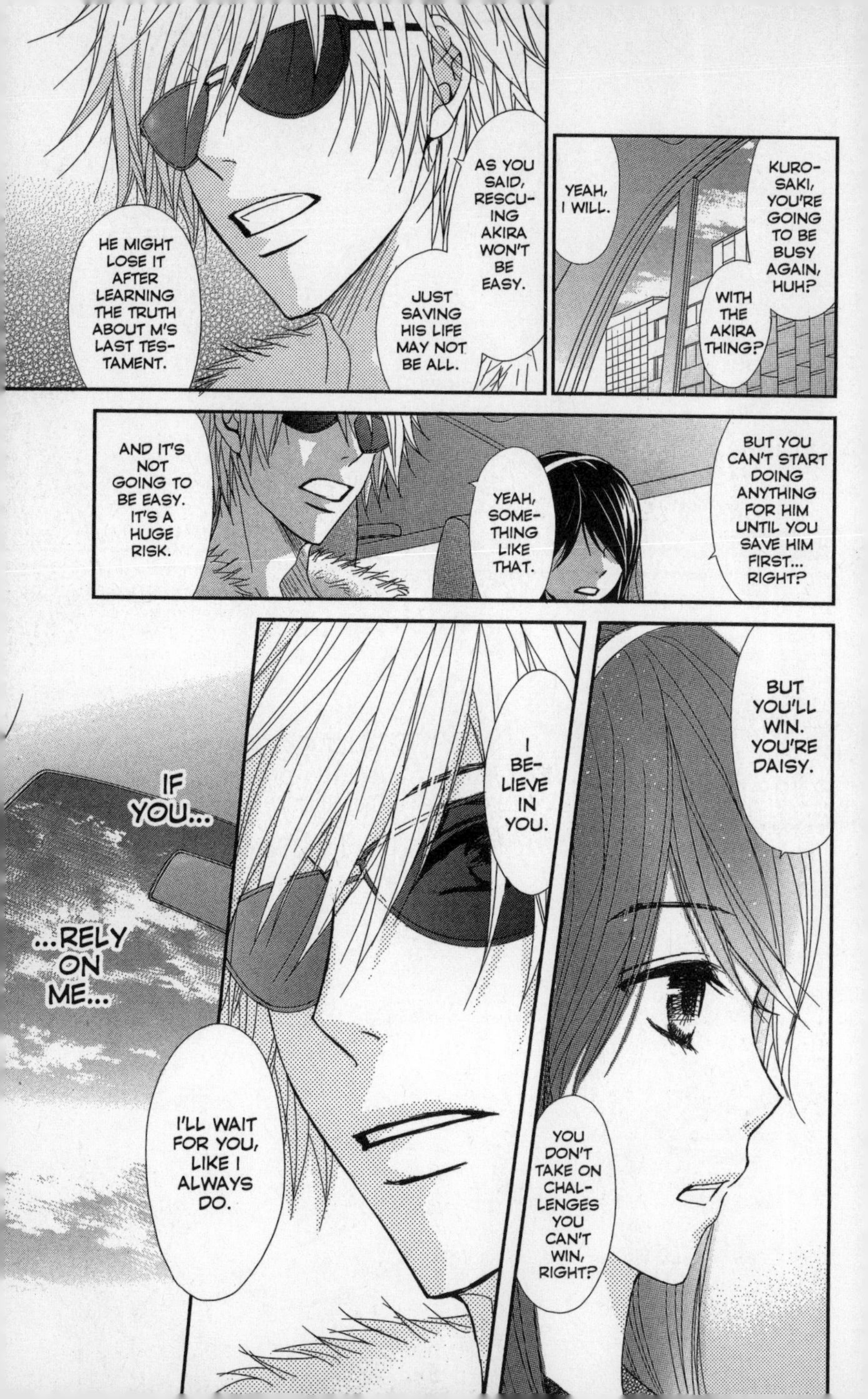
KURO-SAKI, YOU'RE GOING TO BE BUSY AGAIN, HUH?
WITH THE AKIRA THING?
YEAH, I WILL.
AS YOU SAID, RESCU-ING AKIRA WON'T BE EASY.
JUST SAVING HIS LIFE MAY NOT BE ALL.
HE MIGHT LOSE IT AFTER LEARNING THE TRUTH ABOUT M'S LAST TES-TAMENT.
BUT YOU CAN'T START DOING ANYTHING FOR HIM UNTIL YOU SAVE HIM FIRST... RIGHT?
YEAH, SOME-THING LIKE THAT.
AND IT'S NOT GOING TO BE EASY. IT'S A HUGE RISK.
BUT YOU'LL WIN. YOU'RE DAISY.
YOU DON'T TAKE ON CHAL-LENGES YOU CAN'T WIN, RIGHT?
I BE-LIEVE IN YOU.
IF YOU...
...RELY ON ME...
I'LL WAIT FOR YOU, LIKE I ALWAYS DO.

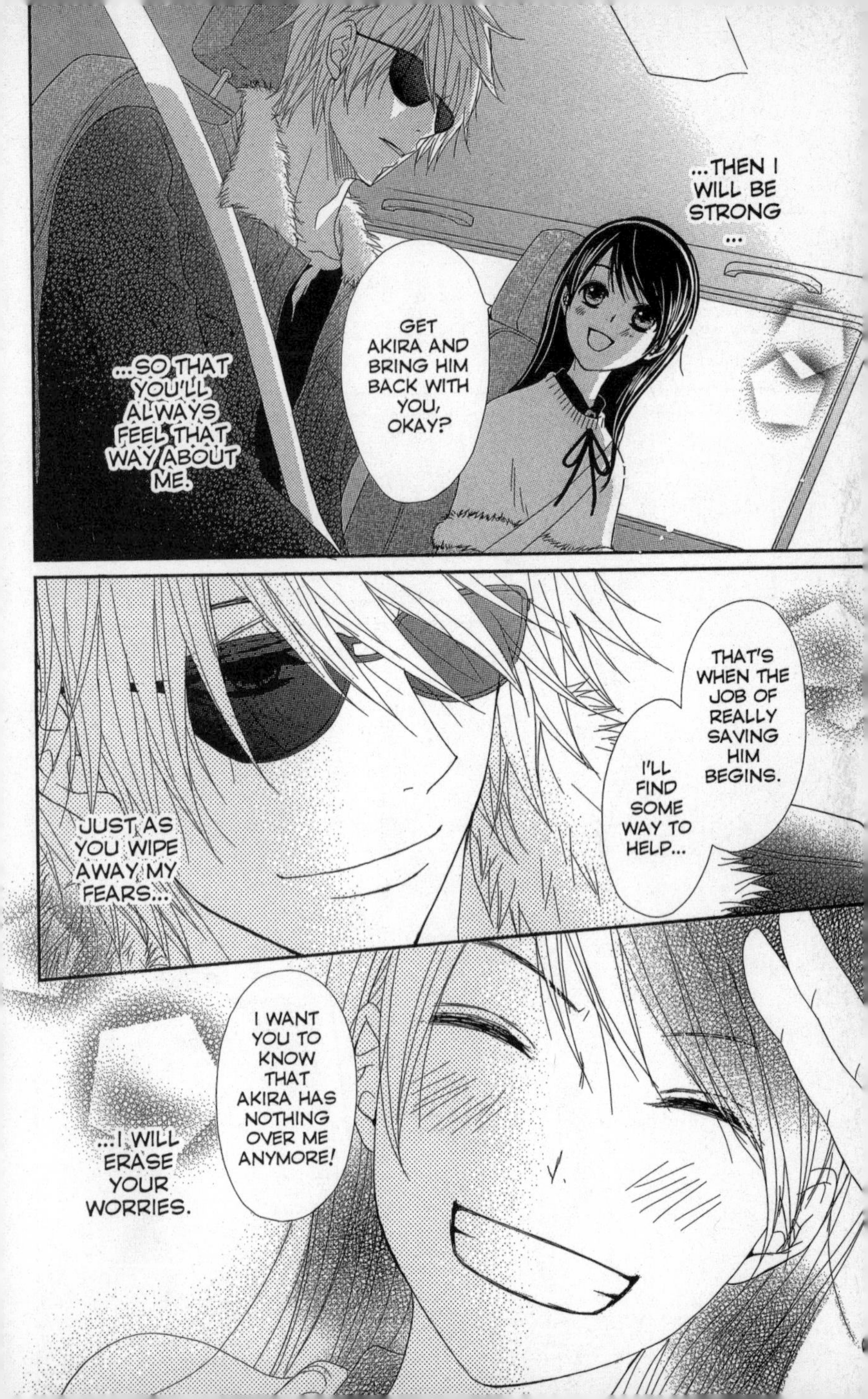
...THEN I WILL BE STRONG...
GET AKIRA AND BRING HIM BACK WITH YOU, OKAY?
...SO THAT YOU'LL ALWAYS FEEL THAT WAY ABOUT ME.
THAT'S WHEN THE JOB OF REALLY SAVING HIM BEGINS.
I'LL FIND SOME WAY TO HELP...
JUST AS YOU WIPE AWAY MY FEARS...
I WANT YOU TO KNOW THAT AKIRA HAS NOTHING OVER ME ANYMORE!
...I WILL ERASE YOUR WORRIES.

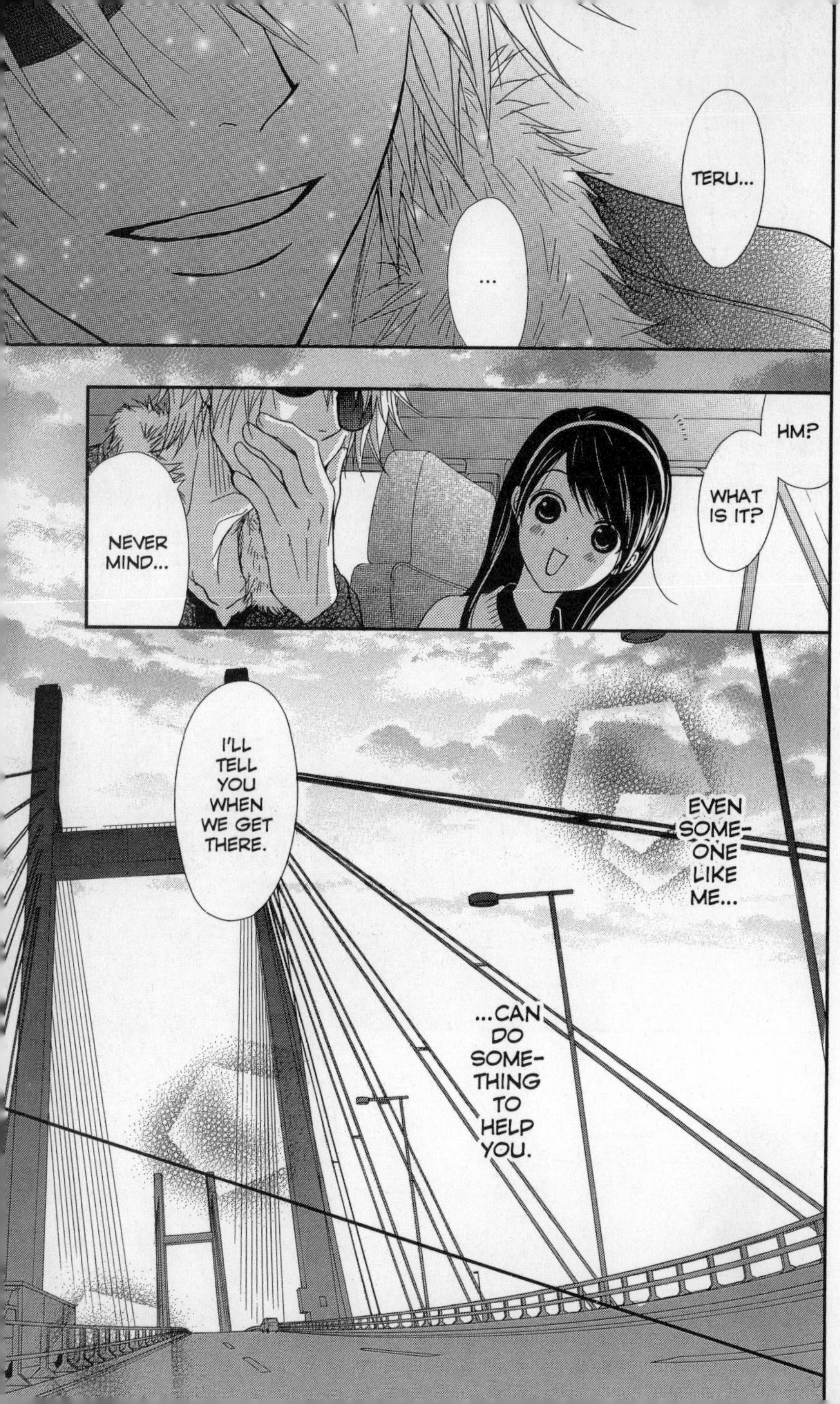
TERU...
...
HM?
WHAT IS IT?
NEVER MIND...
EVEN SOME-ONE LIKE ME...
I'LL TELL YOU WHEN WE GET THERE.
...CAN DO SOME-THING TO HELP YOU.

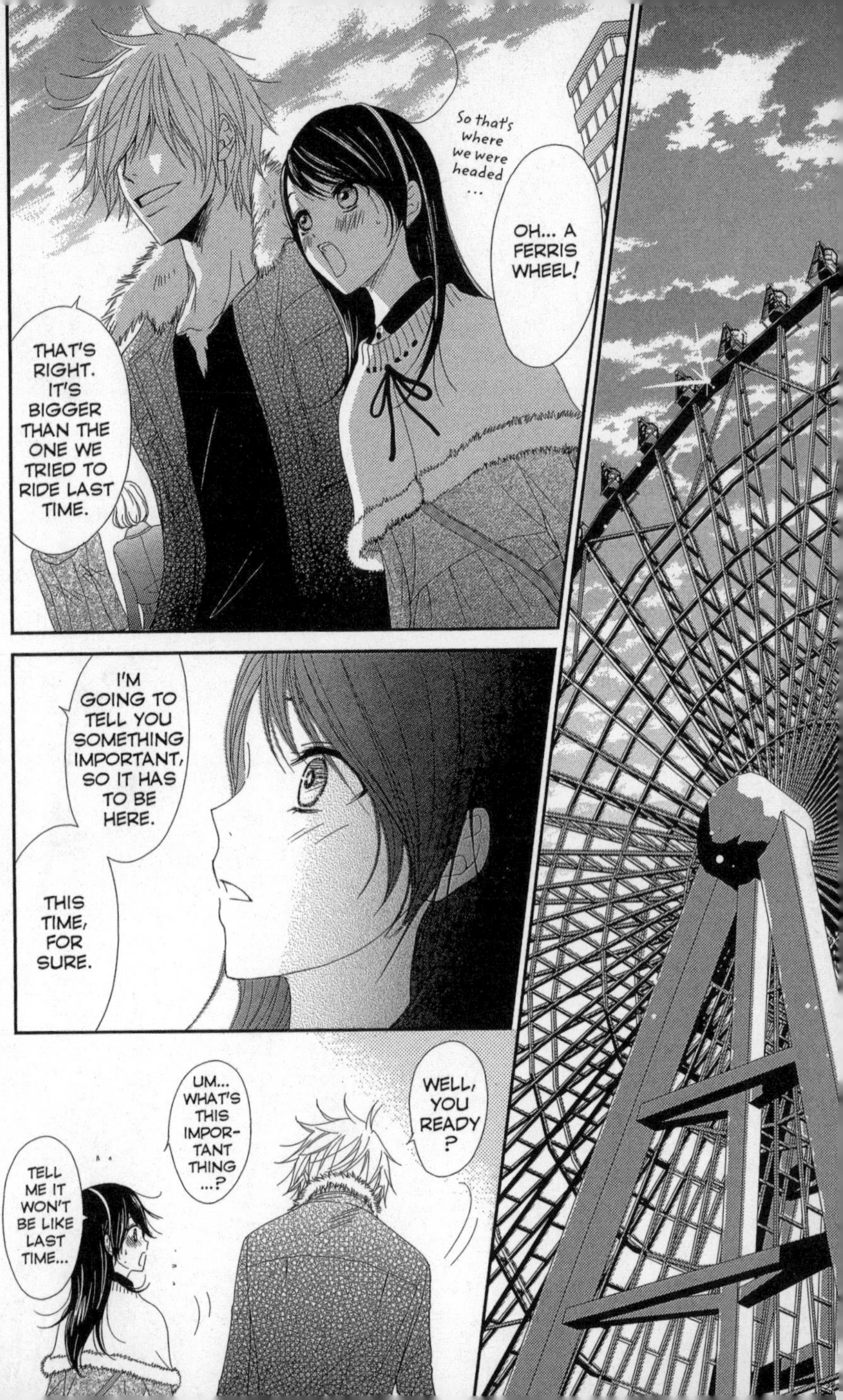
So that's where we were headed...
OH... A FERRIS WHEEL!
THAT'S RIGHT. IT'S BIGGER THAN THE ONE WE TRIED TO RIDE LAST TIME.
I'M GOING TO TELL YOU SOMETHING IMPORTANT, SO IT HAS TO BE HERE.
THIS TIME, FOR SURE.
WELL, YOU READY?
UM... WHAT'S THIS IMPORTANT THING...?
TELL ME IT WON'T BE LIKE LAST TIME...

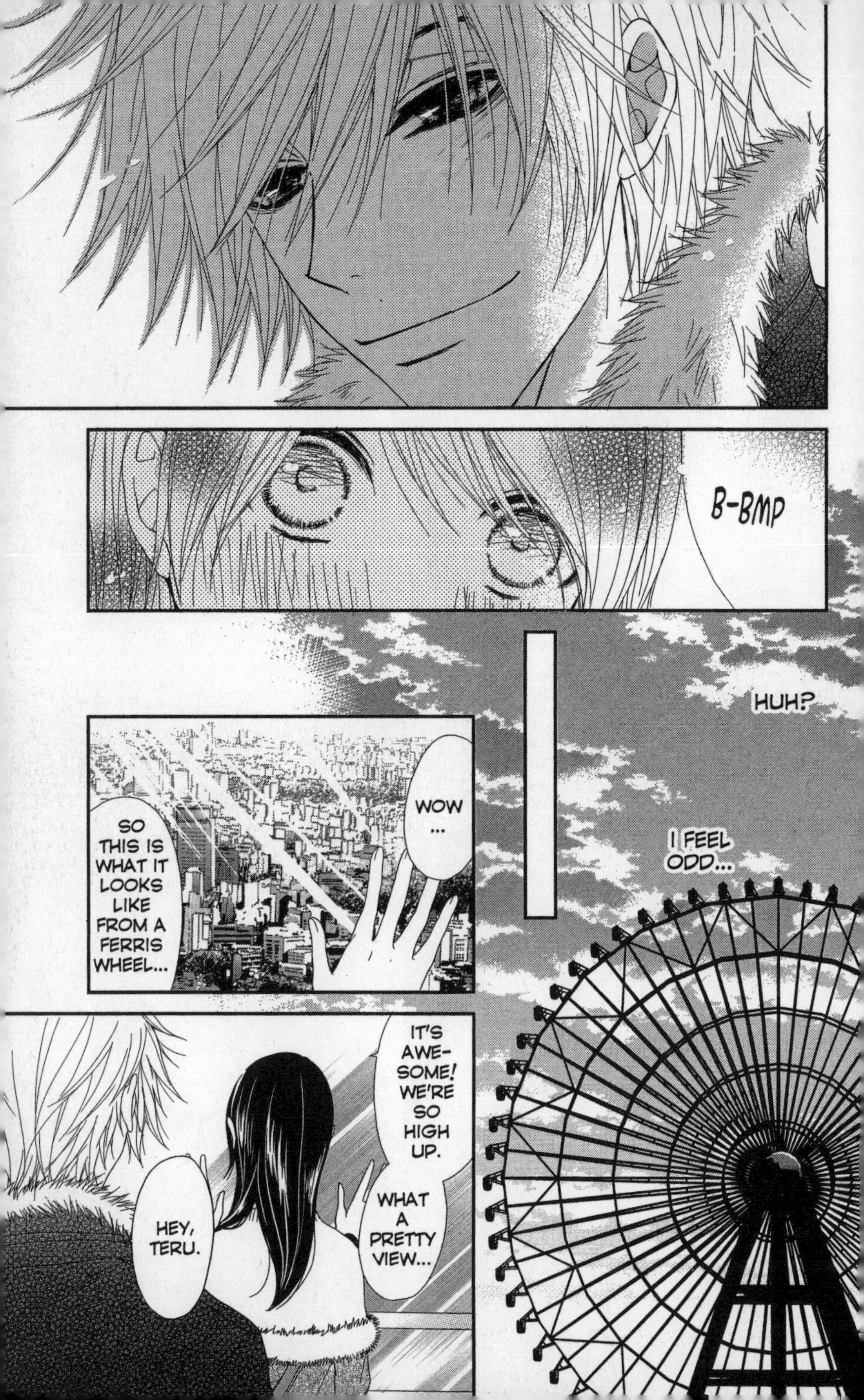
B-BMP
HUH?
I FEEL ODD...
WOW...
SO THIS IS WHAT IT LOOKS LIKE FROM A FERRIS WHEEL...
IT'S AWESOME! WE'RE SO HIGH UP.
WHAT A PRETTY VIEW...
HEY, TERU.

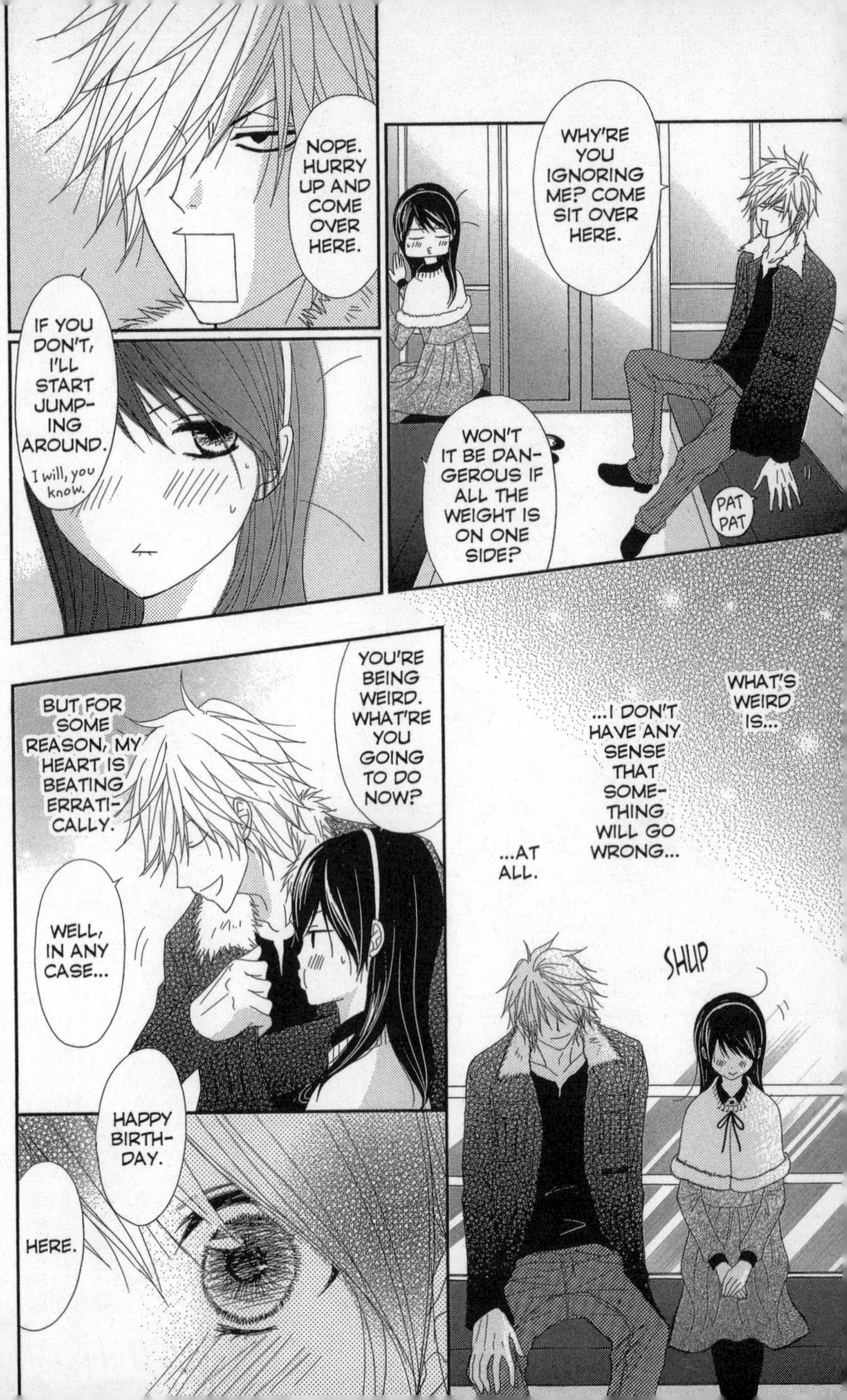
WHY'RE YOU IGNORING ME? COME SIT OVER HERE.
WON'T IT BE DANGEROUS IF ALL THE WEIGHT IS ON ONE SIDE?
PAT PAT
NOPE. HURRY UP AND COME OVER HERE.
IF YOU DON'T, I'LL START JUMPING AROUND.
I will, you know.
WHAT'S WEIRD IS...
...I DON'T HAVE ANY SENSE THAT SOMETHING WILL GO WRONG...
...AT ALL.
SHUP
YOU'RE BEING WEIRD. WHAT'RE YOU GOING TO DO NOW?
BUT FOR SOME REASON, MY HEART IS BEATING ERRATICALLY.
WELL, IN ANY CASE...
HAPPY BIRTHDAY.
HERE.

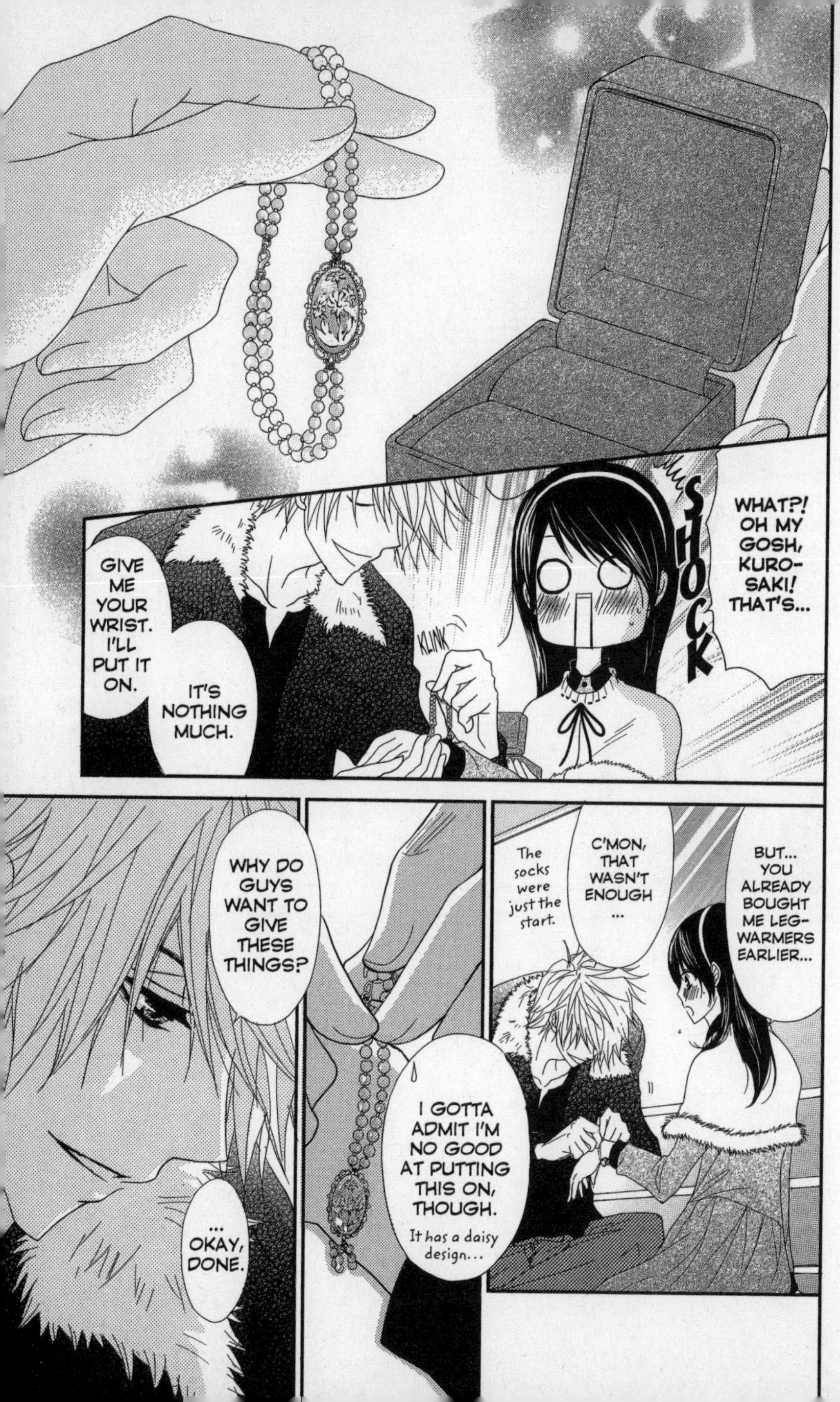
WHAT?! OH MY GOSH, KURO-SAKI! THAT'S...
SHOCK
KLINK
IT'S NOTHING MUCH.
GIVE ME YOUR WRIST. I'LL PUT IT ON.
BUT... YOU ALREADY BOUGHT ME LEG-WARMERS EARLIER...
C'MON, THAT WASN'T ENOUGH ...
The socks were just the start.
WHY DO GUYS WANT TO GIVE THESE THINGS?
I GOTTA ADMIT I'M NO GOOD AT PUTTING THIS ON, THOUGH.
It has a daisy design...
... OKAY, DONE.

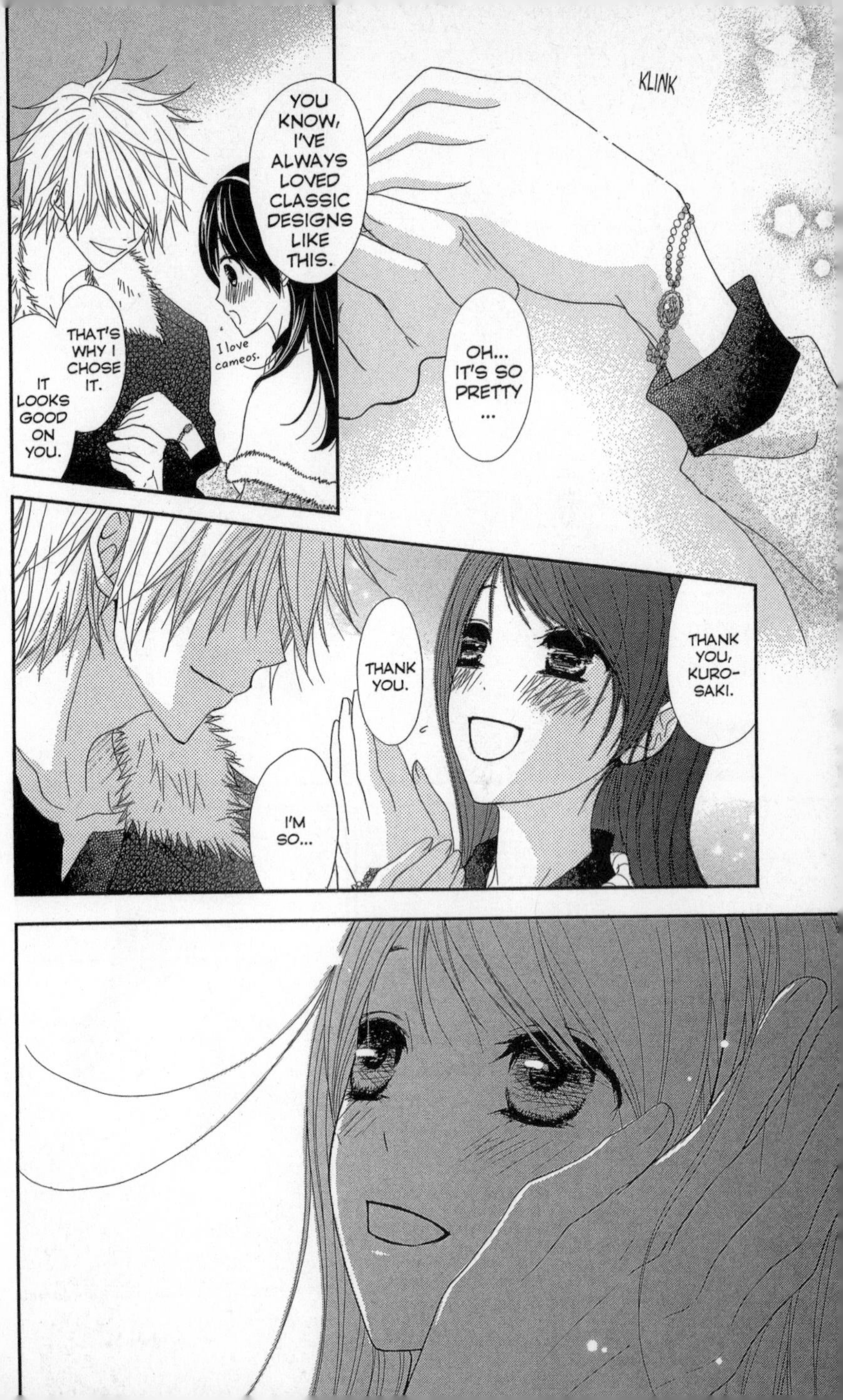
KLINK
OH... IT'S SO PRETTY...
YOU KNOW, I'VE ALWAYS LOVED CLASSIC DESIGNS LIKE THIS.
I love cameos.
THAT'S WHY I CHOSE IT.
IT LOOKS GOOD ON YOU.
THANK YOU, KURO-SAKI.
THANK YOU.
I'M SO...

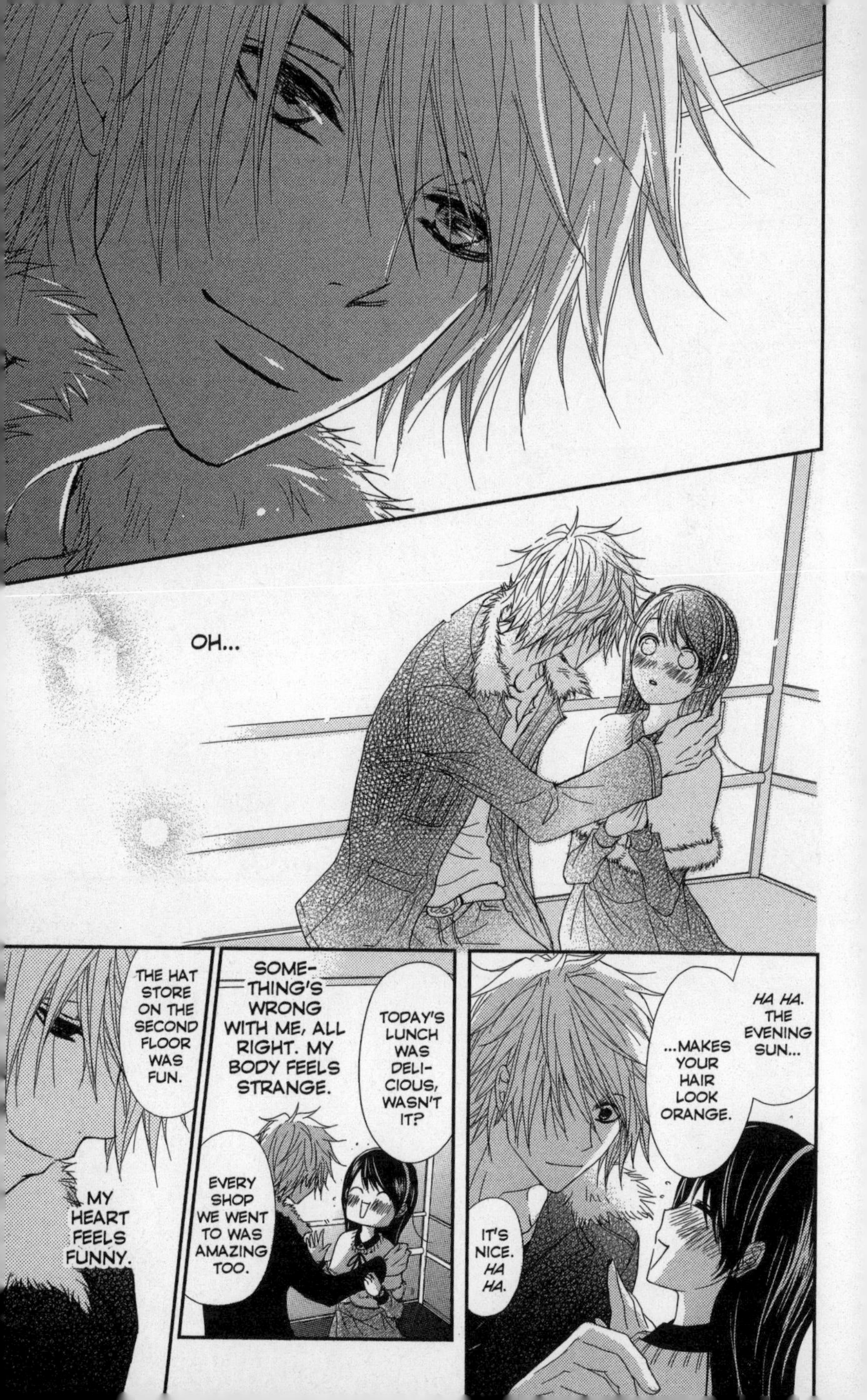
OH...
HA HA. THE EVENING SUN...
...MAKES YOUR HAIR LOOK ORANGE.
IT'S NICE. *HA HA.*
TODAY'S LUNCH WAS DELICIOUS, WASN'T IT?
SOMETHING'S WRONG WITH ME, ALL RIGHT. MY BODY FEELS STRANGE.
EVERY SHOP WE WENT TO WAS AMAZING TOO.
THE HAT STORE ON THE SECOND FLOOR WAS FUN.
MY HEART FEELS FUNNY.

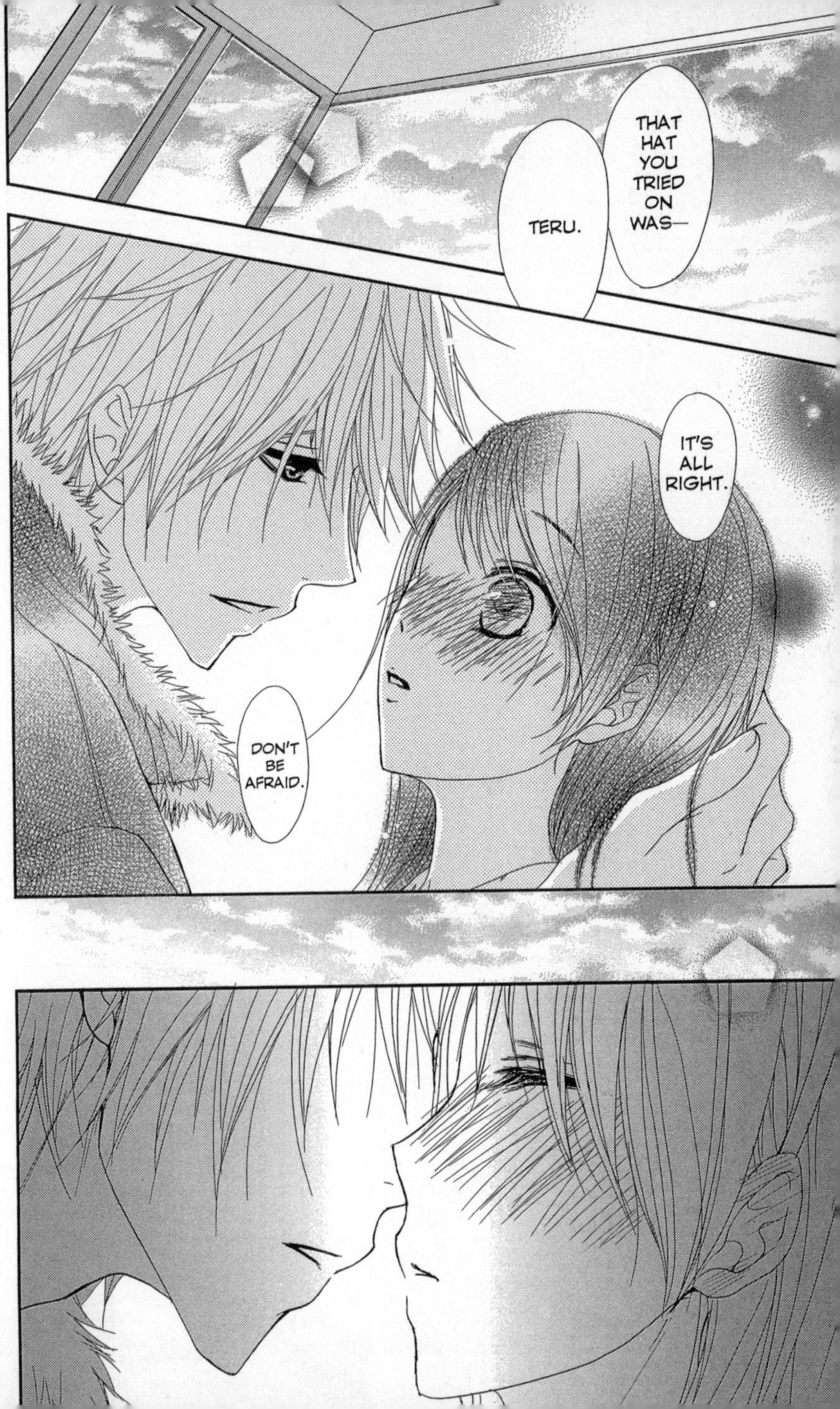
THAT HAT YOU TRIED ON WAS—
TERU.
IT'S ALL RIGHT.
DON'T BE AFRAID.

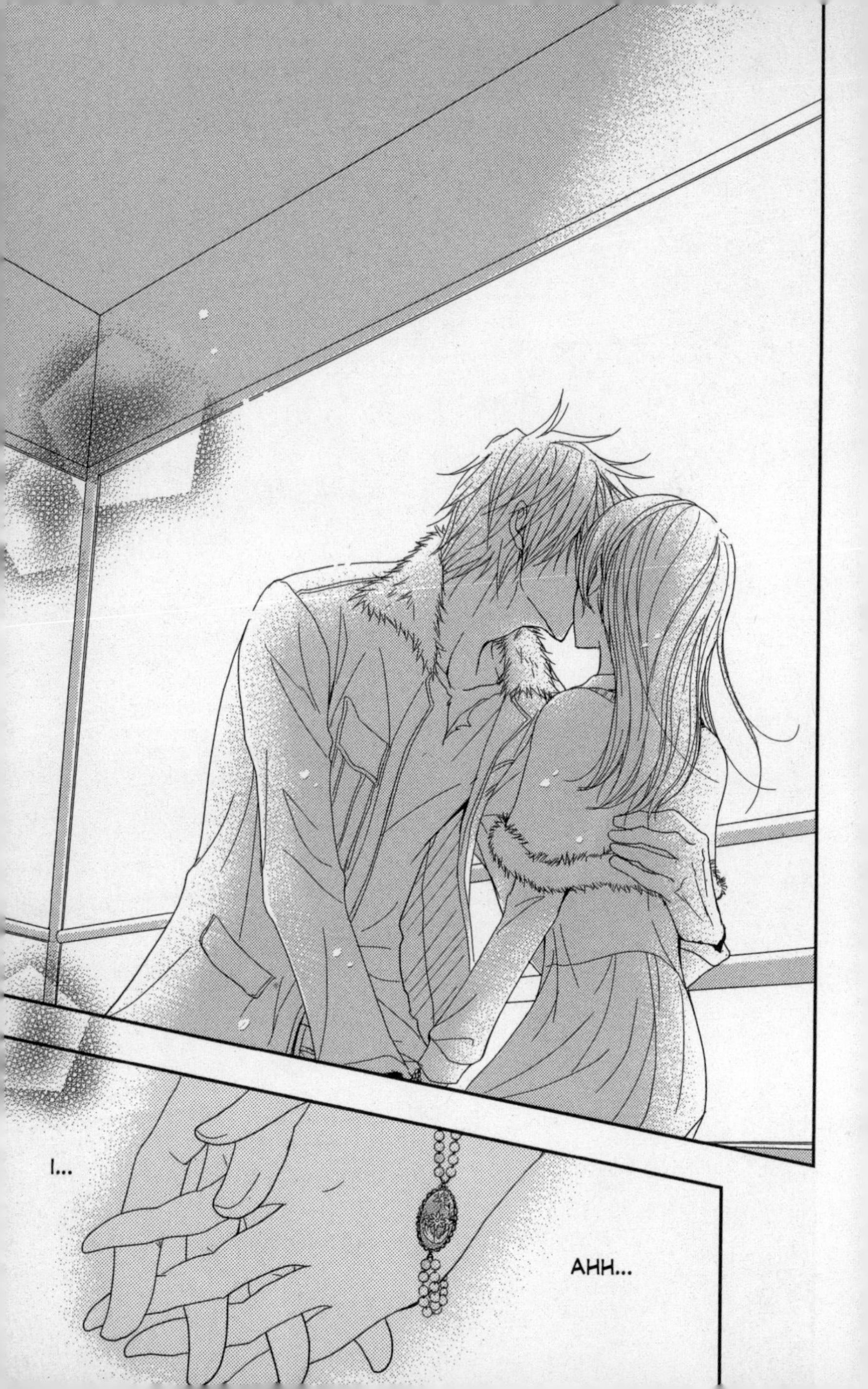
AHH...
I...

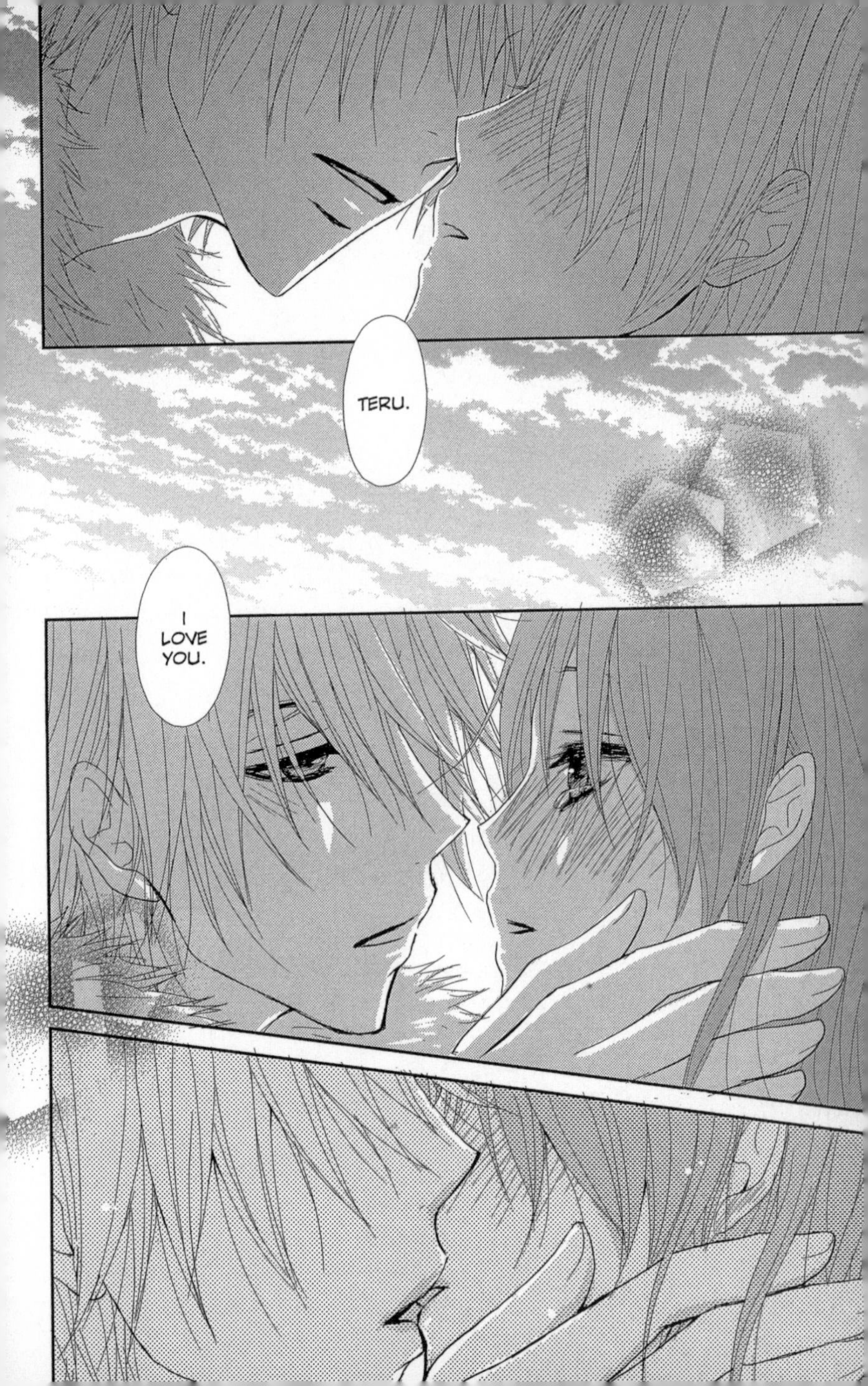
TERU.
I LOVE YOU.

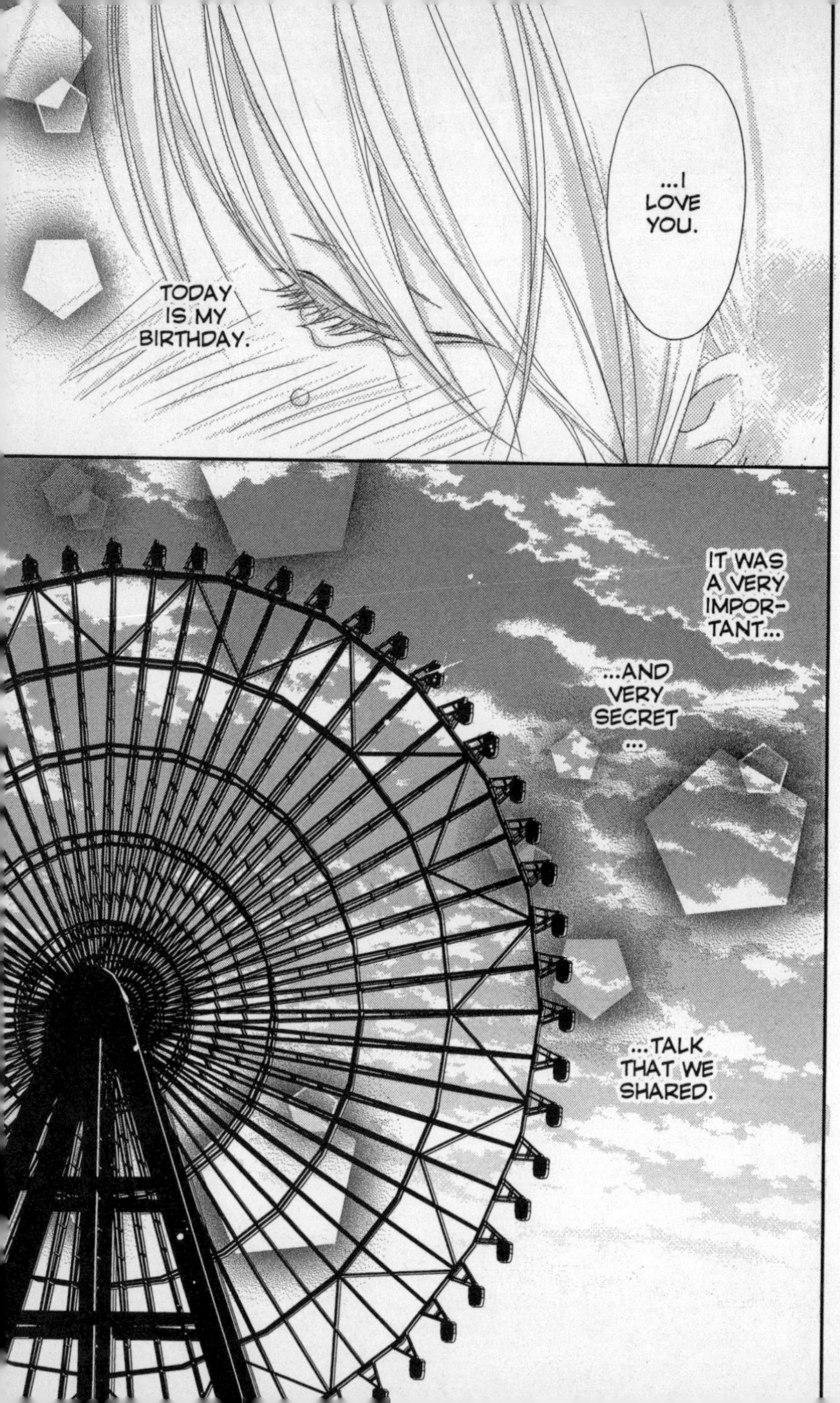
...I LOVE YOU.
TODAY IS MY BIRTHDAY.
IT WAS A VERY IMPORTANT...
...AND VERY SECRET...
...TALK THAT WE SHARED.

THE 9TH ONE OF THIS SUPER POPULAR SECTION ♥

THE BEST OF ☆ THE SECRET SCHOOL CUSTODIAN OFFICE ♥

THERE IS A *DENGEKI DAISY* FAN SEGMENT BOLDLY FEATURED IN *BETSUCOMI* THAT IS APTLY TITLED, "THE SECRET SCHOOL CUSTODIAN OFFICE ♥"!

WITH ARBITRARY EYES, WE EXAMINED ALL THE GREAT WORK FEATURED THERE AND PICKED THE "BEST" AMONG THEM THAT WE WANTED TO LEAVE FOR POSTERITY!

THE "BEST OF" FOR VOLUME 14 IS... "THEATER DAISY—FLOWER COMICS THEATER GUIDE"

HERE, WE PRESENT THE ANNOUNCEMENT OF VOLUME 13 THAT RAN IN THE FEBRUARY 2013 ISSUE OF *BETSUCOMI* AS WELL AS POSTCARDS FROM OUR READERS! ♪

THEATER DAISY-FLOWER COMICS THEATER GUIDE

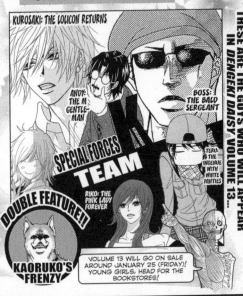

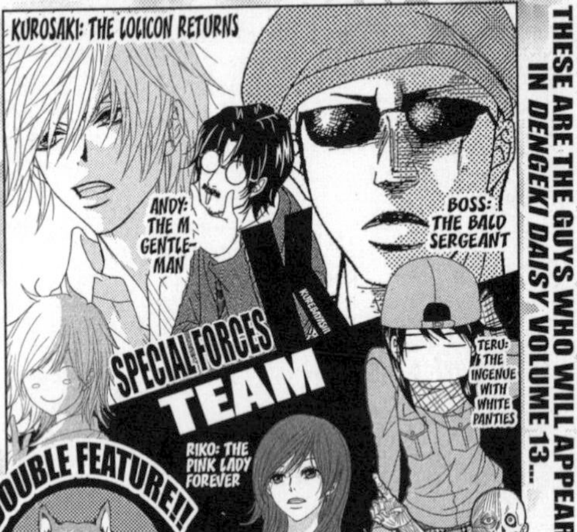
KUROSAKI: THE LOLICON RETURNS
ANDY: THE M GENTLEMAN
BOSS: THE BALD SERGEANT
SPECIAL FORCES TEAM
TERU: THE INGENUE WITH WHITE PANTIES
RIKO: THE PINK LADY FOREVER
DOUBLE FEATURE!!
KAORUKO'S FRENZY
VOLUME 13 WILL GO ON SALE AROUND JANUARY 25 (FRIDAY)! YOUNG GIRLS, HEAD FOR THE BOOKSTORES!
THESE ARE THE GUYS WHO WILL APPEAR IN DENGEKI DAISY VOLUME 13...

ILLUSTRATION CORNER!

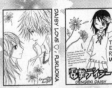

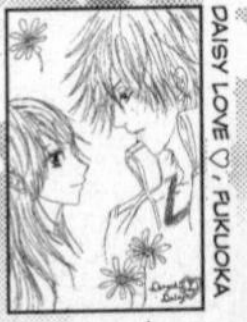
DAISY LOVE ♡, FUKUOKA

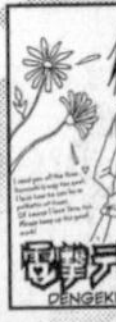
TERU
DENGEKI DAISY
AYAKA, TOKYO

MAIL CORNER!

THIS MONTH, WE HAD A LOT OF PEOPLE WHO COULDN'T WAIT FOR FLOWER COMICS TO GO ON SALE! PLEASE BE WARY OF BECOMING ADDICTED TO *DAISY*. ♪

HOW DO YOU DO! I'M A HUGE FAN OF *DENGEKI DAISY*! I HAVE EVERY VOLUME OF YOUR COMICS! I WANT TO READ VOLUME 13 SOON! I'LL ALWAYS BE ROOTING FOR YOU.
-CHIRURU, HOKKAIDO

AS I KEPT WAITING AND WAITING—IS IT OUT YET? IS IT OUT YET?—FOR THE COMICS TO GO ON SALE, IT WASN'T AUTUMN ANYMORE; IT WAS THE START OF THE NEW YEAR! BUT THAT'S OKAY. I'M SAVING UP MY ANTICIPATION. I'LL BE GRATEFUL BECAUSE IT'LL BE LIKE A NEW YEAR'S PRESENT.
- KYAKKYUUFUFU, TOKYO

I'M A STUDENT STUDYING FOR ENTRANCE EXAMS, SO I'VE SWORN OFF MANGA FOR A YEAR. BUT *DENGEKI DAISY* IS DIFFERENT—I NEED IT FOR LIFE SUPPORT—SO I'VE MADE A SPECIAL EXCEPTION AND CONTINUE TO READ IT. PLEASE KEEP UP THE GOOD WORK.
- CAT-TYPE EMPLOYEE, YAMAGATA

JUDGES' COMMENTS

■ I THINK YELLOW WOULD MATCH THE IMAGE OF "THE LOLICON RETURNS." HE DOES HAVE BLEACHED HAIR, AFTER ALL. BLACK HAS THE FEEL OF A COOL CHARACTER, SO I DON'T WANT KUROSAKI TO HAVE THAT COLOR.
(HEAD JUDGE: KYOUSUKE MOTOMI SENSEI)

■ I WANT TO WATCH THE OTHER HALF OF THE DOUBLE BILL, "KAORUKO'S FRENZY," SO BADLY THAT I CAN'T STAND IT. I'M SURE THERE'S A SCENE THAT WILL MOVE ME TO TEARS.
(JUDGE: *DAISY* EDITOR)

BETSUCOMI, THE MAGAZINE THAT SERIALIZES *DAISY*, GOES ON SALE EVERY MONTH AROUND THE 13TH! PLEASE LOOK FOR IT IF YOU WANT TO READ "THE SECRET SCHOOL CUSTODIAN OFFICE"! ♥

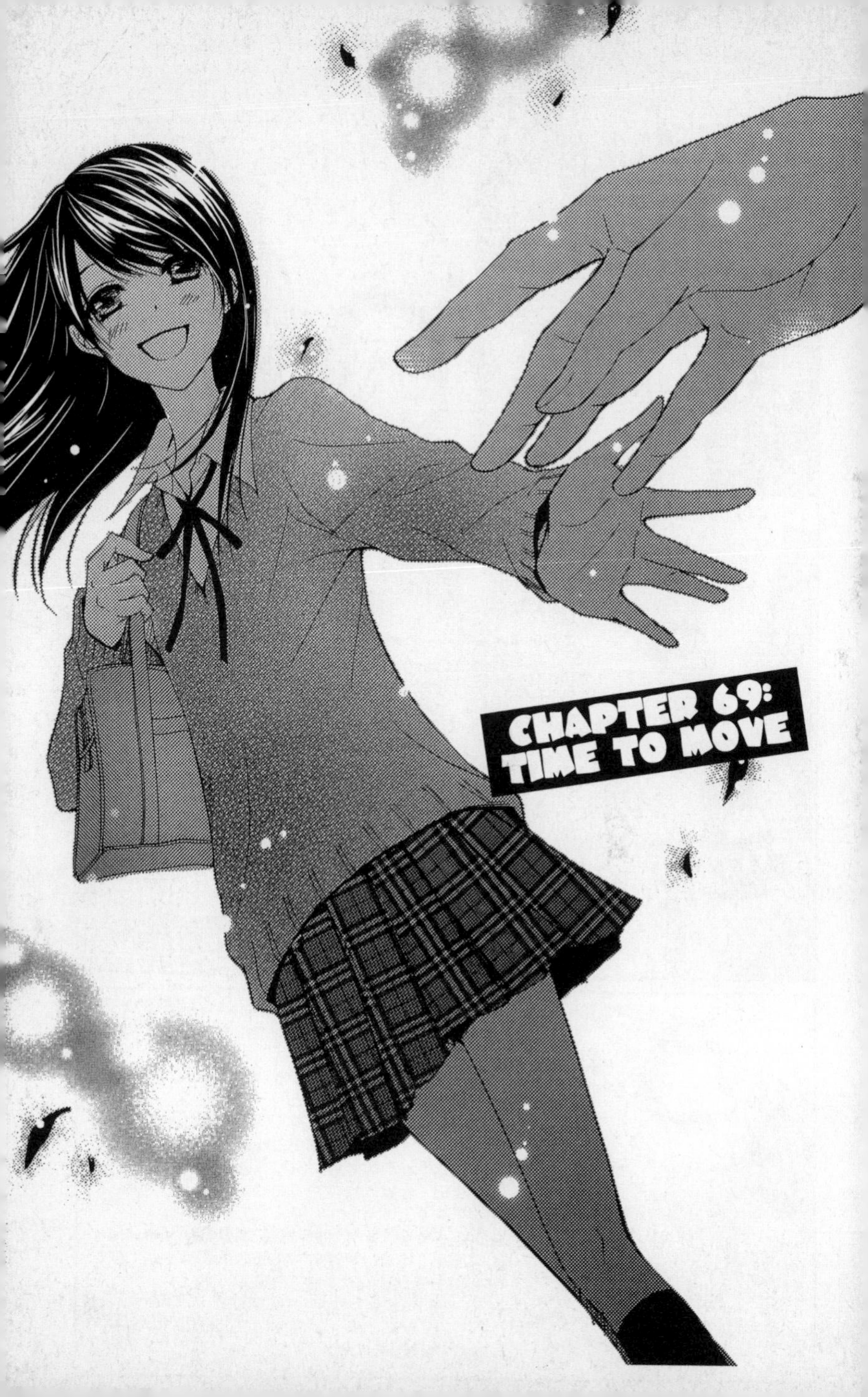
CHAPTER 69:
TIME TO MOVE

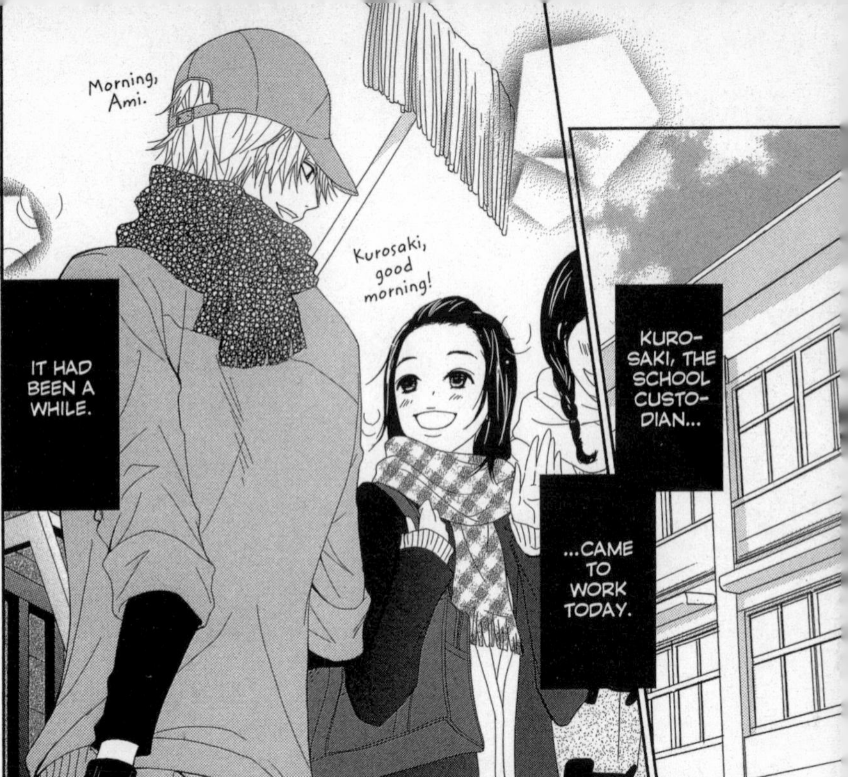
KURO-SAKI, THE SCHOOL CUSTO-DIAN...
...CAME TO WORK TODAY.
Kurosaki, good morning!
Morning, Ami.
IT HAD BEEN A WHILE.

I STILL FEEL AWKWARD ABOUT WHAT WENT ON IN CHAPTER 68, SO I DON'T WANT TO LOOK BACK ON IT TOO MUCH...
THIS COMING FROM A SHOJO MANGA AUTHOR...
SORRY ABOUT THAT...
JUST FOR THE RECORD, IF I DON'T COUNT MOUTH-TO-MOUTH RESUSCITATION AND WHAT HAPPENED WITH AKIRA, THAT WAS THE FIRST KISS SCENE IN SIX YEARS FOR THIS AUTHOR.

THE OPENING DRAWINGS FOR CHAPTERS 66 AND 67 USED TAROT CARDS AS THEIR MOTIF. THE CARDS WERE "THE HERMIT" AND "THE WHEEL OF FORTUNE." I FELT THAT THE STORY IN THOSE CHAPTERS AND THE MEANING OF CARDS SHARED A SLIGHT CONNECTION.

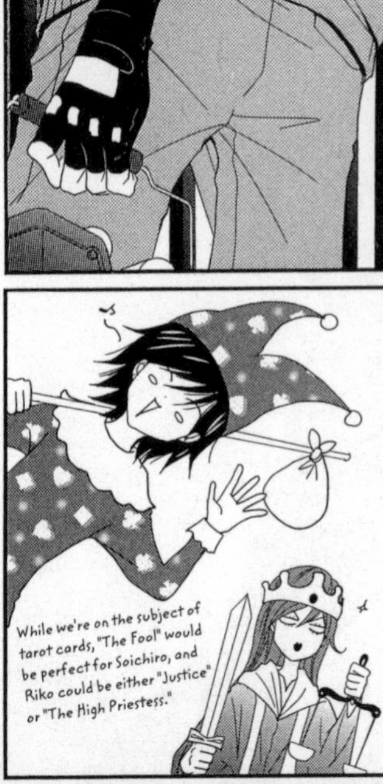
While we're on the subject of tarot cards, "The Fool" would be perfect for Soichiro, and Riko could be either "Justice" or "The High Priestess."

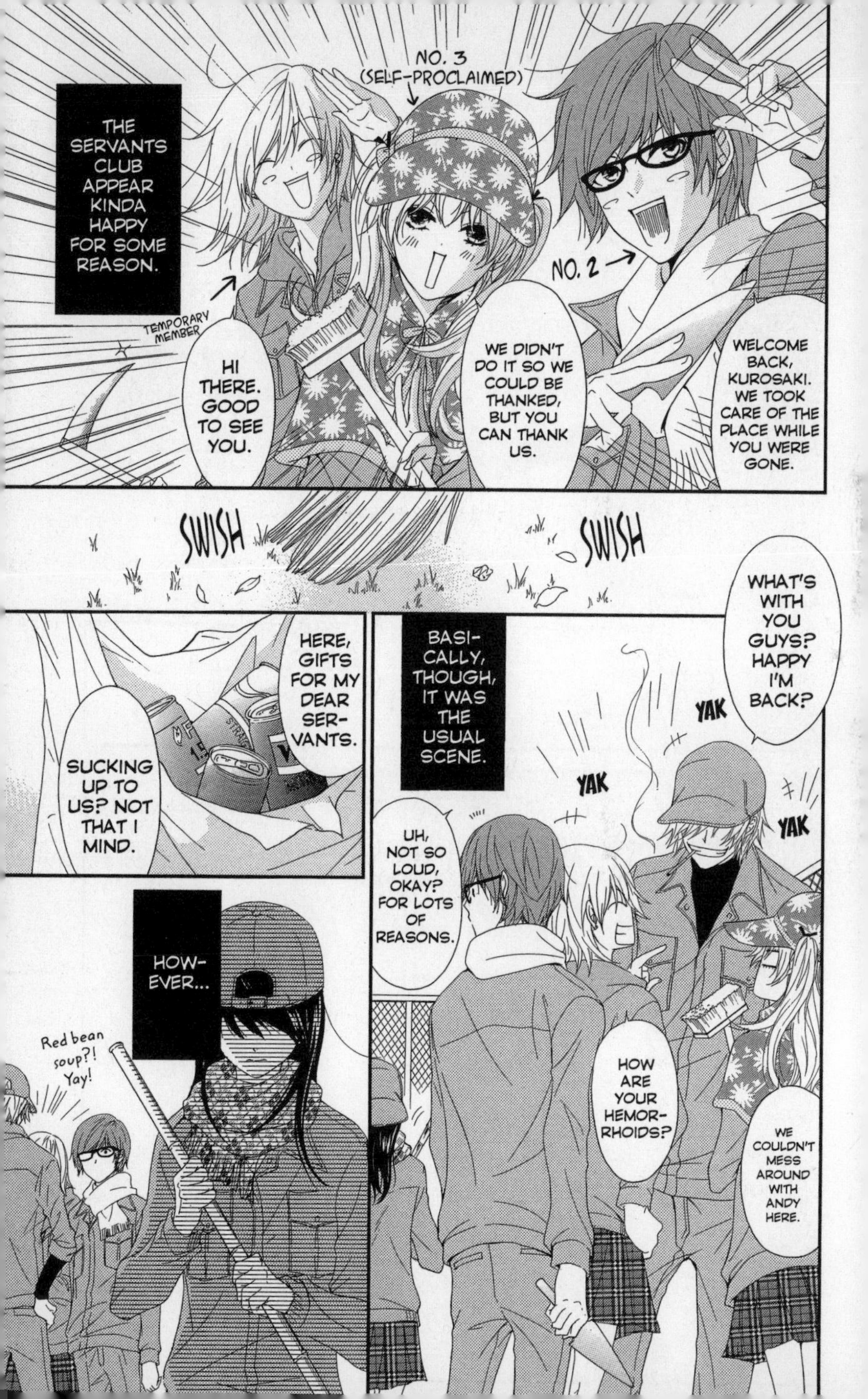
NO. 3 (SELF-PROCLAIMED)
THE SERVANTS CLUB APPEAR KINDA HAPPY FOR SOME REASON.
NO. 2
WELCOME BACK, KUROSAKI. WE TOOK CARE OF THE PLACE WHILE YOU WERE GONE.
WE DIDN'T DO IT SO WE COULD BE THANKED, BUT YOU CAN THANK US.
TEMPORARY MEMBER
HI THERE. GOOD TO SEE YOU.
SWISH
SWISH
WHAT'S WITH YOU GUYS? HAPPY I'M BACK?
BASICALLY, THOUGH, IT WAS THE USUAL SCENE.
YAK
YAK
YAK
UH, NOT SO LOUD, OKAY? FOR LOTS OF REASONS.
HOW ARE YOUR HEMORRHOIDS?
WE COULDN'T MESS AROUND WITH ANDY HERE.
HERE, GIFTS FOR MY DEAR SERVANTS.
SUCKING UP TO US? NOT THAT I MIND.
HOWEVER...
Red bean soup?! Yay!

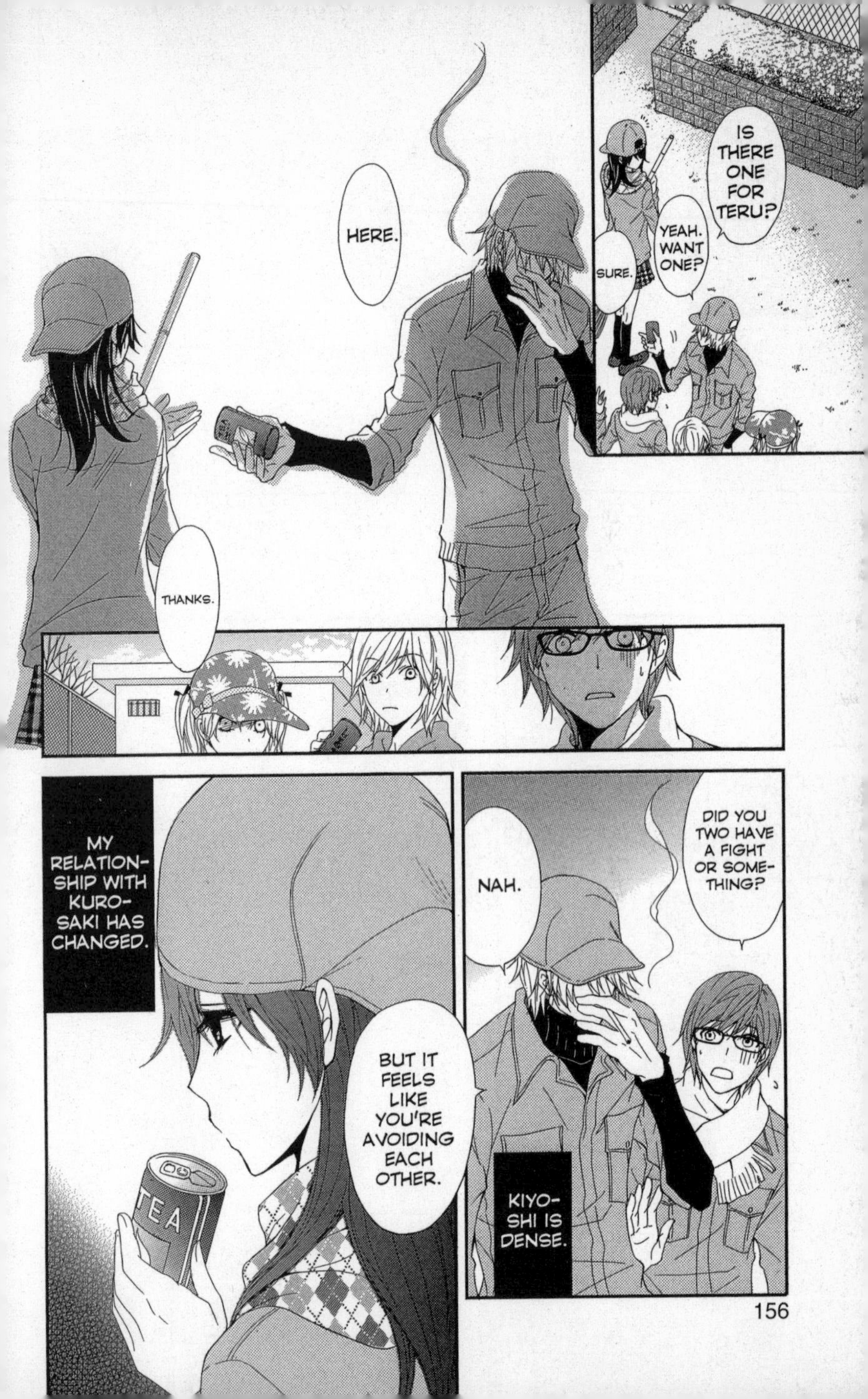

IS THERE ONE FOR TERU?
YEAH. WANT ONE?
SURE.
HERE.
THANKS.
DID YOU TWO HAVE A FIGHT OR SOMETHING?
NAH.
KIYOSHI IS DENSE.
BUT IT FEELS LIKE YOU'RE AVOIDING EACH OTHER.
MY RELATIONSHIP WITH KUROSAKI HAS CHANGED.
TEA

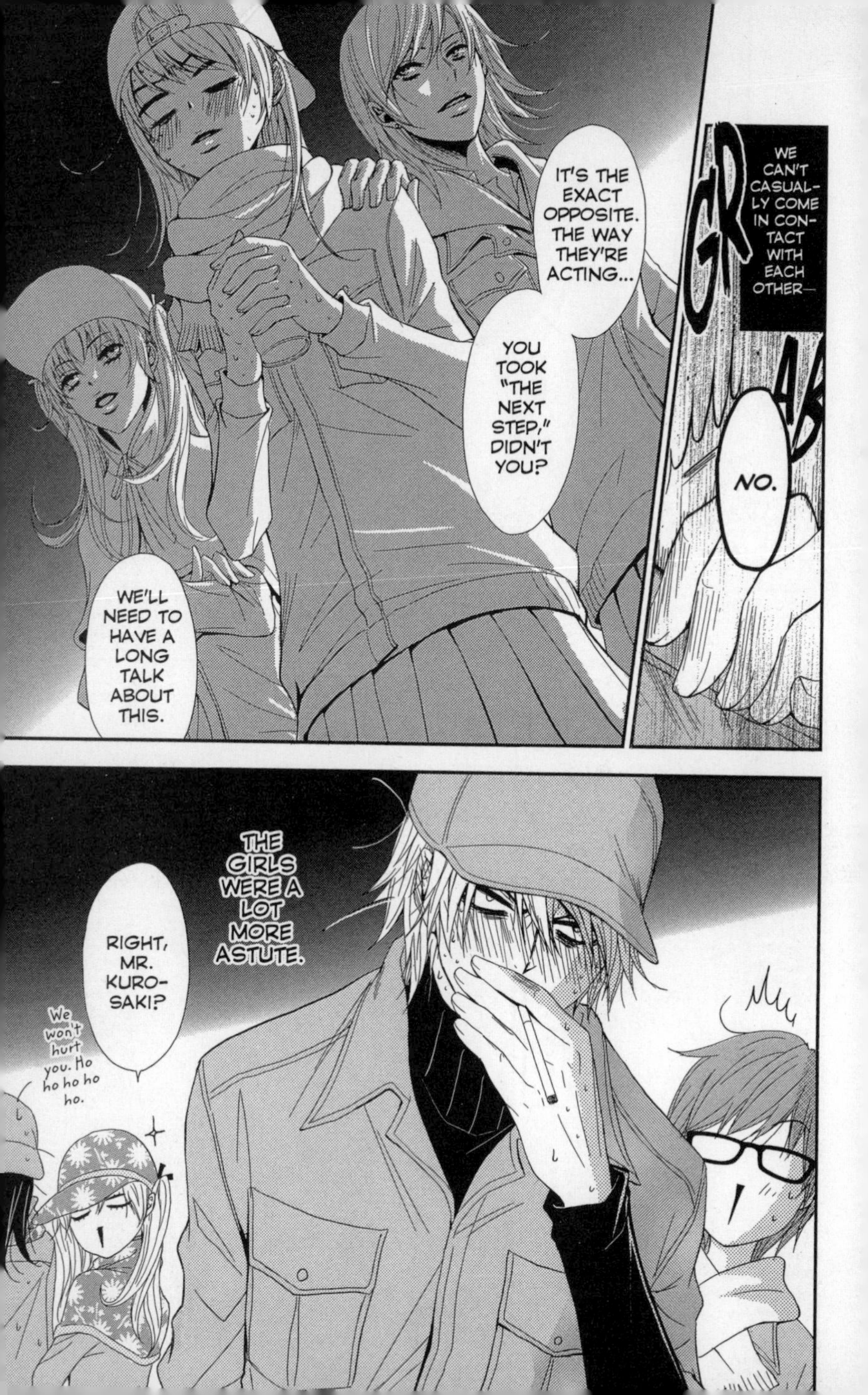
WE CAN'T CASUALLY COME IN CONTACT WITH EACH OTHER—
GR
AB
NO.
IT'S THE EXACT OPPOSITE. THE WAY THEY'RE ACTING...
YOU TOOK "THE NEXT STEP," DIDN'T YOU?
WE'LL NEED TO HAVE A LONG TALK ABOUT THIS.
THE GIRLS WERE A LOT MORE ASTUTE.
RIGHT, MR. KUROSAKI?
We won't hurt you. Ho ho ho ho ho.

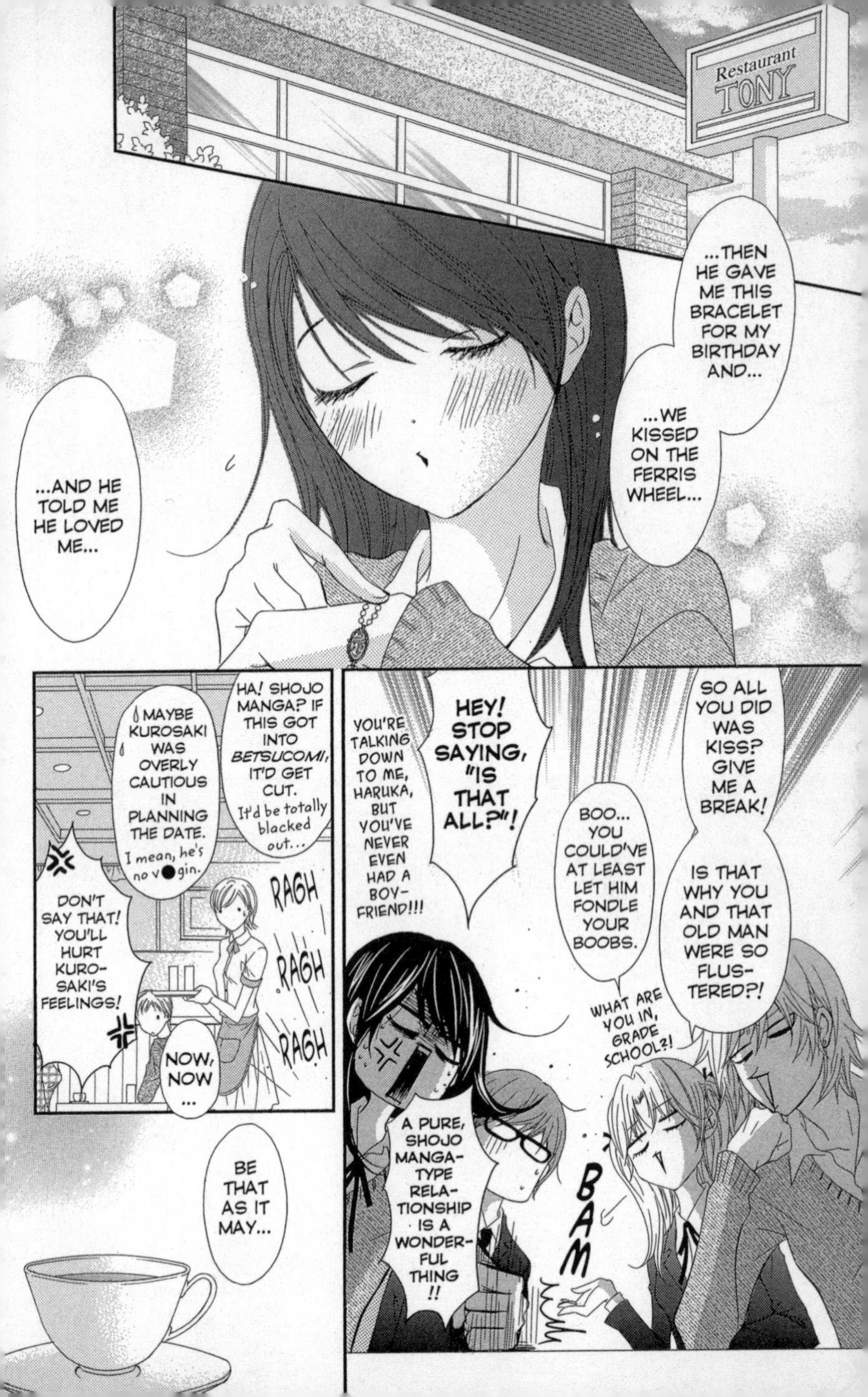

Restaurant TONY
...THEN HE GAVE ME THIS BRACELET FOR MY BIRTHDAY AND...
...WE KISSED ON THE FERRIS WHEEL...
...AND HE TOLD ME HE LOVED ME...
SO ALL YOU DID WAS KISS? GIVE ME A BREAK!
IS THAT WHY YOU AND THAT OLD MAN WERE SO FLUSTERED?!
BOO... YOU COULD'VE AT LEAST LET HIM FONDLE YOUR BOOBS.
WHAT ARE YOU IN, GRADE SCHOOL?!
HEY! STOP SAYING, "IS THAT ALL?"!
YOU'RE TALKING DOWN TO ME, HARUKA, BUT YOU'VE NEVER EVEN HAD A BOY-FRIEND!!!
BAM
A PURE, SHOJO MANGA-TYPE RELATIONSHIP IS A WONDERFUL THING!!
HA! SHOJO MANGA? IF THIS GOT INTO *BETSUCOMI*, IT'D GET CUT. It'd be totally blacked out... I mean, he's no v●gin.
MAYBE KUROSAKI WAS OVERLY CAUTIOUS IN PLANNING THE DATE.
RAGH RAGH RAGH
DON'T SAY THAT! YOU'LL HURT KURO-SAKI'S FEELINGS!
NOW, NOW...
BE THAT AS IT MAY...

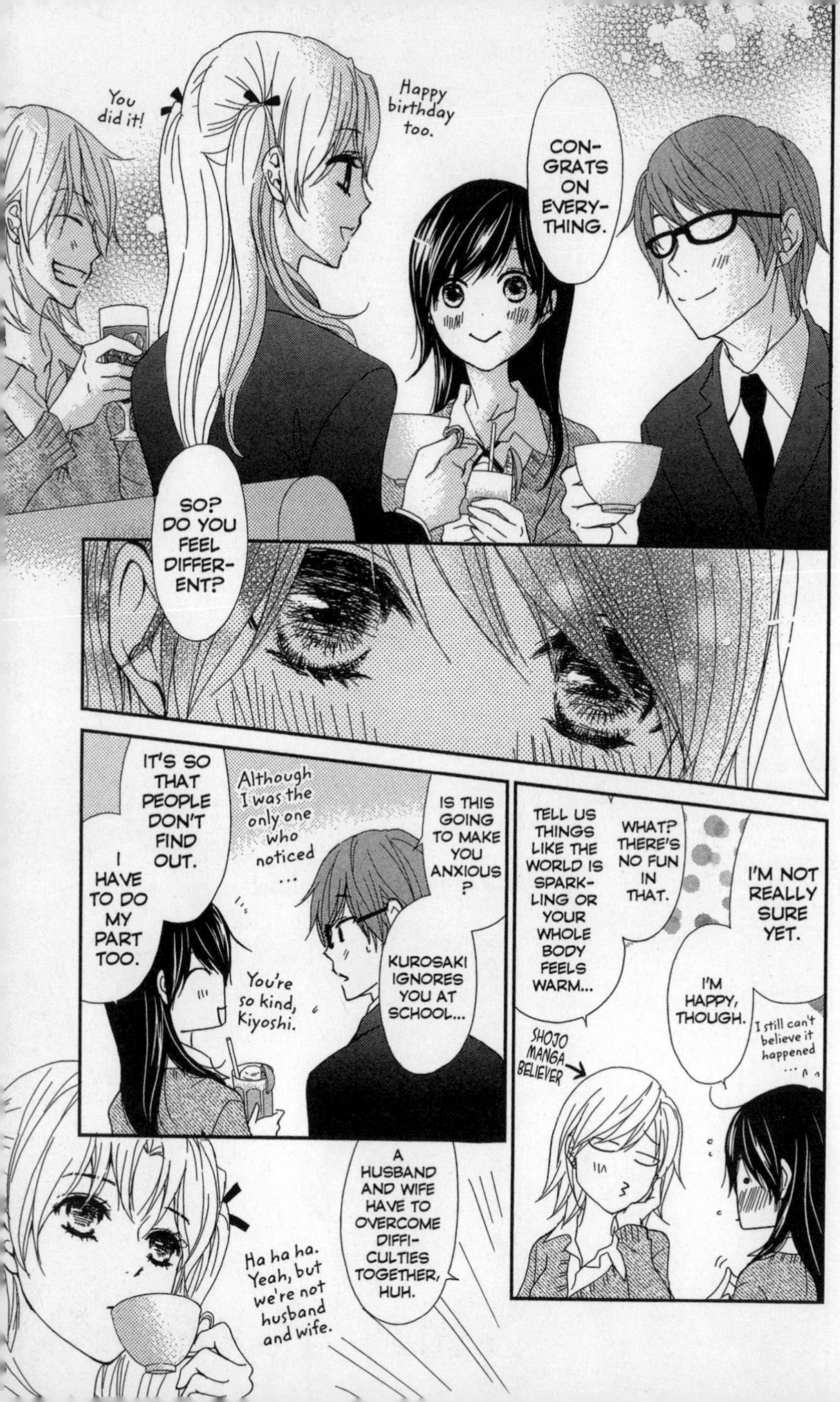
CONGRATS ON EVERYTHING.
Happy birthday too.
You did it!
SO? DO YOU FEEL DIFFERENT?
I'M NOT REALLY SURE YET.
WHAT? THERE'S NO FUN IN THAT.
TELL US THINGS LIKE THE WORLD IS SPARKLING OR YOUR WHOLE BODY FEELS WARM...
I'M HAPPY, THOUGH.
I still can't believe it happened...
SHOJO MANGA BELIEVER
IS THIS GOING TO MAKE YOU ANXIOUS?
KUROSAKI IGNORES YOU AT SCHOOL...
Although I was the only one who noticed...
IT'S SO THAT PEOPLE DON'T FIND OUT.
I HAVE TO DO MY PART TOO.
You're so kind, Kiyoshi.
A HUSBAND AND WIFE HAVE TO OVERCOME DIFFICULTIES TOGETHER, HUH.
Ha ha ha. Yeah, but we're not husband and wife.

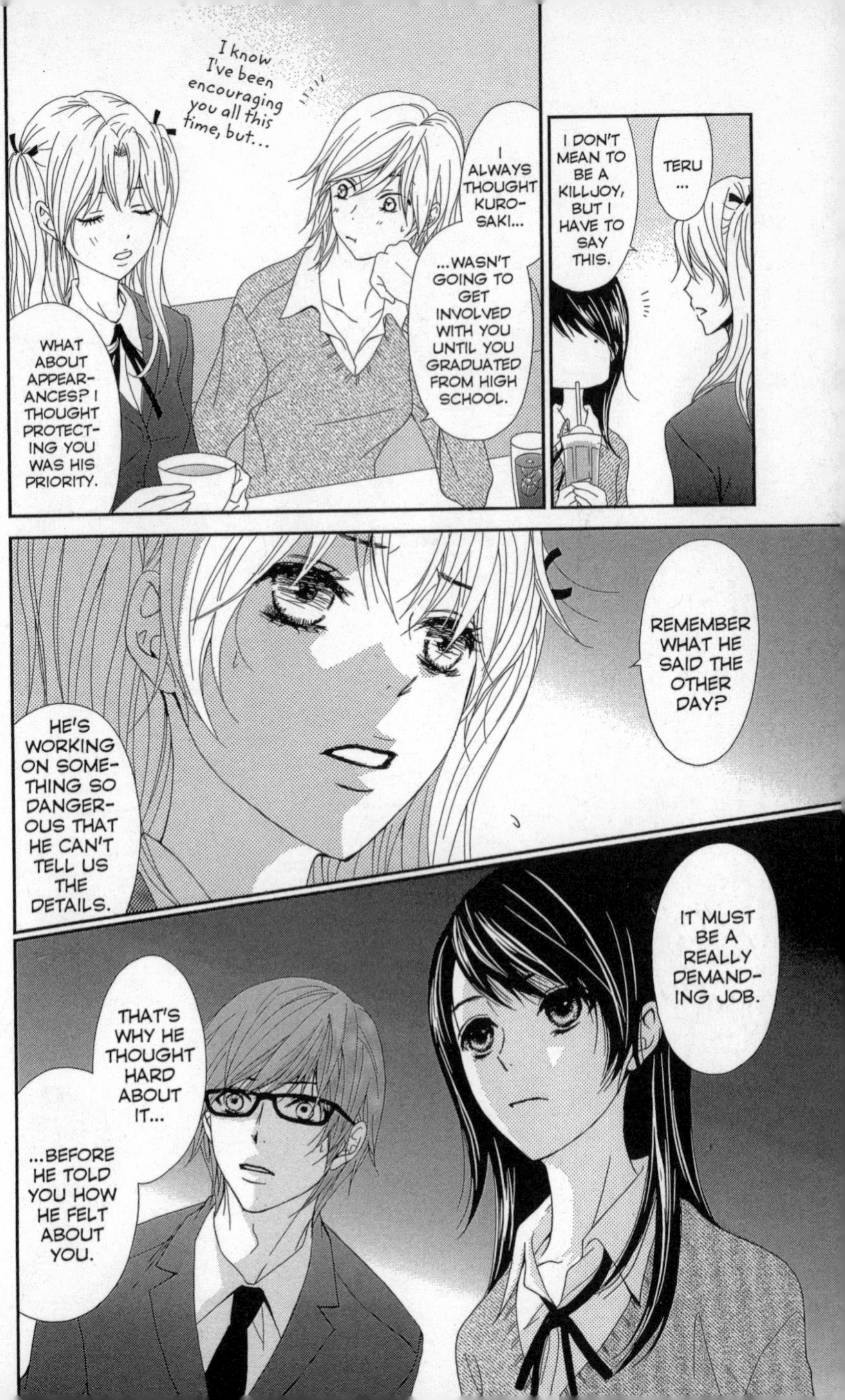
TERU ...
I DON'T MEAN TO BE A KILLJOY, BUT I HAVE TO SAY THIS.
I ALWAYS THOUGHT KURO-SAKI...
...WASN'T GOING TO GET INVOLVED WITH YOU UNTIL YOU GRADUATED FROM HIGH SCHOOL.
I know I've been encouraging you all this time, but...
WHAT ABOUT APPEAR-ANCES? I THOUGHT PROTECT-ING YOU WAS HIS PRIORITY.
REMEMBER WHAT HE SAID THE OTHER DAY?
HE'S WORKING ON SOME-THING SO DANGER-OUS THAT HE CAN'T TELL US THE DETAILS.
IT MUST BE A REALLY DEMAND-ING JOB.
THAT'S WHY HE THOUGHT HARD ABOUT IT...
...BEFORE HE TOLD YOU HOW HE FELT ABOUT YOU.

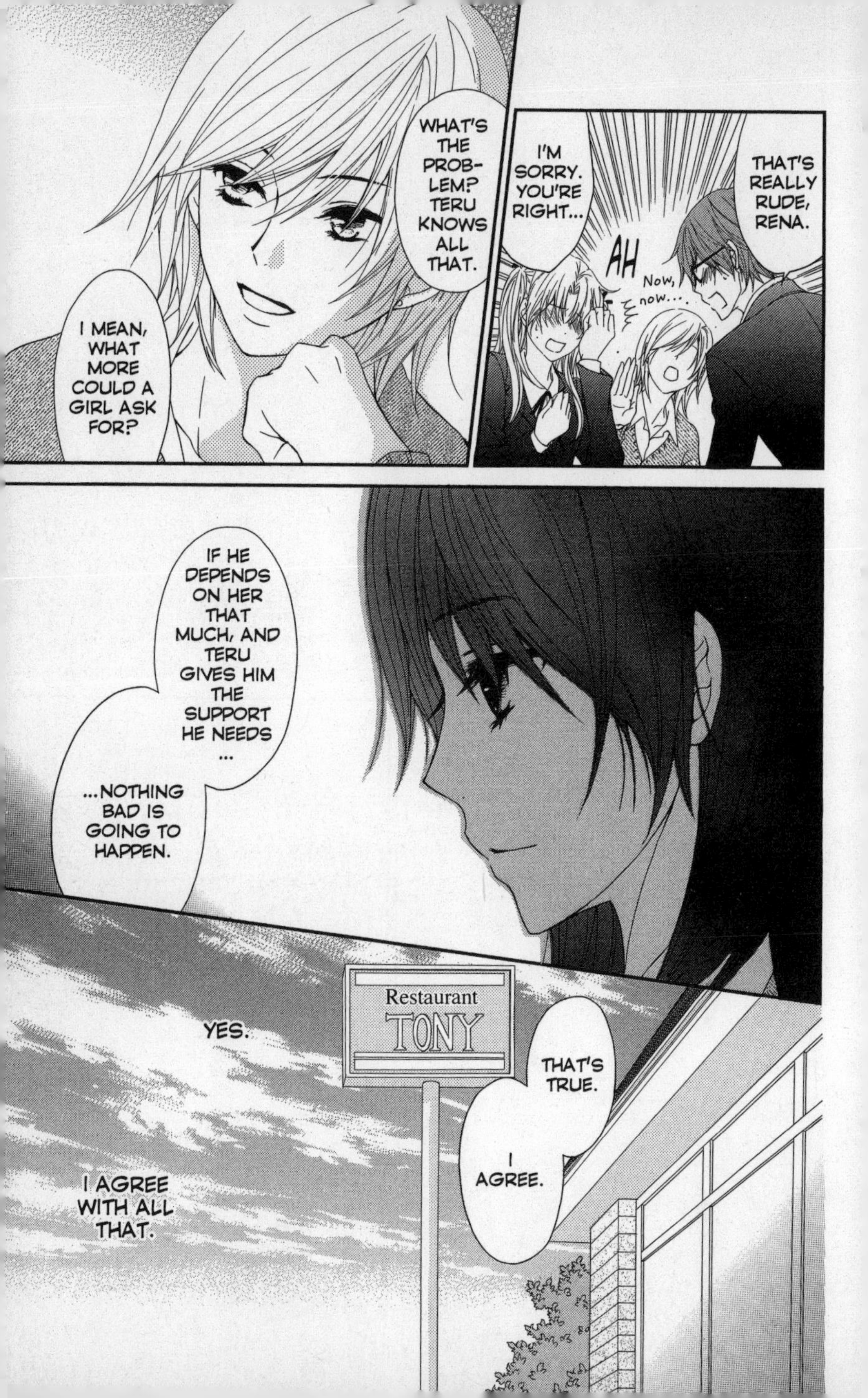
WHAT'S THE PROB-LEM? TERU KNOWS ALL THAT.
I MEAN, WHAT MORE COULD A GIRL ASK FOR?
THAT'S REALLY RUDE, RENA.
AH
Now, now...
I'M SORRY. YOU'RE RIGHT...
IF HE DEPENDS ON HER THAT MUCH, AND TERU GIVES HIM THE SUPPORT HE NEEDS ...
...NOTHING BAD IS GOING TO HAPPEN.
Restaurant
TONY
THAT'S TRUE.
I AGREE.
YES.
I AGREE WITH ALL THAT.

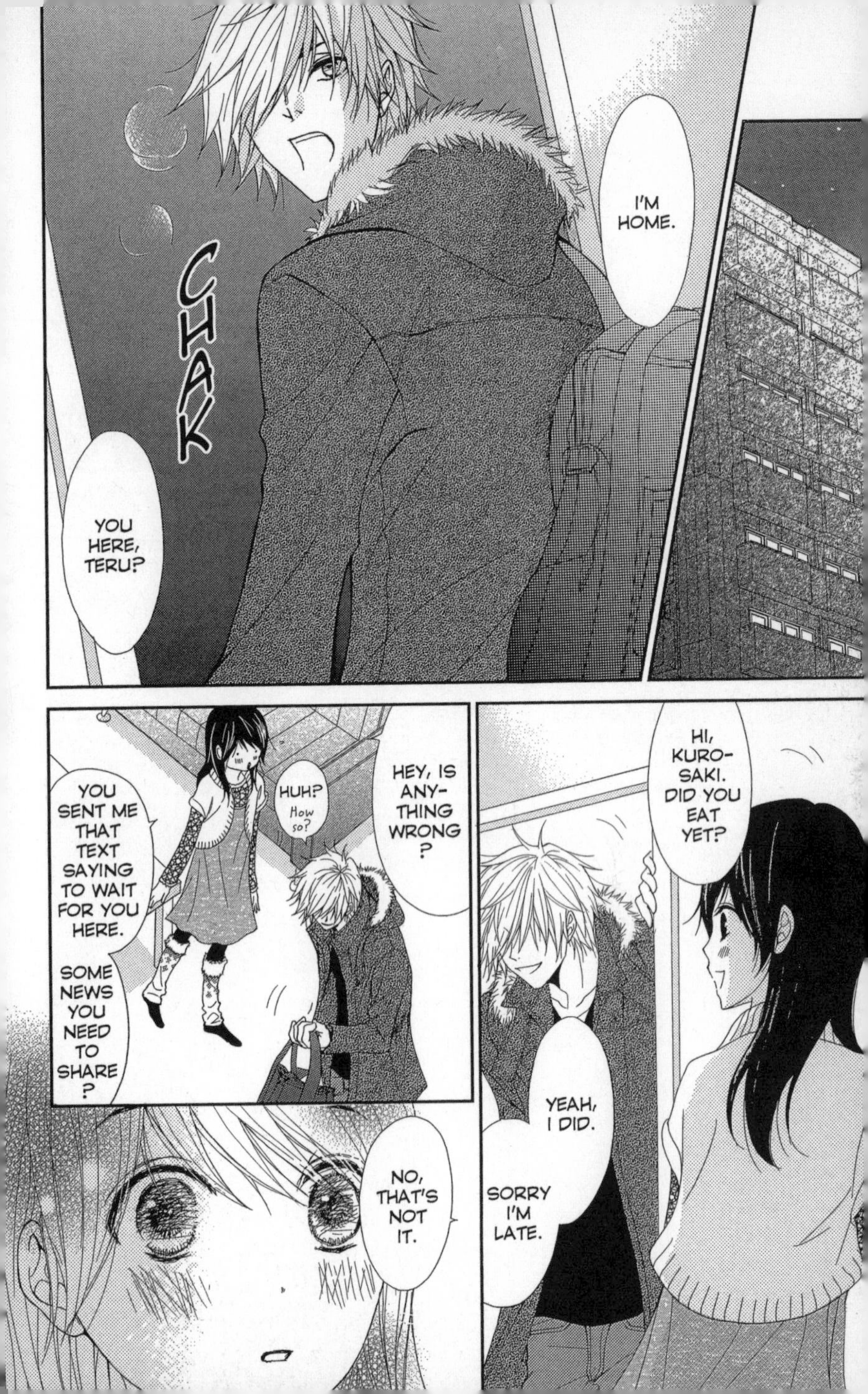
I'M HOME.
CHAK
YOU HERE, TERU?
HI, KURO-SAKI. DID YOU EAT YET?
YEAH, I DID.
SORRY I'M LATE.
HEY, IS ANY-THING WRONG?
HUH?
How so?
YOU SENT ME THAT TEXT SAYING TO WAIT FOR YOU HERE.
SOME NEWS YOU NEED TO SHARE?
NO, THAT'S NOT IT.

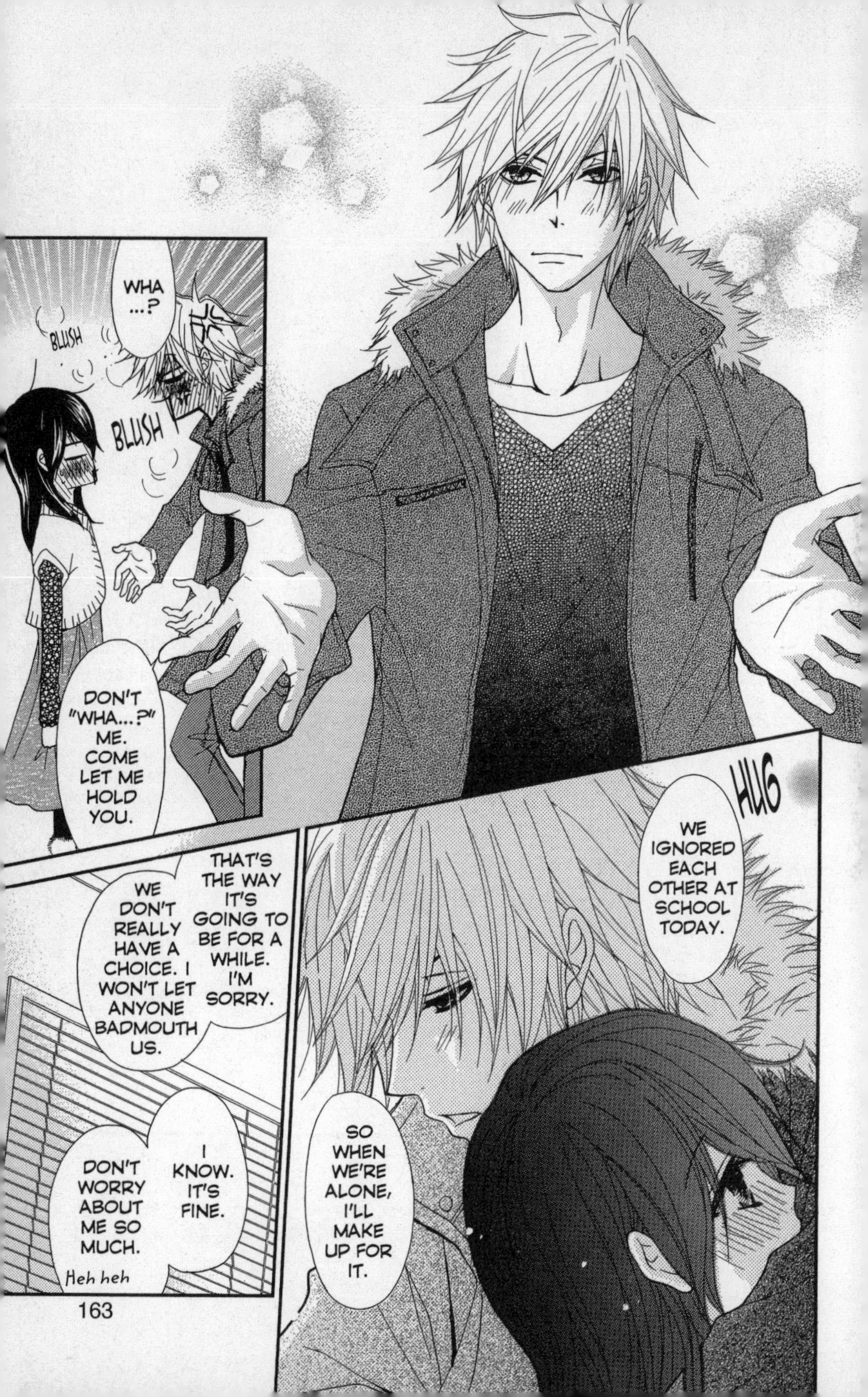
WHA ...?
BLUSH
BLUSH
DON'T "WHA...?" ME. COME LET ME HOLD YOU.
HUG
WE IGNORED EACH OTHER AT SCHOOL TODAY.
SO WHEN WE'RE ALONE, I'LL MAKE UP FOR IT.
THAT'S THE WAY IT'S GOING TO BE FOR A WHILE. I'M SORRY.
WE DON'T REALLY HAVE A CHOICE. I WON'T LET ANYONE BADMOUTH US.
I KNOW. IT'S FINE.
DON'T WORRY ABOUT ME SO MUCH.
Heh heh

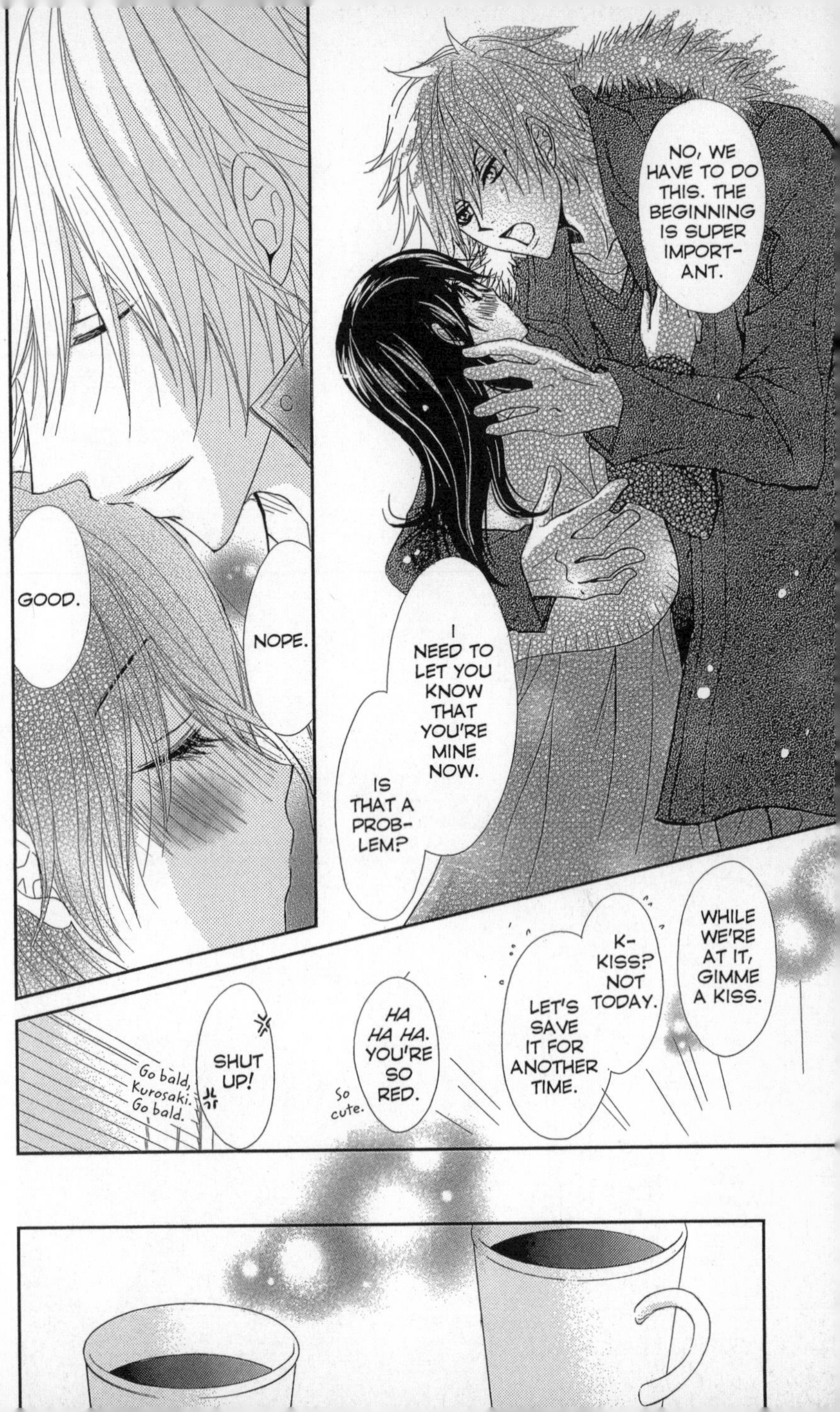
NO, WE HAVE TO DO THIS. THE BEGINNING IS SUPER IMPORT-ANT.
I NEED TO LET YOU KNOW THAT YOU'RE MINE NOW.
IS THAT A PROB-LEM?
NOPE.
GOOD.
WHILE WE'RE AT IT, GIMME A KISS.
K-KISS? NOT TODAY.
LET'S SAVE IT FOR ANOTHER TIME.
HA HA HA. YOU'RE SO RED.
So cute.
SHUT UP!
Go bald, Kurosaki. Go bald.

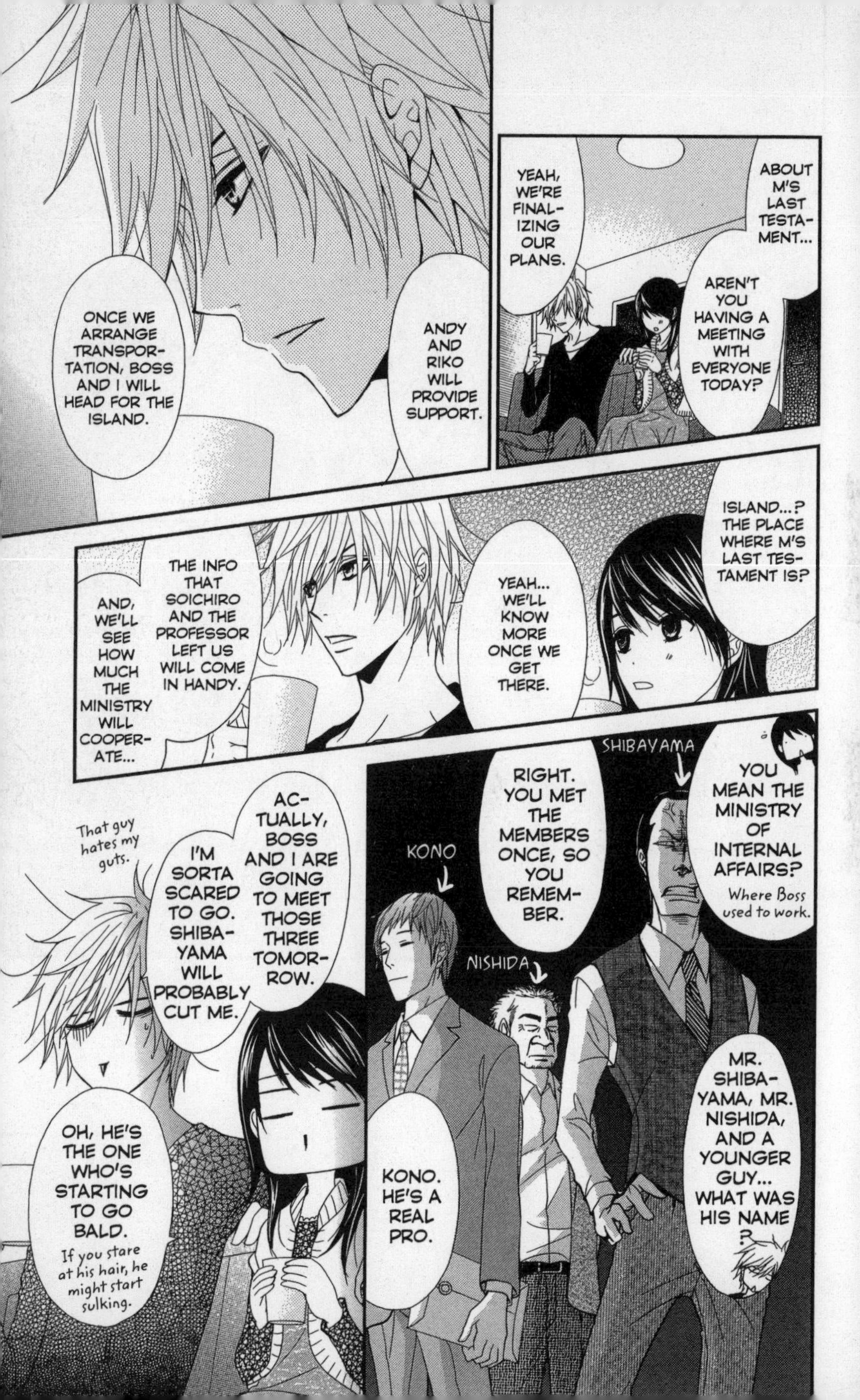
ABOUT M'S LAST TESTAMENT...
AREN'T YOU HAVING A MEETING WITH EVERYONE TODAY?
YEAH, WE'RE FINALIZING OUR PLANS.
ANDY AND RIKO WILL PROVIDE SUPPORT.
ONCE WE ARRANGE TRANSPORTATION, BOSS AND I WILL HEAD FOR THE ISLAND.
ISLAND...? THE PLACE WHERE M'S LAST TESTAMENT IS?
YEAH... WE'LL KNOW MORE ONCE WE GET THERE.
THE INFO THAT SOICHIRO AND THE PROFESSOR LEFT US WILL COME IN HANDY.
AND, WE'LL SEE HOW MUCH THE MINISTRY WILL COOPERATE...
YOU MEAN THE MINISTRY OF INTERNAL AFFAIRS?
Where Boss used to work.
SHIBAYAMA
RIGHT. YOU MET THE MEMBERS ONCE, SO YOU REMEMBER.
KONO
NISHIDA
MR. SHIBAYAMA, MR. NISHIDA, AND A YOUNGER GUY... WHAT WAS HIS NAME?
KONO. HE'S A REAL PRO.
ACTUALLY, BOSS AND I ARE GOING TO MEET THOSE THREE TOMORROW.
I'M SORTA SCARED TO GO. SHIBAYAMA WILL PROBABLY CUT ME.
That guy hates my guts.
OH, HE'S THE ONE WHO'S STARTING TO GO BALD.
If you stare at his hair, he might start sulking.

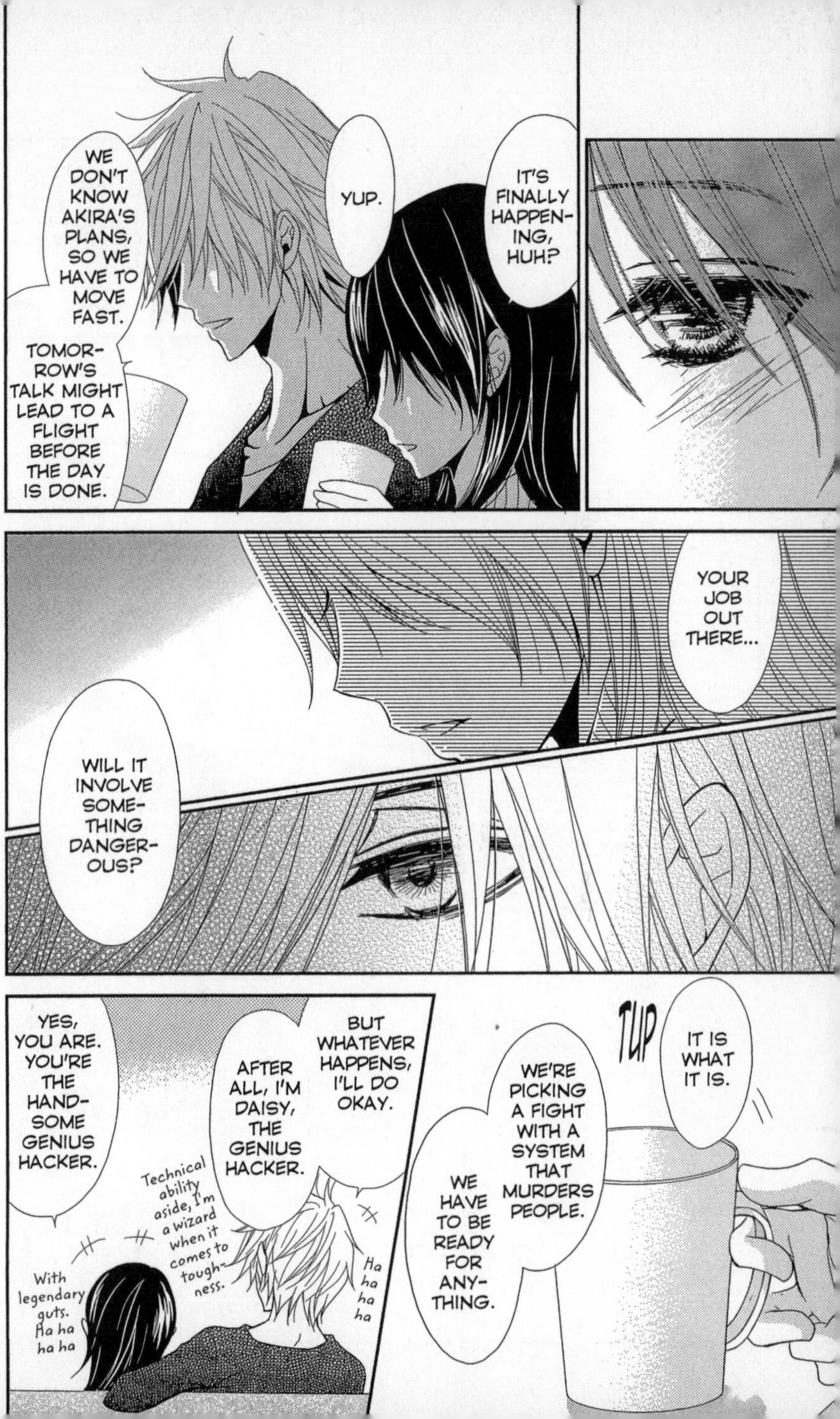
IT'S FINALLY HAPPENING, HUH?
YUP.
WE DON'T KNOW AKIRA'S PLANS, SO WE HAVE TO MOVE FAST.
TOMORROW'S TALK MIGHT LEAD TO A FLIGHT BEFORE THE DAY IS DONE.
YOUR JOB OUT THERE...
WILL IT INVOLVE SOMETHING DANGEROUS?
TUP
IT IS WHAT IT IS.
WE'RE PICKING A FIGHT WITH A SYSTEM THAT MURDERS PEOPLE.
WE HAVE TO BE READY FOR ANYTHING.
BUT WHATEVER HAPPENS, I'LL DO OKAY.
AFTER ALL, I'M DAISY, THE GENIUS HACKER.
Technical ability aside, I'm a wizard when it comes to toughness.
Ha ha ha ha
YES, YOU ARE. YOU'RE THE HANDSOME GENIUS HACKER.
With legendary guts. Ha ha ha ha

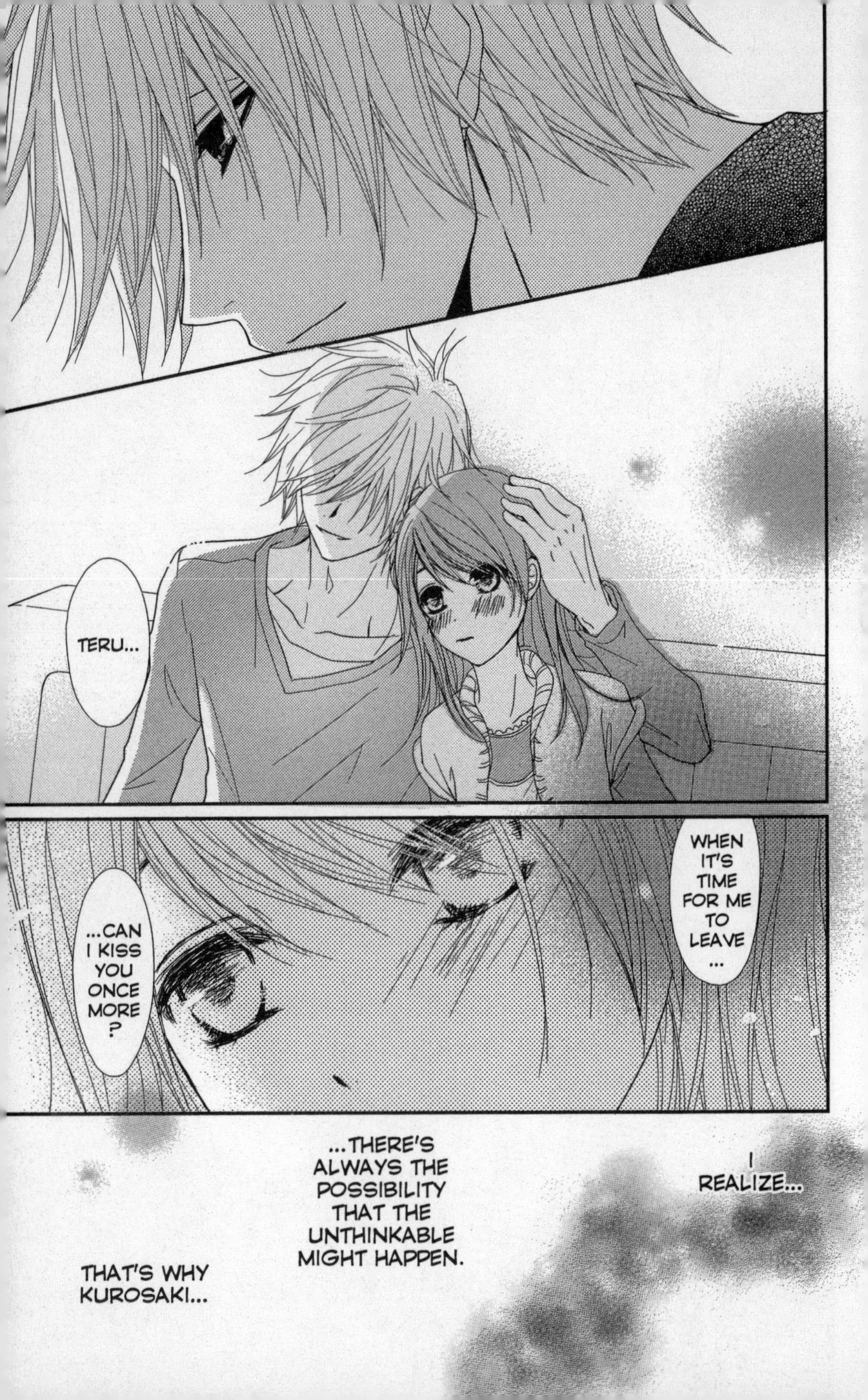
TERU...
WHEN IT'S TIME FOR ME TO LEAVE...
...CAN I KISS YOU ONCE MORE?
I REALIZE...
...THERE'S ALWAYS THE POSSIBILITY THAT THE UNTHINKABLE MIGHT HAPPEN.
THAT'S WHY KUROSAKI...

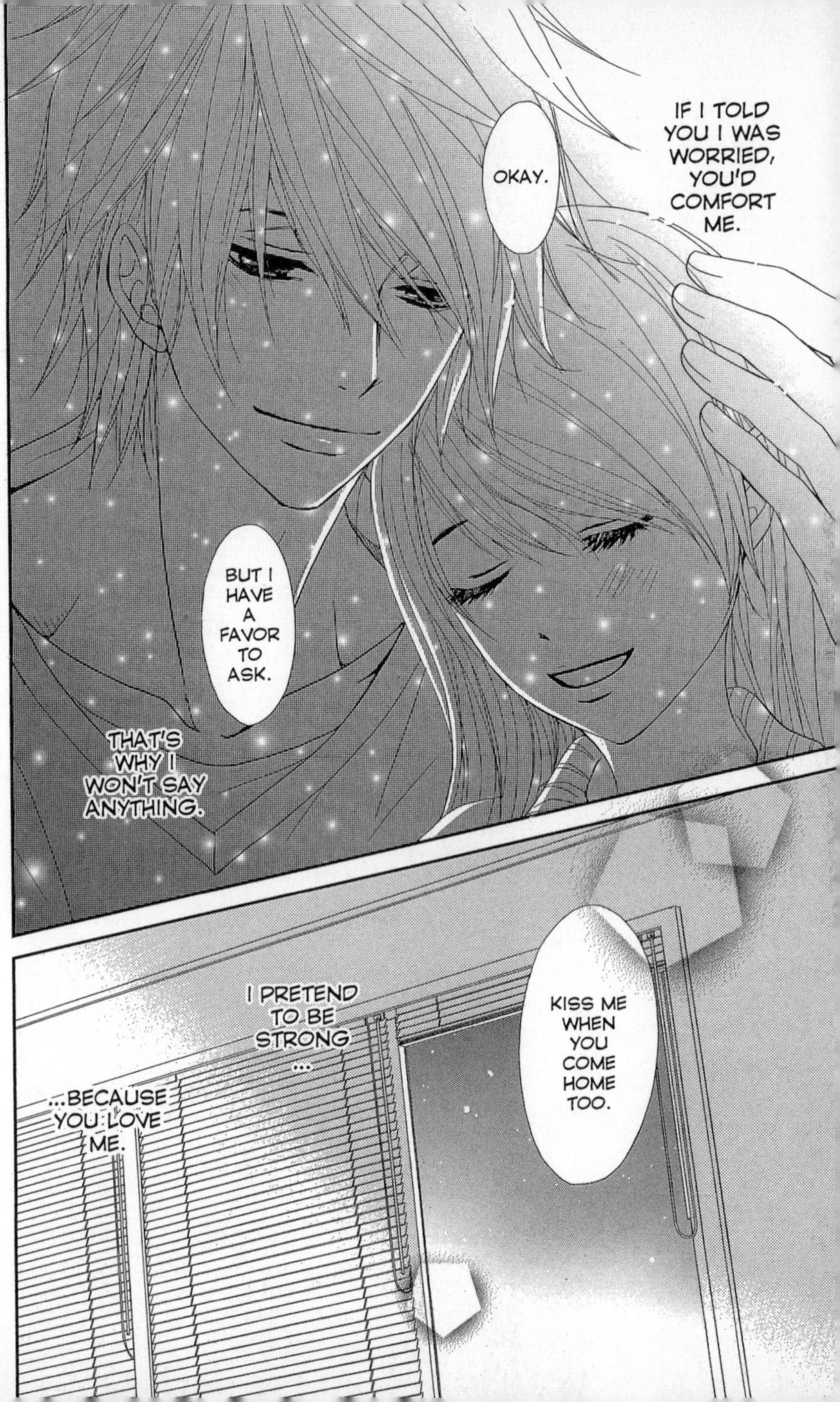
IF I TOLD YOU I WAS WORRIED, YOU'D COMFORT ME.
OKAY.
BUT I HAVE A FAVOR TO ASK.
THAT'S WHY I WON'T SAY ANYTHING.
KISS ME WHEN YOU COME HOME TOO.
I PRETEND TO BE STRONG...
...BECAUSE YOU LOVE ME.

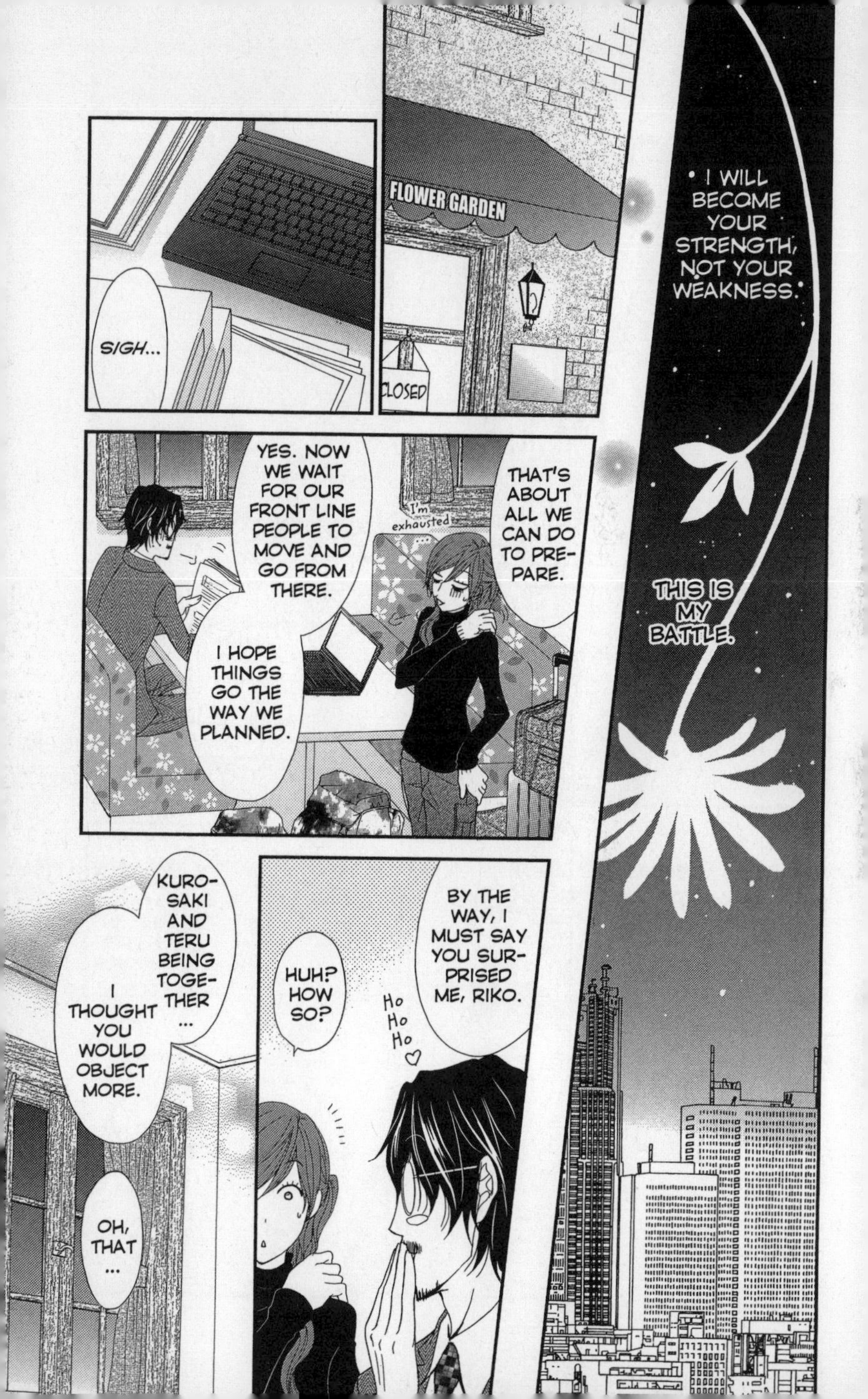
I WILL BECOME YOUR STRENGTH, NOT YOUR WEAKNESS.
THIS IS MY BATTLE.
FLOWER GARDEN
CLOSED
SIGH...
THAT'S ABOUT ALL WE CAN DO TO PREPARE.
I'm exhausted
YES. NOW WE WAIT FOR OUR FRONT LINE PEOPLE TO MOVE AND GO FROM THERE.
I HOPE THINGS GO THE WAY WE PLANNED.
BY THE WAY, I MUST SAY YOU SURPRISED ME, RIKO.
Ho Ho Ho ♡
HUH? HOW SO?
KUROSAKI AND TERU BEING TOGETHER...
I THOUGHT YOU WOULD OBJECT MORE.
OH, THAT...

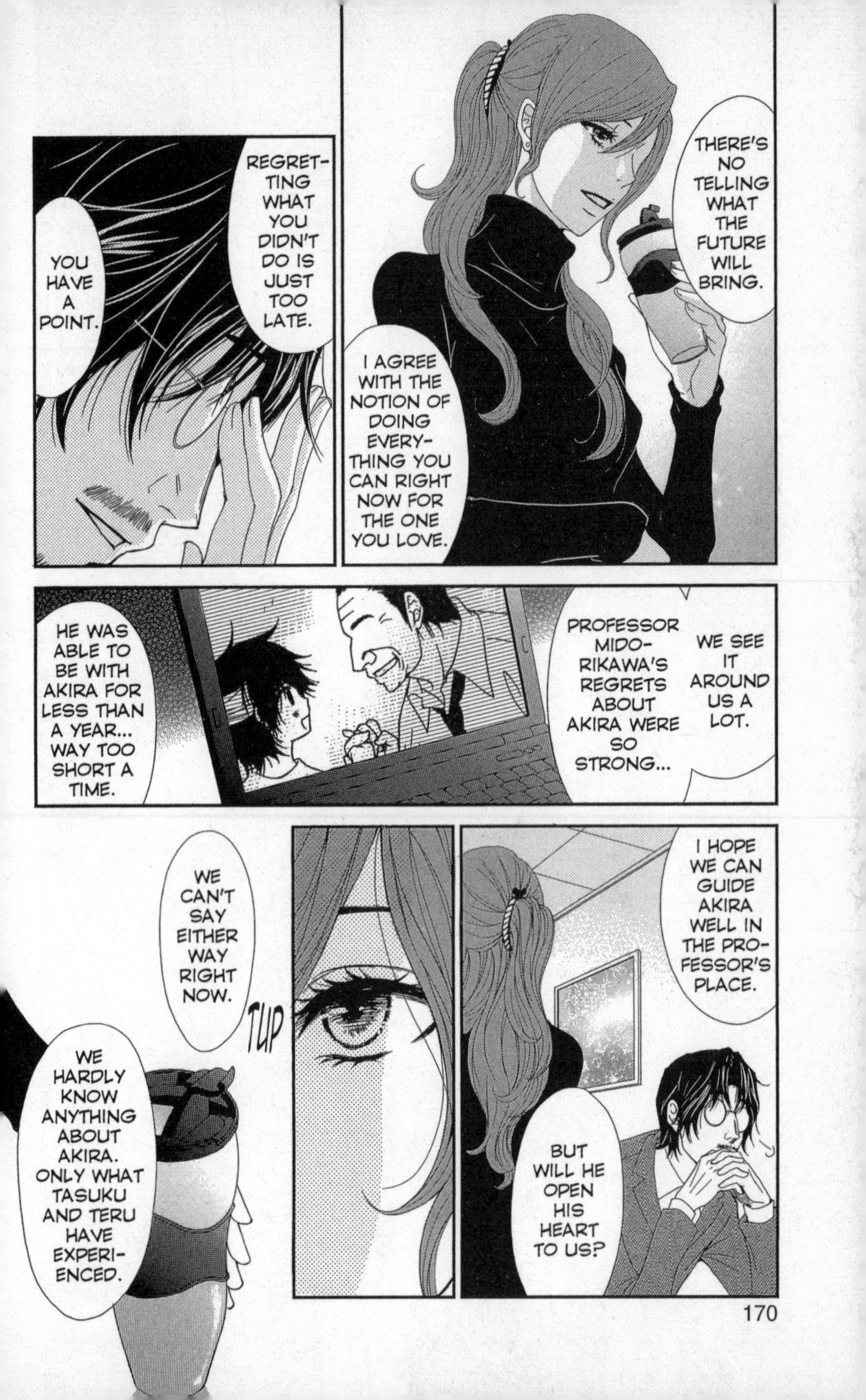
THERE'S NO TELLING WHAT THE FUTURE WILL BRING.
I AGREE WITH THE NOTION OF DOING EVERYTHING YOU CAN RIGHT NOW FOR THE ONE YOU LOVE.
REGRETTING WHAT YOU DIDN'T DO IS JUST TOO LATE.
YOU HAVE A POINT.
WE SEE IT AROUND US A LOT.
PROFESSOR MIDORIKAWA'S REGRETS ABOUT AKIRA WERE SO STRONG...
HE WAS ABLE TO BE WITH AKIRA FOR LESS THAN A YEAR... WAY TOO SHORT A TIME.
I HOPE WE CAN GUIDE AKIRA WELL IN THE PROFESSOR'S PLACE.
BUT WILL HE OPEN HIS HEART TO US?
TUP
WE CAN'T SAY EITHER WAY RIGHT NOW.
WE HARDLY KNOW ANYTHING ABOUT AKIRA. ONLY WHAT TASUKU AND TERU HAVE EXPERIENCED.

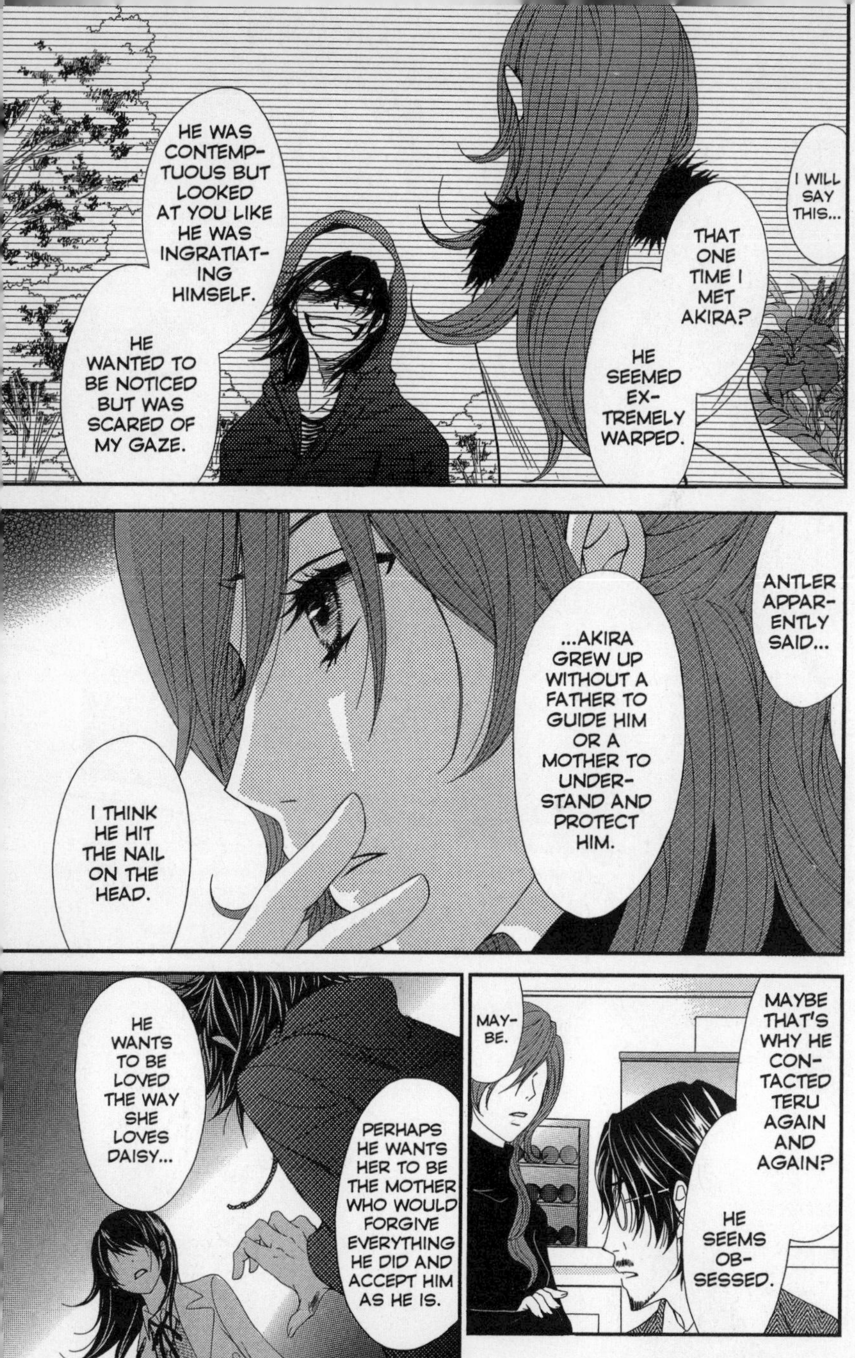
I WILL SAY THIS...
THAT ONE TIME I MET AKIRA?
HE SEEMED EXTREMELY WARPED.
HE WAS CONTEMPTUOUS BUT LOOKED AT YOU LIKE HE WAS INGRATIATING HIMSELF.
HE WANTED TO BE NOTICED BUT WAS SCARED OF MY GAZE.
ANTLER APPARENTLY SAID...
...AKIRA GREW UP WITHOUT A FATHER TO GUIDE HIM OR A MOTHER TO UNDERSTAND AND PROTECT HIM.
I THINK HE HIT THE NAIL ON THE HEAD.
MAYBE THAT'S WHY HE CONTACTED TERU AGAIN AND AGAIN?
MAYBE.
HE SEEMS OBSESSED.
HE WANTS TO BE LOVED THE WAY SHE LOVES DAISY...
PERHAPS HE WANTS HER TO BE THE MOTHER WHO WOULD FORGIVE EVERYTHING HE DID AND ACCEPT HIM AS HE IS.

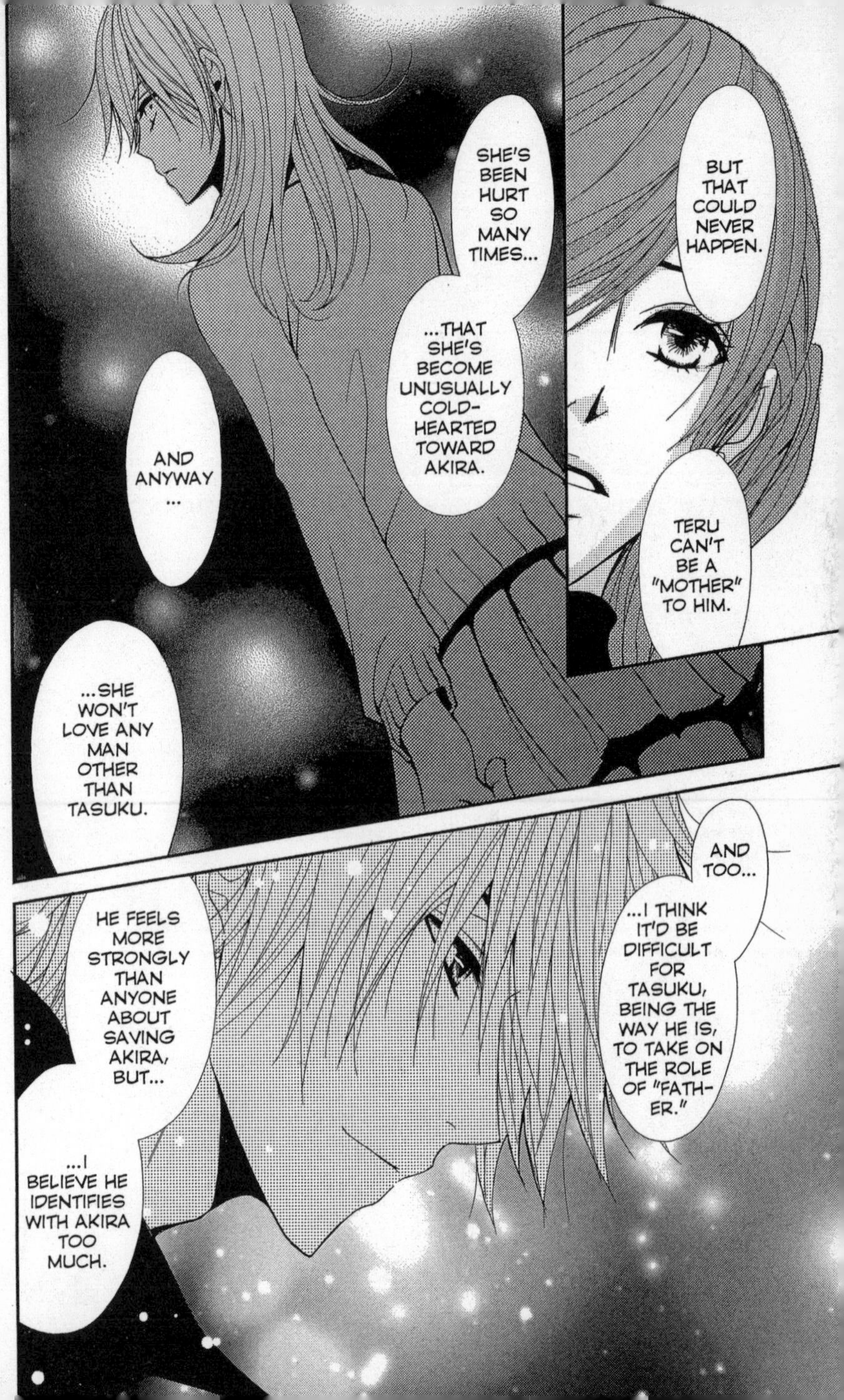
BUT THAT COULD NEVER HAPPEN.
TERU CAN'T BE A "MOTHER" TO HIM.
SHE'S BEEN HURT SO MANY TIMES...
...THAT SHE'S BECOME UNUSUALLY COLD-HEARTED TOWARD AKIRA.
AND ANYWAY ...
...SHE WON'T LOVE ANY MAN OTHER THAN TASUKU.
AND TOO...
...I THINK IT'D BE DIFFICULT FOR TASUKU, BEING THE WAY HE IS, TO TAKE ON THE ROLE OF "FATHER."
HE FEELS MORE STRONGLY THAN ANYONE ABOUT SAVING AKIRA, BUT...
...I BELIEVE HE IDENTIFIES WITH AKIRA TOO MUCH.

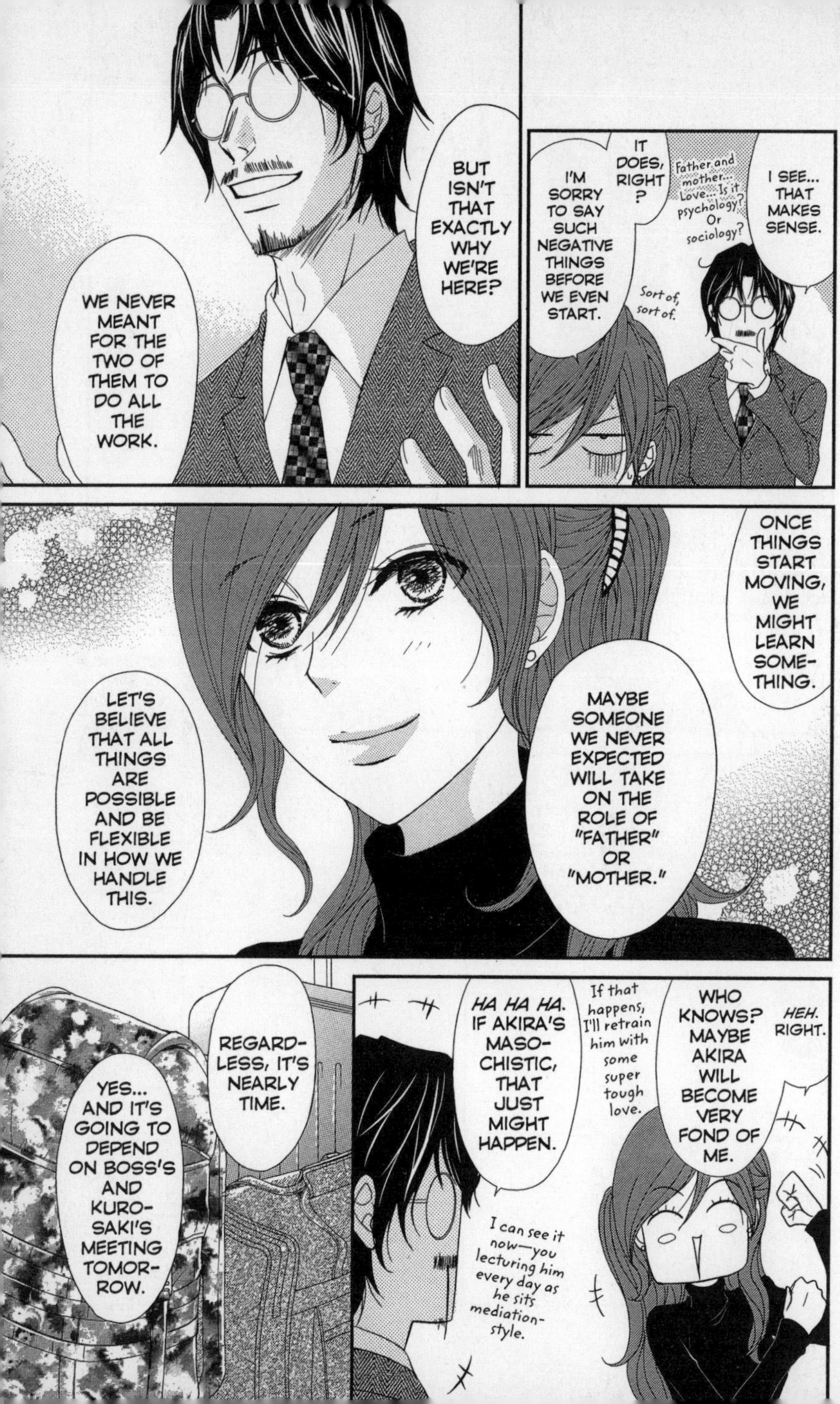
I SEE... THAT MAKES SENSE.
Father and mother... Love... Is it psychology? Or sociology?
IT DOES, RIGHT?
I'M SORRY TO SAY SUCH NEGATIVE THINGS BEFORE WE EVEN START.
Sort of, sort of.
BUT ISN'T THAT EXACTLY WHY WE'RE HERE?
WE NEVER MEANT FOR THE TWO OF THEM TO DO ALL THE WORK.
ONCE THINGS START MOVING, WE MIGHT LEARN SOME-THING.
MAYBE SOMEONE WE NEVER EXPECTED WILL TAKE ON THE ROLE OF "FATHER" OR "MOTHER."
LET'S BELIEVE THAT ALL THINGS ARE POSSIBLE AND BE FLEXIBLE IN HOW WE HANDLE THIS.
HEH. RIGHT.
WHO KNOWS? MAYBE AKIRA WILL BECOME VERY FOND OF ME.
If that happens, I'll retrain him with some super tough love.
HA HA HA. IF AKIRA'S MASO-CHISTIC, THAT JUST MIGHT HAPPEN.
I can see it now—you lecturing him every day as he sits mediation-style.
REGARD-LESS, IT'S NEARLY TIME.
YES... AND IT'S GOING TO DEPEND ON BOSS'S AND KURO-SAKI'S MEETING TOMOR-ROW.

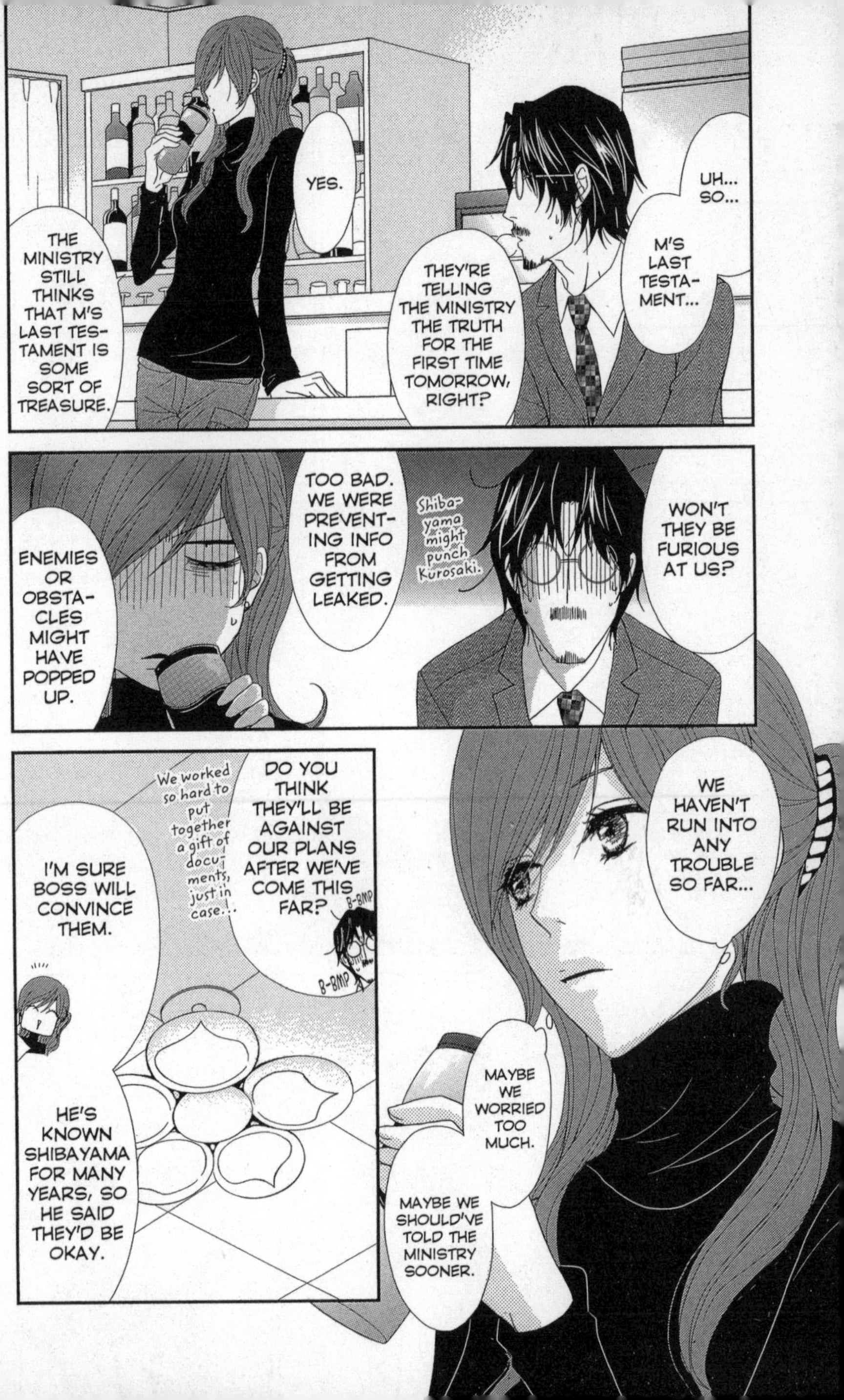
UH... SO...
M'S LAST TESTA-MENT...
THEY'RE TELLING THE MINISTRY THE TRUTH FOR THE FIRST TIME TOMORROW, RIGHT?
YES.
THE MINISTRY STILL THINKS THAT M'S LAST TES-TAMENT IS SOME SORT OF TREASURE.
WON'T THEY BE FURIOUS AT US?
Shiba-yama might punch Kurosaki.
TOO BAD. WE WERE PREVENT-ING INFO FROM GETTING LEAKED.
ENEMIES OR OBSTA-CLES MIGHT HAVE POPPED UP.
WE HAVEN'T RUN INTO ANY TROUBLE SO FAR...
MAYBE WE WORRIED TOO MUCH.
MAYBE WE SHOULD'VE TOLD THE MINISTRY SOONER.
DO YOU THINK THEY'LL BE AGAINST OUR PLANS AFTER WE'VE COME THIS FAR?
We worked so hard to put together a gift of docu-ments, just in case...
B-BMP
B-BMP
I'M SURE BOSS WILL CONVINCE THEM.
HE'S KNOWN SHIBAYAMA FOR MANY YEARS, SO HE SAID THEY'D BE OKAY.

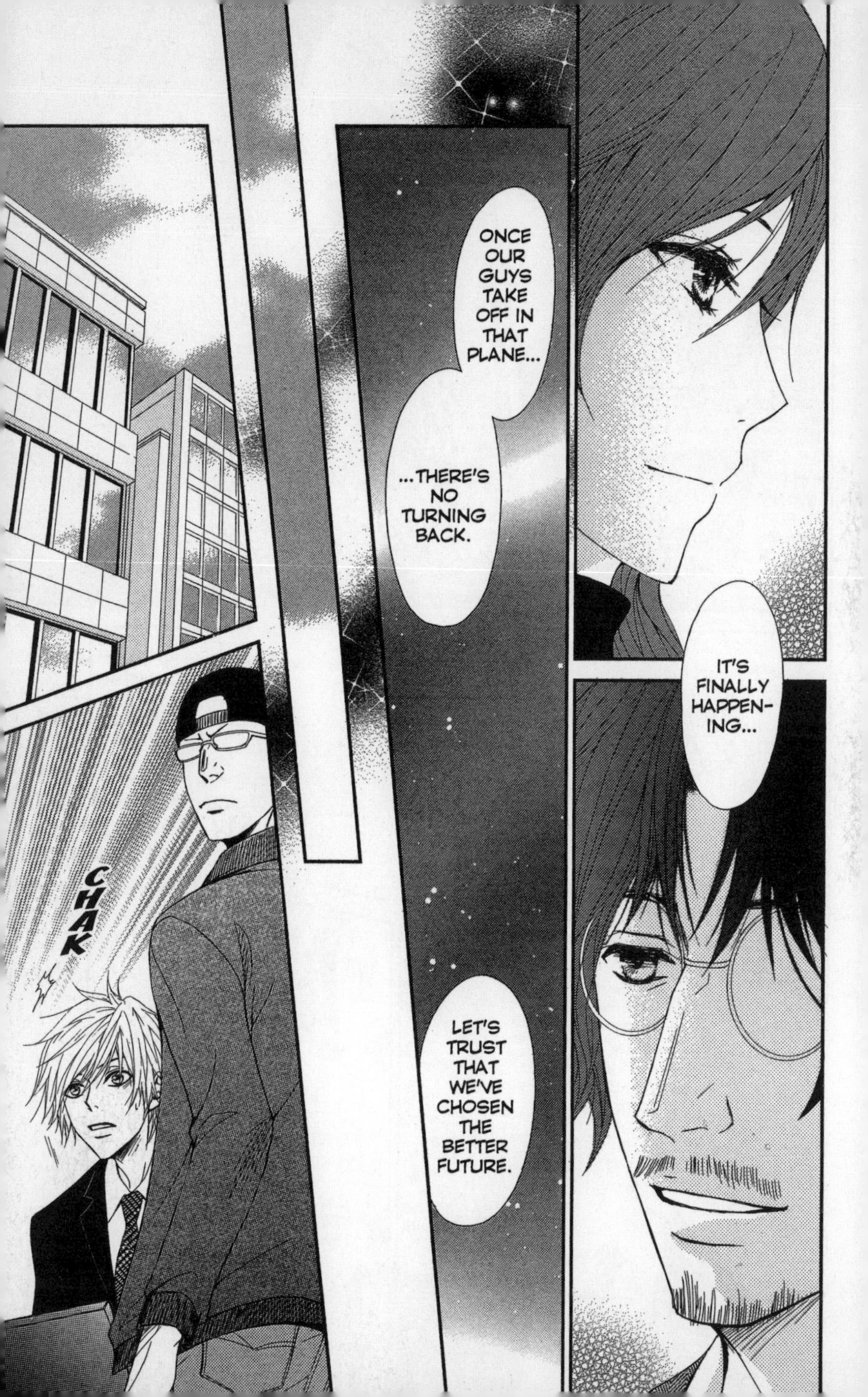
ONCE OUR GUYS TAKE OFF IN THAT PLANE...
...THERE'S NO TURNING BACK.
IT'S FINALLY HAPPENING...
LET'S TRUST THAT WE'VE CHOSEN THE BETTER FUTURE.
CHAK

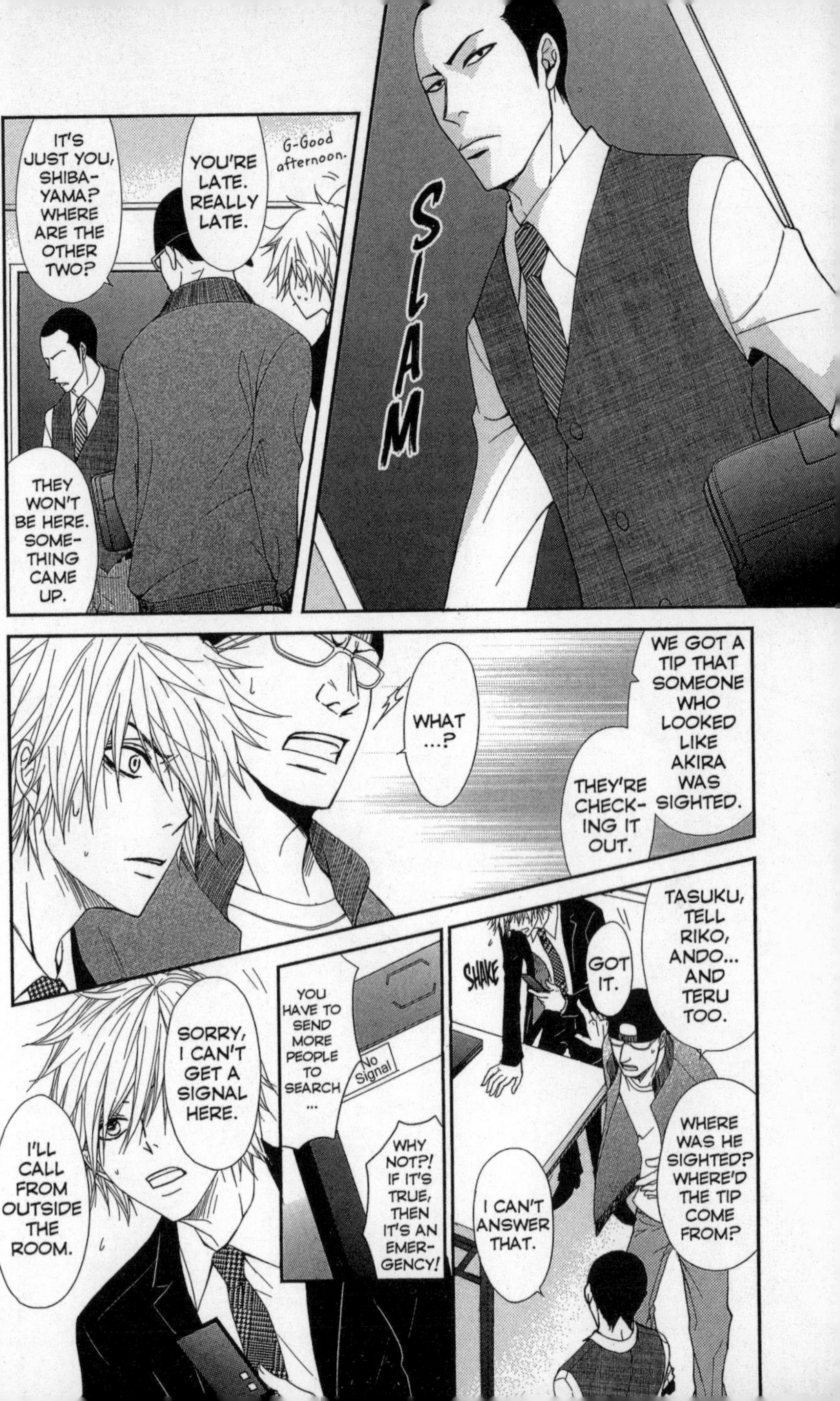
SLAM
G-Good afternoon.
YOU'RE LATE. REALLY LATE.
IT'S JUST YOU, SHIBA-YAMA? WHERE ARE THE OTHER TWO?
THEY WON'T BE HERE. SOME-THING CAME UP.
WE GOT A TIP THAT SOMEONE WHO LOOKED LIKE AKIRA WAS SIGHTED.
THEY'RE CHECK-ING IT OUT.
WHAT ...?
TASUKU, TELL RIKO, ANDO... AND TERU TOO.
GOT IT.
SHAKE
WHERE WAS HE SIGHTED? WHERE'D THE TIP COME FROM?
I CAN'T ANSWER THAT.
YOU HAVE TO SEND MORE PEOPLE TO SEARCH ...
No Signal
WHY NOT?! IF IT'S TRUE, THEN IT'S AN EMER-GENCY!
SORRY, I CAN'T GET A SIGNAL HERE.
I'LL CALL FROM OUTSIDE THE ROOM.

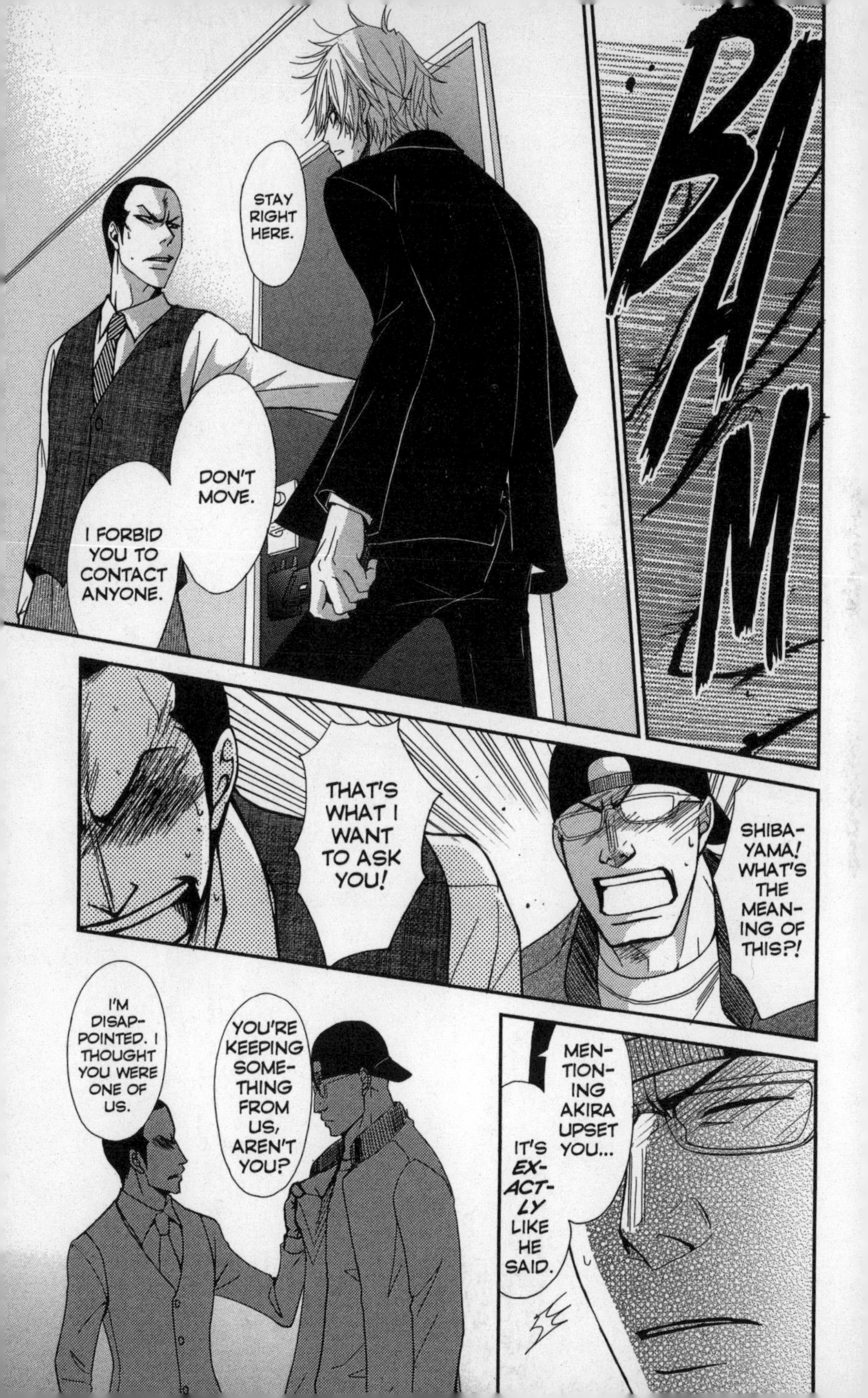
BAM
STAY RIGHT HERE.
DON'T MOVE.
I FORBID YOU TO CONTACT ANYONE.
SHIBAYAMA! WHAT'S THE MEANING OF THIS?!
THAT'S WHAT I WANT TO ASK YOU!
MENTIONING AKIRA UPSET YOU...
IT'S *EXACTLY* LIKE HE SAID.
YOU'RE KEEPING SOMETHING FROM US, AREN'T YOU?
I'M DISAPPOINTED. I THOUGHT YOU WERE ONE OF US.

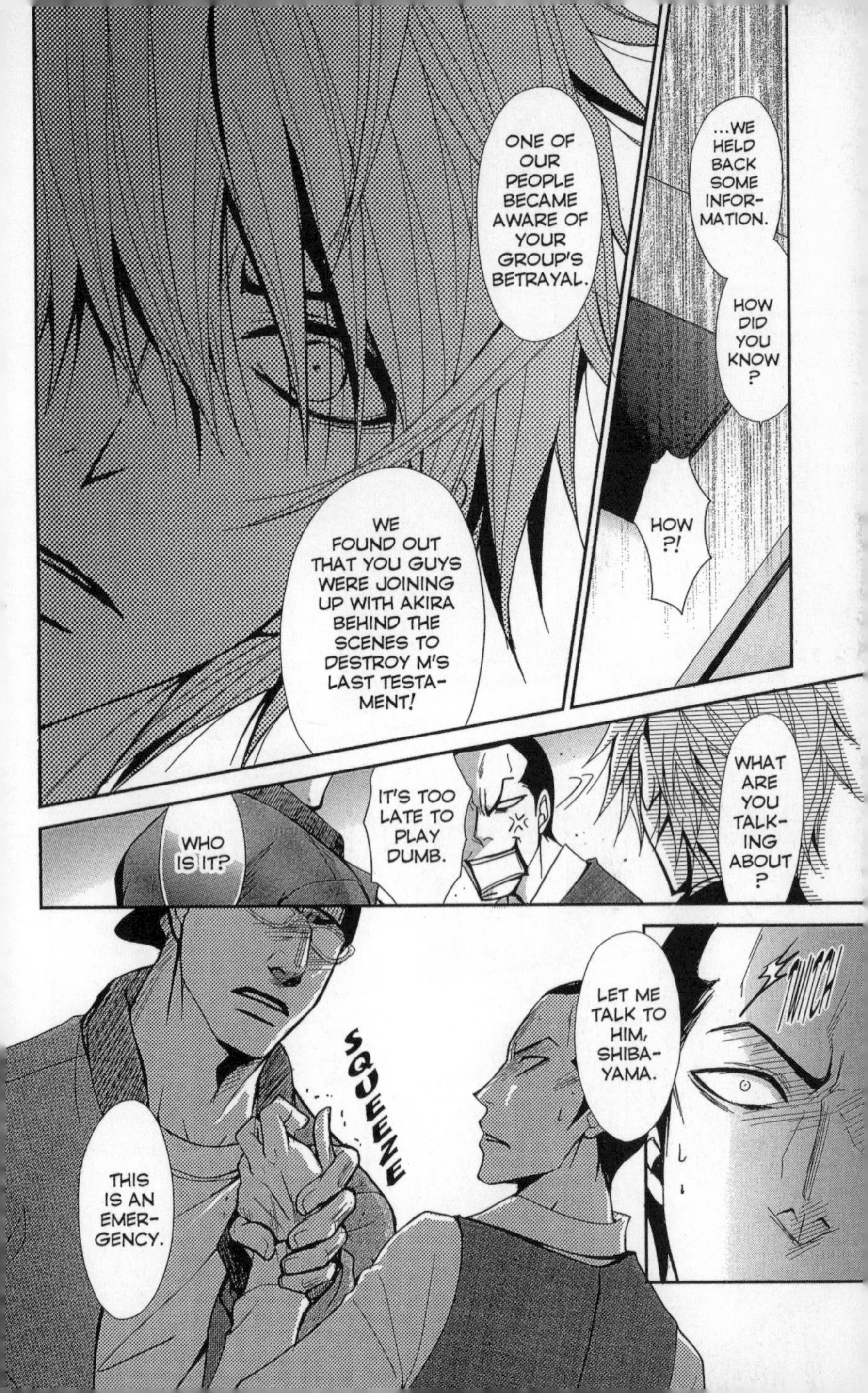
...WE HELD BACK SOME INFORMATION.
HOW DID YOU KNOW?
HOW?!
ONE OF OUR PEOPLE BECAME AWARE OF YOUR GROUP'S BETRAYAL.
WE FOUND OUT THAT YOU GUYS WERE JOINING UP WITH AKIRA BEHIND THE SCENES TO DESTROY M'S LAST TESTAMENT!
WHAT ARE YOU TALKING ABOUT?
IT'S TOO LATE TO PLAY DUMB.
WHO IS IT?
TWITCH
LET ME TALK TO HIM, SHIBAYAMA.
SQUEEZE
THIS IS AN EMERGENCY.

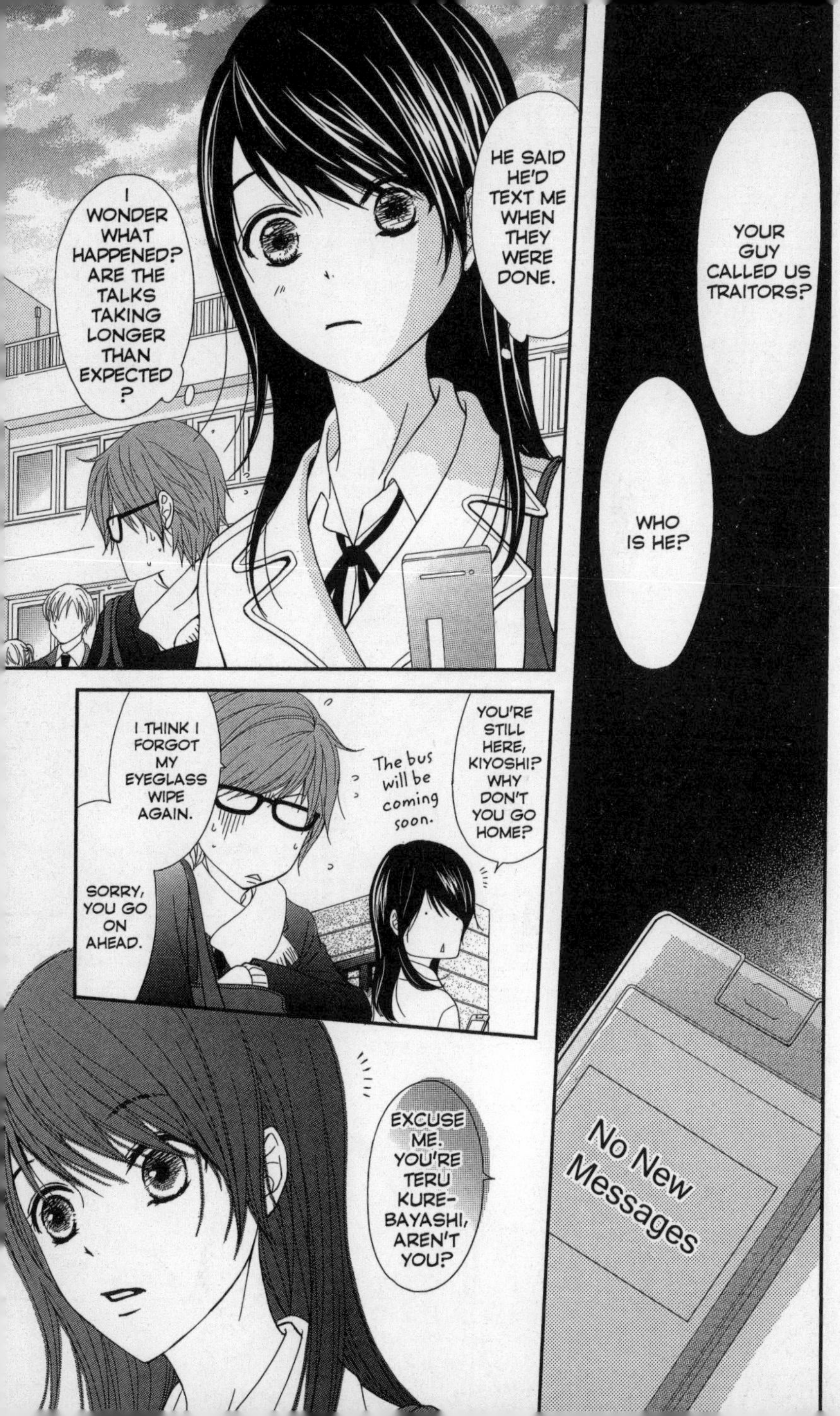
YOUR GUY CALLED US TRAITORS?
WHO IS HE?
No New Messages
HE SAID HE'D TEXT ME WHEN THEY WERE DONE.
I WONDER WHAT HAPPENED? ARE THE TALKS TAKING LONGER THAN EXPECTED?
YOU'RE STILL HERE, KIYOSHI? WHY DON'T YOU GO HOME?
The bus will be coming soon.
I THINK I FORGOT MY EYEGLASS WIPE AGAIN.
SORRY, YOU GO ON AHEAD.
EXCUSE ME. YOU'RE TERU KURE-BAYASHI, AREN'T YOU?

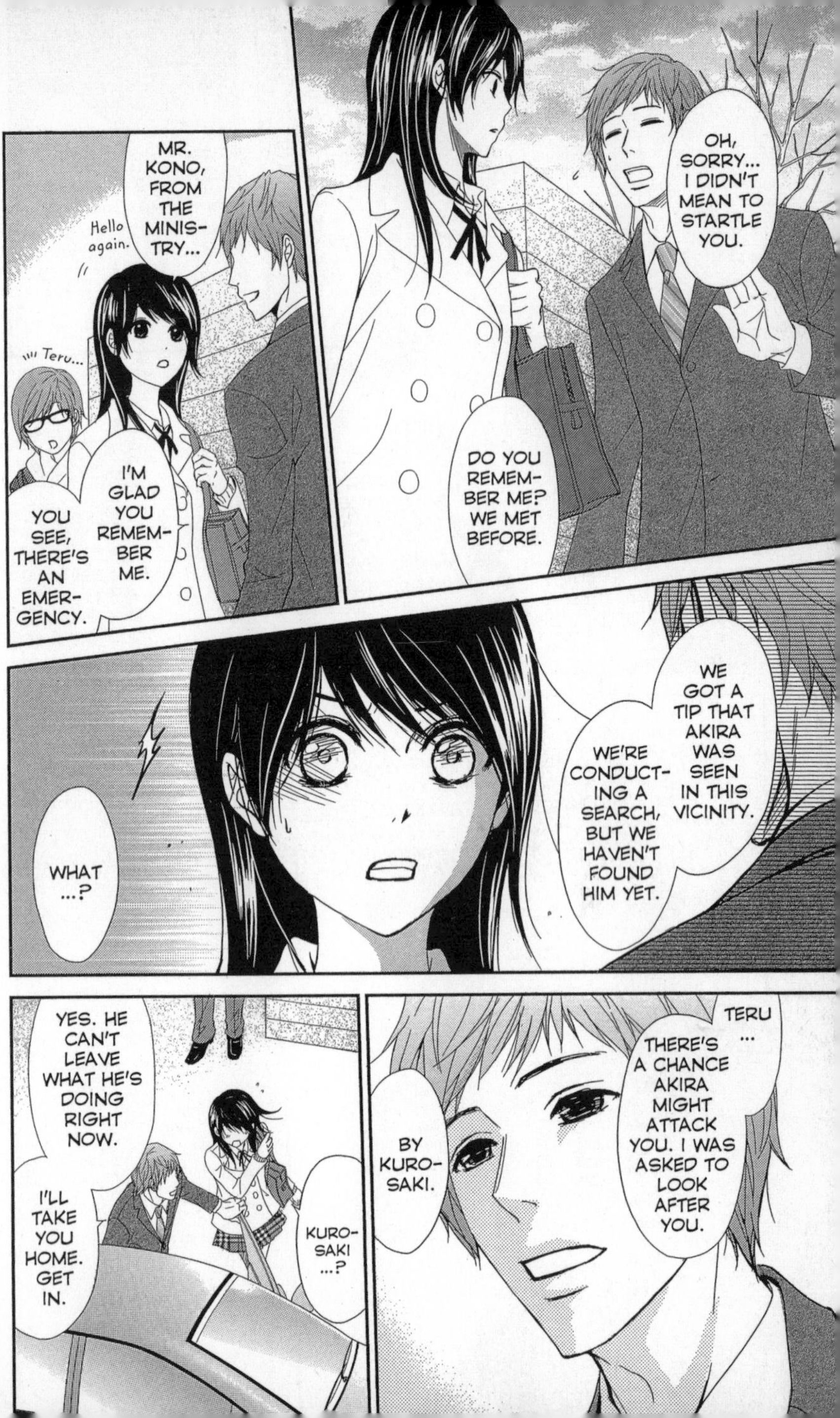
OH, SORRY... I DIDN'T MEAN TO STARTLE YOU.
DO YOU REMEMBER ME? WE MET BEFORE.
MR. KONO, FROM THE MINISTRY...
Hello again.
Teru...
I'M GLAD YOU REMEMBER ME.
YOU SEE, THERE'S AN EMERGENCY.
WE GOT A TIP THAT AKIRA WAS SEEN IN THIS VICINITY.
WE'RE CONDUCTING A SEARCH, BUT WE HAVEN'T FOUND HIM YET.
WHAT ...?
TERU ...
THERE'S A CHANCE AKIRA MIGHT ATTACK YOU. I WAS ASKED TO LOOK AFTER YOU.
BY KUROSAKI.
KUROSAKI ...?
YES. HE CAN'T LEAVE WHAT HE'S DOING RIGHT NOW.
I'LL TAKE YOU HOME. GET IN.

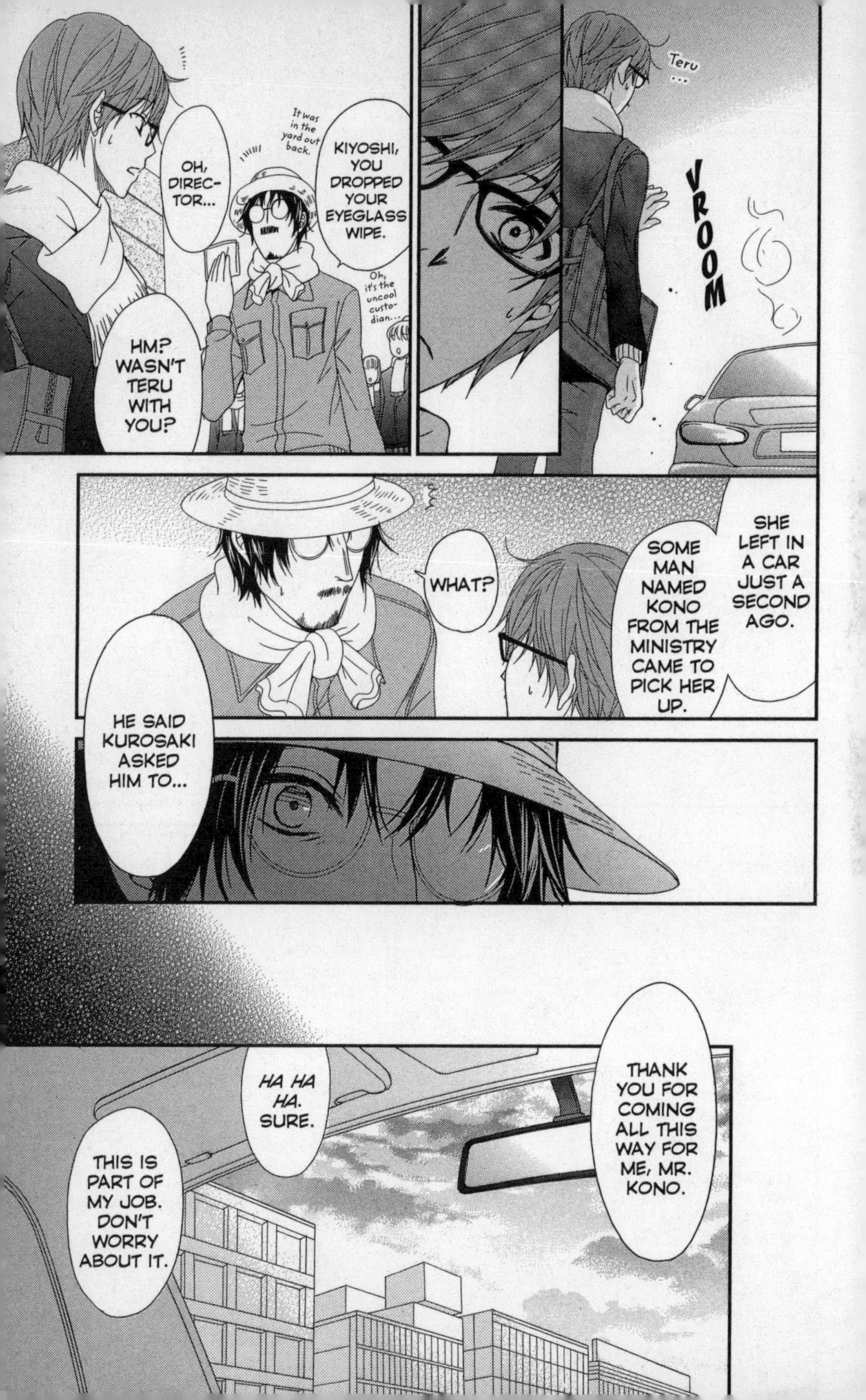
Teru ...
VROOM
KIYOSHI, YOU DROPPED YOUR EYEGLASS WIPE.
It was in the yard out back.
OH, DIRECTOR...
Oh, it's the uncool custodian...
HM? WASN'T TERU WITH YOU?
SHE LEFT IN A CAR JUST A SECOND AGO.
SOME MAN NAMED KONO FROM THE MINISTRY CAME TO PICK HER UP.
WHAT?
HE SAID KUROSAKI ASKED HIM TO...
THANK YOU FOR COMING ALL THIS WAY FOR ME, MR. KONO.
HA HA HA. SURE.
THIS IS PART OF MY JOB. DON'T WORRY ABOUT IT.

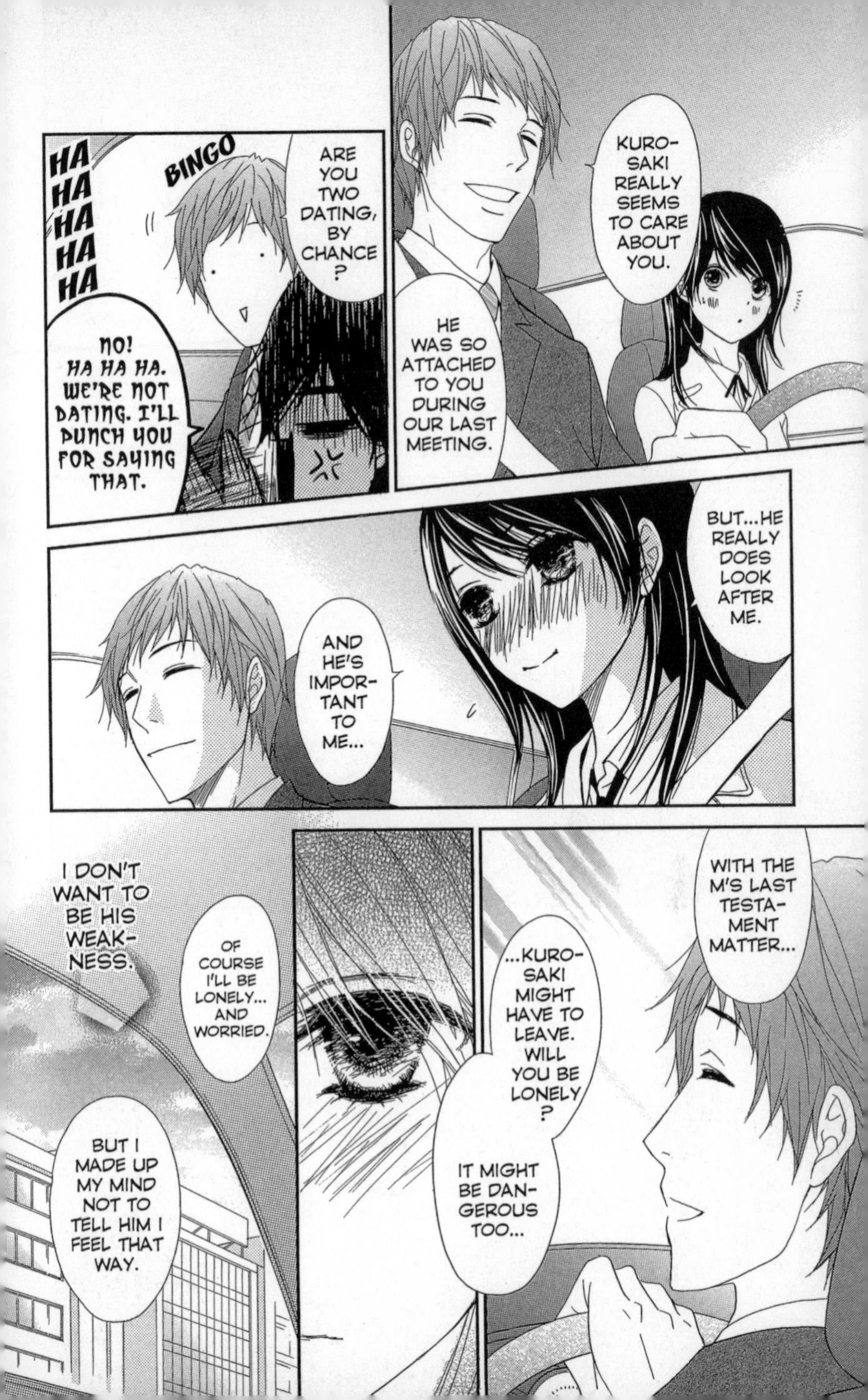
KUROSAKI REALLY SEEMS TO CARE ABOUT YOU.
HE WAS SO ATTACHED TO YOU DURING OUR LAST MEETING.
ARE YOU TWO DATING, BY CHANCE?
BINGO
HA HA HA HA HA
NO! HA HA HA. WE'RE NOT DATING. I'LL PUNCH YOU FOR SAYING THAT.
BUT...HE REALLY DOES LOOK AFTER ME.
AND HE'S IMPORTANT TO ME...
WITH THE M'S LAST TESTAMENT MATTER...
...KUROSAKI MIGHT HAVE TO LEAVE. WILL YOU BE LONELY?
IT MIGHT BE DANGEROUS TOO...
OF COURSE I'LL BE LONELY... AND WORRIED.
BUT I MADE UP MY MIND NOT TO TELL HIM I FEEL THAT WAY.
I DON'T WANT TO BE HIS WEAKNESS.

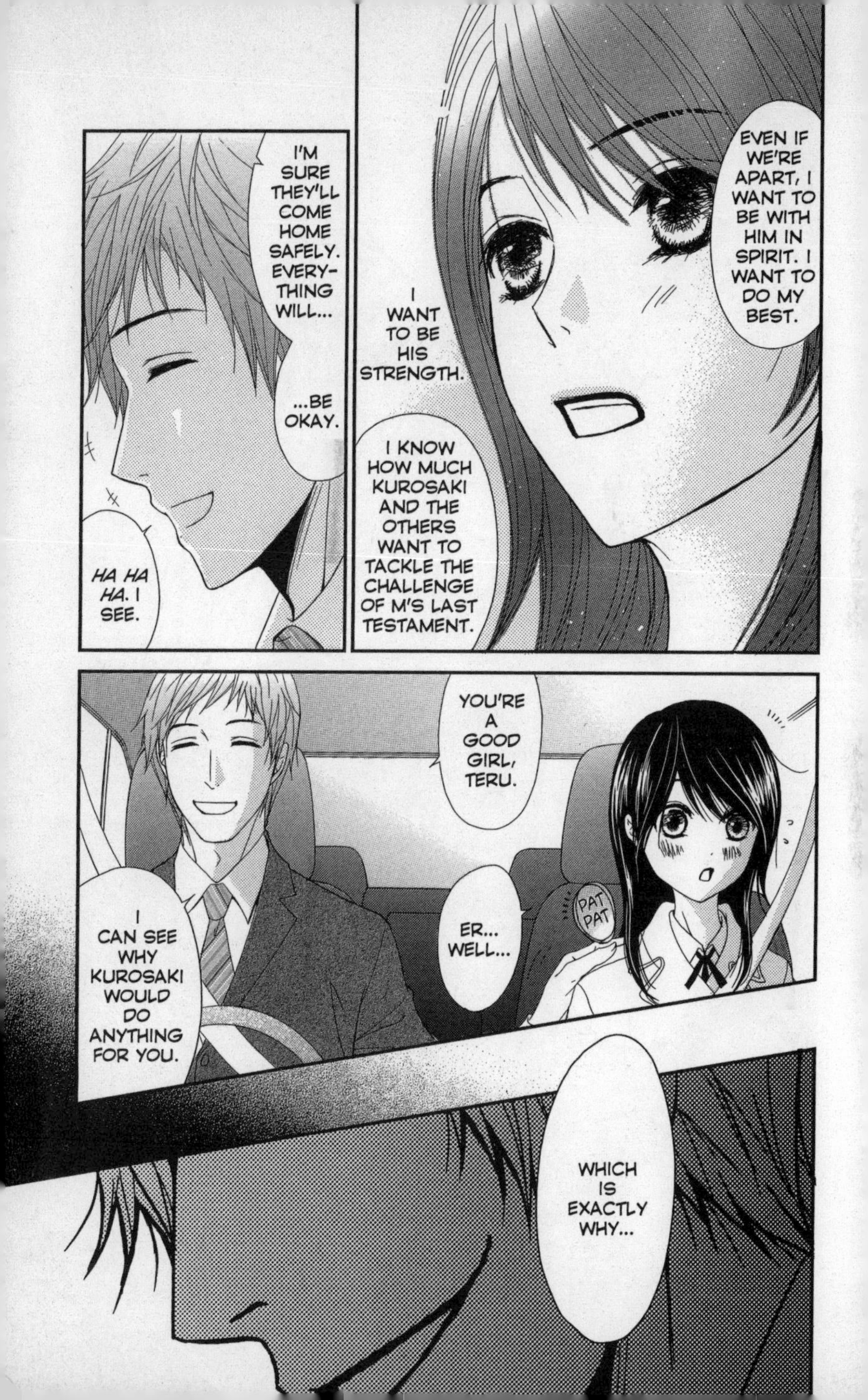
EVEN IF WE'RE APART, I WANT TO BE WITH HIM IN SPIRIT. I WANT TO DO MY BEST.
I WANT TO BE HIS STRENGTH.
I KNOW HOW MUCH KUROSAKI AND THE OTHERS WANT TO TACKLE THE CHALLENGE OF M'S LAST TESTAMENT.
I'M SURE THEY'LL COME HOME SAFELY. EVERYTHING WILL...
...BE OKAY.
HA HA HA. I SEE.
YOU'RE A GOOD GIRL, TERU.
PAT PAT
ER... WELL...
I CAN SEE WHY KUROSAKI WOULD DO ANYTHING FOR YOU.
WHICH IS EXACTLY WHY...

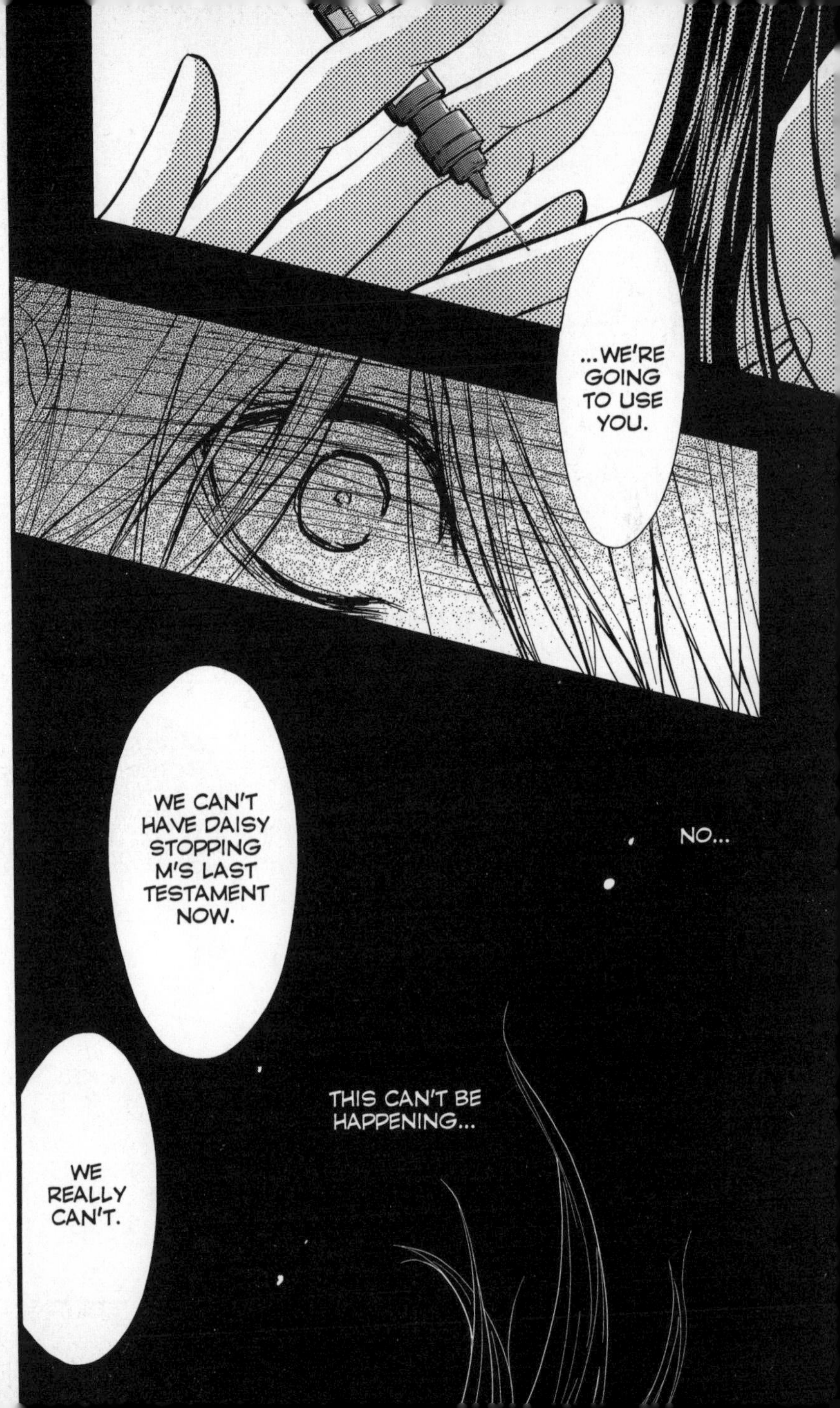
...WE'RE GOING TO USE YOU.
WE CAN'T HAVE DAISY STOPPING M'S LAST TESTAMENT NOW.
NO...
THIS CAN'T BE HAPPENING...
WE REALLY CAN'T.

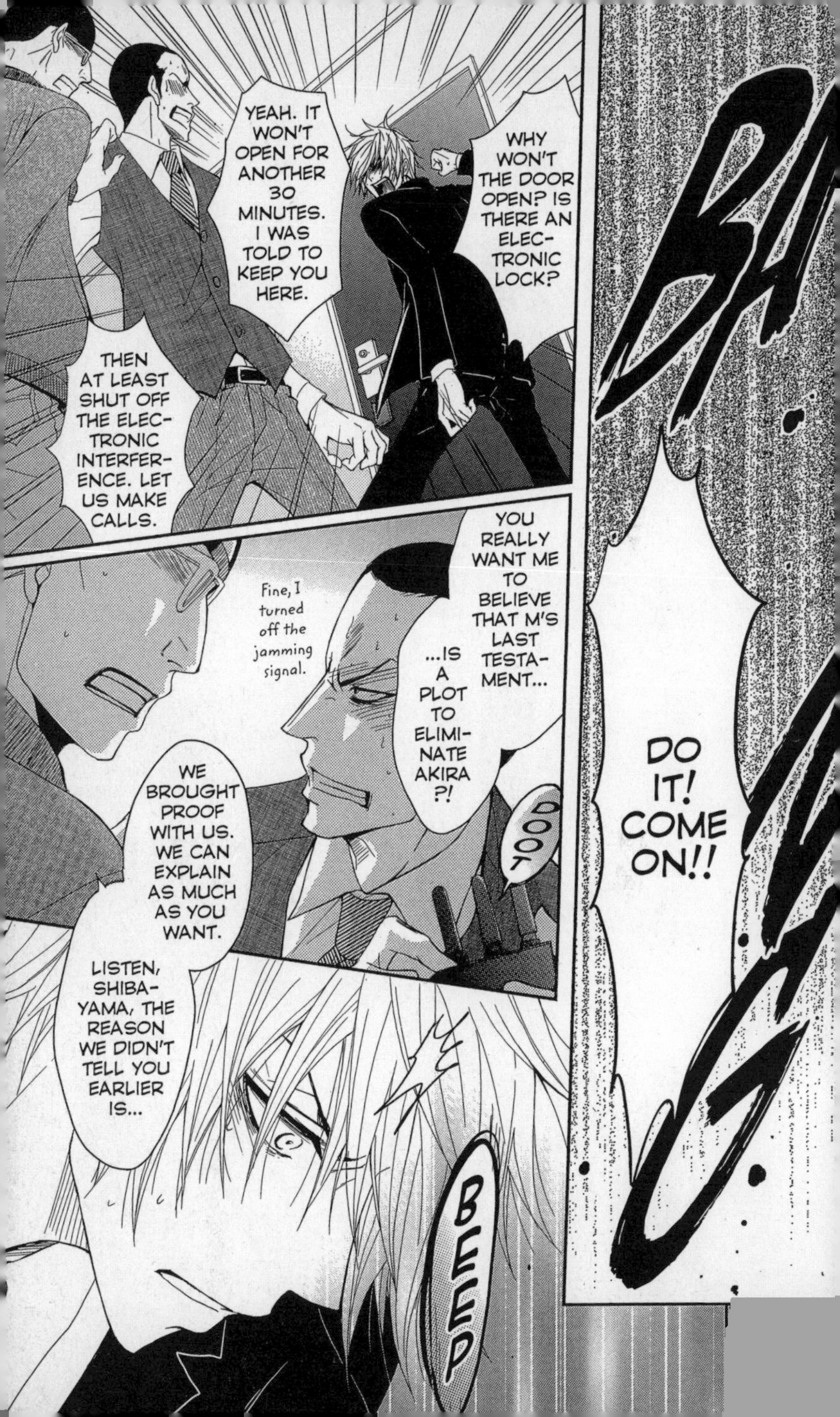
DO IT! COME ON!!
WHY WON'T THE DOOR OPEN? IS THERE AN ELECTRONIC LOCK?
YEAH. IT WON'T OPEN FOR ANOTHER 30 MINUTES. I WAS TOLD TO KEEP YOU HERE.
THEN AT LEAST SHUT OFF THE ELECTRONIC INTERFERENCE. LET US MAKE CALLS.
YOU REALLY WANT ME TO BELIEVE THAT M'S LAST TESTAMENT...
...IS A PLOT TO ELIMINATE AKIRA?!
Fine, I turned off the jamming signal.
DOOT
WE BROUGHT PROOF WITH US. WE CAN EXPLAIN AS MUCH AS YOU WANT.
LISTEN, SHIBAYAMA, THE REASON WE DIDN'T TELL YOU EARLIER IS...
BEEP

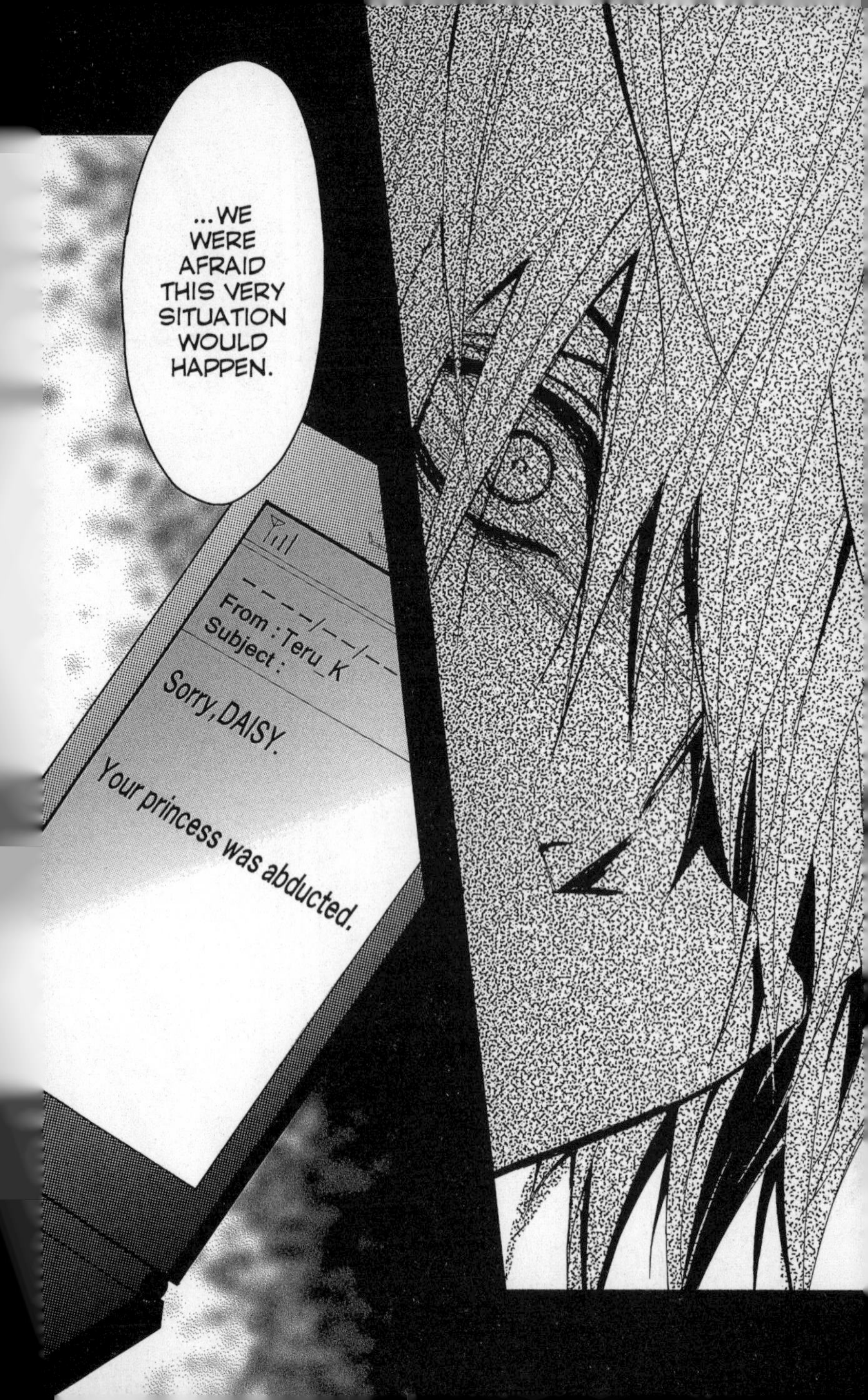
...WE WERE AFRAID THIS VERY SITUATION WOULD HAPPEN.
From : Teru_K
Subject :
Sorry, DAISY.
Your princess was abducted.

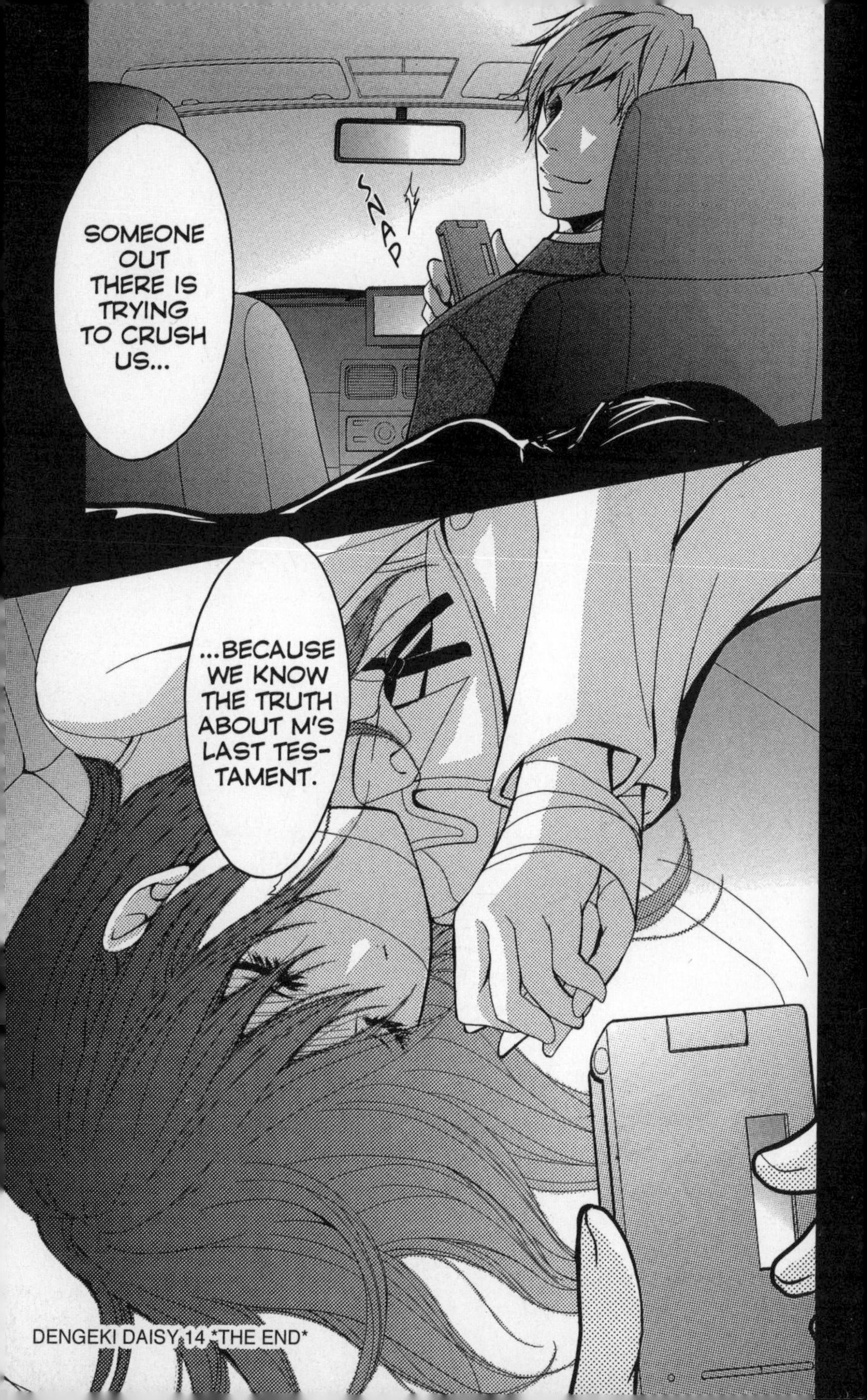
SOMEONE OUT THERE IS TRYING TO CRUSH US...
SNAP
...BECAUSE WE KNOW THE TRUTH ABOUT M'S LAST TES-TAMENT.
DENGEKI DAISY 14 *THE END*

AFTERWORD

AND THERE YOU HAVE IT! THIS IS THE END OF *DENGEKI DAISY* VOLUME 14.

YOU MAY HAVE NOTICED, BUT THE STORY OF *DENGEKI DAISY* IS COMING TO ITS CLIMAX. "BLEACHED HAIR" HAS NOW KISSED "TINY BREASTS," SO WE SHOULD GET CLEAR OUT OF HERE BEFORE WE RUN AFOUL OF REGULATIONS... OKAY, THAT WAS SUPPOSED TO BE A JOKE. I HOPE YOU'LL STICK WITH ME UNTIL THE END. WE'LL CONTINUE JUST A BIT LONGER. THE AUTHOR WILL TIGHTEN THE ELASTIC UNDERWEAR WAISTBAND AND WORK AT AN ALL-OUT SPRINT TO THE FINISH.

ANYWAY, SEE YOU NEXT VOLUME!!

KYOUSUKE MOTOMI

最富キョウスケ

DENGEKI DAISY
C/O VIZ MEDIA
P.O. BOX 77010
SAN FRANCISCO, CA
94107

← IF YOU HAVE ANY QUESTIONS, PLEASE SEND THEM HERE. FOR REGULAR FAN MAIL, PLEASE SEND THEM TO THE SAME ADDRESS BUT CHANGE THE ADDRESSEE TO:

KYOUSUKE MOTOMI
C/O DENGEKI DAISY
EDITOR

...AND THAT'S IT. THANK YOU VERY MUCH!!

Recently, my secret pleasure when working on my storyboard is to polish the kitchen faucet. In a small way, it soothes my frazzled soul. I recommend that you try it... Heh heh heh...

-Kyousuke Motomi

Born on August 1, Kyousuke Motomi debuted in *Deluxe Betsucomi* with *Hetakuso Kyupiddo* (No-Good Cupid) in 2002. She is the creator of *Beast Master* and *Otokomae! Biizu Kurabu* (Handsome! Beads Club). Motomi enjoys sleeping, tea ceremonies and reading Haruki Murakami.

DENGEKI DAISY
VOL. 14
Shojo Beat Edition

STORY AND ART BY
KYOUSUKE MOTOMI

DENGEKI DAISY Vol.14
by Kyousuke MOTOMI
© 2007 Kyousuke MOTOMI
All rights reserved.
Original Japanese edition published by SHOGAKUKAN.
English translation rights in the United States of America
and Canada arranged with SHOGAKUKAN.

Translation & Adaptation/JN Productions
Touch-up Art & Lettering/Rina Mapa
Design/Courtney Utt
Editor/Amy Yu

Printed in the U.S.A.

Published by VIZ Media, LLC
P.O. Box 77010
San Francisco, CA 94107

10 9 8 7 6 5 4 3 2 1
First printing, June 2014

www.viz.com

www.shojobeat.com

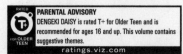

This is the last page.

In keeping with the original Japanese comic format, this book reads from right to left—so action, sound effects, and word balloons are completely reversed. This preserves the orientation of the original artwork—plus, it's fun! Check out the diagram shown here to get the hang of things, and then turn to the other side of the book to get started!